Theories of Human Nature
Classical and Contemporary Readings

Theories of Human Nature

Classical and Contemporary Readings

Donald C. Abel

St. Norbert College

Boston, Massachusetts Burr Ridge, Illinois
Dubuque, Iowa Madison, Wisconsin New York, New York
San Francisco, California St. Louis, Missouri

THEORIES OF HUMAN NATURE
Classical and Contemporary Readings

17 18 19 20   WDD WDD   12 11 10

ISBN-13: 978-0-07-000050-6

ISBN-10: 0-07-000050-6

This book was set in Palatino by Better Graphics, Inc.
The editors were Cynthia Ward and Tom Holton;
the production supervisor was Richard A. Ausburn.
The cover was designed by Elizabeth Harriss.
The photo researcher was Rita Geffert.

Library of Congress Cataloging-in-Publication Data

Theories of human nature: classical and contemporary readings /
   [compiled by] Donald C. Abel.
      p.   cm.
   Includes bibliographical references.
   ISBN 0-07-000050-6
   1. Philosophy.   2. Ethics.   3. Psychology.   I. Abel, Donald C., (date).
   B29.T465   1992
   128—dc20   91-17091

About the Author

Donald C. Abel teaches philosophy at St. Norbert College, where he is an associate professor. Prior to his appointment at St. Norbert, he was an editor at the Great Books Foundation. He holds a B.A. in Philosophy from Gonzaga University, an M.A. in Philosophy from Tulane University, a Ph.L. in Philosophy from St. Michael's Institute, an M.Div. in Theology from Loyola University of Chicago, and a Ph.D. in Philosophy from Northwestern University. He is the author of *Freud on Instinct and Morality* (1989) and the recipient of two awards for excellence in teaching. He is a member of the American Philosophical Association, the American Catholic Philosophical Association, the Society for Ancient Greek Philosophy, and the Medieval Association of the Midwest.

For Diane

Contents

Preface

This anthology is designed as a textbook for a philosophy course that explores human nature. Since studying human nature can be an engaging way for students to be introduced to philosophy, the book can also serve as a text for an introductory course in philosophy.

As a philosophy instructor committed to the use of primary texts but long frustrated by the lack of an anthology on human nature containing substantial selections from a wide spectrum of authors, I decided to compile an anthology that would meet my needs and those of like-minded instructors. This gave me the opportunity to include some pedagogical features I have found particularly useful: a concise introduction to each selection, notes explaining any terms and references likely to be unfamiliar to beginning students, questions for reflection and discussion, and suggestions for further reading. Editing this anthology also afforded me the luxury of selecting what I consider to be the best available English translations of the foreign-language works included. I am pleased to say that I received permission to reprint my first-choice translation in every instance.

The fifteen authors in this anthology represent a broad range of thought about human nature, spanning twenty-four centuries, ten countries, and several disciplines. Criteria for their selection included (1) the extent of their insight into human nature, (2) their historical significance, (3) their diversity, and (4) the accessibility of their writings to undergraduates with little or no background in philosophy. Most of the authors (e.g., Plato, René Descartes) are standard figures in Western philosophy; others fall outside this category, either because they are non-Western (namely, Mencius) or because they are associated primarily with some discipline other than philosophy (e.g., Sigmund Freud, Edward O. Wilson). The selection from each author is taken from a single work and is long enough to give students a substantial introduction to the author's ideas and manner of presentation.

The study of human nature can be approached in many ways. My own experience as a teacher indicates that because beginning philosophy students relate most immediately and energetically to questions concerning ethics, in many cases the most fruitful way to introduce them to an author's views on human nature is to select a work of the author on some broad ethical issue, such as the nature of happiness. Moreover, works on ethics are often more accessible to students than are those that examine human nature more directly. For example, Aristotle's *Nicomachean Ethics* is more readable than *On the Soul*, and David Hume's *Enquiry Concerning the Principles of Morals* is more readable than his *Treatise of Human Nature*. Human values and human nature are, of course, closely related; and students will benefit by thinking about how an author's views on ethics flow from or imply a certain theory of human nature. Many of the selections in this anthology, consequently, are taken from works dealing mainly with ethics.

Not all the readings in the anthology have an ethical orientation. For example, Descartes's *Meditations on First Philosophy* presents a metaphysical theory of mind-body dualism, and Freud's *Five Lectures on Psychoanalysis* sets forth a psychological theory of the unconscious mind. But each selection, regardless of its specific orientation, makes important claims about some aspect of human nature and contains, either explicitly or implicitly, a general theory of what human nature is.

It would be difficult—and inadvisable, in my opinion—to cover all fifteen authors in this anthology in a single semester or quarter. The diversity of readings in the anthology will enable the instructor to select the readings most suitable to his or her objectives. Since each chapter is designed to be accessible on its own, it is possible to omit chapters or to take them in an order different from the chronological sequence in which they appear.

A few comments on the various pedagogical features of the book may be helpful. The introduction to each chapter describes the author's life, principal works, and general philosophy and gives students a brief summary of the main points in the selection. The notes at the end of each section explain terms and references that may be unfamiliar to first-time readers. Some works, such as Plato's *Republic*, required very few notes; others, such as Thomas Aquinas's *Summa theologiae*, required more thorough annotation. I also include some notes written by the editor or translator of the volume from which the selection is taken.

Each selection is followed by five questions. The questions are not designed to check reading comprehension, but to help students reflect critically about the author's views on human nature and begin to formulate their own views. None of the questions has an obviously correct answer; in each case, persuasive arguments can be given for various positions. The questions thus provide students with an opportunity to interpret the text, find textual evidence to support their interpretations, and begin to articulate their own positions on human nature and give reasons for their views. The questions could serve as topics for papers or for classroom discussion or debate.

The final section of each chapter consists of an annotated bibliography of both primary and secondary sources. The primary-source bibliography lists several accessible works (or parts of works) by the author that pertain to human nature. In most cases, the first entry is the work from which the selection is taken. The secondary-source bibliography for each author lists five works, each chosen for its reliability and its accessibility to undergraduates. When I omitted a standard secondary source, such as W. D. Ross's *Aristotle* or Norman Kemp Smith's *Philosophy of David Hume*, I did so because it seemed too difficult or too detailed for most undergraduates. The annotations for the secondary sources briefly describe the content of the work and indicate works written especially for beginners (e.g., the volumes in Oxford's Past Masters Series) and works appropriate for more advanced students. To give students a clearer idea of what to expect in these suggested readings, I state the length of each primary and secondary work.

I wish to thank all those who have helped me with this book, especially Diane Legomsky and Robert J. Vanden Burgt, two of my colleagues at St. Norbert College, and the following readers for McGraw-Hill: David B. Boersema, Pacific University; Deal W. Hudson, Fordham University; Gerald Matross, Merrimack College; Lawrence P. Schrenk, The Catholic University of America; and Raphael T. Waters, Niagara University. I am greatly indebted to Cynthia Ward, my editor at McGraw-Hill, for her support of this project and for her astute editorial advice, which greatly improved the book in both form and content. I thank Tom Holton of McGraw-Hill for his excellent supervision of the copyediting, design, and production of the book. I am also grateful to the St. Norbert College Office of Faculty Development for two summer grants to work on this anthology and to Robert L. Horn, Dean of St. Norbert College, for financial assistance from the Faculty Publications Fund. Finally, I would like to thank the publishers of the books from which the selections are taken (listed on the following pages) for their kind permission to reproduce copyrighted material.

Donald C. Abel

Permissions Acknowledgments

1. Plato

Reprinted from Plato, *The Republic*, A New Translation by Richard W. Sterling and William C. Scott, by permission of W. W. Norton & Company, Inc. Copyright © 1985 by Richard W. Sterling and William C. Scott.

2. Aristotle

Reprinted by permission of Macmillan Publishing Company from Aristotle: *Nicomachean Ethics*, translated by Martin Ostwald. © 1986 by Macmillan Publishing Company. Copyright © 1962.

3. Mencius

From *Mencius*, translated by D. C. Lau, pp. 60, 66–68, 74, 82–84, 106, 111–113, 117, 119, 124–125, 127–131, 133–134, 136, 160–169, 171–174, 182–191, 194–197, 199, 201–202. London: Penguin Classics, 1970. Copyright © D. C. Lau, 1970. Reproduced by permission of Penguin Books Ltd.

4. Lucius Annaeus Seneca

Reprinted by permission of the publishers and the Loeb Classical Library from Seneca, *Moral Essays*, Volume II, translated by John W. Basore, Cambridge, Mass.: Harvard University Press, 1932.

5. Augustine

Reprinted from Saint Augustine, *The Free Choice of the Will*, in *The Teacher, The Free Choice of the Will, Grace and Free Will*, translated by Robert P. Russell, Fathers of the Church Series, Vol. 59, Washington, D.C.: The Catholic University of America Press, 1968.

6. Thomas Aquinas

"Treatise on Man" and "Treatise on Law" reprinted from *Basic Writings of Saint Thomas Aquinas*, edited by Anton C. Pegis, translated by the Fathers of the English Dominican Province, revised by Anton C. Pegis, 2 vols., New York: Random House, Inc., 1945. Reprinted by permission of The Estate of Anton C. Pegis.

"Treatise on Happiness" reprinted from *Summa theologica* by St. Thomas Aquinas, first complete American edition, translated by the Fathers of the English Dominican Province, 3 vols., New York: Benziger Brothers, Inc., 1947–1948. Reprinted by permission of Benziger Publishing Company.

7. René Descartes

From *Meditations on First Philosophy, With Selections from the Objections and Replies* by René Descartes, translated by John Cottingham. © Cambridge University Press 1986. Reprinted with the permission of Cambridge University Press.

8. David Hume

© Oxford University Press 1975. Reprinted from *Enquiries Concerning Human Understanding and the Principles of Morals* by David Hume, edited by L. A. Selby-Bigge, revised by P. H. Nidditch (3rd ed. 1975) by permission of Oxford University Press.

9. Karl Marx

Reprinted from *Economic and Philosophic Manuscripts of 1844* by Karl Marx, edited Dirk J. Struik, translated by Martin Milligan, New York: International Publishers, 1964. Reprinted by permission of International Publishers.

10. Friedrich Nietzsche

Reprinted from *Human, All Too Human: A Book for Free Spirits,* by Friedrich Nietzsche, translated by Marion Faber with Stephen Lehmann, by permission of University of Nebraska Press. Copyright 1984 by the University of Nebraska Press.

11. Sigmund Freud

Reprinted from *Five Lectures on Psycho-Analysis* by Sigmund Freud, translated and edited by James Strachey, by permission of W. W. Norton & Company, Inc. Copyright 1909, 1910 by Sigmund Freud. Copyright © 1961 by James Strachey. Copyright renewed 1989.

12. Jean-Paul Sartre

From *Existentialism* by Jean-Paul Sartre, translated by Bernard Frechtman. Copyright, 1947, by the Philosophical Library, Inc. Reprinted by arrangement with Carol Publishing Group.

13. Simone de Beauvoir

14. B. F. Skinner

15. Edward O. Wilson

Photo Credits

General Introduction

There are many wonders, but none more wondrous than human beings.
Sophocles, *Antigone*

Do human beings have a soul? What is happiness? How do we know if an action is morally right? Do we freely choose our actions, or are they the result of forces beyond our control, such as our genetic makeup, unconscious mind, and environment? Such questions about human nature, difficult as they are, eventually confront every reflective person. Culture and religion usually provide us with our first answers, but as we grow older and gain more experience and knowledge, we may come to question the answers we were given. For example, we may have been taught as children that we have an immortal soul, but as we grow older we might begin to wonder how we can be *sure* we have one or we might want to know just what sort of thing a "soul" is.

The fifteen authors represented in this anthology thought deeply about such questions. Each author approached human nature from his or her own perspective, providing distinctive insights into certain aspects of human nature. Taken together, the readings cover a broad spectrum of views on the soul, happiness, morality, freedom and responsibility, and other important issues regarding human nature. Some of the authors hold that we have a soul, while others argue that the fact that we evolved from animals makes the existence of the soul unlikely. Of those who defend the soul, some maintain that it is immortal and some believe that it ceases to exist when we die. Several authors discuss the nature of happiness and give advice on how to attain it. Some see a close relationship between happiness and morality, arguing that the ultimate purpose of moral rules is to make us happy. Some authors propose other theories of what makes actions moral, while others examine the psychological origin of moral judgments or explore the connections between morality and other topics, such as politics, economics, or evolution. Several of the selections address the question of human freedom and responsibility. Some authors hold that we are utterly free and responsible for our actions; others argue that our actions are partly or even completely

1

determined by genetic, psychological, or environmental factors. Among other issues of human nature addressed in these readings are the relationship of human beings to God, the nature of a just society, and the sources of human motivation.

A principal goal of this anthology is to acquaint readers with interesting, thoughtful, and historically important views on various issues concerning human nature. The authors come from a variety of cultures, disciplines, and personal backgrounds; and each approaches human nature from his or her unique perspective. Most of the authors, such as Plato and David Hume, are typically classified as philosophers, but others are associated primarily with some other discipline. For example, B. F. Skinner is a psychologist and Edward O. Wilson a biologist. Some thinkers do not fall neatly within the boundaries of a single discipline. Augustine, for example, unites theology with philosophy, while Karl Marx combines economics with political theory. Each reading, however, whatever its particular focus or orientation, contains, either explicitly or implicitly, a general view of what human nature is.

A second goal of this anthology is to stimulate readers to reflect critically on the theories presented here. When reading the texts, it is important that we become actively involved with them, noting what we agree with and what we reject and trying to articulate our reasons. We should try to see if the author's conclusions follow from his or her premises. When some point is unclear to us, it helps to note the passage and come back to it later. If an author does not address directly the question of what human nature is, we should try to determine what view he or she implicitly holds. As we progress through the various selections, it is helpful to note similarities and contrasts among the theories and to imagine how one author would respond to another's claims.

The most effective technique, in my opinion, for critically reading the selections is to ask questions along the way and then carefully reread the text in an attempt to answer these questions. To illustrate the kinds of questions I have in mind, at the end of each selection I list five questions that arose for *me* as I reflected on the author's views. The best questions for a reader to ponder, however, are those that derive from his or her own encounter with the text.

The third and ultimate goal of this anthology is to encourage readers to become philosophers of human nature. The word *philosophy* may conjure up notions of hopelessly abstract disputations, but philosophy is not something reserved for specialists. The word comes from a Greek compound that means, literally, "the love of wisdom." To philosophize about human nature, then, means to seek the truth about who (or what) we are. In this sense, all the authors in this anthology—even those who are not usually classified as philosophers—are, in fact, philosophers of human nature. And in this same sense, every reader who seeks a better understanding of who we are is also a philosopher of human nature. The very processes of reading the texts and reflecting critically on them (the first two goals) can themselves be philosophical activities if they are undertaken with a view to attaining wisdom about human nature.

My own experience as a student and as a teacher indicates that the best way to make progress in thinking philosophically about human nature (or about any other topic) is to engage in dialogue. Private reflection and critical reading are important first steps, but real gains in understanding often come only when we articulate our thoughts to other people, hear their views, and challenge each other to defend our respective positions—all in an honest effort to find the truth about the question at hand. We may think that we have a very clear notion about something only to find out otherwise when we try to articulate it to someone else. For example, we may speak easily about the soul but then find ourselves at a loss when we try to explain to someone exactly *what* the soul is or *where* it is. Sometimes a belief that we have may seem obviously true until someone challenges us to defend it. We may, for example, think that human beings can be unselfish but find it difficult to respond to the argument that every apparently unselfish action has some self-interested motive, such as feeling good about oneself, avoiding guilt, receiving gratitude, or gaining merit in heaven.

As we ponder the various arguments presented by the authors in this anthology and try to decide which views to accept and which to reject, we may become aware of so many arguments on every side of every question about human nature that we are tempted to give up all hope of finding any answers; we may decide that "it's all just a matter of opinion." While it may be true that any claim about human nature is just a matter of opinion, we should be aware that this position is, in itself, an opinion that needs to be examined. And I would guess that few readers would maintain that they know nothing *at all* about human nature. I grant that it is unlikely that anyone will ever come up with the whole truth about human nature (no one has done so yet!), but this does not mean that we cannot know something about human nature or that we have no basis for saying that one theory is better than another. If a particular theory seems to explain and illuminate our personal human experience better than other theories we are familiar with, and if it fits in with other ideas that we hold to be true, we have good reasons for preferring this theory to the others. As our human experience grows, we find ourselves continually revising our views of human nature; philosophy is thus a lifelong enterprise. Although philosophy may be frustrating at times, those who pursue it are likely to find it rewarding and worthwhile. The ancient Greek philosopher Socrates went so far as to say that "the unexamined life is not worth living for a human being."

This book includes certain editorial features designed to help readers understand and critically assess the theories of human nature presented here. I have already mentioned the questions following each selection. In addition, each chapter has an introduction that describes the author's life and thought and summarizes the main points in the reading. There are also notes explaining terms and references that may be unfamiliar. Some of the notes are my own; others are by the editor or translator of the book from which the selection is taken. The author of each note is indicated by initials placed in brackets at the end of the note.

To help readers who want to learn more about a particular author's ideas, each chapter includes two lists of additional readings. The first list ("Primary Sources") consists of works (or parts of works) by the author. The second list ("Secondary Sources") consists, in each case, of five books (or articles) *about* the author's theory. A wealth of literature exists on all fifteen authors, and I encourage readers to browse the stacks in their library to find additional works that seem interesting and useful.

As the Greek dramatist Sophocles remarked long ago in the line quoted at the beginning of this introduction, human beings are wondrous creatures. This anthology will have served its purpose if it stimulates readers to delve more deeply into the fascinating reality that is human nature. There is much to ponder—and there is much enrichment to be gained from the pondering.

1

Plato

Plato was born in Athens in about 428 B.C.E. of distinguished parents. As a youth he associated with Socrates (about 470–399 B.C.E.), a philosopher who constantly challenged fellow Athenians to think about virtue and to improve their souls. Plato's initial interest was in politics, but he soon became disillusioned. Under a democratic system, Athens entered into a protracted and devastating war with other Greek states. Upon Athens's defeat in 404, an oligarchy was installed (known as the Thirty Tyrants) and it conducted a reign of terror. Democracy was restored the following year, but the new government proved reactionary: Socrates was arrested on false charges of impiety and the corruption of youth and—to Plato's great distress—was convicted and executed. Plato was present at the trial and later wrote an account of Socrates's defense speech, known as the *Apology*.

After Socrates's execution, Plato moved to nearby Megara for a time and then may have traveled to Egypt. Inspired by Socrates's life (and death) and intellectually convinced by his argument that in order to establish a just political order one must first know what "justice" is, Plato devoted himself to philosophy. In 388 he traveled to Italy and to the city of Syracuse in Sicily. He soon returned to Athens, where he founded a school devoted both to philosophical inquiry and to the philosophically-based education of politicians. The school was located on the outskirts of the city near a grove sacred to the hero Academus; hence it came to be called the Academy. Plato had many illustrious students at the Academy, the most famous of whom was Aristotle (384–322 B.C.E.), who studied under him for twenty years.

Plato spent most of his life teaching at the Academy and writing philosophical works. Most of these works are written as dialogues between Socrates and one or more interlocutors on some topic concerning morality. The dialogue called the *Laches*, for example, depicts Socrates asking the Athenian generals Laches and Nicias about the nature of courage. Plato made two more trips to Syracuse, in 368 and 361, apparently with the intention of turning Dionysius the Younger into a philosopher-king. (If so, he failed.) Plato died in Athens in 347 at the age of eighty-one.

Plato's *dialogues* (the term by which his surviving works are known) are classified chronologically into three groups, each with its distinctive features. To what extent the various dialogues reflect the views of the historical Socrates is a matter of debate. In dialogues of Plato's early period, Socrates typically asks his interlocutors to define a specific moral virtue. For example, in the *Euthyphro* he asks Euthyphro to define *piety*. The interlocutors are quick to give their answers; but Socrates, through probing and persistent questioning, shows them that their responses involve them in contradictions. It thus becomes clear that the interlocutors are not as wise as they claim to be. In these early dialogues, Socrates usually does not propose any solutions of his own to the questions he asks and, at the end of the conversations, the questions remain unresolved. In the dialogues of Plato's middle period, by contrast, Socrates presents his own views on the topic under investigation. In the *Republic*, for example, Socrates gives a detailed answer to the question "What is justice?" In the dialogues of Plato's late period, Socrates plays a lesser role; in fact, in Plato's last dialogue, the *Laws*, Socrates is absent altogether.

Plato had wide-ranging philosophical interests, but his main concern, like Socrates's, was ethics: How should one live one's life? Our selection is from the *Republic*, a dialogue that addresses this question. Everyone wants to live well, and in the *Republic*, Socrates argues that living well means living justly. He examines the nature of justice and depicts an ideal society—one that promotes a just, good life for its citizens.

The dialogue is cast as a report by Socrates of a conversation he had the previous day in the house of his friend Cephalus. Joining Socrates and Cephalus in the conversation are Cephalus's son Polemarchus, the young Sophist Thrasymachus, and Glaucon and Adeimantus (Plato's older brothers).

In Book I Socrates asks his companions to define "justice" and proceeds to point out problems with each definition that is offered. Thrasymachus's definition of justice as "the interest of the stronger" raises the question of whether justice or injustice is more profitable to the individual. Thrasymachus argues that injustice is more profitable, but Socrates exposes inconsistencies in Thrasymachus's position. At the end of Book I, however, Socrates expresses dissatisfaction with his refutation of Thrasymachus: Although he was able to reveal contradictions in Thrasymachus's views, Socrates observes that one cannot be sure whether justice or injustice is more profitable unless one first knows what justice is—and justice had not yet been satisfactorily defined.

Our selection begins with Book II. Here Socrates (who narrates the dialogue) explains how Glaucon urged him to provide a more persuasive refutation of Thrasymachus's view that injustice is more profitable than justice. Glaucon wanted Socrates to show that justice is desirable not simply for its results, such as the benefits accruing from a good reputation, but for its own sake. Socrates states that he will try to meet this challenge by showing what justice is; once this is known, he believes, its intrinsic value will be obvious. In order to understand justice in the soul, Socrates decides first to examine justice in the state. He thus proceeds to construct an imaginary, perfectly just state. In our excerpts from Books III and IV, Socrates argues that as the state has three parts and is just when each part plays its proper role, so the soul has three parts and is just when each of its parts plays its proper role. He then states that justice in the soul, like health in the body, is obviously desirable for its own sake. Our selection ends with an excerpt from Book IX in which Socrates illustrates the intrinsic value of justice by comparing the soul to a composite of a many-headed beast, a lion, and a human being.

THE REPUBLIC

BOOK II

Glaucon . . . went on to ask: Socrates, do you really want to convince us that justice is preferable to injustice, or will you be content if we only seem to be persuaded?

[I responded:] I would really like to persuade you.

Well, so far you haven't succeeded. Consider this question. Is there some kind of good we ought to strive for, not because we expect it to bring about profitable results but simply because we value the good for its own sake? Joy might be an example, or those sorts of harmless pleasures that leave nothing behind except the memory of enjoyment.

These are good pleasures to savor.

And can we agree that there is a second and different kind of good, valuable not only for its own sake but also for the desirable effects it produces? I think of sight, of knowledge, of health.

Of course.

How about a third kind of good? Gymnastic, medicine, the art of making money—all these yield benefits but are tiresome in the doing. Hence we think of them not as goods in themselves but value them only for their effects.

Yes, this is certainly another kind of good. But what is your point?

I want to know in which of these three categories or classes of goods you locate justice.

Justice belongs in the most valuable category. It is the good that the happy man loves both for its own sake and for the effects it produces.

But the multitude does not think so. Most people consider the practice of justice a burdensome affair. They think it a task to be avoided, if possible, and performed only if necessary to maintain one's reputation for propriety—and to collect whatever rewards such a reputation may be worth.

You are right. I know that is the common opinion; it is the opinion just now expressed by Thrasymachus when he scorned justice and praised injustice. But I am too stupid to be convinced of it, Glaucon.

Well, then, Socrates, listen to what I have to say on the subject, too. I think Thrasymachus conceded the argument before he should have. He reminded me of a snake, too soon charmed by the sound of your voice. As for me, neither the nature of justice or injustice is yet clear. I want to consider both of them quite apart from their effects or the rewards they might bring. What are they in themselves? What power do they exert within the confines of a man's soul?

To begin with, Socrates, I should like to revive Thrasymachus's argument. So I will speak first of all of the common view of the nature and origin of justice. Second, I shall argue that all who practice justice do so against their own will. This is so because they regard just behavior as something necessary but not as something good. Third, I shall stress that the rationale for such attitudes is rooted in the common view that the life of the unjust man is far better and happier than the life of the just man.

I do not believe these things myself, Socrates. But I admit that I become perplexed when I listen to the arguments of Thrasymachus and all those who believe as he does. My uncertainty is all the greater when I reflect that I have never yet heard an unambiguous proof that justice is always superior to injustice.

What I desire most, Socrates, is to hear someone praise justice for its own sake, and you are the one most likely to do so. Thus my purpose in praising the unjust life is to provoke a response from you that will effectively repudiate injustice and vindicate justice. Does my proposal please you?

What else could please me more? This is the one subject, more than any other, that a man of sensibility will choose to discuss—and delight in returning to the discussion again and again.

Excellent. I shall begin by discussing the nature of justice and its origin. Most men say that to be unjust is good but to suffer injustice is bad. To this opinion they add another: the measure of evil suffered by one who is wronged is generally greater than the good enjoyed by one who does wrong. Now, once they have learned what it is to wrong others—and also what it is to be wronged—men tend to arrive at this conclusion: justice is unattainable and injustice unavoidable.

Those so lacking in strength that they can neither inflict injustice nor defend themselves against it find it profitable to draw up a compact with one another. The purpose of the compact is to bind them all neither to suffer injustice nor to commit it. From there they proceed to promulgate further contracts and covenants. To all of these they attach the name of justice; indeed, they assert that the true origin and essence of justice is located in their own legislation.

Their lawmaking is clearly a compromise, Socrates. The compromise is between what they say is best of all—to do wrong without incurring punishment—and what is worst of all—to suffer wrong with no possibility of revenge. Hence they conceive of justice not as something good in itself but simply as a midway point between best and worst. Further, they assert that justice is praised only by those too weak to do injustice and that anyone who is a real man with power to do as he likes would never agree to refrain from doing injustice in order not to suffer it. He would be mad to make any such agreement.

As you very well know, Socrates, this is the orthodox account of the nature and origin of justice. Its corollary is that when people practice justice, they do so against their own wills. Only those are just who lack the power to be unjust. Let us test this proposition by altering the power distribution and assigning the just and the unjust equal power to do what they please. We shall then discover that the just man and the unjust man will follow precisely the same path. They will both do what all nature decrees to be good. They will pursue their own interests. Only if constrained by law will they be confined to the path of justice.

The test I propose makes the assumption that both the just and the unjust enjoy the peculiar liberty said to have been granted to Gyges, ancestor of Croesus the Lydian. Tradition has it that Gyges was a shepherd in the service of the king of Lydia. While he was feeding his flock one day, there was a great storm, after which an earthquake opened a chasm directly in front of the place where Gyges stood with his flock. Marveling at the sight, Gyges descended into the chasm. There he beheld many wonders, among them a hollow bronze horse fitted with doors. When he opened one of the doors and looked within, he saw the corpse of a huge man, nude except for a gold ring on his finger. Gyges removed the ring and made his way up and out of the chasm.

Now when the shepherds next met to prepare their customary monthly report to the king concerning their flocks, Gyges attended wearing the ring. While there, he chanced to turn the stone of the ring on his finger inward, toward the palm of his hand. Instantly he became invisible to all eyes. He was amazed to hear those who sat near him speak of him as if he were absent. Fumbling with the ring again, he turned the stone outward, away from the palm, and became visible once more. Now he began to experiment, turning the ring this way and that and always with the same results—turning it inward he became invisible, turning it outward he became visible again. Once he discovered the ring's power, he hastily managed to have himself appointed one of the messengers to the king's court. On arrival he seduced the queen and then, with her help, murdered the king. Thus it was that he became king of Lydia.

Supposing now there were two such rings, the just man wearing one and the unjust man the other. No man is so unyielding that he would remain obedient to justice and keep his hands off what does not belong to him if he could steal with impunity in the very midst of the public market itself. The same if he could enter into houses and lie with whom he chose, or if he could slay—or release from bondage—whom he would, behaving toward other men in these and all other things as if he were the equal of a god. The just man would act no differently from the unjust; both would pursue the same course.

One might argue that here is the great proof that no one is willingly just; men will be just only if constrained. This is because every man believes that justice is really not to his interest. If he has the power to do wrong, he will do wrong, for every man believes in his heart that injustice will profit him far more than justice.

These are the settled convictions of all those who choose to adopt them. They hold that anyone who acquires extraordinary power and then refuses to do wrong and plunder others is truly to be pitied (and a great fool as well). Publicly, however, they praise the fool's example, convinced that they must deny what they really think so that they will not encourage unjust acts against themselves. I think I have spoken sufficiently to this point.

Next, if we are to choose between the lives of justice and injustice, we must be precise in distinguishing the one from the other. Otherwise we cannot choose rightly. We can make the distinction only by treating the two as strictly separate. We must assume the just man to be entirely just and the unjust man entirely unjust. Each must possess all the qualities appropriate to his character and role as a just—or unjust—man.

First, the unjust man: his behavior must be like that of a clever craftsman. Like any good physician or pilot, he must practice his art with an intuitive sense for what is possible and what is impossible, holding fast to the first and shunning the latter. When he makes a mistake, he must be able to recover and correct himself. This means that the unjust man must pursue injustice in the proper way. If he is altogether unjust, he must possess an unerring capacity to escape detection; otherwise, if he fails and is caught, he shows himself to be a mere bungler. After all, the highest form of injustice is to appear just without being so.

Perfect injustice denotes the perfectly unjust man. Nothing belonging to injustice must be withheld from him. He must be allowed to enjoy the greatest reputation for justice all the while he is committing the greatest wrongs. If by mistake any of his misdeeds should become known, he must be endowed with ample powers of persuasion so that he can cover them up. Should he need to use force, let him do so with boldness and manly strength—and by mobilizing friends and money.

Having constructed a model of the unjust man, we must now do the same for the just man. He will be noble and pure—in Aeschylus's words, one who wants to be good rather than to seem good.[1] Accordingly, he must be deprived of the seeming. Should he retain the appearance of being just, he would also enjoy an esteem that brings with it honors and gifts. In that case we could not know whether he serves justice for its own sake or because he covets the honors and gifts. He must therefore be stripped of everything but justice; his situation must be the opposite of his unjust counterpart. Though the best of men, he must be thought the worst. Then let him be put to the test to see whether he will continue resolute in the service of justice, even though all the while he must suffer the opprobrium of an evil reputation. Let him so persevere—just in actuality but unjust in reputation—until death itself.

Here we have charted the full course for both the unjust and the just man and should be in a better position to judge which of the two is happier.

My compliments, Glaucon. You have given your characters high finish and form. One might think you were modeling a pair of sculptures intended to vie for first honors at the exhibition.

I have spoken of them to the best of my ability. And if I have also spoken truly, I think it should be an easy matter to anticipate and describe what life holds in store for each. If I now use language in my description that is sometimes rude—and even brutal—please remember, Socrates, that my words should be attributed not to me but to those who value injustice more than justice.

They will tell you that every man who is just, but whose reputation stamps him as unjust, will learn what it is to feel the lash, the rack, the chains, and the branding iron burning out his eyes. And after suffering all the other agonies he will be impaled on spikes, there finally to learn his lesson that it is better to seem just than to be so.

They will say that those words of Aeschylus apply far better to the unjust man. He who wills to be unjust but not to seem so is the real man of truth. He is the one who does not allow himself to be governed by opinion; instead he orders his affairs in accord with the way life really is:

He plows deep the furrows of his intellect
and brings home prudence as his harvest.[2]

His reputation for justice will bring him high office. He can enter into marriage with whom he will and arrange the same for his children when their time comes. He will do business or not at his option. His contracts and partnerships will always be profitable for he does not hesitate to be unjust. When he becomes involved in law suits or other kinds of disputes, he bests all who stand against him. In gaining the decision in each contest he enters he also augments his wealth. Hence he is increasingly capable of benefiting friends and injuring enemies. He is able to make sacrifices and other gifts to the gods in such a way as will display his magnificence. Consequently, he pays court both to the men he favors and to the gods far more effectively than just men can; he may therefore reasonably expect that heaven will bestow its favors on him rather than on the just.

So do both men and gods favor the unjust man over the just. This is what the multitude believes. . . .

[Adeimantus said:] Socrates, there is a single cause that impels the flow of all these words from me and from my brother, Glaucon. We are astonished at all your self-professed advocates of justice—from the heroes of ancient times and their surviving discourses down to the present day. None has ever awarded blame to injustice or praise to justice except in terms of the gifts, honors, or reputation each of them attracts. Both verse and prose have failed to convey their intrinsic qualities. They do not tell us how justice and injustice do their work within the human soul, out of the sight of both gods and men. No one has ever provided proof that the one is the greatest of goods and the other the greatest of evils. Why did all of you not do this from the beginning and convince us from our youth up? Had you done so, we would not now be guarding against one another's injustices. Instead, each would first of all guard himself; each would banish injustice from his own conduct, so that his own soul might be safeguarded from the taint of evil.

Thrasymachus and perhaps others might well have said all this in debating justice and injustice (and, in my opinion, grossly reversing their roles). But I have no reason to hide anything from you, Socrates. My only purpose in setting forth this argument with some vehemence and with all the intellectual force I could muster is that I want to hear you refute me. Do not only teach us to understand the superiority of justice to injustice, but show us the effect each has on the well-being of the soul, and why the one effect is good and the other evil.

But do also heed what Glaucon said and leave out all references to reputation. For unless you steal from both justice and injustice the reputation proper to each—and make each masquerade in the reputation contrary to its true nature—we shall say that you are not praising the reality of justice but are only dealing with appearances and that you are preoccupied with censuring what injustice is reputed to be and not with what it really is. We shall think that you are actually urging us to be both unjust and hypocritical. In that case there would be nothing to distinguish your arguments from Thrasymachus's opinion that to be just is to serve another's good and to be unjust serves one's own—that justice is the interest of the stronger and so must harm the interest of the weaker.

You have said that justice belongs to that highest class of good things which not only produce good effects but which are, above all, valuable in themselves. Some of these are sight, hearing, health, and intelligence, things whose value is innate and not a matter of opinion. So tell us how justice benefits a man intrinsically, and in the same way how injustice harms him. Let others praise or blame the respective rewards and reputations. I don't say I wouldn't listen to others debate these issues, including the matter of reputation. But you have spent all your life studying the question, and I expect better fare from you, Socrates, unless you tell me in your own words that you are unable to offer it. I repeat, then, disregard outward appearances, and prove to us that justice is better than injustice by showing us the effects each has on a man's soul and how and why each effect can properly be called either good or evil.

I have always admired the brilliance of Glaucon and Adeimantus, but on this occasion their words gave me special pleasure. So I said to them: Sons of a noble father—Glaucon's friend put it well in the elegy he wrote to honor you both for your heroic deeds in the battle of Megara:

Sons of Ariston, you honor the godlike
heritage of a famous father.[3]

There must indeed be some divine spark at work in your natures that you should be able to make such formidable arguments on behalf of injustice and yet resist being convinced by your own reasoning. And I believe that you are really not convinced. I infer this, however, from my knowledge of your characters; if I had to deal with your words alone, I would be suspicious of you.

But the greater my trust in you, the more difficult becomes my task. What can I say when I doubt my ability to offer you satisfactory answers to your questions? And my doubt is well founded, for you have refused to accept the arguments I used against Thrasymachus and which I thought had amply proved the superiority of justice to injustice. Yet I cannot remain silent; that would be a shameful course to take when justice is under attack. As long as there is voice and breath in me, then, I think it is best to give to justice all the help that I can offer.

Glaucon and the others urged me to come to the rescue. They were unwilling to have the argument cut short and insisted on completing the investigation into justice and injustice, including an assessment of the advantages and disadvantages of each.

Well, I think all of you are pressing for an inquiry that is by no means an easy undertaking. We must keep our wits about us. And since our wits are not always sharp, we should do well to adopt a method of examination similar to that used when people without very keen vision are required to read small letters from a distance. This method would draw their attention to the same letters writ large, and I think they would count it a godsend if they could read the larger letters first then check the smaller letters against them to see if they correspond.

Agreed, said Adeimantus, but what kind of analogy are you trying to draw with justice?

I will tell you. We sometimes speak, do we not, of a just man and also of a just city?

Of course.

And the city is larger than the man?

Yes.

Perhaps, then, there would be more of justice in the city; it might also be easier to observe it there. So if it is agreeable to you, let us first inquire into the nature of justice and injustice in the city, and only after that in the individual. In this way we could begin with the larger and then return to the smaller, making comparisons between the two.

A good suggestion.

If we begin our inquiry by examining the beginning of a city, would that not aid us also in identifying the origins of justice and injustice?

Perhaps it would.

So that when our analysis is complete, we should be in a better position to find what we are seeking?

Much better.

Shall we try it, then? But before we do you may want to reconsider. I don't think it will be an easy task.

We have thought about it enough, said Adeimantus. Go ahead. Don't stop now.

Very well. A city—or a state—is a response to human needs. No human being is self-sufficient, and all of us have many wants. Can we discover the origins of the state in any other explanation?

I can imagine no other.

Since each person has many wants, many partners and purveyors will be required to furnish them. One person will turn to another to supply a particular want, and for a different want or need he will seek out still another. Owing to this interchange of services, a multitude of persons will gather and dwell together in what we have come to call the city or the state.

Right.

And so one man trades with another, each assuming he benefits therefrom.

Right.

Come, then, let us construct a city beginning with its origins, keeping in mind that the origin of every real city is human necessity.

That is evident.

Now the first and greatest necessity, on which our very life depends, is food.

Certainly.

Next is a place in which to live; third, clothing and the like.

Yes.

Then we must ask how our city will provide these things. A farmer will be needed, and a builder and a weaver as well. I suppose we should add a shoemaker and still another who can care for the needs of the body.

I agree.

Hence the simplest city or state would count at least four or five people?

Evidently.

Then how should they proceed? Should what each produces be made available to all? I mean, should the individual farmer produce food for himself and also for the rest? That would require him to produce, say, four times as much food as he could use himself. Correspondingly, he would invest four times as much labor in the land than if he were supplying only himself. Or should he decline to concern himself with the others? Should he produce food for his own needs alone, devoting only a fourth of his total effort to that kind of work? Then he could allot the other three-fourths of his time to building a house, making clothes, and cobbling shoes. Choosing the latter, he wouldn't have to bother about associating with others; he could supply his own wants and be his own man.

I don't think he should try to do everything, said Adeimantus. He should concentrate on producing food.

I agree that this would probably be the better way. Your words remind me that we are not all alike. There is a diversity of talents among men; consequently, one man is best suited to one particular occupation and another to another. What do you think?

I think you are right.

Then a man would do better working at one task rather than many?

I think so.

It should also be obvious that work must be done at the proper time; otherwise it will not be work well done.

True.

The reason, I assume, is that commerce will not wait upon the pleasure of the workman. Instead, he must attend first of all to his work and not consider it a pastime.

Of course.

We can conclude, then, that production in our city will be more abundant and the products more easily produced and of better quality if each does the work nature has equipped him to do, at the appropriate time, and is not required to spend time on other occupations.

A sound conclusion.

Then, Adeimantus, we shall need more than our four original citizens to produce all that will be required. If the farmer's plow and hoe and other implements are to be of good quality, he will not be able to make them himself. The builder will also need equipment and supplies, and so will the shoemaker and the weaver.

True.

With carpenters, smiths, and other craftsmen joining our city, it will begin to grow considerably.

Yes.

Still, it wouldn't be a very big city, even if we added cowherds, shepherds, and other kinds of herdsmen in order to furnish oxen to the farmers for plowing and to the builders for hauling, as well as to supply fleece and hides to the weavers and the shoemakers.

But with so many occupations represented it would not be a very small city either.

True. And we must also note that it would be very difficult to establish a city that would not require imports. That means there must be still another class of citizens who import goods from other cities.

Clearly.

It follows that we must have goods to export. If our traders go forth empty-handed, with nothing to exchange for what they want from other cities, they must come home empty-handed.

Inevitably.

Then domestic production must exceed domestic demand, so that there will be a surplus of quality products to exchange with traders from abroad.

True.

Then we shall need more farmers and artisans. There must also be importers and exporters, those whom we call merchants.

We shall certainly need all these.

And if our trade is by sea, there must be sufficient numbers of skilled sailors.

Yes.

Now, if we return to a consideration of the city itself, we must ask how the inhabitants will trade the products of their labor. You will remember that we founded our city in order to facilitate an exchange of production.

Yes. They will trade by buying and selling.

Then there will be a market place and money as a medium of exchange.

Surely.

Supposing the farmer or other craftsman brings his produce to market but does not arrive at the same time as those who would buy from him. Would he sit idly in the market place, wasting time he could otherwise devote to productive work?

Not at all. There will be men at the market who will offer their services to remedy the situation by acting as salesmen. In well-ordered cities they will be those who are generally weakest in physical strength and therefore of little use for any other kind of work. They will take up their place in the agora,[4] offering to exchange money for the goods that sellers bring to market and then, in turn, selling to those who want to buy.

So the need for money in the exchange of goods produces the class we know as tradesmen. Is this not the name we give to those who buy and sell in the agora, just as we give the name merchants to those who perform the same function in trade between cities?

Yes.

Then there is still another class of workers whose intellects are perhaps too weak to count them as full partners in the city but whose bodily strength enables them to perform hard physical labor. They sell their strength for a price, and the price is called wages. Hence they are called wage earners, and they, too, will be part of our city.

True.

Well, Adeimantus, has our city now reached its full growth? Could we call it complete?

Perhaps.

Where, then, do we find justice and injustice? How do they gain entry into the city? Are they brought in by one or more of the groups we have just included among the city's constituents?

I don't know, Socrates. Perhaps they have their origins in the mutual needs of the city's inhabitants.

You may well be right. We must pursue the matter further and not let up now. First, then, let us consider the way of life of the people in the city we have just described. Won't they make bread, wine, clothes, shoes, and houses, too? They will work in the summer for the most part without clothes or shoes, but in the winter they will want to wear both. They will grind meal from barley and flour from wheat; then they will knead and bake cakes and loaves of fine quality and serve them on mats of reeds or on clean leaves. When they eat, they will recline on beds fashioned of yew or myrtle, they and their children feasting together and drinking their wine. All will wear garlands, singing hymns to the gods and enjoying one another's company. But they will take care not to produce too many children in order not to run the risks of poverty or war.

Here Glaucon broke in: But you have provided no relish for the feast.

True, I had forgotten. Relish there must be: salt, of course, and olives and cheese, and there must be boiled roots and herbs of the sort that country people prepare. For a dessert they shall have figs, chick-peas and beans. They will roast myrtle berries and acorns in the fire, all the while drinking in moderation. Living this way in peace and health, they all can probably expect to reach old age and pass on the same life to their children.

But this is fare for a city of pigs, Socrates. Would you provide nothing else?

What do you suggest, Glaucon?

The usual things. If the people are not to be uncomfortable, they must be able to recline on couches and dine from tables. They ought to have sauces and sweetmeats the way we do.

Now I understand what you mean. We are to consider the origins not simply of a city as such but of a luxurious city. Your suggestion is probably a good one because it is in the luxurious city that we are more likely to discover the roots of justice and injustice.

I believe the city I have just described is well founded and that it will prove to be robust. But if you also want to examine a city in a state of fever, we can do that, too. It is in any case evident that many will not be content with simple fare and simple ways. They will want couches and tables and other types of furniture. Sweets and perfumes, incense, courtesans, and cakes—all must be furnished in quantity and variety. And we must go beyond clothing, shoes, houses, and the other necessities I spoke of at first. There will be painting and embroidery, and gold and ivory will be sought after as ornamentation.

True.

Then we must further enlarge our city. The well-founded city we started with will no longer be big enough. It must be extended and filled up with superfluities. There will, for example, be hunters in plenty. There will be crowds of imitators—those who paint and sculpt. Others will make music: there will be poets and their attendants, rhapsodizers, players, dancers, and impresarios. There will be a market for a greater variety of goods, and stylish women will want dressmakers and more servants. Will not tutors be in demand as well, along with wet nurses and dry nurses, barbers and beauticians, cooks and bakers? We shall also require swineherds. There was no need for them in our original city, for there were no pigs there. Now, however, we shall need pigs, as well as other kinds of animals for those who wish to eat them.

You are right.

And this way of life will require many more doctors than were needed before.

That is certain.

Must we also assume that the territory which was at one time sufficient to feed the city will no longer be adequate?

Yes.

So we shall covet some of our neighbor's land in order to expand our pasture and tillage. And if our neighbor has also disregarded the limits set by necessity and has given himself over to the unlimited acquisition of wealth, he will, in turn, covet what belongs to us.

Inevitably.

Then the next step will be war, Glaucon. Or do you see some other outcome?

There can be no other, Socrates.

This is not the time to speak of the good or ill effects of war. What we can say is that we find war originating from the same causes that generate most of the private and public evils in the city.

Agreed.

So our city must be enlarged once more, this time by nothing less than a whole army. We must have it march out to fight our enemies in defense of all the wealth and luxury we have just described.

Does this necessarily follow? Cannot the people defend themselves?

Not if our initial assumptions about constructing the city still hold. Surely you remember our agreement that no man can perform many tasks well?

Yes.

And don't you think that war is an art and fighting a profession?

Yes.

Surely these are matters requiring as much attention as shoemaking.

You are surely right.

And do you recall our reasons for barring the shoemaker from the other crafts such as farming, weaving, or building? Our objective was that he should excel at making shoes. Our purpose was the same with regard to all the other occupations. Each man was assigned an occupation best suited to his nature and was expected to pursue that occupation all his days. He was to be free of all necessity to engage in other pursuits; at the same time, he was not to let opportunities slip in the practice of his own occupation so that he would become a good workman.

Now it is obviously of the first importance that soldiers should do their work well. But is the art of war so easily learned that a soldier can at the same time be a farmer, a shoemaker, or active in some other employment? After all, no one in all the world could become expert at playing dice or checkers if he played only in his spare time, instead of practicing from his earliest childhood to the exclusion of everything else. Is it credible that a man who takes up a shield or any other instrument of war for the first time should forthwith become a competent soldier, ready to fight on line where heavy armor is used or in other forms of warfare? Neither can any kind of instrument or tool by itself turn a man into an artist or an athlete; only learning and practice can do that.

Could we find tools that would teach their own use, we should have discovered something truly beyond price.

But now we approach the most important business in the city, the task of guardians. Accordingly, a guardian would have to spend more time than any other in education—in learning and practice. By the same token, he would have to be freer than any other from tasks extraneous to his work.

I should think so.

And he would also have to have a nature suited to his calling?

Of course. . . .

BOOK III

. . . [I asked Glaucon:] What should we consider next? Must we not decide who shall rule and who shall be ruled?

Clearly.

Well, it should be obvious that the older should rule the younger.

Yes.

And the rulers must be the best of the elders?

Yes.

And are not the best farmers those most skilled in farming?

Yes.

So if we want the best guardians we must choose those most skilled in guarding the city.

Yes.

So they must first of all be intelligent and prudent in managing the affairs of state, and they must be concerned for interests of the city.

Yes.

And will not a man be most concerned for that which he most loves?

He will.

Further, will a man not be likely to love whatever appears to have interests coinciding with his own, whose fortunes for better or worse will affect his own accordingly?

That is the way it is.

It follows that we must set apart from the other guardians those men whose lives convince us that they are the ones most likely to be zealous for the interests of the state and least likely to contravene them.

A suitable selection.

Then I should think that we must keep them under observation at every stage of their lives. We must see whether they are steady in their resolve to guard and serve the state. We must see whether their minds hold fast to the principle of public duty, never permitting either force or deception to make them give up the conviction that they must do what is best for the state. . . .

It will be right to call these men guardians in the fullest sense of the word. They will stand guard against enemies abroad and friends at home, so that the former won't have the power—nor the latter the will—to work injury to the city. The younger ones whom we have so far called guardians will from now on be called auxiliaries, and they will aid the rulers in upholding the principles of their government.

Agreed. . . .

BOOK IV

. . . [I said to Adeimantus:] Son of Ariston, we have finished with founding the city. Next, you, your brother [Glaucon], and Polemarchus, and all the others must find something that will illuminate the city. The light must be clear and strong so that we may discover where justice and injustice are located. We must be able to see what is the difference between them. We want to know whether it is justice or injustice that brings a man happiness. We want to know if justice and injustice are qualities that affect happiness differently according to whether they are practiced openly or in secret.

Socrates, said Glaucon, what is all this nonsense about our having to undertake this search? You promised to search for it yourself. You said you would be ashamed if you failed to serve justice by every means in your power.

You are right to remind me. I will make the search, then, but you must all help.

We will.

I believe we can find what we are looking for by making the following assumption: the city we have founded—if we have built rightly—will be good in the fullest sense of the word.

That is certain.

It means that the city is wise, courageous, temperate, and just.

Necessarily.

Now, if we find some of these qualities in the city, can we assume the ones not yet found will nonetheless be present?

Let us assume it.

Then we can proceed as we would if we were seeking any one element in a set of four. If we discover that one element before the others, we shall have accomplished our task. But if we find the other three first, the one we are looking for will necessarily be the remaining one in the set.

That seems right.

Then let us apply this method as we inquire into the four virtues in our city. Of these virtues, wisdom is evidently the first. But I must add that there appears to be some peculiarity connected with it.

What?

Well, let us see. The city is certainly wise, for it abounds in good counsel. Good counsel, in turn, is a sort of skill or proficiency, something generated from knowledge and not from ignorance.

Of course.

But there are many and diverse skills in the city and many proficiencies. Consider those practiced by carpenters, smiths, and farmers. Are these the skills that produce wisdom and prudence in governing?

No. They could only serve to produce and teach excellence in cabinetry, ironworking, and agriculture.

All right, then. Is there any form of skill or knowledge possessed by some of the citizens of the city we recently founded that attends not to particular interests but to the general interest, to the city as a whole in both its domestic and foreign policies?

Yes.

What is it, and where is it to be found?

It is the art of guardianship practiced by the city's rulers whom we recently described as guardians in the fullest sense.

What description will fit the city possessing this kind of knowledge?

A city that is prudent and truly wise.

Will there be more smiths or guardians in our city?

Far fewer guardians.

They will, in fact, be fewer than all the other groups who are known by the names given their professions. This means that the city built in accordance with the principles we have discussed will be wise thanks to its smallest group, the ruling class. And this is the peculiarity to which I referred earlier: the class whose knowledge is the only knowledge that merits the term *wisdom* seems ordained by nature to be the smallest class of all.

True.

Apparently, then, our discussion of wisdom as one of the four virtues in the city has given us some understanding of its nature and where it is to be found.

If we follow the same approach, I think we can discover the nature of courage, where it is situated, and how it imparts its spirit to the entire city. Now whoever calls a city brave or cowardly will think first about its armed forces. This is so because the character of the city is not determined by the bravery or cowardice of the citizenry as a whole. The city is brave because there is a part of it that is steadfast in its convictions about what is to be feared and what is not to be feared. These convictions constitute an integral part of the education prescribed by the city's founder. They also define the meaning of courage.

Would you please say that again? I don't think I understand.

Courage is a preservative. Strengthened by education, it preserves convictions about the things that are legitimately to be feared and those that are not. Courage makes a man hold fast to these convictions no matter whether he is threatened by danger or lured by desire. Neither pain nor pleasure will move him. . . .

After wisdom and courage we wanted to search out two further virtues in the city. One is temperance—or moderation. The other is justice, the grand object of all our inquiries.

Agreed.

Now, do you think we could go ahead and move directly to a consideration of justice without first inquiring into the nature of temperance?

I don't know. What I do know is that I should regret turning immediately to justice if that meant missing the opportunity for a better understanding of temperance and self-control. So let us look at these first.

It would be wrong of me to refuse.

Go ahead, then.

I will. To begin with, temperance seems more clearly related to peace and harmony than to wisdom and courage.

How so?

It appears to me that temperance is the ordering or controlling of certain pleasures and desires. This is what is implied when one says that a man is master of himself. It is a curious expression because it suggests that a man is both his own master and his own servant. But I believe the proper meaning of the phrase is that there is both good and bad in the soul of man. When the good part governs the bad, a man is praised for being master of himself. But if bad education or bad company subjects the good (and smaller part) of the soul to the bad (and larger) part, a man will be blamed for being unprincipled and a slave of self.

Now look at our newly founded city. If temperance and self-mastery are in charge, if the better part rules the worse, we may well say that the city is master of itself.

I agree.

We may say that the mass of diverse appetites, pleasures, and pains is to be found chiefly among children, women, slaves, and the many so-called freemen from the lower classes. But the simple and temperate desires governed by reason, good sense, and true opinion are to be found only in the few, those who are the best born and the best educated.

Yes.

Both the few and the many have their place in the city. But the meaner desires of the many will be held in check by the virtue and wisdom of the ruling few. It follows that if any city may claim to be master of its pleasures and desires—to be master of itself—it will be ours. For all these reasons, we may properly call our city temperate.

I agree.

There is another point. In our city, if anywhere, rulers and subjects will share a common conviction as to who should rule. What does this agreement suggest about the location of temperance? Will we find it among the rulers or the subjects?

In both, I should think.

Then we were not wrong in detecting a similarity between temperance and some kind of harmony. Temperance is different from wisdom and courage, each of which is associated with a particular part of the city. Temperance, on the other hand, pervades the entire city, producing a harmony of all its parts and inhabitants, from the weakest to the strongest. And this holds true however you want to measure strength and weakness: by force, or numbers, or wealth, or wisdom. Hence we may properly conclude that temperance is a consensual agreement between superior and inferior as to which should rule. And we should note that our conclusion applies both to individuals and to societies.

Agreed.

Now we have inquired into three of the four chief qualities of our city. The fourth and final quality is justice. But here we must take care that it does not elude us. We must be like hunters who surround a thicket to make sure that the quarry doesn't escape. Justice is clearly somewhere hereabouts. Look sharp, and call me if you see it first.

I wish I could. But I am only your follower, with sight just keen enough to see what you show me.

Well, say a prayer and follow me.

Show me the way.

The wood is dark and almost impenetrable. We will have a hard time flushing out the quarry. Still, we must push on. . . . There, I see something. Glaucon! I think we're on the track. Now it won't escape us.

Good news.

But we have really been stupid.

How so?

Because a long time ago, at the beginning of our inquiry, justice was right in front of us, and we never saw it. We were like people who look in the distance for what they already have in their grasp. We looked away from what we were seeking and trained our eyes instead on distant objects. And that is why we did not find it.

What do you mean?

I mean that all this time we have been talking about justice without realizing that our discussion has already begun to disclose its substance.

I am getting weary of your lengthy preambles.

All right. Tell me now whether I am right or wrong. You remember the original principle we laid down at the founding of the city: each citizen should perform that work or function for which his nature best suits him. This is the principle, or some variation of it, that we may properly call justice.

We often said that.

We also said that justice was tending to one's own business and not meddling in others'.

Yes.

So minding one's own business really appears, in one sense, at least, to be justice. Do you know how I reached this conclusion?

No.

You remember we were inquiring into the four cardinal virtues of a city. We examined temperance, courage, and wisdom; now justice remains the one still to be considered. What we will find is that justice sustains and perfects the other three; justice is the ultimate cause and condition of their existence.

Now that we have wisdom, courage, temperance, and justice fairly before us, it would be hard to decide which of the four virtues effectually contributes most to the excellence of the city. Is it the harmony existing between rulers and subjects? Is it the soldier's fidelity to what he has learned about real and fictitious dangers? Or wisdom and watchfulness in the rulers? Or, finally, is it the virtue that is found in everyone—children, women, slaves and freemen, craftsmen, rulers, and subjects—which leads them each to do his own work and not to interfere with others? These are questions not easily answered.

Yes. They are very perplexing.

But we can at least accept the conclusion that the fourth virtue of minding one's own business rivals the other three virtues in contributing to the city's excellence. That is to say that justice is at least the equal of wisdom, courage, and temperance.

Here is something else that points to the same conclusion. You would assign the responsibility for judging lawsuits to the rulers of the city, would you not?

Certainly.

And are lawsuits decided on any other ground than the proposition that a man may neither take what is another's nor be deprived of what is his?

That is the proper principle.

And the just principle.

Yes.

Here, then, is another demonstration that justice commands a man to have and to hold only what is his own.

True.

But see if you agree with me on this point. I would argue that no great harm is done if, say, carpenters and cobblers would decide to exchange tools and occupations, leaving their own businesses and taking on the others'. I don't see much harm even if some attempted to practice both skills at once.

Neither do I.

Suppose, however, that a cobbler or any other man nature designed to be an artisan or tradesman becomes ambitious because he has become rich or because he is physically powerful or has attracted large numbers of followers. Suppose he then attempts to force his way into the warrior class. Or imagine that a warrior, unsuited for the task, seeks to occupy a seat among the guardians. Finally, imagine someone trying to combine into one the roles of artisan, soldier, and statesman. All this kind of behavior can only lead to the ruin of the city.

I agree.

So any person from one class who meddles in another does his city the greatest wrong. This flouting of the maxim to mind one's own business is the very definition of injustice. Conversely, when craftsmen, soldiers, and guardians tend to their own business, that is justice. The city will be just.

How could it be otherwise?

Nonetheless, we had better wait a bit before giving unqualified assent to these propositions. We can be certain about the nature of justice only if its role in the individual turns out to be identical to its role in the city. If we cannot establish the identity, we must make a fresh start. But let us first finish what we have already started.

Remember that we began with the proposition that if we first examined justice on a larger scale, it would be easier to understand justice in the individual. We used the city as our larger measure. We founded the best city we could because we were confident that in a good city we would find justice. Now let us apply our findings to the individual. If they hold for both city and citizen, we will rest our case. But if justice in the individual is shown to be different, we must return to the city for further investigations. Perhaps if we adopted procedures to examine city and citizen simultaneously, we could rub them up against one another and generate enough friction to light the countenance of justice and fix it firmly and forever in our own minds.

The approach seems promising, said Glaucon. Let's try it.

All right. If we use the same name for two things, city and man, one large and one small, they will be alike in that quality to which their common name refers. It follows that as far as the quality of justice is concerned there will be no difference between the just man and the just city.

I agree. The man will resemble the city.

But we must remember that we deemed the city just when each of its three classes attended to its own business. We also called the city temperate, brave, and wise because of the particular qualities and dispositions of the classes. If we now assess the individual in the same way, we must demonstrate that the same three elements from which they spring are actually present in the individual and have the same effects and consequences. In order to do this, of course, we have to halt for a moment to deal with a minor question. Does the individual soul have these three elements or not?

Hardly a minor question, Socrates. But what is worth questioning is seldom easy.

You are right, Glaucon. I must say then that I don't think that our present procedures of inquiry will lead us to the truth of this matter. We need to follow another more difficult and much longer path. But perhaps we can reach at least some useful conclusions based on what we have said so far.

That will satisfy me.

It will satisfy me, too.

Then don't hold back.

Very well. Surely we must admit that the same qualities we observed in the city are also to be found in the individual. Indeed, it is obvious that the individual transmits them to the city. Where else should they come from? Consider the quality of spirit or courage of those who inhabit the northern regions of the Thracians and Scythians. It would be ridiculous to suppose that this collective quality has any other source than the citizens who possess the same quality as individuals. The love of learning, which is a particular characteristic of our society, also originates with individuals. So does the love of money in Egypt and Phoenicia.

So much is easy to see. But the next step is more difficult. Is our whole soul involved in whatever we do? Or is bravery, intellectual effort, and bodily appetite each the exclusive product of a distinct and separate part of the soul? Is our nature an undivided entity, or is it a set of disconnected components?

This is a tricky question. But let's begin by trying to ascertain whether the parts of the soul are identical to each other or different. An example may help. Can something be both at rest and in motion at the same time?

Never.

Then we can infer that nothing acts in opposite ways at the same time. Nor can anything exist simultaneously in two opposing states. If, then, we seem to perceive the soul behaving in contradictory ways or reflecting two opposing states at once, we must conclude that the soul is many and not one.

Now let us tighten up our agreement so that it won't become unraveled again as we go along. Assume a man is standing still but at the same time waving his arms. It would be clearly incorrect to assert that the man is in the same moment at rest and in motion. The correct observation would be that part of the man is moving and part is motionless. Agreed, Glaucon?

Agreed.

If someone is fond of quibbling, however, he might try out some fancy variations on this theme. He might point out, for example, that a spinning top revolves and at the same time remains fixed to a single point. He could then try to dazzle us by concluding that the top as a whole and in all its parts is at once both moving and unmoved and that the same holds for any object circling around a fixed point. But we would refuse to accept the conclusion. A top has an axis and a circumference; the axis, insofar as it remains vertical, stands still while the circumference spins. One part moves and one part does not. On the other hand, of course, should the axis tilt away from the perpendicular during the spin, then it will also be moving.

Right.

Then we won't be hoodwinked or disconcerted by those who argue otherwise.

No.

Very well. Since we don't want to bother to review all the possible objections to our assumption nor take the time to refute them, let us go ahead and assume the correctness of our position. But if we ever come to think otherwise, then we must renounce the assumption and all the inferences we have drawn from it.

Agreed.

Then should we say that the following kinds of pairs are composed of opposites: attraction and repulsion, desire and aversion, agreement and disagreement? And should we observe that any proper discussion of opposites applies to actions as well as emotions?

Yes.

Keeping in mind the pairs we just described, would we not say that thirst, hunger, willing and wishing, and desires in general are examples of the active element in the pairs? The one who desires something actively searches for the object of his desire; he tries to draw to himself the thing he wants to possess. Seeking satisfaction, he will put the question to himself and then answer yes.

That's the way it happens.

What about not wanting, not desiring, not willing? Shall we class them with the passive components of our pairs, along with rejection and repulsion?

Of course.

Then can we classify all desires as belonging to the same element in human nature? Can we also recognize that among the desires the most insistent are hunger and thirst?

Your conclusions seem reasonable. . . .

A thirsty man, insofar as he is only thirsty, desires only to drink. This is what he wants and seeks.

Clearly.

But if a thirsty man refrains from drinking, it must be due to a part of him different from the thirsty part that pulls every animal to water. This conclusion is in accord with our earlier finding that nothing can behave in opposite ways at the same time. We can illustrate the principle with still another example: we do not say that an archer's hands pull and push the bow at the same time. We say rather that one hand pulls and the other pushes.

Of course.

Very well. Have you ever observed people who are thirsty and yet unwilling to drink?

Yes, often.

What are we to conclude in such cases? There must be something in these people that urges them to drink and something else that bids them abstain, something that overpowers and inhibits the initial urge.

Yes.

And what is the inhibiting agent? Is it not reason and reflection? And does not the agent that urges and attracts find its source in passion and sometimes in disease?

Evidently.

Then it would be reasonable to conclude that the soul is composed of at least two distinct parts. One is the reasoning part. The other is appetite or desire, where hunger, thirst, and sexual passion have their abode along with other irrational drives.

The conclusion is reasonable.

Then we are agreed about these two parts of the soul. But is there a third? What about the spirited part which enables us to feel anger or indignation? Is this something separate, or is it identical with one of the other two parts?

I should think it is akin to the desiring part.

A story I once heard may help us find an answer. One day Leontius, the son of Aglaion, was coming up from the Piraeus[5] alongside the north wall when he saw some dead bodies fallen at the hand of the executioner. He felt the urge to look at them; at the same time he was disgusted with himself and his morbid curiosity, and he turned away. For a while he was in inner turmoil, resisting his craving to look and covering his eyes. But finally he was overcome by his desire to see. He opened his eyes wide and ran up to the corpses, cursing his own vision: "Now have your way, damn you. Go ahead and feast at this banquet for sordid appetites."

I have heard that story, too.

Leontius's behavior shows clearly that desire and anger are two different things and sometimes go to war with one another.

Yes, the meaning of the story is obvious.

We often see this kind of behavior where a man's desires overmaster his reason. This results in his reproaching himself for tolerating the violence going on within himself. In this situation a man's soul can resemble a city riven by two warring factions. The spirited part, here in the guise of anger or indignation, will ally with reason against the passions. Indeed, every time reason rejects what the passions propose, neither anger nor indignation nor any other expression of spirit will desert to passion's cause. I don't believe you or anyone else could cite a single instance where spirit and the passions have united against a confident reason.

I could not.

Now think of the man who believes he has committed a wrong. If he is of noble nature, he will not resent it if he subsequently suffers hunger, cold, or other kinds of retribution. He would consider them just punishment. He will not even wish to be angry.

But ponder the opposite situation. A man believes he has been wronged. In response to hunger, cold, and other afflictions he fumes and smarts, regarding himself as a victim of injustice. He grapples with his tormentor in the name of righteousness. He perseveres until victory or death—unless reason, like the shepherd, calls off the dog.

An apt illustration. It parallels the relationship we established between guardians and auxiliaries in our city. The guardians are the shepherds and the auxiliaries the dogs trained to obey their masters.

We understand each other well. But do you see how our position has changed? Just minutes ago the spirited element of the soul appeared to be the ally of the appetites and desires. But now, when the soul is torn by internal divisions, we see spirit arrayed alongside reason.

Yes.

Hence we must now ask whether spirit is distinct from reason or only a function of reason. If the latter, the soul must consist of no more than the two elements of reason and appetite. Or does the soul in fact resemble the city as we have described it, held together by the three classes of craftsmen, auxiliaries, and guardians? If the analogy holds between soul and city, then the spirited part is an authentic third element in the soul. And if it is not corrupted by bad education, spirit will enlist in the service of reason.

No question about it. The soul must be composed of three parts.

Right, but only if spirit, which has already been distinguished from appetite, can now be distinguished from reason.

That is easily proved. Even young children display spirit almost from birth—that is, they frequently display indignation or anger. On the other hand, many of them never seem to discover where it is that reason rules, and most manage it only late in life.

You observe truly. One can say the same thing of animals. Homer makes a similar point in the words we have cited earlier: "He smote his breast and chided his heart."[6] Homer's intention was clearly to mark off the difference between reason and spirit: man's reasoning part judges between better and worse and rebukes that part which harbors unreasoning anger.

You are exactly right.

At last, then, strenuous effort has helped us to reach agreement that the structure of the city corresponds to the structure of the soul; both are composed of three basic elements.

Yes.

Wisdom is the same in the man and in the city. Courage in the city is the same as courage in the individual. Virtue is the same quality in both. A man and a city will be deemed just or unjust according to the same standards.

Yes.

Let us not forget that justice in the city is founded in the good order to which each citizen doing his own work contributes.

We have not forgotten.

Let us not forget either that justice in the individual depends on each of the various elements in his nature doing its own work. It is proper that the reasoning element should rule because it is wise and capable of foresight in planning for the whole. It is clearly appropriate that the spirited element should be the servant and ally of reason. The joint influence of music and gymnastic should be able to harmonize the two. Mental and physical training will cooperate to refine reason and moderate the wildness of the spirit. The reasoning part will be nourished by the study of noble literature; harmony and rhythm will tame the spirit.

Then, when reason and spirit have been trained to understand their proper functions, they must aid each other to govern the appetites that constitute in each of us the largest and most insatiate part of our nature. Here is where we must be watchful lest the appetites wax strong and overbearing by dint of constant indulgence and gratification to the point where they are tempted to defy all limits. Overrunning the territories of soul and city, desire will claim for itself the right to govern. With that the good order of soul and city will be undone and the capitulation to unreason will be complete.

A deplorable outcome.

Only the firm alliance of reason and spirit can prevent it. This alliance is also beautifully designed to guard against the external enemies of both body and soul. Reason would do the planning, and spirit would do the fighting, holding fast to the ruling strategy and courageously accomplishing the mission set by reason.

Note that this is what we have earlier called bravery in the individual, the virtue which permits neither pain nor pleasure to pry him away from the word of reason concerning what to fear and what not to fear.

Right.

And we said a man is wise if that small element in him called reason governs according to what is good for the soul's three elements, for their own sakes and in their mutual relations.

Then we concluded that the temperate man is one in whom the three elements are in harmony. There are no quarrels among the parts because there is agreement among them that the rational element should govern the whole.

That is exactly the nature of temperance in both the man and the city.

And, once again, justice. We have described again and again the qualities that make a man just. Is justice different or less evident in the individual than in the city?

I see no difference between the two, said Glaucon.

Good. But for any who may still doubt, let us see if we can convince them with some simple illustrations. Suppose, for example, a man deposited some money on trust with the government of a just city or with a just man. Would not his money be equally safe with both? Would either embezzle the money?

He need have no concern in either case.

Will the just person, as man or citizen, ever steal from other men or from the state? Would he commit treachery or sacrilege? Would he violate his oath or break agreements? Would he engage in adultery? Would he fail to honor his parents or neglect divine services?

Never.

And are we agreed that the source of this behavior is a soul in which each part is doing its own work with the consequence that the functions of ruling and being ruled are properly allocated?

Yes.

Then justice is nothing else than the power that brings forth well-governed men and well-governed cities. Our dream has come true. We have made real what we only surmised at the outset of our inquiry when we suspected that some divine power was drawing our attention to a basic pattern of justice.

I agree. This is what we have accomplished.

Yes, the first model of justice helped us greatly, Glaucon. We learned from it that justice is somehow related to a division of labor reflecting the natural talents of the city's inhabitants: it is just that he who is naturally a cobbler should stick to cobbling, and the same for carpenters and all the other occupations.

Evidently.

But the early model was analogy, not reality. The reality is that justice is not a matter of external behavior but the way a man privately and truly governs his inner self. The just man does not permit the various parts of his soul to interfere with one another or usurp each other's functions. He has set his own life in order. He is his own master and his own law. He has become a friend to himself. He will have brought into tune the three parts of his soul: high, middle, and low, like the three major notes of a musical scale, and all the intervals between. When he has brought all this together in temperance and harmony, he will have made himself one man instead of many.

Only then will he be ready to do whatever he does in society: making money, training the body, involving himself in politics or in business transactions. In all the public activities in which he is engaged he will call just and beautiful only that conduct which harmonizes with and preserves his own inner order which we have just described. And the knowledge that understands the meaning and importance of such conduct he will call wisdom.

Conversely, behavior that subverts the inner order he will deem unjust. The kind of intellect that sanctions such behavior he will condemn as ignorant and foolish.

Socrates, you have said the exact truth.

Then I believe we could defend the claim that we have discovered the just man and the just city and explained the nature of justice in each of them.

I believe so, too.

Let us stake our claim, then. Our next task is to examine injustice. Here the soul's three parts become contending factions, meddling in one another's business to the point where civil war breaks out. Or one part of the soul rebels against the rest with the purpose of seizing the governing power, usurping the very authority to which it is properly subject. Such anarchy and dissension can only be the product of intemperance, cowardice, ignorance, and every kind of vice. All these evils together concoct the essence of injustice.

Exactly.

If we now understand justice and injustice, we ought to be able to understand the difference between just and unjust behavior.

How can we do that?

By means of an analogy. There are practices that bolster health in the body and practices that lead to illness. Health requires that the body be ordered and governed as intended by nature. Illness disrupts this natural order.

Yes.

So also with justice and injustice. Just behavior produces justice in the soul and unjust behavior injustice. Justice, like health, depends upon the presence of a natural order governing the soul in the relations of its parts and in the conduct of the whole. With injustice, as with illness, the natural order has vanished from the soul, giving place to its opposite.

Agreed.

Then we can agree that virtue is the very health, beauty, and strength of the soul, while vice makes the soul sick, ugly, and weak?

Yes.

What is beautiful, then, must lead to virtue and what is ugly to vice?

Yes.

Well, then, we have only one other matter to consider. Is it profitable to live one's life in the cause of justice and beauty, whether or not anyone takes notice? Or is it more profitable to be unjust, provided you can escape punishment and thus escape repentance, too?

But, Socrates, now you are really asking a ridiculous question. We all know that when our health is irreparably ruined, life is no longer worth living, no matter how much wealth, power, and luxury may be ours. No more would one wish to cling to life if the soul's paramount principle were to be corrupted. With the principle of justice in ruins men are condemned to do whatever they like—except to banish evil and restore themselves to virtue.

Yes, the question is ridiculous. . . .

BOOK IX

. . . [I said to Glaucon:] Having reached this point in the argument, we should do well to return to the things we said first of all and thanks to which we have managed to come this far. Someone, I recall, said that the unjust man will find injustice profitable providing he has a reputation for justice. Was that not said?

Yes, it was said.

Now that we have agreed on the nature of just and unjust conduct, let us try to reason with the one who made that assertion.

How?

By describing the soul in such a way that he will understand the meaning of his words.

What kind of description?

Something like we find in ancient fables about the Chimaera, Scylla, and Cerberus.[7] Many others, too, tell how a multitude of forms grow naturally into one.

That's right. They do.

Imagine, then, a single figure of a multicolored creature with many heads. The ring of heads consists of both tame and wild beasts springing forth from the parent creature, which can produce them and change them at will.

The work of a clever dissembler. Still, speech is more easily twisted than wax and other materials. So let the figure stand.

Then another figure: choose an idea and make it into a lion. Choose still another and make it a man. Make the first far larger than the second.

That is easier. The work is done.

Then unite all three in one in such a way that they will naturally grow together.

I have united them.

Next, encompass them about with the single likeness of a man. Do it so that it looks like one animal, a human being, to anyone who looks only at the surface and is not able to see beneath.

The outer casing is now in place.

Now let us turn back to the one who tells this man that it pays to be unjust and that he will find justice inexpedient. Let us say that all his assertions amount to no more than a recommendation to gorge and exalt the many-colored beast and the lion and all that the lion symbolizes. They offer a recipe that will starve the human being within him to the point where he can be dragged wherever the other parts of his soul want to go. Never do they speak words of friendship and reconciliation; rather do they provoke a man's parts to bite and fight and devour one another.

When a man praises injustice, this is what he really means to say.

His opposite is the man who asserts justice is the more profitable. He tells us that in thought and deed the inner man must govern the entire man. He must deal with the many-headed beast like a farmer who nurtures and cultivates his crops but prevents the growth of weeds. The lion's nature must become his ally, and he must care for all the beasts in common. First he must be friends to all of them and then make them friends to one another. This is the manner in which he must bring them up.

When a man praises justice, this is what he really means to say.

On every count, then, the man who praises justice speaks truth. The man who praises injustice lies. By whatever standard we apply, whether pleasure, profit, or reputation, the friend of justice speaks truly. But the unjust man does not even understand what he dishonors.

No. He cannot understand it.

NOTES

1. Plato here paraphrases Aeschylus, *Seven Against Thebes*, line 592. Aeschylus (525–456 B.C.E.) was a Greek tragedian. [D.C.A.]
2. Aeschylus, *Seven Against Thebes*, lines 593–594 [D.C.A.]
3. The author of this elegy is unknown. [D.C.A.]
4. *agora*: the marketplace in an ancient Greek city [D.C.A.]
5. *Piraeus*: the seaport of Athens, located about 4 miles southwest of the city [D.C.A.]
6. Homer *Odyssey* 20.17. Socrates had quoted this line from Homer earlier, in Book III. [D.C.A.]
7. In Greek mythology, the Chimaera is a fire-breathing monster with the head of a lion, the middle section of a goat, and the tail of a serpent; Scylla is a sea monster with twelve feet and six heads; Cerberus is a three-headed dog that guards the entrance to the lower world. [D.C.A.]

QUESTIONS FOR REFLECTION AND DISCUSSION

1. Does the soul have parts?
2. Is justice in the soul similar to justice in the state?
3. Is justice in the soul, like health in the body, desirable for its own sake?
4. Is a just person with a reputation for injustice better off than an unjust person who is thought to be just?
5. Should reason always control appetite and spirit?

SUGGESTIONS FOR FURTHER READING

I. Primary Sources

The Republic, trans. Richard W. Sterling and William C. Scott. New York: Norton, 1985, 317 pp.

Other good translations of the *Republic* and of the following two dialogues are also available.

Gorgias, trans. Donald J. Zeyl. Indianapolis: Hackett, 1987, 113 pp.

A dialogue on the nature of oratory (rhetoric) and its moral implications. Socrates contrasts the orator-politician with the philosopher and defends philosophy as a way of life. He examines the nature of the true human good, arguing that it is better to suffer injustice than to do it. The *Gorgias* was one of Plato's early dialogues and foreshadows some of the themes in the *Republic*.

Phaedo, trans. R. Hackforth. Cambridge, England: Cambridge University Press, 1955, 200 pp.

A dialogue from Plato's middle period in which Socrates converses with his friends just before he drinks the poison hemlock. Socrates calmly presents arguments to convince his friends that although the poison will kill his body, his soul will live on.

II. Secondary Sources

Annas, Julia. *An Introduction to Plato's Republic.* Oxford, England: Clarendon, 1981, 362 pp.

An examination of the principal themes of the *Republic*. See especially chap. 5, "Parts and Virtues of State and Soul," pp. 109–152, and chap. 6, "The Defence of Justice," pp. 153–169.

Grube, G. M. A. *Plato's Thought.* 1935; reprint ed., with new bibliography, Indianapolis: Hackett, 1980, 346 pp.

A general exposition of Plato's philosophy. Each of the eight chapters treats a separate Platonic theme. See especially chap. 4, "The Nature of the Soul," pp. 120–149.

Hare, R. M. *Plato.* Oxford, England: Oxford University Press, Past Masters Ser., 1982, 82 pp.

A concise introduction to Plato that draws mainly on the dialogues of his early and middle periods. Hare considers the relevance of Plato's views to contemporary social issues.

Melling, David J. *Understanding Plato.* Oxford, England: Oxford University Press, OPUS Ser., 1987, 178 pp.

An exposition of Plato's principal doctrines presented in historical context. Some chapters treat individual dialogues.

White, Nicholas P. *A Companion to Plato's Republic.* Indianapolis: Hackett, 1979, 275 pp.

Contains an introductory essay analyzing the overall argument of the *Republic* (pp. 9–60) and a detailed summary and section-by-section exposition of each of the ten books of the dialogue (pp. 61–266).

2

Aristotle

Aristotle was born in Stagira, a town in the region of Thrace in northern Greece, in 384 B.C.E. His father, a court physician to Amyntas II, king of Macedon, died when Aristotle was young, and Aristotle was raised by a relative. At about the age of seventeen he was sent to Athens to study at Plato's Academy, where he remained until Plato's death twenty years later.

Aristotle then left Athens and went to Assos, a city in Asia Minor, at the invitation of Hermias, the city's tyrant, who was gathering former students of the Academy to help establish Greek philosophy in Asia. Three years later he moved to Mytilene, a city on the island of Lesbos, where he and his student Theophrastus established a school. In 343 or 342, King Philip II of Macedon (son of Amyntas II) invited Aristotle to become the tutor of his thirteen-year-old son, Alexander (later known as Alexander the Great). Aristotle accepted the offer and moved to the royal court in Pella. After a few years as Alexander's tutor, Aristotle returned to his home town of Stagira.

In 335 Aristotle returned to Athens, where he founded a school called the Lyceum—named for its location near the temple of Apollo Lyceus. He ran the Lyceum until 323, when strong anti-Macedonian sentiment arose in Athens. Because of his long-standing connections with Macedon, Aristotle felt it prudent to leave Athens lest, as he reportedly put it, referring to the fate of Socrates, Athens "sin twice against philosophy." He went to Chalcis on the island of Euboea, where he died in 322 of a stomach ailment.

Aristotle is the author of two very different kinds of philosophical writings: polished works, intended for the general reading public, and notes from which he lectured, intended for circulation only among his students and associates. Most of Aristotle's public works were dialogues, probably written when he was a student at the Academy. These works, unfortunately, have been almost entirely lost; only scattered fragments have survived.

The writings of Aristotle that we have today are of the second kind—lecture notes. Since they are notes rather than finished works, they are at times terse and cryptic. Moreover, the person who put the notes in the form in which they have come down to us was not Aristotle himself but Andronicus of Rhodes, a scholar who lived three centuries later. In about 40

B.C.E. Andronicus systematized the various Aristotelian writings, grouping similar ones together, giving them titles, and putting the resultant treatises into what he considered the most logical order.

In these treatises Aristotle explores a wide variety of topics, ranging from logic and metaphysics to biology and ethics. His views were greatly influenced by Plato, but he went on to develop his own distinctive philosophical theories, some of which contradicted Plato's. In the *Nicomachean Ethics*, before presenting arguments against Plato's doctrine that Goodness itself exists, Aristotle explains that it is painful to disagree with his teacher and friend but that he has a duty—especially as a philosopher—to honor truth above friendship (Book I, Chapter 6).

Our selection is taken from Books I, II, and VIII of the *Nicomachean Ethics*, a work that addresses the question of how one should live in order to attain happiness. In Book I Aristotle argues that happiness is what all persons ultimately seek and that happiness consists in living a rational life. A rational life requires that two parts of the soul function well: the intellectual (strictly rational) part and the part containing emotions and desires (while emotions and desires are not in themselves rational, they can obey reason). For each part there is a group of *virtues*—inner dispositions that enable it to function well. The *intellectual* virtues, such as wisdom and understanding, enable the intellectual part to function well, while the *moral* virtues (virtues of character), such as generosity and self-control, enable the emotions and desires to function well. Aristotle argues that a person who lives in accordance with the intellectual and moral virtues attains happiness.

In Book II Aristotle explains how moral virtues are acquired and presents his theory that every moral virtue is a *characteristic* (a state of character) that aims at the mean between two extremes. Virtue lies in the middle; excess and deficiency are vices. To use one of Aristotle's examples, courage is the mean between recklessness and cowardice.

Book VIII examines friendship, which Aristotle says is either a virtue or something that involves virtue. Viewing friendship as "most indispensable for life," Aristotle makes a distinction between friendships based on usefulness or pleasure and friendships based on goodness. He argues that friendships based on goodness are the highest—and rarest—kind because such friends love each other for each other's sake, not for the usefulness or pleasure the other person provides.

NICOMACHEAN ETHICS

BOOK I

Chapter 1

Every art or applied science and every systematic investigation, and similarly every action and choice, seem to aim at some good; the good, therefore, has been well defined as that at which all things aim. But it is clear that there is a difference in the ends at which they aim: in some cases the activity is the end, in others the end is some product beyond the activity. In cases where the end lies beyond the action the product is naturally superior to the activity.

Since there are many activities, arts, and sciences, the number of ends is correspondingly large: of medicine the end is health, of shipbuilding, a vessel, of strategy, victory, and of household management, wealth. In many instances several such pursuits are grouped together under a single capacity: the art of bridle-making, for example, and everything else pertaining to the equipment of a horse are grouped together under horsemanship; horsemanship in turn, along with every other military action, is grouped together under strategy; and other pursuits are grouped together under other capacities. In all these cases the ends of the master sciences are preferable to the ends of the subordinate sciences, since the latter are pursued for the sake of the former. This is true whether the ends of the actions lie in the activities themselves or, as is the case in the disciplines just mentioned, in something beyond the activities.

Chapter 2

Now, if there exists an end in the realm of action which we desire for its own sake, an end which determines all our other desires; if, in other words, we do not make all our choices for the sake of something else—for in this way the

process will go on infinitely so that our desire would be futile and pointless—
then obviously this end will be the good, that is, the highest good. Will not
the knowledge of this good, consequently, be very important to our lives?
Would it not better equip us, like archers who have a target to aim at, to hit
the proper mark? If so, we must try to comprehend in outline at least what
this good is and to which branch of knowledge or to which capacity it
belongs.

This good, one should think, belongs to the most sovereign and most
comprehensive master science, and politics[1] clearly fits this description. For it
determines which sciences ought to exist in states, what kind of sciences each
group of citizens must learn, and what degree of proficiency each must attain.
We observe further that the most honored capacities, such as strategy, household management, and oratory, are contained in politics. Since this science
uses the rest of the sciences, and since, moreover, it legislates what people are
to do and what they are not to do, its end seems to embrace the ends of the
other sciences. Thus it follows that the end of politics is the good for man. For
even if the good is the same for the individual and the state, the good of the
state clearly is the greater and more perfect thing to attain and to safeguard.
The attainment of the good for one man alone is, to be sure, a source of
satisfaction; yet to secure it for a nation and for states is nobler and more
divine. In short, these are the aims of our investigation, which is in a sense an
investigation of social and political matters.

Chapter 3

Our discussion will be adequate if it achieves clarity within the limits of the
subject matter. For precision cannot be expected in the treatment of all
subjects alike, any more than it can be expected in all manufactured articles.
Problems of what is noble and just, which politics examines, present so much
variety and irregularity that some people believe that they exist only by
convention and not by nature. The problem of the good, too, presents a
similar kind of irregularity, because in many cases good things bring harmful
results. There are instances of men ruined by wealth, and others by courage.
Therefore, in a discussion of such subjects, which has to start from a basis of
this kind, we must be satisfied to indicate the truth with a rough and general
sketch: when the subject and the basis of a discussion consist of matters that
hold good only as a general rule, but not always, the conclusions reached
must be of the same order. The various points that are made must be received
in the same spirit. For a well-schooled man is one who searches for that
degree of precision in each kind of study which the nature of the subject at
hand admits: it is obviously just as foolish to accept arguments of probability
from a mathematician as to demand strict demonstrations from an orator.

Each man can judge competently the things he knows, and of these he is
a good judge. Accordingly, a good judge in each particular field is one who

has been trained in it, and a good judge in general, a man who has received an all-round schooling. For that reason, a young man is not equipped to be a student of politics; for he has no experience in the actions which life demands of him, and these actions form the basis and subject matter of the discussion. Moreover, since he follows his emotions, his study will be pointless and unprofitable, for the end of this kind of study is not knowledge but action. Whether he is young in years or immature in character makes no difference; for his deficiency is not a matter of time but of living and of pursuing all his interests under the influence of his emotions. Knowledge brings no benefit to this kind of person, just as it brings none to the morally weak. But those who regulate their desires and actions by a rational principle will greatly benefit from a knowledge of this subject. So much by way of a preface about the student, the limitations which have to be accepted, and the objective before us.

Chapter 4

To resume the discussion: since all knowledge and every choice is directed toward some good, let us discuss what is in our view the aim of politics, i.e., the highest good attainable by action. As far as its name is concerned, most people would probably agree: for both the common run of people and culti-vated men call it happiness, and understand by "being happy" the same as "living well" and "doing well." But when it comes to defining what hap-piness is, they disagree, and the account given by the common run differs from that of the philosophers. The former say it is some clear and obvious good, such as pleasure, wealth, or honor; some say it is one thing and others another, and often the very same person identifies it with different things at different times: when he is sick he thinks it is health, and when he is poor he says it is wealth; and when people are conscious of their own ignorance, they admire those who talk above their heads in accents of greatness. Some thinkers used to believe that there exists over and above these many goods another good, good in itself and by itself, which also is the cause of good in all these things. An examination of all the different opinions would perhaps be a little pointless, and it is sufficient to concentrate on those which are most in evidence or which seem to make some sort of sense. . . .

Chapter 5

. . . It is not unreasonable that men should derive their concept of the good and of happiness from the lives which they lead. The common run of people and the most vulgar identify it with pleasure, and for that reason are satisfied with a life of enjoyment. For the most notable kinds of life are three: the life just mentioned, the political life, and the contemplative life.

The common run of people, as we saw, betray their utter slavishness in their preference for a life suitable to cattle; but their views seem plausible because many people in high places share the feelings of Sardanapallus.[2] Cultivated and active men, on the other hand, believe the good to be honor, for honor, one might say, is the end of the political life. But this is clearly too superficial an answer: for honor seems to depend on those who confer it rather than on him who receives it, whereas our guess is that the good is a man's own possession which cannot easily be taken away from him. Furthermore, men seem to pursue honor to assure themselves of their own worth; at any rate, they seek to be honored by sensible men and by those who know them, and they want to be honored on the basis of their virtue or excellence.[3] Obviously, then, excellence, as far as they are concerned, is better than honor. One might perhaps even go so far as to consider excellence rather than honor as the end of political life. However, even excellence proves to be imperfect as an end: for a man might possibly possess it while asleep or while being inactive all his life, and while, in addition, undergoing the greatest suffering and misfortune. Nobody would call the life of such a man happy, except for the sake of maintaining an argument. . . . In the third place there is the contemplative life, which we shall examine later on. As for the money-maker, his life is led under some kind of constraint: clearly, wealth is not the good which we are trying to find, for it is only useful, i.e., it is a means to something else. Hence one might rather regard the aforementioned objects as ends, since they are valued for their own sake. But even they prove not to be the good, though many words have been wasted to show that they are. Accordingly, we may dismiss them. . . .

Chapter 7

Let us return again to our investigation into the nature of the good which we are seeking. It is evidently something different in different actions and in each art: it is one thing in medicine, another in strategy, and another again in each of the other arts. What, then, is the good of each? Is it not that for the sake of which everything else is done? That means it is health in the case of medicine, victory in the case of strategy, a house in the case of building, a different thing in the case of different arts, and in all actions and choices it is the end. For it is for the sake of the end that all else is done. Thus, if there is some one end for all that we do, this would be the good attainable by action; if there are several ends, they will be the goods attainable by action.

Our argument has gradually progressed to the same point at which we were before,[4] and we must try to clarify it still further. Since there are evidently several ends, and since we choose some of these—e.g., wealth, flutes, and instruments generally—as a means to something else, it is obvious that not all ends are final.[5] The highest good, on the other hand, must be something final. Thus, if there is only one final end, this will be the good we are seeking; if there are several, it will be the most final and perfect of them.

We call that which is pursued as an end in itself more final than an end which is pursued for the sake of something else; and what is never chosen as a means to something else we call more final than that which is chosen both as an end in itself and as a means to something else. What is always chosen as an end in itself and never as a means to something else is called final in an unqualified sense. This description seems to apply to happiness above all else: for we always choose happiness as an end in itself and never for the sake of something else. Honor, pleasure, intelligence, and all virtue we choose partly for themselves—for we would choose each of them even if no further advantage would accrue from them—but we also choose them partly for the sake of happiness, because we assume that it is through them that we will be happy. On the other hand, no one chooses happiness for the sake of honor, pleasure, and the like, nor as a means to anything at all.

We arrive at the same conclusion if we approach the question from the standpoint of self-sufficiency. For the final and perfect good seems to be self-sufficient. However, we define something as self-sufficient not by reference to the "self" alone. We do not mean a man who lives his life in isolation, but a man who also lives with parents, children, a wife, and friends and fellow citizens generally, since man is by nature a social and political being. But some limit must be set to these relationships; for if they are extended to include ancestors, descendants, and friends of friends, they will go on to infinity. However, this point must be reserved for investigation later. For the present we define as "self-sufficient" that which taken by itself makes life something desirable and deficient in nothing. It is happiness, in our opinion, which fits this description. Moreover, happiness is of all things the one most desirable, and it is not counted as one good thing among many others. But if it were counted as one among many others, it is obvious that the addition of even the least of the goods would make it more desirable; for the addition would produce an extra amount of good, and the greater amount of good is always more desirable than the lesser. We see then that happiness is something final and self-sufficient and the end of our actions.

To call happiness the highest good is perhaps a little trite, and a clearer account of what it is, is still required. Perhaps this is best done by first ascertaining the proper function[6] of man. For just as the goodness and performance of a flute player, a sculptor, or any kind of expert, and generally of anyone who fulfills some function or performs some action, are thought to reside in his proper function, so the goodness and performance of man would seem to reside in whatever is his proper function. Is it then possible that while a carpenter and a shoemaker have their own proper functions and spheres of action, man as man has none, but was left by nature a good-for-nothing without a function? Should we not assume that just as the eye, the hand, the foot, and in general each part of the body clearly has its own proper function, so man too has some function over and above the functions of his parts? What can this function possibly be? Simply living? He shares that even with plants, but we are now looking for something peculiar to man. Accordingly, the life of nutrition and growth must be excluded. Next in line there is a life of sense perception. But this, too, man has in common with the horse, the ox, and every animal. There remains then an active life of the rational element. The rational element has two parts: one is rational in that it obeys the rule of reason, the other in that it possesses and conceives rational rules. Since the expression "life of the rational element" also can be used in two senses, we must make it clear that we mean a life determined by the activity, as opposed to the mere possession, of the rational element. For the activity, it seems, has a greater claim to be the function of man.

The proper function of man, then, consists in an activity of the soul in conformity with a rational principle or, at least, not without it. In speaking of the proper function of a given individual we mean that it is the same in kind as the function of an individual who sets high standards for himself: the proper function of a harpist, for example, is the same as the function of a harpist who has set high standards for himself. The same applies to any and every group of individuals: the full attainment of excellence must be added to the mere function. In other words, the function of the harpist is to play the harp; the function of the harpist who has high standards is to play it well. On these assumptions, if we take the proper function of man to be a certain kind of life, and if this kind of life is an activity of the soul and consists in actions performed in conjunction with the rational element, and if a man of high standards is he who performs these actions well and properly, and if a function is well performed when it is performed in accordance with the excellence appropriate to it—we reach the conclusion that the good of man is an activity of the soul in conformity with excellence or virtue, and if there are several virtues, in conformity with the best and most complete.

But we must add "in a complete life." For one swallow does not make a spring, nor does one sunny day; similarly, one day or a short time does not make a man blessed and happy.

This will suffice as an outline of the good: for perhaps one ought to make a general sketch first and fill in the details afterwards. Once a good outline has been made, anyone, it seems, is capable of developing and completing it in detail, and time is a good inventor or collaborator in such an effort. Advances in the arts, too, have come about in this way, for anyone can fill in gaps. We must also bear in mind what has been said above, namely that one should not require precision in all pursuits alike, but in each field precision varies with the matter under discussion and should be required only to the extent to which it is appropriate to the investigation. A carpenter and a geometrician both want to find a right angle, but they do not want to find it in the same sense: the former wants to find it to the extent to which it is useful for his work, the latter, wanting to see truth, [tries to ascertain] what it is and what sort of thing it iş. We must, likewise, approach other subjects in the same spirit, in order to prevent minor points from assuming a greater importance than the major tasks. Nor should we demand to know a causal explanation in all matters alike; in some instances, e.g., when dealing with fundamental principles, it is sufficient to point out convincingly that such-and-such is in fact the case. The fact here is the primary thing and the fundamental principle. Some fundamental principles can be apprehended by induction, others by sense perception, others again by some sort of habituation,[7] and others by still other means. We must try to get at each of them in a way naturally appropriate to it, and must be scrupulous in defining it correctly, because it is of great importance for the subsequent course of the discussion. Surely, a good beginning is more than half the whole, and as it comes to light, it sheds light on many problems.

Chapter 8

We must examine the fundamental principle with which we are concerned, [happiness,] not only on the basis of the logical conclusion we have reached and on the basis of the elements which make up its definition, but also on the basis of the views commonly expressed about it. For in a true statement, all the facts are in harmony; in a false statement, truth soon introduces a discordant note.

Good things are commonly divided into three classes: (1) external goods, (2) goods of the soul, and (3) goods of the body. Of these, we call the goods pertaining to the soul goods in the highest and fullest sense. But in speaking of "soul," we refer to our soul's actions and activities. Thus, our definition tallies with this opinion which has been current for a long time and to which philosophers subscribe. We are also right in defining the end as consisting of actions and activities; for in this way the end is included among the goods of the soul and not among external goods.

Also the view that a happy man lives well and fares well fits in with our definition: for we have all but defined happiness as a kind of good life and well-being.

Moreover, the characteristics which one looks for in happiness are all included in our definition. For some people think that happiness is virtue, others that it is practical wisdom, others that it is some kind of theoretical wisdom; others again believe it to be all or some of these accompanied by, or not devoid of, pleasure; and some people also include external prosperity in its definition. Some of these views are expressed by many people and have come down from antiquity, some by a few men of high prestige, and it is not reasonable to assume that both groups are altogether wrong; the presumption is rather that they are right in at least one or even in most respects.

Now, in our definition we are in agreement with those who describe happiness as virtue or as some particular virtue, for our term "activity in conformity with virtue" implies virtue. But it does doubtless make a considerable difference whether we think of the highest good as consisting in the possession or in the practice of virtue, viz., as being a characteristic or an activity. For a characteristic may exist without producing any good result, as for example, in a man who is asleep or incapacitated in some other respect. An activity, on the other hand, must produce a result: [an active person] will necessarily act and act well. Just as the crown at the Olympic Games is not awarded to the most beautiful and the strongest but to the participants in the contests—for it is among them that the victors are found—so the good and noble things in life are won by those who act rightly.

The life of men active in this sense is also pleasant in itself. For the sensation of a pleasure belongs to the soul, and each man derives pleasure from what he is said to love: a lover of horses from horses, a lover of the theater from plays, and in the same way a lover of justice from just acts, and a lover of virtue in general from virtuous acts. In most men, pleasant acts conflict with one another because they are not pleasant by nature, but men who love what is noble derive pleasure from what is naturally pleasant. Actions which conform to virtue are naturally pleasant, and, as a result, such actions are not only pleasant for those who love the noble but also pleasant in themselves. The life of such men has no further need of pleasure as an added attraction, but it contains pleasure within itself. We may even go so far as to state that the man who does not enjoy performing noble actions is not a good man at all. Nobody would call a man just who does not enjoy acting justly, nor generous who does not enjoy generous actions, and so on. If this is true, actions performed in conformity with virtue are in themselves pleasant.

Of course it goes without saying that such actions are good as well as noble, and they are both in the highest degree, if the man of high moral standards displays any right judgment about them at all; and his judgment corresponds to our description. So we see that happiness is at once the best, noblest, and most pleasant thing, and these qualities are not separate, as the inscription at Delos makes out:

The most just is most noble, but health is the best,
and to win what one loves is pleasantest.

For the best activities encompass all these attributes, and it is in these, or in the best one of them, that we maintain happiness consists.

Still, happiness, as we have said, needs external goods as well. For it is impossible or at least not easy to perform noble actions if one lacks the wherewithal. Many actions can only be performed with the help of instruments, as it were: friends, wealth, and political power. And there are some external goods the absence of which spoils supreme happiness, e.g., good birth, good children, and beauty: for a man who is very ugly in appearance or ill-born or who lives all by himself and has no children cannot be classified as altogether happy; even less happy perhaps is a man whose children and friends are worthless, or one who has lost good children and friends through death. Thus, as we have said, happiness also requires well-being of this kind, and that is the reason why some classify good fortune with happiness, while others link it to virtue.

Chapter 9

This also explains why there is a problem whether happiness is acquired by learning, by discipline, or by some other kind of training, or whether we attain it by reason of some divine dispensation or even by chance. Now, if there is anything at all which comes to men as a gift from the gods, it is reasonable to suppose that happiness above all else is god-given; and of all things human it is the most likely to be god-given, inasmuch as it is the best. But although this subject is perhaps more appropriate to a different field of study, it is clear that happiness is one of the most divine things, even if it is not god-sent but attained through virtue and some kind of learning or training. For the prize and end of excellence and virtue is the best thing of all, and it is something divine and blessed. Moreover, if happiness depends on excellence, it will be shared by many people; for study and effort will make it accessible to anyone whose capacity for virtue is unimpaired. And if it is better that happiness is acquired in this way rather than by chance, it is reasonable to assume that this is the way in which it is acquired. For, in the realm of nature, things are naturally arranged in the best way possible—and the same is also true of the products of art and of any kind of causation, especially the highest. To leave the greatest and noblest of things to chance would hardly be right.

A solution of this question is also suggested by our earlier definition, according to which the good of man, happiness, is some kind of activity of the soul in conformity with virtue. All the other goods are either necessary prerequisites for happiness, or are by nature co-workers with it and useful instruments for attaining it. Our results also tally with what we said at the outset: for we stated that the end of politics is the best of ends; and the main concern of politics is to engender a certain character in the citizens and to make them good and disposed to perform noble actions.

We are right, then, when we call neither a horse nor an ox nor any other animal happy, for none of them is capable of participating in an activity of this kind. For the same reason, a child is not happy, either; for, because of his age, he cannot yet perform such actions. When we do call a child happy, we do so by reason of the hopes we have for his future. Happiness, as we have said, requires completeness in virtue as well as a complete lifetime. Many changes and all kinds of contingencies befall a man in the course of his life, and it is possible that the most prosperous man will encounter great misfortune in his old age, as the Trojan legends tell about Priam.[8] When a man has met a fate such as his and has come to a wretched end, no one calls him happy.

Chapter 10

Must we, then, apply the term "happy" to no man at all as long as he is alive? Must we, as Solon[9] would have us do, wait to see his end? And, on this assumption, is it also true that a man is actually happy after he is dead? Is this not simply absurd, especially for us who define happiness as a kind of activity? Suppose we do not call a dead man happy, and interpret Solon's words to mean that only when a man is dead can we safely say that he has been happy, since he is now beyond the reach of evil and misfortune—this view, too, is open to objection. For it seems that to some extent good and evil really exist for a dead man, just as they may exist for a man who lives without being conscious of them, for example, honors and disgraces, and generally the successes and failures of his children and descendants. This presents a further problem. A man who has lived happily to his old age and has died as happily as he lived may have many vicissitudes befall his descendants: some of them may be good and may be granted the kind of life which they deserve, and others may not. It is, further, obvious that the descendants may conceivably be removed from their ancestors by various degrees. Under such circumstances, it would be odd if the dead man would share in the vicissitudes of his descendants and be happy at one time and wretched at another. But it would also be odd if the fortunes of their descendants did not affect the ancestors at all, not even for a short time.

But we must return to the problem raised earlier, for through it our present problem perhaps may be solved. If one must look to the end and praise a man not as being happy but as having been happy in the past, is it not paradoxical that at a time when a man actually is happy this attribute, though true, cannot be applied to him? We are unwilling to call the living happy because changes may befall them and because we believe that happiness has permanence and is not amenable to changes under any circumstances, whereas fortunes revolve many times in one person's lifetime. For obviously, if we are to keep pace with a man's fortune, we shall frequently have to call the same man happy at one time and wretched at another and demonstrate that the happy man is a kind of chameleon, and that the foundations [of his life] are unsure. Or is it quite wrong to make our judgment depend on fortune? Yes, it is wrong, for fortune does not determine whether we fare well or ill, but is, as we said, merely an accessory to human life; activities in conformity with virtue constitute happiness, and the opposite activities constitute its opposite.

The question which we have just discussed further confirms our definition. For no function of man possesses as much stability as do activities in conformity with virtue: these seem to be even more durable than scientific knowledge. And the higher the virtuous activities, the more durable they are, because men who are supremely happy spend their lives in these activities most intensely and most continuously, and this seems to be the reason why such activities cannot be forgotten.

The happy man will have the attribute of permanence which we are discussing, and he will remain happy throughout his life. For he will always or to the highest degree both do and contemplate what is in conformity with virtue; he will bear the vicissitudes of fortune most nobly and with perfect decorum under all circumstances, inasmuch as he is truly good and "foursquare beyond reproach."[10]

But fortune brings many things to pass, some great and some small. Minor instances of good and likewise of bad luck obviously do not decisively tip the scales of life, but a number of major successes will make life more perfectly happy; for, in the first place, by their very nature they help to make life attractive, and secondly, they afford the opportunity for noble and good actions. On the other hand, frequent reverses can crush and mar supreme happiness in that they inflict pain and thwart many activities. Still, nobility shines through even in such circumstances, when a man bears many great misfortunes with good grace not because he is insensitive to pain but because he is noble and high-minded.

If, as we said, the activities determine a man's life, no supremely happy man can ever become miserable, for he will never do what is hateful and base. For in our opinion, the man who is truly good and wise will bear with dignity whatever fortune may bring, and will always act as nobly as circumstances permit, just as a good general makes the most strategic use of the troops at his disposal, and a good shoemaker makes the best shoe he can from the leather available, and so on with experts in all other fields. If this is true, a happy man will never become miserable; but even so, supreme happiness will not be his if a fate such as Priam's befalls him. And yet, he will not be fickle and changeable; he will not be dislodged from his happiness easily by any misfortune that comes along, but only by great and numerous disasters such as will make it impossible for him to become happy again in a short time; if he recovers his happiness at all, it will be only after a long period of time, in which he has won great distinctions.

Is there anything to prevent us, then, from defining the happy man as one whose activities are an expression of complete virtue, and who is sufficiently equipped with external goods, not simply at a given moment but to the end of his life? Or should we add that he must die as well as live in the manner which we have defined? For we cannot foresee the future, and happiness, we maintain, is an end which is absolutely final and complete in every respect. If this be granted, we shall define as "supremely happy" those living men who fulfill and continue to fulfill these requirements, but blissful only as human beings. So much for this question. . . .

Chapter 13

Since happiness is a certain activity of the soul in conformity with perfect virtue, we must now examine what virtue or excellence is. For such an inquiry will perhaps better enable us to discover the nature of happiness. Moreover, the man who is truly concerned about politics seems to devote special attention to excellence, since it is his aim to make the citizens good and law-abiding. We have an example of this in the lawgivers of Crete and Sparta and in other great legislators. If an examination of virtue is part of politics, this question clearly fits into the pattern of our original plan.

There can be no doubt that the virtue which we have to study is human virtue. For the good which we have been seeking is a human good and the happiness a human happiness. By human virtue we do not mean the excellence of the body, but that of the soul, and we define happiness as an activity of the soul. If this is true, the student of politics must obviously have some knowledge of the workings of the soul, just as the man who is to heal eyes must know something about the whole body. In fact, knowledge is all the more important for the former, inasmuch as politics is better and more valuable than medicine, and cultivated physicians devote much time and trouble to gain knowledge about the body. Thus, the student of politics must study the soul, but he must do so with his own aim in view, and only to the extent that the objects of his inquiry demand: to go into it in greater detail would perhaps be more laborious than his purposes require.

Some things that are said about the soul in our less technical discussions are adequate enough to be used here, for instance, that the soul consists of two elements, one irrational and one rational. Whether these two elements are separate, like the parts of the body or any other divisible thing, or whether they are only logically separable though in reality indivisible, as convex and concave are in the circumference of a circle, is irrelevant for our present purposes.

Of the irrational element, again, one part seems to be common to all living things and vegetative in nature: I mean that part which is responsible for nurture and growth. We must assume that some such capacity of the soul exists in everything that takes nourishment, in the embryonic stage as well as when the organism is fully developed; for this makes more sense than to assume the existence of some different capacity at the latter stage. The excellence of this part of the soul is, therefore, shown to be common to all living things and is not exclusively human. This very part and this capacity seem to be most active in sleep. For in sleep the difference between a good man and a bad is least apparent—whence the saying that for half their lives the happy are no better off than the wretched. This is just what we would expect, for sleep is an inactivity of the soul in that it ceases to do things which cause it to be called good or bad. However, to a small extent some bodily movements do penetrate to the soul in sleep, and in this sense the dreams of honest men are better than those of average people. But enough of this subject: we may pass by the nutritive part, since it has no natural share in human excellence or virtue.

In addition to this, there seems to be another integral element of the soul which, though irrational, still does partake of reason in some way. In morally strong and morally weak men we praise the reason that guides them and the rational element of the soul, because it exhorts them to follow the right path and to do what is best. Yet we see in them also another natural strain different from the rational, which fights and resists the guidance of reason. The soul behaves in precisely the same manner as do the paralyzed limbs of the body. When we intend to move the limbs to the right, they turn to the left, and similarly, the impulses of morally weak persons turn in the direction opposite to that in which reason leads them. However, while the aberration of the body is visible, that of the soul is not. But perhaps we must accept it as a fact, nevertheless, that there is something in the soul besides the rational element, which opposes and reacts against it. In what way the two are distinct need not concern us here. But, as we have stated, it too seems to partake of reason; at any rate, in a morally strong man it accepts the leadership of reason, and is perhaps more obedient still in a self-controlled and courageous man, since in him everything is in harmony with the voice of reason.

Thus we see that the irrational element of the soul has two parts: the one is vegetative and has no share in reason at all, the other is the seat of the appetites and of desire in general and partakes of reason insofar as it complies with reason and accepts its leadership; it possesses reason in the sense that we say it is "reasonable" to accept the advice of a father and of friends, not in the sense that we have a "rational" understanding of mathematical propositions. That the irrational element can be persuaded by the rational is shown by the fact that admonition and all manner of rebuke and exhortation are possible. If it is correct to say that the appetitive part, too, has reason, it follows that the rational element of the soul has two subdivisions: the one possesses reason in the strict sense, contained within itself, and the other possesses reason in the sense that it listens to reason as one would listen to a father.

Virtue, too, is differentiated in line with this division of the soul. We call some virtues "intellectual" and others "moral": theoretical wisdom, understanding, and practical wisdom are intellectual virtues, generosity and self-control moral virtues. In speaking of a man's character, we do not describe him as wise or understanding, but as gentle or self-controlled; but we praise the wise man, too, for his characteristic, and praiseworthy characteristics are what we call virtues.

BOOK II

Chapter 1   How do The Virtues work together

Virtue, as we have seen, consists of two kinds, intellectual virtue and moral virtue. Intellectual virtue or excellence owes its origin and development chiefly to teaching, and for that reason requires experience and time. Moral virtue, on the other hand, is formed by habit, *ethos*, and its name, *ēthikē*, is therefore derived, by a slight variation, from *ethos*. This shows, too, that none of the moral virtues is implanted in us by nature, for nothing which exists by nature can be changed by habit. For example, it is impossible for a stone, which has a natural downward movement, to become habituated to moving upward, even if one should try ten thousand times to inculcate the habit by throwing it in the air; nor can fire be made to move downward, nor can the direction of any nature-given tendency be changed by habituation. Thus, the virtues are implanted in us neither by nature nor contrary to nature: we are by nature equipped with the ability to receive them, and habit brings this ability to completion and fulfillment.

Furthermore, of all the qualities with which we are endowed by nature, we are provided with the capacity first, and display the activity afterward. That this is true is shown by the senses: it is not by frequent seeing or frequent hearing that we acquired our senses, but on the contrary we first possess and then use them; we do not acquire them by use. The virtues, on the other hand, we acquire by first having put them into action, and the same is also true of the arts. For the things which we have to learn before we can do them we learn by doing: men become builders by building houses, and harpists by playing the harp. Similarly, we become just by the practice of just actions, self-controlled by exercising self-control, and courageous by performing acts of courage.

This is corroborated by what happens in states. Lawgivers make the citizens good by inculcating [good] habits in them, and this is the aim of every lawgiver; if he does not succeed in doing that, his legislation is a failure. It is in this that a good constitution differs from a bad one.

Moreover, the same causes and the same means that produce any excellence or virtue can also destroy it, and this is also true of every art. It is by playing the harp that men become both good and bad harpists, and correspondingly with builders and all the other craftsmen: a man who builds well will be a good builder, one who builds badly a bad one. For if this were not so, there would be no need for an instructor, but everybody would be born as a good or a bad craftsman. The same holds true of the virtues: in our transactions with other men it is by action that some become just and others unjust, and it is by acting in the face of danger and by developing the habit of feeling fear or confidence that some become brave men and others cowards. The same applies to the appetites and feelings of anger: by reacting in one way or in another to given circumstances some people become self-controlled and gentle, and others self-indulgent and short-tempered. In a word, characteristics develop from corresponding activities. For that reason, we must see to it that our activities are of a certain kind, since any variations in them will be reflected in our characteristics. Hence it is no small matter whether one habit or another is inculcated in us from early childhood; on the contrary; it makes a considerable difference, or, rather, all the difference. . . .

Chapter 6

It is not sufficient, however, merely to define virtue in general terms as a characteristic: we must also specify what kind of characteristic it is. It must, then, be remarked that every virtue or excellence (1) renders good the thing itself of which it is the excellence, and (2) causes it to perform its function well. For example, the excellence of the eye makes both the eye and its function good, for good sight is due to the excellence of the eye. Likewise, the excellence of a horse makes it both good as a horse and good at running, at carrying its rider, and at facing the enemy. Now, if this is true of all things, the virtue or excellence of man, too, will be a characteristic which makes him a good man, and which causes him to perform his own function well. To some extent we have already stated how this will be true; the rest will become clear if we study what the nature of virtue is.

Of every continuous entity that is divisible into parts it is possible to take the larger, the smaller, or an equal part, and these parts may be larger, smaller, or equal either in relation to the entity itself, or in relation to us. The "equal" part is something median between excess and deficiency. By the median of an entity I understand a point equidistant from both extremes, and this point is one and the same for everybody. By the median relative to us I understand an amount neither too large nor too small, and this is neither one nor the same for everybody. To take an example: if ten is many and two is few, six is taken as the median in relation to the entity, for it exceeds and is exceeded by the same amount, and is thus the median in terms of arithmetical proportion. But the median relative to us cannot be determined in this manner: if ten pounds of food is much for a man to eat and two pounds little, it does not follow that the trainer will prescribe six pounds, for this may in turn be much or little for him to eat; it may be little for Milo[11] and much for someone who has just begun to take up athletics. The same applies to

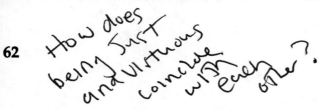

running and wrestling. Thus we see that an expert in any field avoids excess and deficiency, but seeks the median and chooses it—not the median of the object but the median relative to us.

If this, then, is the way in which every science perfects its work, by looking to the median and by bringing its work up to that point—and this is the reason why it is usually said of a successful piece of work that it is impossible to detract from it or to add to it, the implication being that excess and deficiency destroy success while the mean safeguards it (good craftsmen, we say, look toward this standard in the performance of their work)—and if virtue, like nature, is more precise and better than any art, we must conclude that virtue aims at the median. I am referring to moral virtue: for it is moral virtue that is concerned with emotions and actions, and it is in emotions and actions that excess, deficiency, and the median are found. Thus we can experience fear, confidence, desire, anger, pity, and generally any kind of pleasure and pain either too much or too little, and in either case not properly. But to experience all this at the right time, toward the right objects, toward the right people, for the right reason, and in the right manner—that is the median and the best course, the course that is a mark of virtue.

Similarly, excess, deficiency, and the median can also be found in actions. Now virtue is concerned with emotions and actions; and in emotions and actions excess and deficiency miss the mark, whereas the median is praised and constitutes success. But both praise and success are signs of virtue or excellence. Consequently, virtue is a mean in the sense that it aims at the median. This is corroborated by the fact that there are many ways of going wrong, but only one way which is right—for evil belongs to the indeterminate . . . but good to the determinate. This, by the way, is also the reason why the one is easy and the other hard: it is easy to miss the target but hard to hit it. Here, then, is an additional proof that excess and deficiency characterize vice, while the mean characterizes virtue: for "bad men have many ways, good men but one."[12]

We may thus conclude that virtue or excellence is a characteristic involving choice, and that it consists in observing the mean relative to us, a mean which is defined by a rational principle, such as a man of practical wisdom would use to determine it. It is the mean by reference to two vices: the one of excess and the other of deficiency. It is, moreover, a mean because some vices exceed and others fall short of what is required in emotion and in action, whereas virtue finds and chooses the median. Hence, in respect of its essence and the definition of its essential nature virtue is a mean, but in regard to goodness and excellence it is an extreme.

Not every action nor every emotion admits of a mean. There are some actions and emotions whose very names connote baseness, e.g., spite, shamelessness, envy; and among actions, adultery, theft, and murder. These and similar emotions and actions imply by their very names that they are bad; it is not their excess nor their deficiency which is called bad. It is, therefore,

How can virtue exist in action and emotion.

impossible ever to do right in performing them: to perform them is always to do wrong. In cases of this sort, let us say adultery, rightness and wrongness do not depend on committing it with the right woman at the right time and in the right manner, but the mere fact of committing such action at all is to do wrong. It would be just as absurd to suppose that there is a mean, an excess, and a deficiency in an unjust or a cowardly or a self-indulgent act. For if there were, we would have a mean of excess and a mean of deficiency, and an excess of excess and a deficiency of deficiency. Just as there cannot be an excess and a deficiency of self-control and courage—because the intermediate is, in a sense, an extreme—so there cannot be a mean, excess, and deficiency in their respective opposites: their opposites are wrong regardless of how they are performed; for, in general, there is no such thing as the mean of an excess or a deficiency, or the excess and deficiency of a mean.

Chapter 7

However, this general statement is not enough; we must also show that it fits particular instances. For in a discussion of moral actions, although general statements have a wider range of application, statements on particular points have more truth in them: actions are concerned with particulars and our statements must harmonize with them. Let us now take particular virtues and vices from the following table.[13]

In feelings of fear and confidence courage is the mean. As for the excesses, there is no name that describes a man who exceeds in fearlessness—many virtues and vices have no name; but a man who exceeds in confidence is reckless, and a man who exceeds in fear and is deficient in confidence is cowardly.

In regard to pleasures and pains—not all of them and to a lesser degree in the case of pains—the mean is self-control and the excess self-indulgence. Men deficient in regard to pleasure are not often found, and there is therefore no name for them, but let us call them "insensitive."

In giving and taking money, the mean is generosity, the excess and deficiency are extravagance and stinginess. In these vices excess and deficiency work in opposite ways: an extravagant man exceeds in spending and is deficient in taking, while a stingy man exceeds in taking and is deficient in spending. For our present purposes, we may rest content with an outline and a summary. . . .

BOOK VIII

Chapter 1

The next subject which we shall have to discuss is friendship.[14] For it is some sort of excellence or virtue, or involves virtue, and it is, moreover, most

Eudaimonia

indispensable for life. No one would choose to live without friends, even if he had all other goods. Rich men and those who hold office and power are, above all others, regarded as requiring friends. For what good would their prosperity do them if it did not provide them with the opportunity for good works? And the best works done and those which deserve the highest praise are those that are done to one's friends. How could prosperity be safeguarded and preserved without friends? The greater it is the greater are the risks it brings with it. Also, in poverty and all other kinds of misfortune men believe that their only refuge consists in their friends. Friends help young men avoid error; to older people they give the care and help needed to supplement the failing powers of action which infirmity brings in its train; and to those in their prime they give the opportunity to perform noble actions. [This is what is meant when men quote Homer's verse:] "When two go together . . .":[15] friends enhance our ability to think and to act. Also, it seems that nature implants friendship in a parent for its offspring and in offspring for its parent, not only among men, but also among birds and most animals. [Not only members of the same family group but] also members of the same race feel it for one another, especially human beings, and that is why we praise men for being humanitarians or "lovers of their fellow men." Even when traveling abroad one can see how near and dear and friendly every man may be to another human being.

Friendship also seems to hold states together, and lawgivers apparently devote more attention to it than to justice. For concord seems to be something similar to friendship, and concord is what they most strive to attain, while they do their best to expel faction, the enemy of concord. When people are friends, they have no need of justice, but when they are just, they need friendship in addition. In fact, the just in the fullest sense is regarded as constituting an element of friendship. Friendship is noble as well as necessary: we praise those who love their friends and consider the possession of many friends a noble thing. And further, we believe of our friends that they are good men. . . .

Chapter 2

. . . We do not feel affection for everything, but only for the lovable, and that means what is good, pleasant, or useful. However, since we regard a thing as useful when it serves as a means to some good or pleasure, we can say that as ends [only] the good and the pleasant are worthy of affection. Which good, then, is it that men love? Is it the good [in general] or is it what is good for them? For there is sometimes a discrepancy between these two, and a discrepancy also in the case of what is pleasant. Now it seems that each man loves what is good for him: in an unqualified sense it is the good which is worthy of affection, but for each individual it is what is good for him. Now in fact every man does not love what is really good for him, but what appears to

what good would sucess do, It
you dean't have tilends?
Best works are done with those of hijrest praise, hijrest
praise, comes from frlends.

him to be good. But that makes no difference [for our discussion]. It simply
follows that what appears good will appear worthy of affection.

While there are three causes of affection or friendship, we do not speak
of "friendship" to describe the affection we feel for inanimate objects, since
inanimate objects do not reciprocate affection and we do not wish for their
good. It would surely be ridiculous to wish for the good of wine: if one wishes
it at all, it is that the wine may keep, so that we can have it ourselves. But men
say that we ought to wish for the good of our friend for the friend's sake.
When people wish for our good in this way, we attribute good will to them, if
the same wish is not reciprocated by us. If the good will is on a reciprocal
basis, it is friendship. Perhaps we should add: "provided that we are aware of
the good will." For many people have good will toward persons they have
never seen, but whom they assume to be decent and useful, and one of these
persons may well reciprocate this feeling. Accordingly, the two parties appear
to have good will toward one another; but how can they be called "friends"
when they are unaware how they are disposed toward one another? We
conclude, therefore, that to be friends men must have good will for one
another, must each wish for the good of the other on the basis of one of the
three motives mentioned, and must each be aware of one another's good will.

Chapter 3

These three motives differ from one another in kind, and so do the corresponding types of affection and friendship. In other words, there are three
kinds of friendship, corresponding in number to the objects worthy of affection. In each of these, the affection can be reciprocated so that the partner is
aware of it, and the partners wish for each other's good in terms of the motive
on which their affection is based.[16] Now, when the motive of the affection is
usefulness, the partners do not feel affection for one another *per se* but in
terms of the good accruing to each from the other. The same is also true of
those whose friendship is based on pleasure: we love witty people not for
what they are, but for the pleasure they give us.

So we see that when the useful is the basis of affection, men love
because of the good they get out of it, and when pleasure is the basis, for the
pleasure they get out of it. In other words, the friend is loved not because he
is a friend, but because he is useful or pleasant. Thus, these two kinds are
friendship only incidentally, since the object of affection is not loved for being
the kind of person he is, but for providing some good or pleasure. Consequently, such friendships are easily dissolved when the partners do not
remain unchanged: the affection ceases as soon as one partner is no longer
pleasant or useful to the other. Now, usefulness is not something permanent,
but differs at different times. Accordingly, with the disappearance of the
motive for being friends, the friendship, too, is dissolved, since the friendship
owed its existence to these motives.

Friendships of this kind seem to occur most commonly among old people, because at that age men do not pursue the pleasant but the beneficial. They are also found among young men and those in their prime who are out for their own advantage. Such friends are not at all given to living in each other's company, for sometimes they do not even find each other pleasant. Therefore, they have no further need of this relationship, if they are not mutually beneficial. They find each other pleasant only to the extent that they have hopes of some good coming out of it. The traditional friendship between host and guest is also placed in this group.

Friendship of young people seems to be based on pleasure. For their lives are guided by emotion, and they pursue most intensely what they find pleasant and what the moment brings. As they advance in years, different things come to be pleasant for them. Hence they become friends quickly and just as quickly cease to be friends. For as another thing becomes pleasant, the friendship, too, changes, and the pleasure of a young man changes quickly. Also, young people are prone to fall in love, since the greater part of falling in love is a matter of emotion and based on pleasure. That is why they form a friendship and give it up again so quickly that the change often takes place within the same day. But they do wish to be together all day and to live together, because it is in this way that they get what they want out of their friendship.

The perfect form of friendship is that between good men who are alike in excellence or virtue. For these friends wish alike for one another's good because they are good men, and they are good *per se* [that is, their goodness is something intrinsic, not incidental]. Those who wish for their friends' good for their friends' sake are friends in the truest sense, since their attitude is determined by what their friends are and not by incidental considerations. Hence their friendship lasts as long as they are good, and [that means it will last for a long time, since] goodness or virtue is a thing that lasts. In addition, each partner is both good in the unqualified sense and good for his friend. For those who are good, i.e., good without qualification, are also beneficial to one another. In the same double sense, they are also pleasant to one another: for good men are pleasant both in an unqualified sense and to one another, since each finds pleasure in his own proper actions and in actions like them, and the actions of good men are identical with or similar to one another. That such a friendship is lasting stands to reason, because in it are combined all the qualities requisite for people to be friends. For, [as we have seen,] every friendship is based on some good or on pleasure—either in the unqualified sense or relative to the person who feels the affection—and implies some similarity [between the friends]. Now this kind of friendship has all the requisite qualities we have mentioned and has them *per se*, that is, as an essential part of the characters of the friends. For in this kind of friendship the partners are like one another, and the other objects worthy of affection—the unqualified good and the unqualified pleasant—are also found in it, and these are the highest objects worthy of affection. It is, therefore, in the friendship of good men that feelings of affection and friendship exist in their highest and best form.

Such friendships are of course rare, since such men are few. Moreover, time and familiarity are required. For, as the proverb has it, people cannot know each other until they have eaten the specified [measure of] salt together. One cannot extend friendship to or be a friend of another person until each partner has impressed the other that he is worthy of affection, and until each has won the other's confidence. Those who are quick to show the signs of friendship to one another are not really friends, though they wish to be; they are not true friends unless they are worthy of affection and know this to be so. The wish to be friends can come about quickly, but friendship cannot. . . .

Chapter 5

As in the case of virtues, some men are called "good" because of a characteristic they have and others because of an activity in which they engage, so in the case of friendship there is a distinction [between the activity of friendship and the lasting characteristic]. When friends live together, they enjoy each other's presence and provide each other's good. When, however, they are asleep or separated geographically, they do not actively engage in their friendship, but they are still characterized by an attitude which could express itself in active friendship. For it is not friendship in the unqualified sense but only its activity that is interrupted by distance. But if the absence lasts for some time, it apparently also causes the friendship itself to be forgotten. Hence the saying: "Out of sight, out of mind."[17]

Neither old nor sour people are apparently disposed to forming friendships. There is only little pleasure one can get from them, and no one can spend his days in painful or unpleasant company: we see that nature avoids what is painful more than anything else and aims at what is pleasant. Those who extend friendship to one another without living together are more like men of good will than like friends. For nothing characterizes friends as much as living in each other's company. Material advantage is desired by those who stand in need, but company is something which is wanted even by men who are supremely happy, for they are the least suited to live in isolation. But it is impossible for men to spend their time together unless they are pleasant [in one another's eyes] and find joy in the same things. It is this quality which seems typical of comradeship.

The highest form of friendship, then, is that between good men, as we have stated repeatedly. For what is good or pleasant without qualification is regarded as an object of affection and of choice, while for each individual it is what is good or pleasant to him. But for a good man, a good man is the object of affection and of choice for both these reasons.

Now, affection resembles an emotion, while friendship is rather a characteristic or lasting attitude. For it is equally possible to feel affection for inanimate objects, [which cannot reciprocate the affection,] but mutual affection involves choice, and choice springs from a characteristic. Also, men wish their friends' good for the sake of those for whom they feel friendship, and this attitude is not determined by an emotion but by a characteristic. Also, in loving a friend they love their own good. For when a good man becomes a friend he becomes a good to the person whose friend he is. Thus, each partner both loves his own good and makes an equal return in the good he wishes for his partner and in the pleasure he gives him.

NOTES

1. To the Greeks, the city-state (*polis*) was the most advanced form of community, and *politics* was the enterprise of achieving the good of the city-state (*polis*). [D.C.A.]
2. *Sardanapallus*: the Hellenized name of King Ashurbanipal of Assyria (668–627 B.C.E.), famous for his sensual excesses [D.C.A., after M.O.]
3. *virtue or excellence*: This phrase is a translation of the single Greek word *aretē*. As Aristotle explains later (Book II, Chapter 6), *aretē* is the quality that makes a thing good and enables it to perform its distinctive function well. In the present translation, *aretē* is usually rendered either "virtue" *or* "excellence" (not both), depending on the context. [D.C.A.]
4. The reference is to the beginning of Chapter 2. [M.O.]
5. *final*: pertaining to a goal. The English word derives from the Latin *finis* (end, goal), the counterpart of the Greek *telos*. [D.C.A.]
6. *function*: a translation of the Greek word *ergon*, which means, literally, "work" [D.C.A.]
7. This, according to Aristotle, is the way in which fundamental principles of ethics are learned, and for that reason a person must be mature in order to be able to study ethics properly. It is most important for the modern reader to note that Aristotle is not trying to persuade his listener of the truth of these principles, but takes it for granted that he has learned them at home. [M.O.]
8. According to mythology, Priam was king of Troy when the city was destroyed by the Greeks in the Trojan War. Priam, who was very wealthy and the father of many children, was killed by a Greek soldier at an altar of Zeus in his own palace. [D.C.A.]
9. Solon (about 630–559 B.C.E.) was an Athenian lawgiver and poet. The Greek historian Herodotus (about 484–425 B.C.E.) recounts Solon's views on calling a person happy during his or her lifetime (Herodotus *Histories* 1.32). [D.C.A.]
10. The quotation is from the Greek poet Simonides of Ceos (about 556–486 B.C.E.). [D.C.A., after M.O.]
11. Milo of Croton was a famous Greek wrestler of the latter half of the sixth century B.C.E. [D.C.A., after M.O.]

12. The author of this verse is unknown. [M.O.]
13. Aristotle evidently used a table here to illustrate graphically the various virtues and their opposite extremes. [M.O.]
14. *friendship*: a translation of the Greek word *philia*, which designates a relationship that exists not only among friends but also among family members and members of civic, social, and business associations [D.C.A.]
15. Homer *Iliad* 10.224 [M.O.]
16. E.g., if the basis of their affection is the pleasant, they try to contribute each to the pleasure of the other. [M.O.]
17. The author of this hexameter verse is unknown. A more literal translation is: "A lack of converse spells the end of friendships." [M.O.]

QUESTIONS FOR REFLECTION AND DISCUSSION

1. Is happiness the ultimate goal that everyone seeks?
2. Does happiness consist in living in accordance with reason?
3. Does happiness depend in part on things beyond our control?
4. Can moral virtue ever be an extreme rather than a mean between extremes?
5. In loving a friend, do we love our own good?

SUGGESTIONS FOR FURTHER READING

I. Primary Sources

Nicomachean Ethics, trans. Martin Ostwald. Indianapolis: Bobbs-Merrill, Library of Liberal Arts, 1962, 316 pp.

Other good translations of the *Nicomachean Ethics* and of the following two treatises are also available.

The Politics, trans. T. A. Sinclair. Revised by Trevor J. Saunders. Harmondsworth, England: Penguin, 1981, 506 pp.

The *Politics* takes up where the *Nicomachean Ethics* leaves off. The subject matter of both treatises is the good life, and while the *Nicomachean Ethics* focuses on the individual, the *Politics* discusses the state (*polis*). Aristotle argues that human beings naturally live in political society and examines what type of state best promotes the happiness of its members.

De Anima (On the Soul), trans. Hugh Lawson-Tancred. Harmondsworth, England: Penguin, 1986, 253 pp.

A difficult work, but important for a fuller understanding of Aristotle's theory of human nature. In this treatise Aristotle presents his theory of the soul as the principle of life of an organism. More specifically, he maintains that the soul is that which makes the body what it is. He establishes a hierarchy of the faculties of the human soul—proceeding from the nutritive to the perceptive to the intellective—and analyzes the bodily senses, imagination, animal movement, and the human intellect.

II. Secondary Sources

Ackrill, J. L. *Aristotle the Philosopher*. Oxford, England: Oxford University Press, OPUS Ser., 1981, 160 pp.

> An introduction to the main topics of Aristotle's philosophy that focuses on his arguments and way of philosophizing rather than on his conclusions. See the sections on the soul-body relation (pp. 55–63) and on the nature of the soul (pp. 68–78).

Allan, D. J. *The Philosophy of Aristotle*, 2d ed., Oxford, England: Oxford University Press, OPUS Ser., 1970, 175 pp.

> A clear introduction to Aristotle's principal doctrines presented in historical context.

Barnes, Jonathan. *Aristotle*. Oxford, England: Oxford University Press, Past Masters Ser., 1982, 101 pp.

> A brief overview of Aristotle's philosophy, divided into twenty concise chapters.

Lear, Jonathan. *Aristotle: The Desire to Understand*. Cambridge, England: Cambridge University Press, 1988, 328 pp.

> A detailed introduction to major themes in Aristotle's philosophy. See chap. 4, "Man's Nature," pp. 96–151, and chap. 5, "Ethics and the Organization of Desire," pp. 152–208.

Lloyd, G. E. R. *Aristotle: The Growth and Structure of His Thought*. Cambridge, England: Cambridge University Press, 1968, 324 pp.

> An account of how Aristotle's thought developed over time (pp. 3–108) and an exposition of his fundamental doctrines (pp. 111–315).

3

Mencius

Mencius is the Latinized form of the Chinese name Meng-tzu, which means "Master Meng." Mencius (whose full Chinese name was Meng K'o) was born in about 371 B.C.E. in Tsou, a small Chinese state located in what is now Shantung province. He was three when his father died, and his mother was very concerned about his proper upbringing. According to legend, his mother moved three times until she found a proper environment: She moved near a cemetery but was displeased when she found him playing at being a grave-digger; she then moved near a market, but there he mimicked the sellers; at last she moved near a school and there was satisfied to find him pretending to perform ceremonial rituals. Legend also states that Mencius studied under a disciple of Tzu Ssu, the grandson of Confucius (551–479 B.C.E.). Whether or not Mencius was actually taught by a disciple of Tzu Ssu, he was greatly inspired by Confucius's teachings and was acknowledged by the Confucian thinkers of his time as their most learned scholar. He later became known as "the second sage," the wisest thinker after Confucius.

Mencius lived at a time of great social and political upheaval. The feudal ritual system in China was giving way to centralized governments, and wars were frequent (the era from about 400 to 221 is known as the Period of the Warring States). Politics was based on power and wealth rather than on morality, and the people suffered greatly as a result. Mencius thought that the key to restoring political stability and to improving the lives of the people was for rulers to follow Confucian moral principles. He emphasized that rulers must govern for the good of the people; a ruler who failed to govern humanely lost the "Mandate of Heaven" and could legitimately be deposed— even killed—by the people. An outspoken critic of tyranny, he taught that the people were the most important element in the state and the rulers the least important. As a teacher, Mencius's goal was to train a class of Confucian scholar-officials who would teach rulers the principles of humane government.

At one point in his life, Mencius served briefly as a minister of King Hsüan (reigned 319–301) of Ch'i, but he spent most of his life traveling from state to state as a teacher-scholar, offering his counsel to rulers on social and political matters. Rulers paid him little heed, however; they were more interested in power and riches than in humanitarian principles. Near the end of his life, disappointed that his message kept falling on deaf ears, Mencius returned to his native state of Tsou and spent his final years writing and teaching. He died in about 289.

The writings of Mencius are gathered in a work known simply as *The Book of Mencius*. The book records conversations between Mencius and various rulers, officials, friends, and students and also includes some of his brief sayings. It seems to have been compiled by his disciples rather than by Mencius himself, but in either case we can be confident that the text accurately preserves his teachings. The conversations and sayings are grouped in seven books, each of which is divided into two parts. For the most part, the material is not arranged in any strict chronological or thematic order—a fact that has led some modern translators to rearrange the text (see the bibliography at the end of this chapter).

The central topic of Mencius's philosophy is human nature, and his most famous teaching is that human beings are by nature good. Confucius himself did not directly say whether human nature is good or bad, and the question became a subject of debate among his followers. Mencius argues against those Confucians who hold that (1) human nature is neither good nor bad, (2) human nature is initially neutral but eventually becomes good or bad, or (3) by nature some people are good and others bad. He maintains that all people are good at birth, in the sense of being endowed with tendencies toward benevolence, dutifulness, observance of rites (propriety), and wisdom (the ability to distinguish right from wrong). But these tendencies need to be preserved and developed; they can be corrupted by a bad environment or by allowing one's heart to be overcome by lower desires or appetites. An important implication of Mencius's doctrine of the innate goodness of human nature is that everyone, given the proper environment and with sustained personal effort, can become a sage.

Mencius's political philosophy flows from his theory of human nature. Since a proper environment is essential for the proper development of one's human potential, he argues, the state must be structured so as to foster moral growth. Much of *The Book of Mencius*, consequently, consists of proposals to various rulers for political reforms. While our selection omits passages proposing specific reforms, it does include texts that indicate, in general terms, the connection between Mencius's view of human nature and his political philosophy.

THE BOOK OF MENCIUS

BOOK I

Part B

6. Mencius said to King Hsüan of Ch'i,[1] "Suppose a subject of Your Majesty's, having entrusted his wife and children to the care of a friend, were to go on a trip to Ch'u, only to find, upon his return, that his friend had allowed his wife and children to suffer cold and hunger, then what should he do about it?"

"Break with his friend."

"If the Marshal of the Guards was unable to keep his guards in order, then what should be done about it?"

"Remove him from office."

"If the whole realm within the four borders was ill-governed, then what should be done about it?"

The King turned to his attendants and changed the subject. . . .

8. King Hsüan of Ch'i asked, "Is it true that T'ang banished Chieh and King Wu marched against Tchou?"[2]

"It is so recorded," answered Mencius.

"Is regicide permissible?"

"A man who mutilates benevolence is a mutilator, while one who cripples rightness is a crippler. He who is both a mutilator and a crippler is an 'outcast.' I have indeed heard of the punishment of the 'outcast Tchou,' but I have not heard of any regicide." . . .

BOOK II

Part A

6. Mencius said, "No man is devoid of a heart sensitive to the suffering of others. Such a sensitive heart was possessed by the Former Kings and this

manifested itself in compassionate government. With such a sensitive heart behind compassionate government, it was as easy to rule the Empire as rolling it on your palm.

"My reason for saying that no man is devoid of a heart sensitive to the suffering of others is this. Suppose a man were, all of a sudden, to see a young child on the verge of falling into a well. He would certainly be moved to compassion, not because he wanted to get in the good graces of the parents, nor because he wished to win the praise of his fellow villagers or friends, nor yet because he disliked the cry of the child. From this it can be seen that whoever is devoid of the heart of compassion is not human, whoever is devoid of the heart of shame is not human, whoever is devoid of the heart of courtesy and modesty is not human, and whoever is devoid of the heart of right and wrong is not human. The heart of compassion is the germ of benevolence; the heart of shame, of dutifulness; the heart of courtesy and modesty, of observance of the rites; the heart of right and wrong, of wisdom. Man has these four germs just as he has four limbs. For a man possessing these four germs to deny his own potentialities is for him to cripple himself; for him to deny the potentialities of his prince is for him to cripple his prince. If a man is able to develop all these four germs that he possesses, it will be like a fire starting up or a spring coming through. When these are fully developed, he can take under his protection the whole realm within the Four Seas,[3] but if he fails to develop them, he will not be able even to serve his parents." . . .

8. Mencius said, "When anyone told him that he had made a mistake, Tzu-lu[4] was delighted. When he heard a fine saying, Yü bowed low before the speaker. The Great Shun went even further.[5] He was ever ready to fall into line with others, giving up his own way for theirs, and glad to take from others that by which he could do good. From the time he was a farmer, a potter and a fisherman to the time he became Emperor, there was nothing he did that he did not take from others. To take from others that by which one can do good is to help them do good. Hence there is nothing more important to a gentleman[6] than helping others do good." . . .

BOOK III

Part B

6. Mencius said to Tai Pu-sheng,[7] "Do you wish your King[8] to be good? I shall speak to you plainly. Suppose a Counsellor of Ch'u wished his son to speak the language of Ch'i. Would he have a man from Ch'i to tutor his son? Or would he have a man from Ch'u?"

"He would have a man from Ch'i to tutor his son."

"With one man from Ch'i tutoring the boy and a host of Ch'u men chattering around him, even though you caned him every day to make him speak Ch'i, you would not succeed. Take him away to some district like Chuang and Yüeh[9] for a few years, then even if you caned him every day to make him speak Ch'u, you would not succeed. You have placed Hsüeh Chü-chou[10] near the King because you think him [Hsüeh Chü-chou] a good man. If everyone around the King, old or young, high or low, is a Hsüeh Chü-chou, then who will help the King to do evil? But if no one around the King is a Hsüeh Chü-chou, then who will help the King to do good? What difference can one Hsüeh Chü-chou make to the King of Sung?" . . .

8. Tai Ying-chih[11] said, "We are unable in the present year to change over to a tax of one in ten and to abolish custom and market duties. What would you think if we were to make some reductions and wait till next year before putting the change fully into effect?"

"Here is a man," said Mencius, "who appropriates one of his neighbour's chickens every day. Someone tells him, 'This is not how a gentleman behaves.' He answers, 'May I reduce it to one chicken every month and wait until next year to stop altogether?'

"When one realizes that something is morally wrong, one should stop it as soon as possible. Why wait for next year?" . . .

BOOK IV

Part A

3. Mencius said, "The Three Dynasties[12] won the Empire through benevolence and lost it through cruelty. This is true of the rise and fall, survival and collapse, of states as well. An Emperor cannot keep the Empire within the Four Seas unless he is benevolent; a feudal lord cannot preserve the altars to the gods of earth and grain unless he is benevolent; a Minister or a Counsellor cannot preserve his ancestral temple unless he is benevolent; a Gentleman or a Commoner cannot preserve his four limbs unless he is benevolent. To dislike death yet revel in cruelty is no different from drinking beyond your capacity despite your dislike of drunkenness."

4. Mencius said, "If others do not respond to your love with love, look into your own benevolence; if others fail to respond to your attempts to govern them with order, look into your own wisdom; if others do not return your courtesy, look into your own respect. In other words, look into yourself whenever you fail to achieve your purpose." . . .

15. Mencius said, "There is in man nothing more ingenuous than the pupils of his eyes. They cannot conceal his wickedness. When he is upright within his breast, a man's pupils are clear and bright; when he is not, they are clouded and murky. How can a man conceal his true character if you listen to his words and observe the pupils of his eyes?" . . .

17. Ch'un-yü K'un[13] said, "Is it prescribed by the rites that, in giving and receiving, man and woman should not touch each other?"

"It is," said Mencius.

"When one's sister-in-law is drowning, does one stretch out a hand to help her?"

"Not to help a sister-in-law who is drowning is to be a brute. It is prescribed by the rites that, in giving and receiving, man and woman should not touch each other, but in stretching out a helping hand to the drowning sister-in-law one uses one's discretion." . . .

19. Mencius said, "What is the most important duty? One's duty towards one's parents. What is the most important thing to watch over? One's own character. I have heard of a man who, not having allowed his character to be morally lost, is able to discharge his duties toward his parents; but I have not heard of one morally lost who is able to do so. There are many duties one should discharge, but the fulfilment of one's duty towards one's parents is the most basic. There are many things one should watch over, but watching over one's character is the most basic." . . .

27. Mencius said, "The content of benevolence is the serving of one's parents; the content of dutifulness is obedience to one's elder brothers; the content of wisdom is to understand these two and to hold fast to them; the content of the rites is the regulation and adornment of them; the content of music is the joy that comes of delighting in them. When joy arises how can one stop it? And when one cannot stop it, then one begins to dance with one's feet and wave one's arms without knowing it." . . .

Part B

5. Mencius said, "When the prince is benevolent, everyone else is benevolent; when the prince is dutiful, everyone else is dutiful."

6. Mencius said, "A great man will not observe a rite that is contrary to the spirit of the rites, nor will he perform a duty that goes against the spirit of dutifulness." . . .

8. Mencius said, "Only when a man will not do some things is he capable of doing great things." . . .

11. Mencius said, "A great man need not keep his word nor does he necessarily see his action through to the end. He aims only at what is right."

12. Mencius said, "A great man is one who retains the heart of a new-born babe." . . .

14. Mencius said, "A gentleman steeps himself in the Way because he wishes to find it in himself. When he finds it in himself, he will be at ease in it; when he is at ease in it, he can draw deeply upon it; when he can draw deeply upon it, he finds its source wherever he turns. That is why a gentleman wishes to find the Way in himself." . . .

19. Mencius said, "Slight is the difference between man and the brutes. The common man loses this distinguishing feature, while the gentleman retains it. Shun understood the way of things and had a keen insight into human relationships. He followed the path of morality. He did not just put morality into practice." . . .

26. Mencius said, "In talking about human nature people in the world merely follow former theories. They do so because these theories can be explained with ease. What they dislike in clever men is that they bore their way through. If clever men could act as Yü did in guiding the flood waters, then there would be nothing to dislike in them. Yü guided the water by imposing nothing on it that was against its natural tendency." . . .

28. Mencius said, "A gentleman differs from other men in that he retains his heart. A gentleman retains his heart by means of benevolence and the rites. The benevolent man loves others, and the courteous man respects others. He who loves others is always loved by them; he who respects others is always respected by them. Suppose a man treats one in an outrageous manner. Faced with this, a gentleman will say to himself, 'I must be lacking in benevolence and courtesy, or how could such a thing happen to me?' When, looking into himself, he finds that he has been benevolent and courteous, and yet this outrageous treatment continues, then the gentleman will say to himself, 'I must have failed to do my best for him.' When, on looking into himself, he finds that he has done his best and yet this outrageous treatment continues, then the gentleman will say, 'This man does not know what he is doing. Such a person is no different from an animal. One cannot expect an animal to know any better.' Hence while a gentleman has perennial worries, he has no unexpected vexations. His worries are of this kind: Shun was a man; I am also a man. Shun set an example for the Empire worthy of being handed down to posterity, yet here am I, just an ordinary man. That is something worth worrying about. If one worries about it, what should one do? One should become like Shun. That is all. On the other hand, the

gentleman is free from vexations. He never does anything that is not benev-olent; he does not act except in accordance with the rites. Even when unex-pected vexations come his way, the gentleman refuses to be perturbed by them." . . .

32. Ch'u Tzu[14] said, "The King sent someone to spy on you to see whether you were at all different from other people."

"In what way," said Mencius, "should I be different from other people? Even Yao and Shun were the same as anyone else." . . .

BOOK VI

Part A

1. Kao Tzu[15] said, "Human nature is like the *ch'i* willow. Dutifulness is like cups and bowls. To make morality out of human nature is like making cups and bowls out of the willow."

"Can you," said Mencius, "make cups and bowls by following the nature of the willow? Or must you mutilate the willow before you can make it into cups and bowls? If you have to mutilate the willow to make it into cups and bowls, must you, then, also mutilate a man to make him moral? Surely it will be these words of yours men in the world will follow in bringing disaster upon morality."

2. Kao Tzu said, "Human nature is like whirling water. Give it an outlet in the east and it will flow east; give it an outlet in the west and it will flow west. Human nature does not show any preference for either good or bad just as water does not show any preference for either east or west."

"It certainly is the case," said Mencius, "that water does not show any preference for either east or west, but does it show the same indifference to high and low? Human nature is good just as water seeks low ground. There is no man who is not good; there is no water that does not flow downwards.

"Now in the case of water, by splashing it one can make it shoot up higher than one's forehead, and by forcing it one can make it stay on a hill. How can that be the nature of water? It is the circumstances being what they are. That man can be made bad shows that his nature is no different from that of water in this respect."

3. Kao Tzu said, "The inborn is what is meant by 'nature.'"

"Is that," said Mencius, "the same as 'white is what is meant by "white"'?"

"Yes."

"Is the whiteness of white feathers the same as the whiteness of white snow and the whiteness of white snow the same as the whiteness of white jade?"

"Yes."

"In that case, is the nature of a hound the same as the nature of an ox and the nature of an ox the same as the nature of a man?" . . .

6. Kung-tu Tzu[16] said, "Kao Tzu said, 'There is neither good nor bad in human nature,' but others say, 'Human nature can become good or it can become bad, and that is why with the rise of King Wen and King Wu, the people were given to goodness, while with the rise of King Yu and King Li,[17] they were given to cruelty.' Then there are others who say, 'There are those who are good by nature, and there are those who are bad by nature. For this reason, Hsiang could have Yao as prince, and Shun could have the Blind Man as father, and Ch'i, Viscount of Wei, and Prince Pi Kan could have Tchou as nephew as well as sovereign.'[18] Now you say human nature is good. Does this mean that all the others are mistaken?"

"As far as what is genuinely in him is concerned, a man is capable of becoming good," said Mencius. "That is what I mean by good. As for his becoming bad, that is not the fault of his native endowment. The heart of compassion is possessed by all men alike; likewise the heart of shame, the heart of respect, and the heart of right and wrong. The heart of compassion pertains to benevolence, the heart of shame to dutifulness, the heart of respect to the observance of the rites, and the heart of right and wrong to wisdom. Benevolence, dutifulness, observance of the rites, and wisdom are not welded on to me from the outside; they are in me originally. Only this has never dawned on me. That is why it is said, 'Seek and you will find it; let go and you will lose it.' There are cases where one man is twice, five times or countless times better than another man, but this is only because there are people who fail to make the best of their native endowment. The *Book of Odes*[19] says,

> Heaven produces the teeming masses,
> And where there is a thing there is a norm.
> If the people held on to their constant nature,
> They would be drawn to superior virtue.

Confucius commented, 'The author of this poem must have had knowledge of the Way.'[20] Thus where there is a thing there is a norm, and because the people hold on to their constant nature they are drawn to superior virtue."

7. Mencius said, "In good years the young men are mostly lazy, while in bad years they are mostly violent. Heaven has not sent down men whose endowment differs so greatly. The difference is due to what ensnares their hearts.

Take the barley for example. Sow the seeds and cover them with soil. The place is the same and the time of sowing is also the same. The plants shoot up and by the summer solstice they all ripen. If there is any unevenness, it is because the soil varies in richness and there is no uniformity in the fall of rain and dew and the amount of human effort devoted to tending it. Now things of the same kind are all alike. Why should we have doubts when it comes to man? The sage and I are of the same kind. Thus Lung Tzu[21] said, 'When someone makes a shoe for a foot he has not seen, I am sure he will not produce a basket.' All shoes are alike because all feet are alike. All palates show the same preferences in taste. Yi Ya[22] was simply the man first to discover what would be pleasing to my palate. Were the nature of taste to vary from man to man in the same way as horses and hounds differ from me in kind, then how does it come about that all palates in the world follow the preferences of Yi Ya? The fact that in taste the whole world looks to Yi Ya shows that all palates are alike. It is the same also with the ear. The whole world looks to Shih K'uang,[23] and this shows that all ears are alike. It is the same also with the eye. The whole world appreciates the good looks of Tzu-tu;[24] whoever does not is blind. Hence it is said: all palates have the same preference in taste; all ears in sound; all eyes in beauty. Should hearts prove to be an exception by possessing nothing in common? What is common to all hearts? Reason and rightness. The sage is simply the man first to discover this common element in my heart. Thus reason and rightness please my heart in the same way as meat pleases my palate."

8. Mencius said, "There was a time when the trees were luxuriant on the Ox Mountain. As it is on the outskirts of a great metropolis, the trees are constantly lopped by axes. Is it any wonder that they are no longer fine? With the respite they get in the day and in the night, and the moistening by the rain and dew, there is certainly no lack of new shoots coming out, but then the cattle and sheep come to graze upon the mountain. That is why it is as bald as it is. People, seeing only its baldness, tend to think that it never had any trees. But can this possibly be the nature of a mountain? Can what is in man be completely lacking in moral inclinations? A man's letting go of his true heart is like the case of the trees and the axes. When the trees are lopped day after day, is it any wonder that they are no longer fine? If, in spite of the respite a man gets in the day and in the night and of the effect of the morning air on him, scarcely any of his likes and dislikes resemble those of other men, it is because what he does in the course of the day once again dissipates what he has gained. If this dissipation happens repeatedly, then the influence of the air in the night will no longer be able to preserve what was originally in him, and when that happens, the man is not far removed from an animal. Others, seeing his resemblance to an animal, will be led to think that he never had any native endowment. But can that be what a man is genuinely like? Hence, given the right nourishment there is nothing that will not grow, and deprived

of it there is nothing that will not wither away. Confucius said, 'Hold on to it and it will remain; let go of it and it will disappear. One never knows the time it comes or goes, neither does one know the direction.' It is perhaps to the heart this refers."

9. Mencius said, "Do not be puzzled by the King's lack of wisdom. Even a plant that grows most readily will not survive if it is placed in the sun for one day and exposed to the cold for ten. It is very rarely that I have an opportunity of seeing the King, and as soon as I leave, those who expose him to the cold arrive on the scene. What can I do with the few new shoots that come out? Now take *yi*,[25] which is only an art of little consequence. Yet if one does not give one's whole mind to it, one will never master it. Yi Ch'iu is the best player in the whole country. Get him to teach two people to play, one of whom concentrates his mind on the game and listens only to what Yi Ch'iu has to say, while the other, though he listens, dreams of an approaching swan and wants to take up his bow and corded arrow to shoot at it. Now even though this man shares the lessons with the first, he will never be as good. Is this because he is less clever? The answer is, 'No.'"

10. Mencius said, "Fish is what I want; bear's palm is also what I want. If I cannot have both, I would rather take bear's palm than fish. Life is what I want; dutifulness is also what I want. If I cannot have both, I would rather take dutifulness than life. On the one hand, though life is what I want, there is something I want more than life. That is why I do not cling to life at all costs. On the other hand, though death is what I loathe, there is something I loathe more than death. That is why there are troubles I do not avoid. If there is nothing a man wants more than life, then why should he have scruples about any means, so long as it will serve to keep him alive? If there is nothing a man loathes more than death, then why should he have scruples about any means, so long as it helps him to avoid trouble? Yet there are ways of remaining alive and ways of avoiding death to which a man will not resort. In other words, there are things a man wants more than life and there are also things he loathes more than death. This is an attitude not confined to the moral man but common to all men. The moral man simply never loses it.

"Here is a basketful of rice and a bowlful of soup. Getting them will mean life; not getting them will mean death. When these are given with abuse, even a wayfarer would not accept them; when these are given after being trampled upon, even a beggar would not accept them. Yet when it comes to ten thousand bushels of grain one is supposed to accept without asking if it is in accordance with the rites or if it is right to do so. What benefit are ten thousand bushels of grain to me? [Do I accept them] for the sake of beautiful houses, the enjoyment of wives and concubines, or for the sake of the gratitude my needy acquaintances will show me? What I would not accept in the first instance when it was a matter of life and death I now accept for the sake of beautiful houses; what I would not accept when it was a matter of life and death and I now accept for the enjoyment of wives and concubines; what I would not accept when it was a matter of life and death I now accept for the sake of the gratitude my needy acquaintances will show me. Is there no way of putting a stop to this? This way of thinking is known as losing one's original heart."

11. Mencius said, "Benevolence is the heart of man, and rightness his road. Sad it is indeed when a man gives up the right road instead of following it and allows his heart to stray without enough sense to go after it. When his chickens and dogs stray, he has sense enough to go after them, but not when his heart strays. The sole concern of learning is to go after this strayed heart. That is all."

12. Mencius said, "Now if one's third finger is bent and cannot stretch straight, though this neither causes any pain nor impairs the use of the hand, one would think nothing of the distance between Ch'in and Ch'u if someone able to straighten it could be found. This is because one's finger is inferior to other people's. When one's finger is inferior to other people's, one has sense enough to resent it, but not when one's heart is inferior. This is known as failure to see that one thing is the same in kind as another."

13. Mencius said, "Even with a *t'ung* or a *tzu* tree one or two spans thick, anyone wishing to keep it alive will know how it should be tended, yet when it comes to one's own person, one does not know how to tend it. Surely one does not love one's person any less than the *t'ung* or the *tzu*. This is unthinking to the highest degree."

14. Mencius said, "A man loves all parts of his person without discrimination. As he loves them all without discrimination, he nurtures them all without discrimination. If there is not one foot or one inch of his skin that he does not love, then there is not one foot or one inch that he does not nurture. Is there any other way of telling whether what a man does is good or bad than by the choice he makes? The parts of the person differ in value and importance. Never harm the parts of greater importance for the sake of those of smaller importance, or the more valuable for the sake of the less valuable. He who nurtures the parts of smaller importance is a small man; he who nurtures the parts of greater importance is a great man. Now consider a gardener. If he tends the common trees while neglecting the valuable ones, then he is a bad gardener. A man who takes care of one finger to the detriment of his shoulder and back without realizing his mistake is a muddled man. A man who cares only about food and drink is despised by others because he takes care of the parts of smaller importance to the detriment of the parts of greater importance. If a man who cares about food and drink can do so without neglecting

any other part of his person, then his mouth and belly are much more than just a foot or an inch of his skin."

15. Kung-tu Tzu asked, "Though equally human, why are some men greater than others?"

"He who is guided by the interests of the parts of his person that are of greater importance is a great man; he who is guided by the interests of the parts of his person that are of smaller importance is a small man."

"Though equally human, why are some men guided one way and others guided another way?"

"The organs of hearing and sight are unable to think and can be misled by external things. When one thing acts on another, all it does is to attract it. The organ of the heart can think. But it will find the answer only if it does think; otherwise, it will not find the answer. This is what Heaven has given me. If one makes one's stand on what is of greater importance in the first instance, what is of smaller importance cannot displace it. In this way, one cannot but be a great man."

16. Mencius said, "There are honours bestowed by Heaven, and there are honours bestowed by man. Benevolence, dutifulness, conscientiousness, truthfulness to one's word, unflagging delight in what is good,—these are honours bestowed by Heaven. The position of a Ducal Minister, a Minister, or a Counsellor is an honour bestowed by man. Men of antiquity bent their efforts towards acquiring honours bestowed by Heaven, and honours bestowed by man followed as a matter of course. Men of today bend their efforts towards acquiring honours bestowed by heaven in order to win honours bestowed by man, and once the latter is won they discard the former. Such men are deluded to the extreme, and in the end are sure only to perish."

17. Mencius said, "All men share the same desire to be exalted. But as a matter of fact, every man has in him that which is exalted. The fact simply never dawned on him. What man exalts is not truly exalted. Those Chao Meng[26] exalts, Chao Meng can also humble. The *Book of Odes* says,

> Having filled us with drink,
> Having filled us with virtue . . .[27]

The point is that, being filled with moral virtue, one does not envy other people's enjoyment of fine food and, enjoying a fine and extensive reputation, one does not envy other people's fineries."

18. Mencius said. "Benevolence overcomes cruelty just as water overcomes fire. Those who practise benevolence today are comparable to someone trying to put out a cartload of burning firewood with a cupful of water. When the fire fails to be extinguished, they say water cannot overcome fire. For a man to

do this is for him to place himself on the side of those who are cruel to the extreme, and in the end he is sure only to perish."

19. Mencius said, "The five types of grain[28] are the best of plants, yet if they are not ripe they are worse than the wild varieties. With benevolence the point, too, lies in seeing to its being ripe." . . .

Part B

1. A man from Jen asked Wu-lu Tzu,[29] "Which is more important, the rites or food?"

"The rites."

"Which is more important, the rites or sex?"

"The rites."

"Suppose you would starve to death if you insisted on the observance of the rites, but would manage to get something to eat if you did not. Would you still insist on their observance? Again, suppose you would not get a wife if you insisted on the observance of ch'in ying,[30] but would get one if you did not. Would you still insist on its observance?"

Wu-lu Tzu was unable to answer. The following day he went to Tsou and gave an account of the discussion to Mencius.

"What difficulty is there," said Mencius, "in answering this? If you bring the tips to the same level without measuring the difference in the bases, you can make a piece of wood an inch long reach a greater height than a tall building. In saying that gold is heavier than feathers, surely one is not referring to the amount of gold in a clasp and a whole cartload of feathers? If you compare a case where food is important with a case where the rite is inconsequential, then the greater importance of food is not the only absurd conclusion you can draw. Similarly with sex. Go and reply to the questioner in this way, 'Suppose you would manage to get something to eat if you took the food from your elder brother by twisting his arm, but would not get it if you did not. Would you twist his arm? Again, suppose you would get a wife if you climbed over the wall of your neighbour on the east side and dragged away the daughter of the house by force, but would not if you did not. Would you drag her away by force?'"[31]

2. Ts'ao Chiao[32] asked, "Is it true that all men are capable of becoming a Yao or a Shun?"

"Yes," said Mencius.

"I heard that King Wen was ten foot tall, while T'ang was nine. Now I am a little more than nine foot four inches,[33] yet all I can do is to eat rice. What should I do?"[34]

"What difficulty is there? All you have to do is to make an effort. Here is a man who cannot lift a chicken. He is, indeed, a weak man. Now if he were to lift a ton, then he would, indeed, be a strong man. In other words, whoever can lift the same weight as Wu Huo[35] is himself a Wu Huo. The trouble with a man is surely not his lack of sufficient strength, but his refusal to make the effort. One who walks slowly, keeping behind his elders, is considered a well-mannered younger brother. One who walks quickly, over-taking his elders, is considered an ill-mannered younger brother. Walking slowly is surely not beyond the ability of any man. It is simply a matter of his not making the effort. The way of Yao and Shun is simply to be a good son and a good younger brother. If you wear the clothes of Yao, speak the words of Yao and behave the way Yao behaved, then you *are* a Yao. On the other hand, if you wear the clothes of Chieh, speak the words of Chieh and behave the way Chieh behaved, then you *are* a Chieh. That is all.''

"If the ruler of Tsou receives me and I am given a place to lodge, then I should like to stay and be a disciple of yours.''

"The Way is like a wide road. It is not at all difficult to find. The trouble with people is simply that they do not look for it. You go home and look for it and there will be teachers enough for you.'' . . .

4. Sung K'eng[36] was on his way to Ch'u. Mencius, meeting him at Shih Ch'iu, asked him, "Where are you going, sir?"

"I heard that hostilities had broken out between Ch'in and Ch'u. I am going to see the king of Ch'u and try to persuade him to bring an end to them. If I fail to find favour with the king of Ch'u I shall go to see the king of Ch'in and try to persuade him instead. I hope I shall have success with one or other of the two kings.''

"I do not wish to know the details, but may I ask about the gist of your argument? How are you going to persuade the kings?''

"I shall explain to them the unprofitability of war.''

"Your purpose is lofty indeed, but your slogan is wrong. If you place profit before the kings of Ch'in and Ch'u, and they call off their armies because they are drawn to profit, then it means that the soldiers in their armies retire because they are drawn to profit. If a subject, in serving his prince, cherished the profit motive, and a son, in serving his father, and a younger brother, in serving his elder brother, did likewise, then it would mean that in their mutual relations, prince and subject, father and son, elder brother and younger brother, all cherished the profit motive to the total exclusion of morality. The prince of such a state is sure to perish. If, on the other hand, you placed morality before the kings of Ch'in and Ch'u and they called off their armies because they were drawn to morality, then it would mean that the soldiers in their armies retired because they were drawn to morality. If a subject, in serving his prince, cherished morality, and a son, in serving his father, and a younger brother, in serving his elder brother, did likewise, then it would mean that in their mutual relations, prince and subject, father and son, elder brother and younger brother, all cherished morality to the exclusion of profit. The prince of such a state is sure to become a true King. What is the point of mentioning the word 'profit'?" . . .

BOOK VII

Part A

1. Mencius said, "For a man to give full realization to his heart is for him to understand his own nature, and a man who knows his own nature will know Heaven. By retaining his heart and nurturing his nature he is serving Heaven. Whether he is going to die young or to live to a ripe old age makes no difference to his steadfastness of purpose. It is through awaiting whatever is to befall him with a perfected character that he stands firm on his proper destiny."

2. Mencius said, "Though nothing happens that is not due to destiny, one accepts willingly only what is one's proper destiny. That is why he who understands destiny does not stand under a wall on the verge of collapse. He who dies after having done his best in following the Way dies according to his proper destiny. It is never anyone's proper destiny to die in fetters."

3. Mencius said, "Seek and you will get it; let go and you will lose it. If this is the case, then seeking is of use to getting and what is sought is within yourself. But if there is a proper way to seek it and whether you get it or not depends on destiny, then seeking is of no use to getting and what is sought lies outside yourself."

4. Mencius said, "All the ten thousand things are there in me. There is no greater joy for me than to find, on self-examination, that I am true to myself. Try your best to treat others as you would wish to be treated yourself, and you will find that this is the shortest way to benevolence."

5. Mencius said, "The multitude can be said never to understand what they practise, to notice what they repeatedly do, or to be aware of the path they follow all their lives."

6. Mencius said, "A man must not be without shame, for the shame of being without shame is shamelessness indeed." . . .

9. Mencius said to Sung Kou-chien,[37] "You are fond of travelling from state to state, offering advice. I shall tell you how this should be done. You should be content whether your worth is recognized by others or not."

   "What must a man be before he can be content?"

"If he reveres virtue and delights in rightness, he can be content. Hence a Gentleman never abandons rightness in adversity, nor does he depart from the Way in success. By not abandoning rightness in adversity, he finds delight in himself; by not departing from the Way in success, he does not disappoint the people. Men of antiquity made the people feel the effect of their bounty when they realized their ambition, and, when they failed to realize their ambition, were at least able to show the world an exemplary character. In obscurity a man makes perfect his own person, but in prominence he makes perfect the whole Empire as well."

10. Mencius said, "Those who make the effort only when there is a King Wen are ordinary men. Outstanding men make the effort even without a King Wen."

11. Mencius said, "To look upon oneself as deficient even though the possessions of the families of Han and Wei be added to one's own is to surpass other men by a long way." . . .

15. Mencius said, "What a man is able to do without having to learn it is what he can truly do; what he knows without having to reflect on it is what he truly knows. There are no young children who do not know loving their parents, and none of them when they grow up will not know respecting their elder brothers. Loving one's parents is benevolence; respecting one's elders is rightness. What is left to be done is simply the extension of these to the whole Empire." . . .

20. Mencius said, "A gentleman delights in three things, and being ruler over the Empire is not amongst them. His parents are alive and his brothers are well. This is the first delight. Above, he is not ashamed to face Heaven; below, he is not ashamed to face man. This is the second delight. He has the good fortune of having the most talented pupils in the Empire. This is the third delight. A gentleman delights in three things and being ruler over the Empire is not amongst them."

21. Mencius said, "An extensive territory and a vast population are things a gentleman desires, but what he delights in lies elsewhere. To stand in the centre of the Empire and bring peace to the people within the Four Seas is what a gentleman delights in, but that which he follows as his nature lies elsewhere. That which is a gentleman follows as his nature is not added to when he holds sway over the Empire, nor is it detracted from when he is reduced to straitened circumstances. This is because he knows his allotted station. That which a gentleman follows as his nature, that is to say, benevolence, rightness, the rites and wisdom, is rooted in his heart, and manifests

itself in his face, giving it a sleek appearance. It also shows in his back and extends to his limbs, rendering their message intelligible without words." . . .

25. Mencius said, "He who gets up with the crowing of the cock and never tires of doing good is the same kind of man as Shun; he who gets up with the crowing of the cock and never tires of working for profit is the same kind of man as Chih.[38] If you wish to understand the difference between Shun and Chih, you need look no further than the gap separating the good and the profitable."

26. Mencius said, "Yang Tzu chooses egoism. Even if he could benefit the Empire by pulling out one hair he would not do it. Mo Tzu advocates love without discrimination. If by shaving his head and showing his heels he could benefit the Empire, he would do it. Tzu-mo holds on to the middle, half way between the two extremes.[39] Holding on to the middle is closer to being right, but to do this without the proper measure is no different from holding to one extreme. The reason for disliking those who hold to one extreme is that they cripple the Way. One thing is singled out to the neglect of a hundred others."

27. Mencius said, "A hungry man finds his food delectable; a thirsty man finds his drink delicious. Both lack the proper measure of food and drink because hunger and thirst interfere with his judgement. The palate is not the only thing which is open to interference by hunger and thirst. The human heart, too, is open to the same interference. If a man can prevent hunger and thirst from interfering with his heart, then he does not need to worry about being inferior to other men." . . .

33. Prince Tien[40] asked, "What is the business of a Gentleman?"
    "To set his mind on high principles."
    "What do you mean by this?"
    "To be moral. That is all. It is contrary to benevolence to kill one innocent man; it is contrary to rightness to take what one is not entitled to. Where is one's dwelling? In benevolence. Where is one's road? In rightness. To dwell in benevolence and to follow rightness constitute the sum total of the business of a great man." . . .

36. Mencius went to Ch'i from Fan. When he saw the son of the King of Ch'i from a distance, he sighed and said, "A man's surroundings transform his air just as the food he eats changes his body. Great indeed are a man's surroundings. Otherwise, are we not all the son of some man or another?" . . .

41. Kung-sun Ch'ou[41] said, "The Way is indeed lofty and beautiful, but to

attempt it is like trying to climb up to Heaven which seems beyond one's reach. Why not substitute for it something which men have some hopes of attaining so as to encourage them constantly to make the effort?"

"A great craftsman," said Mencius, "does not put aside the plumb-line for the benefit of the clumsy carpenter. Yi[42] did not compromise on his standards of drawing the bow for the sake of the clumsy archer." . . .

Part B

1. Mencius said, "How ruthless was King Hui of Liang![43] A benevolent man extends his love from those he loves to those he does not love. A ruthless man extends his ruthlessness from those he does not love to those he loves."

"What do you mean?" asked Kung-sun Ch'ou.

"King Hui of Liang sent his people to war, making pulp of them, for the sake of gaining further territory. He suffered a grave defeat and when he wanted to go to a war a second time he was afraid he would not be able to win, so he herded the young men he loved to their death as well. This is what I meant when I said he extended his ruthlessness from those he did not love to those he loved." . . .

7. Mencius said, "Only now do I realize how serious it is to kill a member of the family of another man. If you killed his father, he would kill your father; if you killed his elder brother, he would kill your elder brother. This being the case, though you may not have killed your father and brother with your own hands, it is but one step removed." . . .

10. Mencius said, "He who never misses a chance for profit cannot be killed by a bad year; he who is equipped with every virtue cannot be led astray by a wicked world."

11. Mencius said, "A man who is out to make a name for himself will be able to give away a state of a thousand chariots, but reluctance would be written all over his face if he had to give away a basketful of rice and a bowlful of soup when no such purpose was served." . . .

14. Mencius said, "The people are of supreme importance; the altars to the gods of earth and grain come next; last comes the ruler." . . .

16. Mencius said, " 'Benevolence' means 'man.'[44] When these two are conjoined, the result is 'the Way.'" . . .

25. Hao-sheng Pu-hai[45] asked, "What sort of a man is Yüeh-cheng Tzu?"[46]

"A good man," said Mencius. "A true man."

"What do you mean by 'good' and 'true'?"

"The desirable is called 'good.' To have it in oneself is called 'true.' To possess it fully in oneself is called 'beautiful,' but to shine forth with this full possession is called 'great.' To be great and be transformed by this greatness is called 'sage'; to be sage and to transcend the understanding is called 'divine.' Yüeh-cheng Tzu has something of the first two qualities but has not quite reached the last four." . . .

33. Mencius said, "Yao and Shun had it as their nature; T'ang and King Wu returned to it.[47] To be in accord with the rites in every movement is the highest of virtue. When one mourns sorrowfully over the dead it is not to impress the living. When one follows unswervingly the path of virtue it is not to win advancement. When one invariably keeps one's word it is not to establish the rectitude of one's actions. A gentleman merely follows the norm and awaits his destiny." . . .

35. Mencius said, "There is nothing better for the nurturing of the heart than to reduce the number of one's desires. When a man has but few desires, even if there is anything he fails to retain in himself, it cannot be much; but when he has a great many desires, then even if there is anything he manages to retain in himself, it cannot be much."

NOTES

1. King Hsüan of Ch'i is the king in whose court Mencius served as a minister. [D.C.A.]
2. Chieh was an evil tyrant, the last emperor of the Hsia dynasty. He was over-thrown by T'ang, who began the Shang, or Yin, dynasty, which ruled from about the sixteenth to the eleventh centuries B.C.E. Tchou (Chou Hsin) was the last emperor of the Shang dynasty, notorious for his depravity. King Wu (reigned 1027–1005) overthrew Tchou and began the Chou dynasty, which ruled from about the eleventh to the eighth centuries. [D.C.A.]
3. In ancient times, China was thought to be square, surrounded by seas on the east, west, north, and south. The "whole realm within the Four Seas" thus denotes all of China. [D.C.A.]
4. *Tzu-lu*: a disciple of Confucius [D.C.A.]
5. In Mencius's view of history, Yü and Shun, along with Yao, were ancient heroes who made the world habitable after a great deluge and then became the first emperors. Mencius sees them as model rulers, governing "under Heaven," with Yao ruling first, then Shun, and then Yü. Yü was considered the first emperor of the Hsia dynasty. [D.C.A.]
6. In this translation, "gentleman" and "Gentleman" translate two different Chinese terms. The uncapitalized form designates a man of moral excellence or a man in authority; capitalized, the word means a member of the lowest rank of officials. [D.C.A.]

7. *Tai Pu-sheng*: a minister of the state of Sung [D.C.A.]
8. This is Yen, the King of Sung. [D.C.L.]
9. It is possible that these are the names of streets in Ch'i. [D.C.L.]
10. *Hsüeh Chü-chou*: a minister in the state of Sung [D.C.A.]
11. *Tai Ying-chih*: another minister in the state of Sung [D.C.A.]
12. *the Three Dynasties*: the Hsia, Shang, and Chou dynasties [D.C.A.]
13. *Ch'un-yü K'un*: a clever thinker from the state of Ch'i [D.C.A.]
14. *Ch'u Tzu*: a minister of the state of Ch'i [D.C.A.]
15. *Kao Tzu*: a philosopher contemporary with Mencius [D.C.A.]
16. *Kung-tu Tzu*: a disciple of Mencius [D.C.A.]
17. King Wen (died 1027 B.C.E.) and his son, King Wu (who, as noted earlier, overthrew the tyrant Tchou), were both good kings. King Li (reigned 857–842 B.C.E.) and King Yu (reigned 781–772 B.C.E.) were both tyrants. [D.C.A.]
18. In Chinese legend, Hsiang was an evil prince of Emperor Yao, and the "Blind Man" (so called because of his mental blindness) was the evil father of the Emperor Shun. Ch'i was a good elder brother (not an uncle, as this text states) of the tyrant Tchou, and Prince Pi Kan was a good uncle of Tchou. [D.C.A.]
19. *Book of Odes*: the earliest anthology of Chinese poetry, dating from the eighth and seventh centuries B.C.E. The poem cited here is Ode 260. [D.C.A.]
20. *the Way*: Way (*tao*) means, literally, "road" or "path." Confucius uses the term metaphorically to designate the correct path to follow—both on the individual level (personal morality) and the group level (the ideal social and political order). [D.C.A.]
21. Nothing is known about Lung Tzu. [D.C.A.]
22. *Yi Ya*: the skillful cook of Duke Huan of Ch'i [D.C.A.]
23. *Shih K'uang*: the court musician of Duke P'ing of Chin, known for his perfect sense of pitch [D.C.A.]
24. *Tzu-tu*: a man of legendary beauty [D.C.A.]
25. *yi*: an Oriental game, still played today, known in the West as "go" [D.C.A., after D.C.L.]
26. Four members of the family of Chao were called by the name Chao Meng; all were politically influential. [D.C.A.]
27. Ode 247 [D.C.L.]
28. *the five types of grain*: rice, wheat, pulse, and two kinds of millet (the five edible crops) [D.C.A.]
29. *Wu-lu Tzu*: a disciple of Mencius [D.C.A.]
30. *ch'in ying*: the part of the marriage rite in which the groom goes to the home of the bride to fetch her [D.C.A., after D.C.L.]
31. Mencius's assumption here is that it would be morally inconceivable to twist an elder brother's arm or to drag away a neighbor's daughter by force. [D.C.A.]
32. Nothing certain is known about Ts'ao Chiao. [D.C.A.]
33. The Chinese foot in this period was, needless to say, much shorter than the English foot. [D.C.L.]
34. Ts'ao Chiao's point seems to be that since he is comparable in height to King Wen and T'ang, and since these men became good like Yao and Shun, then perhaps he, too, can become good like Yao and Shun. [D.C.A.]
35. *Wu Huo*: a byword for a strong man [D.C.L.]

36. *Sung K'eng*: a traveling scholar who offered his advice to various rulers [D.C.A.]
37. All we know of Sung Kou-chien is that he traveled to offer his counsel to rulers. [D.C.A.]
38. *Chih*: a byword for robbers [D.C.L.]
39. Yang Tzu (Yang Chu) and Mo Tzu were influential philosophers whose ethical doctrines Mencius criticized. Mo Tzu lived in the fifth, Yang Tzu in the fourth century B.C.E. All we know of Tzu-Mo is that he was from the state of Lu. [D.C.A.]
40. *Prince Tien*: the son of King Hsüan of Ch'i [D.C.A.]
41. *Kung-sun Ch'ou*: a disciple of Mencius [D.C.A.]
42. *Yi*: a famous archer in ancient times [D.C.A.]
43. King Hui reigned from 370 to 319 B.C.E. [D.C.A.]
44. The Chinese words for *benevolence* and *man* have the same pronunciation; the written form of *benevolence* derives in part from the written form of *man*. [D.C.A.]
45. All we know of Hao-sheng Pu-hai is that he was from Ch'i. [D.C.A.]
46. *Yüeh-cheng Tzu*: a disciple of Mencius [D.C.A.]
47. "It" here refers to benevolence. [D.C.A., after D.C.L.]

QUESTIONS FOR REFLECTION AND DISCUSSION

1. Is the tendency to be moral inherent in human nature?
2. Are there any evil tendencies inherent in human nature?
3. Is our environment chiefly responsible for whether we end up "good" or "bad"?
4. Is everyone capable of moral perfection?
5. Is it profitable to be moral?

SUGGESTIONS FOR FURTHER READING

I. Primary Sources

Mencius, trans. D. C. Lau. Harmondsworth, England: Penguin, 1970, 280 pp.

Mencius: A New Translation Arranged and Annotated for the General Reader, trans. W. A. C. H. Dobson. 1963; reprint ed., Ann Arbor, Mich.: Books on Demand, 215 pp.

> A translation of *The Book of Mencius* that rearranges the passages and groups them under seven headings: "Mencius at Court," "Mencius in Public Life," "Mencius and His Disciples," "Mencius and His Rivals," "Comment on the Times," "The Teachings of Mencius," and "Maxims." Includes an introduction to each group.

"The Works of Mencius, or Meng Tzu," in *The Sacred Books of Confucius and Other Confucian Classics*, ed. and trans. Ch'u Chai and Winberg Chai. Hyde Park, N.Y.: University Books, 1965, pp. 95–220.

A translation of *The Book of Mencius* that rearranges the passages under four headings: "The Doctrine of Human Nature," "The Political and Economic Measures," "The Way of Life," and "The Comments of Mencius." Each category is divided into chapters.

II. Secondary Sources

Chai, Ch'u, and Winberg Chai. *Confucianism*. Woodbury, N.Y.: Barron's Educational Ser., 1973, 202 pp.

Chap. 3, "The Idealistic School of Confucianism: Mencius," pp. 48–64, gives a clear overview of Mencius's philosophy.

Fung Yu-Lan. *A History of Chinese Philosophy*, Vol. I, *The Period of the Philosophers (From the Beginnings to circa 100 B.C.)*, trans. Derk Bodde. 1937; 2d English ed., Princeton, N.J.: Princeton University Press, 1952, 455 pp.

The exposition of Mencius in chap. 6, "Mencius and His School of Confucianism," pp. 106–131, contains many substantial quotations from Mencius.

Ivanhoe, Philip J. *Ethics in the Confucian Tradition: The Thought of Mencius and Wang Yang-ming*. Atlanta: Scholars Press, American Academy of Religion Academy Ser., 1990, 186 pp.

A comparison of the ethical views of Mencius and the Neo-Confucian thinker Wang Yang-Ming (1472–1529 C.E.). There are brief expository sections on five aspects of Mencius's thought, which may be read independently.

Schwartz, Benjamin I. *The World of Thought in Ancient China*. Cambridge, Mass.: Harvard University Press, 1985, 490 pp.

Chap. 7, "The Defense of Confucian Faith: Mencius and Hsün-tzu," pp. 255–320, contains a thorough analysis of Mencius's philosophy, placed in cultural context. (Hsün-tzu, another important Confucian thinker, lived from about 300 to 230 B.C.E.). See especially the section entitled "Mencius' 'Philosophic Anthropology,'" pp. 263–278.

Verwilghen, Albert Felix. *Mencius: The Man and His Ideas*. New York: St. John's University Press, Asian Philosophical Studies, 1967, 122 pp.

A sympathetic study of the character and doctrines of Mencius.

4

Lucius Annaeus Seneca

Lucius Annaeus Seneca was born in about 4 B.C.E. in Córdoba, Spain, where his father was a Roman official and a noted orator. While still an infant, he was brought to Rome by an aunt, who nursed him through a sickly childhood and got him started in his political career. In school he studied rhetoric and then philosophy. Even while pursuing a career as a lawyer and politician, he continued his study of philosophy.

Seneca's eloquence in the Senate aroused the jealousy of Caligula, Roman emperor from 37–41 C.E. Caligula planned to execute Seneca but changed his mind when someone told him that Seneca (always in poor health) was about to die anyway of natural causes. He did not die, but he did continue to have political troubles under the next two emperors. When Claudius became emperor in 41, his wife accused Seneca of committing adultery with Claudius's niece. The Senate condemned Seneca to death, but Claudius commuted the sentence to banishment, and Seneca was exiled to the island of Corsica. Eight years later, Claudius's new wife (the previous one was executed) had Seneca recalled to Rome to tutor the young Nero, her son by a previous marriage. When Nero became emperor in 54, he made Seneca one of his principal advisers. But in 65 Seneca was accused of conspiracy and, presented with the choice of execution or suicide, calmly slashed his veins.

Seneca was a prolific and versatile author. He wrote twelve essays on practical moral philosophy (his main area of interest), examining such topics as happiness, leisure, mercy, and anger. He wrote a work on natural science entitled *Natural Questions*, which examines phenomena such as thunder and lightning, earthquakes, and comets. Seneca is also the author of three *consolations*, works intended to comfort individuals who have suffered a personal loss. His dramatic works include nine tragedies, and he is believed to have written the satirical skit on the deification of Claudius entitled *Apocolocyntosis* ("The Pumpkinification"). Near the end of his life he wrote numerous letters to his friend Lucilius (124 of them survive) on a wide range of philosophical and personal topics.

Seneca's philosophy continues the tradition of Stoicism, which began with the philosopher Zeno of Citium (about 335–263 B.C.E.). The first Stoics were so called because they met in the Stoa Poikile ("painted porch"), the public hall in Athens in which Zeno lectured. Historians divide Stoicism into three periods, the Early Stoa (from Zeno until the second century B.C.E.), the Middle Stoa (first and second centuries B.C.E.), and the Late Stoa (first and second centuries C.E.). Seneca, accordingly, is considered a late Stoic.

The Stoics studied logic, physics (natural science), and ethics. Their central ethical doctrine was that human beings should imitate the order of the cosmos by following nature. There was a clear connection, therefore, between natural science and ethics. Members of the Late Stoa focused their attention on ethics; while they had some interest in natural science (as we see from Seneca's *Natural Questions*), they were concerned above all with the practical question of how to live one's life.

Our selection is from Seneca's treatise *On the Happy Life*, written about 58 C.E. and addressed to Gallio, his older brother. (Gallio, incidentally, was the Roman official who refused to judge Paul; see Acts 18:12–17.) Seneca begins with the observation that by nature all human beings desire happiness. The question, then, is what happiness is and how it can be attained. Seneca presents the Stoic doctrine that to be happy is to follow the guidance of nature. *Nature* has a twofold sense: the divine power that rules the universe and the rational nature of the individual person, which is a portion of the divine power. To follow nature means to live a life of virtue. A virtuous life is one of tranquillity and harmony of soul: One is content with one's lot, indifferent to the vagaries of fortune, and beyond both fear and desire.

Since many people mistakenly identify happiness with pleasure, Seneca explains how pleasure is related to the happy life. He maintains that a virtuous life will have a certain type of pleasure as a by-product but that it would be a serious mistake to devote one's life to the pursuit of pleasure. Finally, Seneca (who was himself very wealthy) explains that it is not contradictory for a Stoic to possess wealth: Material riches, although not necessary for a virtuous life, enable one to engage in certain virtuous activities and add a certain joy to life. The moral error lies not in owning riches but in letting riches own us.

ON THE HAPPY LIFE

To live happily, my brother Gallio, is the desire of all men, but their minds are blinded to a clear vision of just what it is that makes life happy; and so far from its being easy to attain the happy life, the more eagerly a man strives to reach it, the farther he recedes from it if he has made a mistake in the road; for when it leads in the opposite direction, his very speed will increase the distance that separates him.

First, therefore, we must seek what it is that we are aiming at; then we must look about for the road by which we can reach it most quickly, and on the journey itself, if only we are on the right path, we shall discover how much of the distance we overcome each day, and how much nearer we are to the goal toward which we are urged by a natural desire. But so long as we wander aimlessly, having no guide, and following only the noise and discordant cries of those who call us in different directions, life will be consumed in making mistakes—life that is brief even if we should strive day and night for sound wisdom. Let us, therefore, decide both upon the goal and upon the way, and not fail to find some experienced guide who has explored the region towards which we are advancing; for the conditions of this journey are different from those of most travel. On most journeys some well-recognized road and inquiries made of the inhabitants of the region prevent you from going astray; but on this one all the best beaten and the most frequented paths are the most deceptive. Nothing, therefore, needs to be more emphasized than the warning that we should not, like sheep, follow the lead of the throng in front of us, travelling, thus, the way that all go and not the way that we ought to go. Yet nothing involves us in greater trouble than the fact that we adapt ourselves to common report in the belief that the best things are those that have met with great approval,—the fact that, having so many to follow, we live after the rule, not of reason, but of imitation. The result of this is that people are piled high, one above another, as they rush to destruction. And just as it happens that in a great crush of humanity, when the people

push against each other, no one can fall down without drawing along another, and those that are in front cause destruction to those behind—this
same thing you may see happening everywhere in life. No man can go wrong
to his own hurt only, but he will be both the cause and the sponsor of
another's wrongdoing. For it is dangerous to attach one's self to the crowd in
front, and so long as each one of us is more willing to trust another than to
judge for himself, we never show any judgement in the matter of living, but
always a blind trust, and a mistake that has been passed on from hand to
hand finally involves us and works our destruction. It is the example of other
people that is our undoing; let us merely separate ourselves from the crowd,
and we shall be made whole. But as it is, the populace, defending its own
iniquity, pits itself against reason. And so we see the same thing happening
that happens at the elections, where, when the fickle breeze of popular favour
has shifted, the very same persons who chose the praetors[1] wonder that
those praetors were chosen. The same thing has one moment our favour, the
next our disfavour; this is the outcome of every decision that follows the
choice of the majority.

When the happy life is under debate, there will be no use for you to
reply to me, as if it were a matter of votes: "This side seems to be in a
majority." For that is just the reason it is the worse side. Human affairs are
not so happily ordered that the majority prefer the better things; a proof of the
worst choice is the crowd. Therefore let us find out what is best to do, not
what is most commonly done—what will establish our claim to lasting happiness, not what finds favour with the rabble, who are the worst possible
exponents of the truth. But by the rabble I mean no less the servants of the
court than the servants of the kitchen; for I do not regard the colour of the
garments that clothe the body. In rating a man I do not rely upon eyesight; I
have a better and surer light, by which I may distinguish the false from the
true. Let the soul discover the good of the soul. If the soul ever has leisure to
draw breath and to retire within itself—ah! to what self-torture will it come,
and how, if it confesses the truth to itself, it will say: "All that I have done
hitherto, I would were undone; when I think of all that I have said, I envy the
dumb; of all that I have prayed for, I rate my prayers as the curses of my
enemies; of all that I have feared—ye gods! how much lighter it would have
been than the load of what I have coveted! With many I have been at enmity,
and, laying aside hatred, have been restored to friendship with them—if only
there can be any friendship between the wicked; with myself I have not yet
entered into friendship. I have made every effort to remove myself from the
multitude and to make myself noteworthy by reason of some endowment.
What have I accomplished save to expose myself to the darts of malice and
show it where it can sting me? See you those who praise your eloquence, who
trail upon your wealth, who court your favour, who exalt your power? All
these are either now your enemies, or—it amounts to the same thing—can
become such. To know how many are jealous of you, count your admirers.

Why do I not rather seek some real good—one which I could feel, not one which I could display? These things that draw the eyes of men, before which they halt, which they show to one another in wonder, outwardly glitter, but are worthless within."

Let us seek something that is a good in more than appearance—something that is solid, constant, and more beautiful in its more hidden part; for this let us delve. And it is placed not far off; you will find it—you need only to know where to stretch out your hand. As it is, just as if we groped in darkness, we pass by things near at hand, stumbling over the very objects we desire.

Not to bore you, however, with tortuous details, I shall pass over in silence the opinions of other philosophers, for it would be tedious to enumerate and refute them all. Do you listen to ours. But when I say "ours," I do not bind myself to some particular one of the Stoic masters; I, too, have the right to form an opinion. Accordingly, I shall follow so-and-so, I shall request so-and-so to divide the question; perhaps, too, when called upon after all the rest, I shall impugn none of my predecessors' opinions, and shall say: "I simply have this much to add." Meantime, I follow the guidance of Nature—a doctrine upon which all Stoics are agreed. Not to stray from Nature and to mould ourselves according to her law and pattern—this is true wisdom.

The happy life, therefore, is a life that is in harmony with its own nature, and it can be attained in only one way. First of all, we must have a sound mind and one that is in constant possession of its sanity; second, it must be courageous and energetic, and, too, capable of the noblest fortitude, ready for every emergency, careful of the body and of all that concerns it, but without anxiety; lastly, it must be attentive to all the advantages that adorn life, but with over-much love for none—the user, but not the slave, of the gifts of Fortune. You understand, even if I do not say more, that, when once we have driven away all that excites or affrights us, there ensues unbroken tranquillity and enduring freedom; for when pleasures and fears have been banished, then, in place of all that is trivial and fragile and harmful just because of the evil it works, there comes upon us first a boundless joy that is firm and unalterable, then peace and harmony of the soul and true greatness coupled with kindliness; for all ferocity is born from weakness.

It is possible also to define this good of ours in other terms—that is, the same idea may be expressed in different language. Just as an army remains the same, though at one time it deploys with a longer line, now is massed into a narrow space and either stands with hollowed centre and wings curved forward, or extends a straightened front, and, no matter what its formation may be, will keep the selfsame spirit and the same resolve to stand in defence of the selfsame cause,—so the definition of the highest good may at one time be given in prolix and lengthy form, and at another be restrained and concise. So it will come to the same thing if I say: "The highest good is a mind that scorns the happenings of chance, and rejoices only in virtue," or say: "It is the power of the mind to be unconquerable, wise from experience, calm in action, showing the while much courtesy and consideration in intercourse with others." It may also be defined in the statement that the happy man is he who recognizes no good and evil other than a good and an evil mind—one who cherishes honour, is content with virtue, who is neither puffed up, nor crushed, by the happenings of chance, who knows of no greater good than that which he alone is able to bestow upon himself, for whom true pleasure will be the scorn of pleasures. It is possible, too, if one chooses to be discursive, to transfer the same idea to various other forms of expression without injuring or weakening its meaning. For what prevents us from saying that the happy life is to have a mind that is free, lofty, fearless and steadfast— a mind that is placed beyond the reach of fear, beyond the reach of desire, that counts virtue the only good, baseness the only evil, and all else but a worthless mass of things, which come and go without increasing or diminishing the highest good, and neither subtract any part from the happy life nor add any part to it?

A man thus grounded must, whether he wills or not, necessarily be attended by constant cheerfulness and a joy that is deep and issues from deep within, since he finds delight in his own resources, and desires no joys greater than his inner joys. Should not such joys as these be rightly matched against the paltry and trivial and fleeting sensations of the wretched body? The day a man becomes superior to pleasure, he will also be superior to pain; but you see in what wretched and baneful bondage he must linger whom pleasures and pains, those most capricious and tyrannical of masters, shall in turn enslave. Therefore we must make our escape to freedom. But the only means of procuring this is through indifference to Fortune. Then will be born the one inestimable blessing, the peace and exaltation of a mind now safely anchored, and, when all error is banished, the great and stable joy that comes from the discovery of truth, along with kindliness and cheerfulness of mind; and the source of a man's pleasure in all of these will not be that they are good, but that they spring from a good that is his own.

Seeing that I am employing some freedom in treating my subject, I may say that the happy man is one who is freed from both fear and desire because of the gift of reason; since even rocks are free from fear and sorrow, and no less are the beasts of the field, yet for all that no one could say that these things are "blissful," when they have no comprehension of bliss. Put in the same class those people whose dullness of nature and ignorance of themselves have reduced them to the level of beasts of the field and of inanimate things. There is no difference between the one and the other, since in one case they are things without reason, and in the other their reason is warped, and works their own hurt, being active in the wrong direction; for no man can be said to be happy if he has been thrust outside the pale of truth. Therefore, the life that is happy has been founded on correct and trustworthy judgement, and is unalterable. Then, truly, is the mind unclouded and freed from every ill, since it knows how to escape not only deep wounds, but even scratches, and, resolved to hold to the end whatever stands it has taken, it will defend its position even against the assaults of an angry Fortune. For so far as sensual pleasure is concerned, though it flows about us on every side, steals in through every opening, softens the mind with its blandishments, and employs one resource after another in order to seduce us in whole or in part, yet who of mortals, if he has left in him one trace of a human being, would choose to have his senses tickled night and day, and, forsaking the mind, devote his attention wholly to the body?

"But the mind also," it will be said, "has its own pleasures." Let it have them, in sooth, and let it pose as a judge of luxury and pleasures; let it gorge itself with all the things that are wont to delight the senses, then let it look back upon the past, and, recalling faded pleasures, let it intoxicate itself with former experiences and be eager now for those to come, and let it lay its plans, and, while the body lies helpless from present cramming, let it direct its thoughts to that to come—yet from all this, it seems to me, the mind will be more wretched than ever, since it is madness to choose evils instead of goods. But no man can be happy unless he is sane, and no man can be sane who searches for what will injure him in place of what is best. The happy man, therefore, is one who has right judgement; the happy man is content with his present lot, no matter what it is, and is reconciled to his circumstances; the happy man is he who allows reason to fix the value of every condition of existence.

Even those who declare that the highest good is in the belly see in what a dishonourable position they have placed it. And so they say that it is not possible to separate pleasure from virtue, and they aver that no one can live virtuously without also living pleasantly, nor pleasantly without also living virtuously. But I do not see how things so different can be cast in the same mould. What reason is there, I beg of you, why pleasure cannot be separated from virtue? Do you mean, since all goods have their origin in virtue, even the things that you love and desire must spring from its roots? But if the two were inseparable, we should not see certain things pleasant, but not honourable, and certain things truly most honourable, but painful and capable of being accomplished only through suffering. Then, too, we see that pleasure enters into even the basest life, but, on the other hand, virtue does not permit life to be evil, and there are people who are unhappy not without pleasure—nay, are so on account of pleasure itself—and this could not happen if pleasure were indissolubly joined to virtue; virtue often lacks pleasure, and never needs it. Why do you couple things that are unlike, nay, even opposites? Virtue is something lofty, exalted and regal, unconquerable, and unwearied; pleasure is something lowly, servile, weak, and perishable, whose haunt and abode are the brothel and the tavern. Virtue you will find in the temple, in the forum, in the senate-house—you will find her standing in front of the city walls, dusty and stained, and with calloused hands; pleasure you will more often find lurking out of sight, and in search of darkness, around the public baths and the sweating rooms and the places that fear the police—soft, enervated, reeking with wine and perfume, and pallid, or else painted and made up with cosmetics like a corpse. The highest good is immortal, it knows no ending, it permits neither surfeit nor regret; for the right-thinking mind never alters, it neither is filled with self-loathing nor suffers any change in its life, that is ever the best. But pleasure is extinguished just when it is most enjoyed; it has but small space, and thus quickly fills it—it grows weary and is soon spent after its first assault. Nor is anything certain whose nature consists in movement. So it is not even possible that there should be any substance in that which comes and goes most swiftly and will perish in the very exercise of its power; for it struggles to reach a point at which it may cease, and it looks to the end while it is beginning.

What, further, is to be said of the fact that pleasure belongs alike to the good and the evil, and that the base delight no less in their disgrace than do the honourable in fair repute? And therefore the ancients have enjoined us to follow, not the most pleasant, but the best life, in order that pleasure should be, not the leader, but the companion of a right and proper desire. For we must use Nature as our guide; she it is that Reason heeds, it is of her that it takes counsel. Therefore to live happily is the same thing as to live according to Nature. What this is, I shall proceed to make clear. If we shall guard the endowments of the body and the needs of Nature with care and fearlessness, in the thought that they have been given but for a day and are fleeting, if we shall not be their slaves, nor allow these alien things to become our masters, if we shall count that the gratifications of the body, unessential as they are, have a place like to that of the auxiliaries and light-armed troops in camp—if we let them serve, not command—thus and thus only will these things be profitable to the mind. Let a man not be corrupted by external things, let him be unconquerable and admire only himself, courageous in spirit and ready for any fate, let him be the moulder of his own life; let not his confidence be without knowledge, nor his knowledge without firmness; let his decisions once made abide, and let not his decrees be altered by any erasure. It will be understood, even without my adding it, that such a man will be poised and well ordered, and will show majesty mingled with courtesy in all his actions. Let reason search into external things at the instigation of the senses, and, while it derives from them its first knowledge—for it has no other base from which it may operate, or begin its assault upon truth—yet let it fall back upon itself. For God also, the all-embracing world and the ruler of the universe, reaches forth into outward things, yet, withdrawing from all sides, returns into himself. And our mind should do the same; when, having followed the senses that serve it, it has through them reached to things without, let it be the master both of them and of itself. In this way will be born an energy that is united, a power that is at harmony with itself, and that dependable reason which is not divided against itself, nor uncertain either in its opinions, or its perceptions, or in its convictions; and this reason, when it has regulated itself, and established harmony between all its parts, and, so to speak, is in tune, has attained the highest good. For no crookedness, no slipperiness is left to it, nothing that will cause it to stumble or fall. It will do everything under its own authority and nothing unexpected will befall it, but whatever it does will turn out a good, and that, too, easily and readily and without subterfuge on the part of the doer; for reluctance and hesitation are an indication of conflict and instability. Wherefore you may boldly declare that the highest good is harmony of the soul; for where concord and unity are, there must the virtues be. Discord accompanies the vices.

"But even you," it is retorted, "cultivate virtue for no other reason than because you hope for some pleasure from it." But, in the first place, even though virtue is sure to bestow pleasure, it is not for this reason that virtue is sought; for it is not this, but something more than this that she bestows, nor does she labour for this, but her labour, while directed toward something else, achieves this also. As in a ploughed field, which has been broken up for corn, some flowers will spring up here and there, yet it was not for these poor little plants, although they may please the eye, that so much toil was expended—the sower had a different purpose, these were superadded—just so pleasure is neither the cause nor the reward of virtue, but its by-product, and we do not accept virtue because she delights us, but if we accept her, she also delights us. The highest good lies in the very choice of it, and the very attitude of a mind made perfect, and when the mind has completed its course and fortified itself within its own bounds, the highest good has now been perfected, and nothing further is desired; for there can no more be anything outside of the whole than there can be some point beyond the end. Therefore you blunder when you ask what it is that makes me seek virtue; you are looking for something beyond the supreme. Do you ask what it is that I seek in virtue? Only herself. For she offers nothing better—she herself is her own reward. Or does this seem to you too small a thing? When I say to you, "The highest good is the inflexibility of an unyielding mind, its foresight, its sublimity, its soundness, its freedom, its harmony, its beauty," do you require of me something still greater to which these blessings may be ascribed? Why do you mention to me pleasure? It is the good of man that I am searching for, not that of his belly—the belly of cattle and wild beasts is more roomy!

"You are misrepresenting what I say," you retort; "for I admit that no man can live pleasantly without at the same time living virtuously as well, and this is patently impossible for dumb beasts and for those who measure their good by mere food. Distinctly, I say, and openly I testify that the life that I denominate pleasant is impossible without the addition of virtue." Yet who does not know that those who are most apt to be filled with your sort of pleasure are all the greatest fools, and that wickedness abounds in enjoyments, and that the mind itself supplies many kinds of pleasure that are vicious? Foremost are haughtiness, a too high opinion of one's self and a puffed-up superiority to others, a blind and unthinking devotion to one's own interests, dissolute luxury, extravagant joy springing from very small and childish causes, and, besides a biting tongue and the arrogance that takes pleasure in insults, sloth, and the degeneracy of a sluggish mind that falls asleep over itself. All these things Virtue tosses aside, and she plucks the ear,[2] and appraises pleasures before she permits them, and those that she approves she sets no great store by, or even just permits them, and it is not her use of them, but her temperance that gives her joy. Since, however, temperance reduces our pleasures, injury results to your highest good. You embrace pleasure, I enchain her; you enjoy pleasure, I use it; you think it the highest good, I do not think it even a good; you do everything for the sake of pleasure, I, nothing.

When I say that "I" do nothing for the sake of pleasure, I am speaking of the ideal wise man, to whom alone you are willing to concede pleasure. But I do not call him a wise man who is dominated by anything, still less by pleasure. And yet if he is engrossed by this, how will he withstand toil and danger and want and all the threatening ills that clamour about the life of man? How will he endure the sight of death, how grief, how the crashes of the universe and all the fierce foes that face him, if he has been subdued by so soft an adversary? You say: "He will do whatever pleasure advises." But come, do you not see how many things it will be able to advise? "It will not be able to advise anything base," you say, "because it is linked with virtue." But once more, do you not see what sort of thing that highest good must be if it needs a guardian in order to become a good? And how shall Virtue guide Pleasure if she follows her, since it is the part of one who obeys to follow, of one who commands to guide? Do you station in the rear the one that commands? Truly a fine office that you assign to Virtue—to be the foretaster[3] of your pleasures! We shall see later whether to those who have treated virtue so contemptuously she still remains virtue; for she cannot keep her name if she yields her place. Meanwhile—for this is the point here—I shall show that there are many who are besieged by pleasures, upon whom Fortune has showered all her gifts, and yet, as you must needs admit, are wicked men. Look at Nomentanus and Apicius,[4] digesting, as they say, the blessings of land and sea, and reviewing the creations of every nation arrayed upon their board! See them, too, upon a heap of roses, gloating over their rich cookery, while their ears are delighted by the sound of music, their eyes by spectacles, their palates by savours; soft and soothing stuffs caress with their warmth the length of their bodies, and, that the nostrils may not meanwhile be idle, the room itself, where sacrifice is being made to Luxury, reeks with varied perfumes. You will recognize that these are living in the midst of pleasures, and yet it will not be well with them, because what they delight in is not a good.

"It will be ill with them," you say, "because many things will intrude that perturb the soul, and opinions, conflicting with one another, will disquiet the mind." That this is so I grant; but none the less these very men, foolish as they are and inconsistent and subject to the pangs of remorse, will have experience of very great pleasures, so that you must admit that, while in that state they lack all pain, they no less lack a sound mind, and, as is the case with very many others, that they make merry in madness and laugh while they rave. But, on the other hand, the pleasures of the wise man are calm, moderate, almost listless and subdued, and scarcely noticeable inasmuch as they come unsummoned, and, although they approach of their own accord, are not held in high esteem and are received without joy on the part of those who experience them; for they only let them mingle now and then with life as we do amusements and jests with serious affairs.

Let them cease, therefore, to join irreconcilable things and to link pleasure with virtue—a vicious procedure which flatters the worst class of men. The man who has plunged into pleasures, in the midst of his constant belching and drunkenness, because he knows that he is living with pleasure, believes that he is living with virtue as well; for he hears first that pleasure cannot be separated from virtue, then dubs his vices wisdom, and parades what ought to be concealed. And so it is not Epicurus[5] who has driven them to debauchery, but they, having surrendered themselves to vice, hide their debauchery in the lap of philosophy and flock to the place where they may hear the praise of pleasure, and they do not consider how sober and abstemious[6] the "pleasure" of Epicurus really is—for so, in all truth, I think it— but they fly to a mere name seeking some justification and screen for their lusts. And thus they lose the sole good that remained to them in their wickedness—shame for wrongdoing. For they now praise the things that used to make them blush, and they glory in vice; and therefore they cannot even recover their youth,[7] when once an honourable name has given warrant to their shameful laxity. The reason why your praise of pleasure is pernicious is that what is honourable in your teaching lies hid within, what corrupts is plainly visible.

Personally I hold the opinion—I shall express it though the members of our school may protest—that the teachings of Epicurus are upright and holy and, if you consider them closely, austere; for his famous doctrine of pleasure is reduced to small and narrow proportions, and the rule that we Stoics lay down for virtue, this same rule he lays down for pleasure—he bids that it obey Nature. But it takes a very little luxury to satisfy Nature! What then is the case? Whoever applies the term "happiness" to slothful idleness and the alternate indulgence in gluttony and lust, looks for a good sponsor for his evil course, and when, led on by an attractive name, he has found this one,[8] the pleasure he pursues is not the form that he is taught, but the form that he has brought, and when he begins to think that his vices accord with the teacher's maxims, he indulges in them no longer timidly, and riots in them, not now covertly, but from this time on in broad daylight. And so I shall not say, as do most of our sect, that the school of Epicurus is an academy of vice, but this is what I say—it has a bad name, is of ill repute, and yet undeservedly. How can anyone know this who has not been admitted to the inner shrine? Its mere outside gives ground for scandal and incites to evil hopes. The case is like that of a strong man dressed up in a woman's garb; you maintain your chastity, your virility is unimpaired, your body is free from base submission—but in your hand is a tambourine![9] Therefore you should choose some honourable superscription and a motto that in itself appeals to the mind; the one that stands has attracted only the vices.

Whosoever has gone over to the side of virtue, has given proof of a noble nature; he who follows pleasure is seen to be weakly, broken, losing his manhood, and on the sure path to baseness unless someone shall establish for him some distinction between pleasures, so that he may know which of them lie within the bounds of natural desire, which sweep headlong onward and are unbounded and are the more insatiable the more they are satisfied. Come then! let virtue lead the way, and every step will be safe. Then, too, it is the excess of pleasure that harms; but in the case of virtue there need be no fear of any excess, for in virtue itself resides moderation. That cannot be a good that suffers from its own magnitude. Besides, to creatures endowed with a rational nature what better guide can be offered than reason? Even if that combination[10] pleases you, if you are pleased to proceed toward the happy life in such company, let virtue lead the way, let pleasure attend her— let it hover about the body like its shadow. To hand over virtue, the loftiest of mistresses, to be the handmaid of pleasure is the part of a man who has nothing great in his soul.

Let virtue go first, let her bear the standard. We shall none the less have pleasure, but we shall be the master and control her; at times we shall yield to her entreaty, never to her constraint. But those who surrender the leadership to pleasure, lack both; for they lose virtue, and yet do not possess pleasure, but are possessed by it, and they are either tortured by the lack of it or strangled by its excess—wretched if it deserts them, more wretched if it overwhelms them—they are like sailors who have been caught in the waters around the Syrtes,[11] and now are left on the dry shore, and again are tossed by the seething waves. But this results from a complete lack of self-control and blind love for an object; for, if one seeks evils instead of goods, success becomes dangerous. As the hunt for wild beasts is fraught with hardship and danger, and even those that are captured are an anxious possession—for many a time they rend their masters—so it is as regards great pleasures; for they turn out to be a great misfortune, and captured pleasures become now the captors. And the more and the greater the pleasures are, the more inferior will that man be whom the crowd calls happy, and the more masters will he have to serve. I wish to dwell still further upon this comparison. Just as the man who tracks wild animals to their lairs, and counts it a great delight

> With noose the savage beasts to snare,

and

> Around the spreading woods to fling a line of hounds,[12]

in order that he may follow upon their tracks, leaves things that are more worth while and forsakes many duties, so he who pursues pleasures makes everything else secondary, and first of all gives up liberty, and he pays this price at the command of his belly; nor does he buy pleasures for himself, but he sells himself to pleasures.

"Nevertheless," someone asks, "what is there to prevent the blending of virtue and pleasure into one, and constituting the highest good in such a way that the honourable and the agreeable may be the same thing?" The answer is that the honourable can have no part that is not honourable, nor will the highest good preserve its integrity if it sees in itself something that is different from its better part. Even the joy that springs from virtue, although it is a good, is not nevertheless a part of the absolute good, any more than are cheerfulness and tranquillity, although they spring from the noblest origins; for goods they are, yet they only attend on the highest good but do not consummate it. But whoever forms an alliance between virtue and pleasure— and that too, not an equal one—by the frailty of one good dulls whatever power the other may have, and sends beneath the yoke that liberty[13] which remains unconquered only so long as it finds nothing more precious than itself. For it begins to need the help of Fortune, and this is the depth of servitude; there follows a life of anxiety, suspicion, and alarm, a dread of mishap and worry over the changes time brings. You do not give to virtue a foundation solid and immovable, but bid her stand on unstable ground; yet what is so unstable as trust in the hazards of chance and the vicissitudes of the body and the things that affect the body? How is such a man able to obey God and to receive in cheerful spirit whatever happens, and, interpreting his mishaps indulgently, never to complain of Fate, if he is agitated by the petty prickings of pleasure and pain? But he is not even a good guardian or avenger of his country, nor a defender of his friends, if he has a leaning toward pleasures. Therefore let the highest good mount to a place from which no force can drag it down, where neither pain nor hope nor fear finds access, nor does any other thing that can lower the authority of the highest good; but Virtue alone is able to mount to that height. We must follow her footsteps to find that ascent easy; bravely will she stand, and she will endure whatever happens, not only patiently, but even gladly; she will know that every hardship that time brings comes by a law of Nature, and like a good soldier she will submit to wounds, she will count her scars, and, pierced by darts, as she dies she will love him for whose sake she falls—her commander; she will keep in mind that old injunction, "Follow God!" But whoever complains and weeps and moans is compelled by force to obey commands, and, even though he is unwilling, is rushed none the less to the bidden tasks. But what madness to prefer to be dragged rather than to follow! As much so, in all faith, as it is great folly and ignorance of one's lot to grieve because of some lack or some rather bitter happening, and in like manner to be surprised or indignant at those ills that befall the good no less than the bad—I mean sickness and death and infirmities and all the other unexpected ills that invade human life. All that the very constitution of the universe obliges us to suffer, must be borne with high courage. This is the sacred obligation by which we are bound—to submit to the human lot, and not to be disquieted by those things which we have no power to avoid. We have been born under a monarchy; to obey God is freedom.

Therefore true happiness is founded upon virtue. And what is the counsel this virtue will give to you? That you should not consider anything either a good or an evil that will not be the result of either virtue or vice; then, that you should stand unmoved both in the face of evil and by the enjoyment of good, to the end that—as far as is allowed—you may body forth God. And what does virtue promise you for this enterprise? Mighty privileges and equal to the divine. You shall be bound by no constraint, nothing shall you lack, you shall be free, safe, unhurt; nothing shall you essay in vain, from nothing be debarred; all things shall happen according to your desire, nothing adverse shall befall you, nothing contrary to your expectations and wish. "What! does virtue alone suffice for living happily?" Perfect and divine as it is, why should it not suffice—nay, suffice to overflowing? For if a man has been placed beyond the reach of any desire, what can he possibly lack? If a man has gathered into himself all that is his, what need does he have of any outside thing? But the man who is still on the road to virtue, who, even though he has proceeded far, is still struggling in the toils of human affairs, does have need of some indulgence from Fortune until he has loosed that knot and every mortal bond. Where then lies the difference? In that some are closely bound, others fettered—even hand and foot. He who has advanced toward the higher realm and has lifted himself to higher levels drags a loosened chain; he is not yet free, but still is as good as free. . . .

"Philosophers do not practise what they preach," you say. Yet they do practise much that they preach, much that their virtuous minds conceive. For indeed if their actions always matched their words, who would be more happy than they? Meanwhile you have no reason to despise noble words and hearts that are filled with noble thoughts. The pursuit of salutary studies is praiseworthy, even if they have no practical result. What wonder that those who essay the steep path do not mount to the summit? But if you are a man, look up to those who are attempting great things, even though they fall. The man that measures his effort, not by his own strength, but by the strength of his nature, that aims at high things, and conceives in his heart greater undertakings than could possibly be accomplished even by those endowed with gigantic courage, shows the mark of nobility. The man who has set before himself such ideals as these: "As for me, I shall look upon death or a comedy with the same expression of countenance. As for me, I shall submit to all hardships, no matter how great they be, staying my body by the spirit. As for me, I shall despise riches alike when I have them and when I have them not, being neither cast down if they shall lie elsewhere, nor puffed up if they shall glitter around me. As for me, I shall pay no heed to Fortune, either when she comes or when she goes. As for me, I shall view all lands as my own, my own as belonging to all others. As for me, I shall always live as if I were aware that I had been born for service to others, and on this account I shall render my thanks to Nature; for how could she better have served my interest? She has given me, the individual, to all men and all men to me, the individual. Whatever I may possess, I shall neither hoard as a miser, nor as a spendthrift squander. Nothing shall seem to me so truly my possessions as the gifts I have wisely bestowed. I shall not estimate my benefactions by their number, nor by their size, nor by anything except my estimation of the recipient; never shall what a worthy man receives seem great in my eyes. Nothing shall I ever do for the sake of opinion, everything for the sake of my conscience. Whatever I shall do when I alone am witness I shall count as done beneath the gaze of the Roman people. In eating and drinking my aim shall be to quench the desires of Nature, not to fill and empty my belly. I shall be agreeable to my friends, to my enemies mild and indulgent. I shall give pardon before it is asked, and hasten to grant all honourable requests. I shall know that the whole world is my country, that its rulers are the gods, and that they abide above me and around me, the censors of my words and deeds. And whenever Nature demands back my breath, or my reason releases[14] it, I shall depart, bearing witness that I have loved a good conscience and all good endeavour, that I have been guilty of nothing that impaired the liberty of any man, least of all my own"—the man who shall resolve, shall wish, and shall essay to do these things will be following the path toward the gods—ah! such a man, even if he shall not reach them,

> Yet fails in a high emprise.[15] . . .

The wise man does not deem himself undeserving of any of the gifts of Fortune. He does not love riches, but he would rather have them; he does not admit them to his heart, but to his house, and he does not reject the riches he has, but he keeps them and wishes them to supply ampler material for exercising his virtue.

Who, however, can doubt that the wise man finds in riches, rather than in poverty, this ampler material for displaying his powers, since in poverty there is room for only one kind of virtue—not to be bowed down and crushed by it—while in riches moderation and liberality and diligence and orderliness and grandeur all have a wide field? The wise man will not despise himself even if he has the stature of a dwarf, but nevertheless he will wish to be tall. And if he is feeble in body, or deprived of one eye, he will be strong,[16] but nevertheless he will prefer to have strength of body, and this too, though he knows that there is something else in him that is stronger than body. If his health is bad he will endure it, but he will wish for good health. For certain things, even if they are trifles in comparison with the whole, and can be withdrawn without destroying the essential good, nevertheless contribute something to the perpetual joy that springs from virtue. As a favourable wind, sweeping him on, gladdens the sailor, as a bright day and a sunny spot in the midst of winter and cold give cheer, just so riches have their influence upon the wise man and bring him joy. And besides, who among wise men—I mean those of our school, who count virtue the sole good—denies that even those things which we call "indifferent"[17] do have some inherent value, and that some are more desirable than others? To some of them we accord little honour, to others much. Do not, therefore, make a mistake—riches are among the more desirable things. "Why then," you say, "do you make game of me, since they occupy the same place in your eyes that they do in mine?" Do you want to know what a different place they occupy? In my case, if riches slip away, they will take from me nothing but themselves, while if they leave you, you will be dumbfounded, and you will feel that you have been robbed of your real self; in my eyes riches have a certain place, in yours they have the highest; in fine, I own my riches, yours own you.

NOTES

1. *praetors*: elected Roman magistrates with judicial duties [D.C.A.]
2. *"plucks the ear"*: a Latin expression meaning "reminds someone of something" [D.C.A.]
3. *foretaster*: a slave who tasted food to test it for poison before serving it to the master [D.C.A.]
4. *Nomentanus*: a well-known Roman spendthrift
   Apicius: a Roman gourmet who wrote a book on cooking and later poisoned himself out of fear of starving [D.C.A.]
5. *Epicurus*: a Greek philosopher (341–270 B.C.E.) who held that pleasure is the ultimate good. He taught that we should choose only those pleasures that are not outweighed by accompanying or subsequent pains and recommended the traditional virtues as means of attaining pleasure. His ethical ideal was *ataraxia*, which means peace of mind or, more literally, "freedom from disturbance." [D.C.A.]
6. Although the word *epicure* has come to mean "gourmet," Epicurus himself said he was content to live on bread and water. [D.C.A.]
7. i.e., their youthful point of view [J.W.B.]
8. i.e., has become an Epicurean [J.W.B.]

9. *tambourine*: here a symbol of something enervated and effeminate. The tambourine was associated with the orgiastic worship of the goddess Cybele, whose priests were emasculated. [D.C.A., after J.W.B.]
10. i.e., a life combining virtue and pleasure [J.W.B.]
11. *Syrtes*: sandbanks off the northern coast of Africa, proverbially perilous to the sailor [J.W.B.]
12. Virgil *Georgics* 1.139–140. Virgil (70–19 B.C.E.) was a Roman poet. [D.C.A.]
13. i.e., which belongs to virtue; virtue frees, pleasure enslaves [J.W.B.]
14. Suicide was recognized by the Stoics as a desirable and heroic release from unbearable misfortune. [J.W.B.]
15. Ovid *Metamorphoses* 2.328. Ovid (43 B.C.E.–about 17 C.E.) was a Roman poet. *emprise*: a daring enterprise [D.C.A.]
16. The author contrasts physical and mental well-being; the latter may exist without the former, but it is desirable to have both. [J.W.B.]
17. In Stoic moral philosophy, something that makes no difference to a person's moral worth is called "indifferent"—a category that encompasses everything other than virtue and vice. But the Stoics also held that some "indifferent" things (e.g., riches) are preferable to others (e.g., poverty). [D.C.A.]

QUESTIONS FOR REFLECTION AND DISCUSSION

1. Is virtue its own reward?
2. Is virtue all one needs to be happy?
3. Is pleasure necessary for happiness?
4. Is only a virtuous person free?
5. Do "indifferent" things, such as riches or health, make any difference to a person's moral worth?

SUGGESTIONS FOR FURTHER READING

I. Primary Sources

The Stoic Philosophy of Seneca: Essays and Letters of Seneca, trans. Moses Hadas. 1958; reprint ed., New York: Norton, 1968, 261 pp.

Contains the essays *On Providence, On the Shortness of Life, On Tranquillity of Mind, Consolation to Helvia,* and *On Clemency* and eighteen of the letters to Lucilius.

Letters From a Stoic: Epistulae Morales ad Lucilium, trans. Robin Campbell. Harmondsworth, England: Penguin, 1969, 254 pp.

Forty-one letters on various topics, selected on the basis of how well they "set out a philosophy and contribute to a picture of a man and his times."

On Anger, Books 1 and 2, in *Moral Essays 1*, ed. and trans. John W. Basore. Cambridge, Mass., Harvard University Press, Loeb Classical Library, 1928, pp. 107–251.

Seneca examines the nature and origin of anger, explains why anger is not in accordance with nature, and gives advice on how to master this harmful emotion. (The selection is only half as long as the page numbers indicate; the Latin text and English translation are on facing pages.)

II. Secondary Sources

Currie, H. MacL. "Seneca As Philosopher," in *Neronians and Flavians: Silver Latin 1*, ed. D. R. Dudley. London: Routledge, 1972, pp. 24–61.

A clear exposition of Seneca's philosophy that focuses on his interest in the practical question of how one should live one's life. Includes a brief general account of Stoicism.

Long, A. A. *Hellenistic Philosophy: Stoics, Epicureans, Sceptics*, 2d ed. Berkeley and Los Angeles: University of California Press, 1986, 274 pp.

The section entitled "Stoics Ethics" (pp. 179–209) gives a general exposition of this topic. There are specific references to Seneca.

Motto, Anna Lydia. *Seneca*. New York: Twayne, Twayne's World Authors Ser., 1973, 173 pp.

A study of Seneca's life, philosophy, and dramatic works. See chap. 3, "The Keystones of Senecan Philosophy," pp. 49–81.

Sandbach, F. H. *The Stoics*. New York: Norton, Ancient Culture and Society Ser., 1975, 190 pp.

The section on Seneca, pp. 149–162, summarizes several of Seneca's philosophical works, including *On Anger, On Clemency*, and *On the Happy Life*.

Timothy, H. B. *The Tenets of Stoicism, Assembled and Systematized, from the Works of L. Annaeus Seneca*. Amsterdam: Hakkert, 1973, 118 pp.

Timothy presents a general exposition of Stoic philosophy (especially ethics) through the writings of Seneca, arguing that Seneca is a much more systematic thinker than is commonly assumed. See chap. 2, "Living and Living Well," pp. 19–40.

5

Augustine

Augustine, son of a pagan father and a Christian mother, was born in 354 in the town of Tagaste in northern Africa (now Souk-Ahras, Algeria). As a youth he received instruction in Christianity but was not baptized. When he was seventeen he began studying rhetoric in Carthage, financially supported by a friend of the family. There his interest in philosophy was aroused when he read the *Hortensius*, a dialogue (now lost) by the Roman orator and author Cicero (106–43 B.C.E.) that praises the pursuit of wisdom.

As a young man Augustine showed little interest in Christianity; its doctrines seemed to him either superficial or unclear, especially with regard to the origin of evil in the world and the compatibility of evil with an all-good and all-powerful God. The Manichaean religion, which had been founded by the Babylonian Mani around the year 240 and was spreading to northern Africa, offered an explanation that Augustine found, for a time, intellectually satisfying: There are two equally powerful forces at work in the universe, Light (goodness) and Darkness (evil). Augustine became a Manichaean in 373 and remained one for ten years. But he began to question some of its doctrines, especially its claims regarding certain scientific facts. When the Manichaean leader Faustus proved unable to answer his questions, Augustine left the religion.

Meanwhile, he had begun teaching rhetoric, first at Tagaste and then at Carthage. In 383 (the same year he abandoned Manichaeism), he went to teach in Rome, and the following year he moved to Milan. At this time Augustine became attracted to skepticism, the view that it is impossible to attain truth. Augustine then began reading works of the Roman (Egyptian-born) philosopher Plotinus (205–270), who saw himself as carrying forward the theories of Plato. (Augustine refers to Plotinus's philosophy as "Platonism," but since it differs importantly from Plato's own theories, the philosophy of Plotinus and his successors is now called, more accurately, Neoplatonism.)

Augustine was deeply influenced by Neoplatonism. Its doctrines that God is a nonmaterial being and that evil is a lack of being rather than a positive entity helped prepare Augustine intellectually for his return to Christianity. Another major influence was Ambrose (339–397), bishop of Milan. Augustine attended Ambrose's sermons to study their rhetorical style, but when he began paying attention to their content, he found that the sermons made Christian doctrine seem reasonable. After a dramatic moral conversion (recounted in the *Confessions*, his autobiography), he was baptized by Ambrose in 387.

After his conversion, Augustine returned to Tagaste, where he and some friends set up a sort of monastery. In 391 he was ordained a priest at the seaport town of Hippo (now Annaba, Algeria). Four years later he became bishop of Hippo, a position he held for thirty-five years, until his death in 430.

Augustine wrote over a hundred works in addition to his numerous sermons and letters. His earlier writings are more philosophical in character than are his later, more theological, works, which rely more heavily on the authority of Scripture. Many of the later works are refutations of contemporary heresies, especially Donatism and Pelagianism. In addition to the *Confessions*, written between 397 and 401, Augustine's best-known works are *On The Trinity*, a treatise written between 399 and 419, and *The City of God*, his Christian interpretation of history, written between 413 and 426.

Our selection is from one of Augustine's early works, his dialogue *The Free Choice of the Will*, which was begun in 388 and finished in 395. The work is cast as a conversation between Augustine and his friend Evodius. The topic is stated by Evodius in the opening line: "Tell me, please, whether God is not the cause of evil."

Augustine begins his response to Evodius's question by distinguishing the evil that people suffer from the evil that they commit. God causes the former as just punishment for people's sins, according to Augustine, but He does not cause the latter: When people commit evil, they do so of their own free will (hence the title of the dialogue).

What does it mean to choose evil? Augustine argues that moral evil consists in pursuing what is temporal and changeable rather than what is eternal and unchangeable. Our will is naturally oriented toward the eternal realm, and therefore a will that chooses temporal things lacks its own perfection, its own full being. Augustine thus uses the Neoplatonic doctrine that evil is a 'negation' (a 'lack of being') to reject the Manichaean position that evil is something positive (a being).

Since it is our free will that enables us to sin, is free will itself something evil? Augustine argues that God gave us free will to enable us to choose rightly (and thereby attain happiness); the fact that we can abuse free will by choosing wrongly (thereby becoming unhappy) does not make free will itself evil. In the course of defending the goodness of free will, Augustine presents an argument for the existence of God, the source of all good things. The argument for God involves an analysis of sensation, a capacity we share with animals, and of understanding, which sets us above the animals.

THE FREE CHOICE OF THE WILL

BOOK I

Chapter 1

Evodius. Tell me, please, whether God is not the cause of evil.

Augustine. I will tell you if you make it clear what kind of evil you are inquiring about, for we usually speak of evil in two ways: first, when we say that someone has done evil; second, when someone has suffered something evil.

Ev. I am eager to know about both kinds.

Aug. But if you know or take it on faith that God is good (and it would be irreligious to think differently), then He does no evil. Again, if we acknowledge that God is just (and to deny this would be sacrilegious), then, as He bestows rewards upon the good, so does He mete out punishments to the wicked. To those who suffer them, such punishments are of course evil. Accordingly, if no one suffers penalties unjustly (and this we must believe since we believe that the universe is ruled by Divine Providence), God is not at all the Cause of the first kind of evil, though He is of the second.

Ev. Is there not, therefore, some other cause of that evil which we have found cannot be God?

Aug. There certainly is, for, without a cause, it could not come to exist. But if you ask me who that cause is, no answer is possible, for it is no one person but rather each evil man that is the author of his own misdeeds. If you have any doubt of this, take note of our earlier remark that evil deeds are punished by God's justice. For unless they were committed voluntarily, their punishment would not be just.

Ev. I fail to see how anyone can sin who has not learned to do so. If this

119

is true, I want to know who that someone is from whom we have learned to sin.

Aug. Do you look upon learning as something good?

Ev. Who would dare say that learning is something evil?

Aug. What if it is neither good nor evil?

Ev. I think it is good.

Aug. It certainly is, since, in fact, knowledge is imparted or awakened in us by learning, and it is only in this way that something is learned. Or do you have a different idea?

Ev. I think that only good things come to us by learning.

Aug. See to it then that you do not say that evil is learned, for the word "learning" derives solely from the verb "to learn."

Ev. If evil things are not learned, then how is it that man can do them?

Aug. Possibly, evil comes about from the fact that man turns his back upon learning and estranges himself from it. But whether this, or something else, is the reason, this much is certainly clear, that since learning is something good, and "learning" comes from "to learn," it is altogether impossible to learn things evil. For, if evil is learned, it is included in learning and thus, learning will not be something good. But learning is, according to your own admission, something good. Consequently, evil is not something learned, and it is pointless for you to ask who it is that teaches us wrongdoing. But if evil is something learned, we learn how to avoid it, not how to do it. Hence, to do evil is nothing else than to stray from the path of learning.

Ev. I really think there are two kinds of learning: one, teaching us to do good; the other, to do evil. But when you asked whether learning was something good, I replied that it was, for the love of this very good had taken such hold on my mind that I was thinking of that kind of learning which concerns good conduct. But now I realize that there is another kind of learning which I declare, beyond any shadow of doubt, to be something evil, and I am looking for its author.

Aug. Do you at least think that understanding is something that can only be good?

Ev. So good, in fact, that I fail to see how anything else in man can be better, and I could not possibly say that any kind of understanding is evil.

Aug. Suppose the person being taught does not understand. Can you think of him as having learned?

Ev. Not at all.

Aug. If, then, every kind of understanding is good and no one learns who does not understand, then whoever is learning is doing good. For everyone who learns, understands, and everyone who understands is doing good. Consequently, whoever is looking for the author through whom we learn something is really looking for the author of our good actions. Put an end, therefore, to your wish to find an evil teacher of some kind or other. For if he is evil, he is not a teacher; if he is a teacher, he is not evil.

Chapter 2

Ev. Now that you force me to admit that we do not learn how to do evil, go on and tell me the reason why we do evil.

Aug. You raise a question which sorely perplexed me while yet a young man, and one which in my weariness drove me into the company of heretics[1] and resulted in my fall. I was so injured by this fall, so weighed down by the vast accumulation of nonsensical fables that, had not the love of finding the truth obtained divine aid for me, I would have been unable to rise from this fall and to breathe again in the former atmosphere of free inquiry. And as I took great pains to extricate myself from this perplexity, so I will follow the same procedure with you that led to my liberation. For God will be at hand and will enable us to understand what we have believed. We know well that we are following the course enjoined by the Prophet who says: "Unless you believe, you shall not understand."[2] We believe that all things in existence are from the one God, though He is not the author of sin. But this problem confronts the mind: if sins come from souls created by God, while these souls in turn come from God, how is it that sins are not at once chargeable to God?

Ev. You have just stated very clearly the problem which plagued my mind so much and which forcibly drew me into this inquiry.

Aug. Take courage, and go on believing what you believe, for there is no better belief even though the reason for it is hidden from me. To hold God in the highest esteem is most truly the beginning of all piety. Anyone who does not believe that God is Almighty or absolutely unchangeable, or that He is the Creator of all things good, though surpassing them in excellence, or that He is also a most just Ruler of all that He has created, or that He had need of no other nature in creating, as if He were not sufficient unto Himself—such a one does not hold God in the highest esteem.

It follows, therefore, that God created all things from nothing. But Him who is equal to the Father, and whom we call the Only Son of God, He did not create but begot Him from His own substance. When we try to represent Him more clearly, we call Him the Power and Wisdom of God through whom He made all that He created from nothing.

Having set down these points, let us strive with the help of God to understand the problem you raise in the following manner.

Chapter 3

Since your question has to do with the cause of our doing evil, we must first have a discussion on the nature of evil. State your opinion on this matter. If you cannot express it fully, all at once and in a few words, let me at least know what you think by mentioning, in particular, some evil deeds themselves.

Ev. Adultery, murder, and sacrilege, to say nothing of others which time and my memory do not allow me to mention. Can anyone think that these are not evil?

Aug. Tell me first, then, why you think it is wrong to commit adultery. Is it because the law forbids it?

Ev. It is not wrong just because the law forbids it; rather, the law forbids it because it is wrong.

Aug. What if someone with an exaggerated idea of the delights of adultery should press us further and ask us why we judge it wrong and reprehensible? Do you think that, for men who are eager not only to believe but also to understand, we must fall back on the authority of the law? I am one with you in this belief, and I do firmly believe and I call upon all peoples and nations to believe that adultery is wrong. But right now we are trying to acquire a rational understanding and a firm grasp of something that we have accepted on faith. Think it over, then, as best you can, and tell me the reason why you think adultery is wrong.

Ev. I know it is wrong for the very reason that I myself would be unwilling to tolerate it in my own wife. But anyone who does to another what he is unwilling to have done to himself is certainly doing wrong.

Aug. What if a man's lust leads him to offer his wife to another to have her willingly violated by him, and he, in turn, desires the same liberty with the other's wife? Do you think he is doing nothing wrong?

Ev. On the contrary. He is doing great wrong.

Aug. But, according to that rule of yours, such a man commits no sin, for he is doing nothing that he is unwilling to have done to him. Accordingly, you must find another reason to show why adultery is wrong.

Ev. I think it is wrong for the reason that I have often seen men condemned for such a crime.

Aug. What of the fact that men have often been condemned for good deeds? Without sending you to other books, examine that history which owes its excellence to divine authority. You will find what a bad opinion we should have of the Apostles and all the martyrs if we agree that being condemned is a sure indication of wrongdoing, for they were all judged as deserving of condemnation for having confessed their faith. Consequently, if whatever is condemned is evil, then it was evil at that time to believe in Christ and to confess the faith itself. On the other hand, if not everything that is condemned is evil, you must look for another reason for teaching that adultery is wrong.

Ev. I cannot find any answer to give you.

Aug. Perhaps it is passion [*libido*] that is evil in adultery. But as long as you look for the evil in the outward act itself, which can be seen, you will run into difficulties. To give you an idea how the evil of adultery is passion, let us suppose that there is no opportunity for intercourse with another man's wife, though it is somehow evident that one has the desire and would do the act if he could. In this case, he is no less guilty than if he were caught in the act.

Ev. Nothing could be clearer. I see now that there is no need for a long discussion to convince me of this in the case of murder and sacrilege, and, in fact, for all kinds of sin. It is now clear that passion alone is the ruling factor in every kind of wrongdoing.

Chapter 4

Aug. Do you know too that another name for passion is desire [*cupiditas*]?

Ev. I do.

Aug. Do you think there is any difference between this and fear?

Ev. Indeed. I think there is a great difference between them.

Aug. I believe you think so for the reason that desire seeks its object, while fear avoids it.

Ev. It is just as you say.

Aug. But suppose someone kills a man, not out of desire to gain possession of something, but because he fears that some evil may befall him—will he not be a murderer?

Ev. He will, indeed. Yet his act is not thereby free of the ruling passion of desire, because whoever kills a man out of fear, certainly desires to live free of fear.

Aug. Do you think it is a small good to live free of fear?

Ev. It is a great good, but it cannot possibly come to the murderer through his crime.

Aug. I am not asking you what can come to him but what it is that he himself desires. Whoever desires a life free of fear certainly desires a good and, consequently, the desire is not blameworthy; otherwise we shall be placing blame upon all who love what is good. Hence we are forced to admit that there can be murder where we are unable to discover evil desire as the dominant factor, and it will no longer be true that the malice in all sins stems from the dominant influence of passion; otherwise there will be some form of murder that cannot possibly be sinful.

Ev. If murder means taking the life of a man, this can sometimes happen without any sin. When a soldier slays the enemy, when a judge, or his deputy, executes a criminal, when, by chance, a deadly weapon leaves someone's hand unintentionally or thoughtlessly, I do not think that these are guilty of sin in killing a man.

Aug. I agree, but such men are not usually called murderers. Answer me this question. If a slave kills his master from whom he was in fear of grave torture, do you think we should include him among those who take a man's life in a way that does not warrant their being called murderers?

Ev. I see a great difference between the two. The first are acting either according to the law or in a way not opposed to the law. But there is no law to sanction this man's crime.

Aug. You are bringing me back to authority again. But you must keep in mind that we have presently undertaken to understand what we believe. We take the laws on faith, and therefore, we must try to understand, if this is at all possible, whether the law may not be doing wrong in punishing such an act.

Ev. It is not wrong at all when it punishes a man who knowingly and willingly slays his master, which is something that none of the others did.

Aug. Do you recall having said a while ago that in every evil deed passion is the dominant factor whereby an act is made evil?

Ev. Yes, I do.

Aug. Well, did you not also grant that a man who desires to live free from fear is not harboring an evil desire?

Ev. I remember that too.

Aug. Therefore, when a master is slain by his servant from this kind of desire, it is not done by a desire that is blameworthy. Consequently, we have not yet found out why this deed is evil. For we agree that all wrongdoing becomes such only by passion, namely, by a desire that is blameworthy.

Ev. It now seems to me that this servant was condemned unjustly. I would not venture this opinion if I could think of something else to say.

Aug. Have you then convinced yourself that such a serious crime should go unpunished before you stop to consider whether that servant desired to be free from fear of his master in order to gratify his passions? The desire to live free from fear is characteristic not only of the good but also of evil men, with this difference, that good men desire it by turning their love from whatever cannot be possessed without fear of loss, while evil men, bent upon enjoying such things securely, try to remove whatever hindrances stand in their way. As a result, they lead a life of crime and wickedness which should be called death rather than life.

Ev. I have come to my senses, and am very glad to have a clear understanding of the nature of that blameworthy desire called passion. I now see that it is the love of things which each one can lose against his will.

Chapter 5

Let us now inquire, if you will, whether passion is also the dominant factor in acts of sacrilege which we see frequently committed out of superstition.

Aug. Take note whether this question be not premature. I think we should first inquire whether an on-rushing enemy or a stealthy assassin may be slain, in the absence of passion, to defend one's life or liberty or virtue.

Ev. How am I to judge that these men are free of passion who take up the sword in defense of things that can be lost against their will? On the other hand, if they cannot lose them, what need is there to go to the extreme of killing a man to defend them?

Aug. Then the law is not just which gives a traveler the right to kill a robber to avoid being killed himself, or the right to any man or woman to destroy, if they can, an assailant about to attack with violence before the injury is inflicted. Soldiers, too, are commanded by law to kill the enemy, and if a soldier refrains from doing this, he is punished by the commander. Can we be rash enough to assert that these laws are unjust, or rather that they are no laws at all? For an unjust law, it seems to me, is no law.

Ev. I think the law is well protected against any such accusation since, for those people whom it governs, the law allows for minor transgressions to prevent the commission of more serious crimes. It is a far lesser evil that one who plots another's death should be slain rather than the person who is protecting his own life. And it is a much greater crime that a man should be the victim of a violent attack than that the attacker should be killed by the victim of the attempted attack. In the slaying of any enemy, the soldier is an agent of the law and consequently readily discharges his duty apart from any passion. A law which itself has been enacted for the protection of the people, cannot be charged with passion. Actually, if the lawgiver enacts a law, and does so at God's command, namely, in compliance with eternal justice, he may have done so completely free of passion. But if he did enact this law under the influence of passion, it does not follow that compliance with the law must be accompanied by passion, since a good law can be enacted by a lawgiver who is not good. If, for example, a ruler who has seized tyrannical power should accept a bribe from an interested party to issue a decree making it unlawful to carry off a woman forcibly, even for the purpose of marriage, the law is not evil just because it was made by an unjust and corrupt lawmaker. One can, therefore, without passion, obey a law enacted for the protection of its citizens when it commands that an enemy force be met by the same kind of force. The same may be said of all public servants who are subject to the ruling powers according to the existing law and established order.

But I fail to see how these men mentioned before can be without blame, though they are blameless in the sight of the law. For the law does not compel them to kill, but leaves it within their power. Consequently, they are not at liberty to kill anyone to defend those things which can be lost against their will and which, on this account, ought not be loved at all. As for life, there may be a doubt on the part of some as to whether it can be taken away from the soul at all when the body is destroyed. But if it can be taken away, it is worthless; if not, there is nothing to fear. But as for chastity, who could doubt that it is rooted in the soul itself, seeing that it is a virtue? It cannot, therefore, be snatched away by the violence of an assailant. Whatever the slain attacker was going to snatch from us is something not entirely within our power and, consequently, I fail to see how we can call it our own. Accordingly, I certainly am not blaming the law which permits such assailants to be slain, yet I can find no way to defend those who kill them. . . .

Chapter 10

. . . *Aug.* Do you think that the power of passion is greater than the mind, which we know has been given mastery over the passions? Personally, I do not think so. For there could be no perfect order if the weaker should lord it over the stronger. Consequently, I feel that the power of the mind must be greater than desire for the very reason that it is only right and just that it should hold sway over desire.

Ev. I feel the same way, too.

Aug. We can have no hesitation, then, in preferring every virtue to all vices, so that a virtue is more perfect and sublime to the extent that it becomes stronger and more invincible?

Ev. Unquestionably.

Aug. It follows that a soul infected with vice cannot overcome one fortified by virtue.

Ev. Very true.

Aug. I think you will not deny that any kind of soul at all is better and stronger than any body.

Ev. No one denies this who understands (and it is readily understandable) that a living substance should be more highly valued than a non-living substance, or that what imparts life should be esteemed more than that which receives it.

Aug. It is then far less possible for any kind of body at all to overcome a soul endowed with virtue.

Ev. That is perfectly evident.

Aug. What of a just soul and mind that keeps its natural right to rule? Could it ever dethrone some other mind possessed of equal power and virtue, and make it subject to desire?

Ev. This is impossible, not merely because both souls have the same degree of excellence but also because, in its attempt to degrade the other soul, the first will defect from its just state and become a wicked mind, thereby becoming the weaker of the two.

Aug. You have grasped this point very well. Consequently, you have only to tell me, if you can, whether you think there is anything more excellent than a mind endowed with reason and wisdom.

Ev. Nothing, I think, apart from God.

Aug. I think so too. But the question is a difficult one, and this is not the opportune time to seek a proper understanding of it. And, though we accept this matter with a firm faith, a full discussion of this problem must be undertaken by us with care and diligence.

Chapter 11

For the time being we can be sure that whatever that nature is which rightfully excels a mind adorned with virtue, it cannot possibly be unjust. Consequently, though it were within its power to do so, not even this nature will force the mind to become a slave to passion.

Ev. Anyone could see that right away.

Aug. Whatever, therefore, is the equal of mind, or superior to it, will not make it a slave to lust because of its own justice, provided the mind is in control and is strong in virtue. On the other hand anything inferior to the mind cannot do so because of its own weakness, as we have learned from what we already agreed upon. We are faced with the conclusion, then, that nothing else can make the mind the companion of evil desire except its own will and free choice.

Ev. Nothing, I see, could be more logical.

Aug. It follows that you feel it is only just that such a mind should suffer punishment for so great a sin.

Ev. I cannot deny it.

Aug. Well, then, are we to take lightly a punishment entailing such consequences as these, where passion lords it over the mind, dragging it about, poor and needy, in different directions, stripped of its wealth of virtue, now mistaking the false for the true, even defending something vigorously at one time only to reject at another what it had previously demonstrated, while all the while it rushes headlong into other false judgments; now withholding all assent, while fearful for the most part of the clearest demonstrations; now in despair of the whole business of finding the truth while it clings tenaciously to the darkness of its folly; now at pains to see the light and understand, and again falling back out of weariness to the darkness? And all the while, the cruel tyranny of evil desire holds sway, disrupting the entire soul and life of man by various and conflicting surges of passion; here by fear, there by desire; here by anxiety, there by empty and spurious delights; here by torment over the loss of a loved object, there by a burning desire to acquire something not possessed; here by pain for an injury received, there by the urge to revenge an injury. On every possible side, the mind is shriveled up by greed, wasted away by sensuality, a slave to ambition, is inflated by pride, tortured by envy, deadened by sloth, kept in turmoil by obstinacy, and distressed by its condition of subjection. And so with other countless impulses that surround and plague the rule of passion. How could we ever think that this is not a punishment when, as you see, it is something that all have to suffer who do not hold fast to wisdom? . . .

Chapter 12

. . . I [ask] you whether we have a will.

Ev. I do not know.

Aug. Do you want to know?

Ev. Even that I do not know.

Aug. Then do not ask me any more questions.

Ev. Why?

Aug. Because I do not have to answer your questions unless you want to know what you are asking. Furthermore, if you have no desire to attain wisdom, there should be no discussion with you about such matters. Finally, you can be no friend of mine unless you wish me well. Furthermore, look into yourself and see whether you do not will a happy life for yourself.

Ev. I acknowledge there can be no denying that we have a will. Go on now, and let us see what you are going to conclude from this.

Aug. I shall, but tell me first whether you think you also have a good will.

Ev. What is a good will?

Aug. It is a will by which we seek to live a good and upright life and to attain unto perfect wisdom. See now whether you are not seeking after a good and upright life and whether you do not have a strong desire to be wise, or whether, in any case, you can dare deny that we have a good will when we choose these things.

Ev. I do not deny any of this, and I agree, therefore, not only that I have a will but also that it is now a good will.

Aug. Please tell me what value you set on this will. Do you think that riches or honors or bodily pleasures, or all three together, can be compared in any way with the will?

Ev. God forbid such wicked folly!

Aug. Should we not then rejoice a little that we have something in the soul—I am referring to this good will itself—in comparison with which all the things we mentioned are worthless, though we see how men in great numbers spare no effort or risk to acquire them?

Ev. Rejoice we should, indeed, and very much so.

Aug. Do you think that those who fail to experience this joy suffer only a small loss when they are deprived of so great a good?

Ev. On the contrary, they suffer a very great loss.

Aug. I believe you see then that it lies within our will either to enjoy or to lack so great and true a good as this. For what is more within the power of the will than the will itself? When anyone has a good will, he really possesses something which ought to be esteemed far above all earthly kingdoms and all the delights of the body. On the other hand, if he does not have a good will, he is truly deprived of something which the will alone can of itself bestow upon him and which is more excellent than all those goods which lie beyond our control. Accordingly, when he thinks himself most unhappy if he loses his fine name, vast wealth, and various kinds of bodily goods, will you not rather think him most unhappy for clinging to goods he can lose so easily and which he cannot have when he wants them, even though he possesses all these things in abundance? For he lacks a good will which should not even be compared with these, and though it is so great a good, one has only to will it in order to possess it.

Ev. Very true.

Aug. It is, therefore, only right and just that foolish men should suffer such misery, even though there was never a time when they were wise—and this is an uncertain and baffling question.

Ev. I agree. . . .

Chapter 14

Aug. . . . Do you not think that every man wills and desires the happy life in every way possible?

    Ev. Undoubtedly.

    Aug. Then why do they not all attain it? We had agreed in our discussion that men merit a happy life by their will and an unhappy life also by their will, so that they deserve what they get. But now a kind of contradiction suddenly appears, which, unless we examine it carefully, threatens to upset our previous careful and clear line of reasoning. How, for example, can anyone endure an unhappy life because of his own will when there is no one at all who wills to live unhappily? Or how does man by his will attain the happy life when there are so many unhappy, and yet they all will to be happy?

    Does it come about because it is one thing to will what is good or bad, but another to merit something in virtue of a good or bad will? For those who are happy—and they must also be good—are not happy simply because they willed to live the happy life, for bad men do this too, but because they wished to live upright lives, which bad men are unwilling to do. It is little wonder, therefore, that unhappy men do not attain what they want, namely, the happy life, for they do not also will what must be its companion, and without which no one can deserve to attain it, namely, an upright life. Certainly . . . merit is in the will, whereas reward and punishment are identified with happiness and unhappiness. Hence, when we say that men are unhappy by their own choice, we are not saying they want to be unhappy but that their will is such that unhappiness results of necessity and even against their will. Hence this does not go counter to our earlier conclusion that all men want to be happy, though not all succeed because they do not all have the will to lead an upright life, and it is this will which alone can merit the happy life. Do you have any objections to raise here?

    Ev. No, I have none. . . .

Chapter 16

Aug. . . . We have . . . made a clear enough distinction between two classes of things, eternal and temporal, and again between two classes of men, those who pursue and love things eternal, and those who pursue and love temporal things. But we also agreed that what each man chooses to pursue and embrace is within the power of the will to determine, and that it is only the will that can dethrone the mind from its citadel and despoil it of its right order. It is also clear that when someone puts a thing to bad use, we are not to blame the thing itself but the one who makes bad use of it. Let us go back, if you will, to the question proposed at the start of this discussion and see whether it has been solved. We had set out to inquire about the nature of wrongdoing and our entire discussion has been directed to this end.

    We may now, then, turn our attention to this question and inquire whether wrongdoing is anything else than the pursuit of temporal things to the neglect of things eternal, namely, the pursuit of things, as if they were great and wonderful, which are perceived by the lowest part of man, his body, and which we can never be sure of, and the neglect of those things which the mind enjoys and perceives of itself, and which cannot be lost to the man who loves them. For every kind of wrongdoing, namely, sin, is included, it seems to me, under this one class. But I am waiting to find out what you think.

Ev. It is just as you say, and I agree that all sins fall under this one class and occur when a man turns away from what is divine and truly abiding and turns to what is changing and uncertain. And though these latter have been assigned their rightful place and achieve a kind of beauty all their own, nevertheless, it is the mark of a wicked and perverse soul to become a slave to the pursuit of those things which should rather be regulated according to the good pleasure of the soul whose right to rule derives from divine order and law. I think we have at the same time found a solution to the problem of why we do evil, which we proposed to examine after the question on the nature of wrongdoing. For, unless I am mistaken, we do evil from the free choice of the will, as was shown by the argument already advanced. But now I am asking whether He who created us should have given us that very freedom of choice by which it has been shown that we have the power to sin. For, without this power, we apparently would not have been capable of sinning, and there is thus reason to fear that God will be adjudged the cause even of our evil deeds.

Aug. Have no fear of this. But we will have to find another time to examine this matter more carefully since the discussion at hand needs to be kept within limits and brought to an end. I would have you believe that we have, so to speak, knocked at the door of great and abstruse questions that warrant our inquiry. When we have begun, with God's help, to penetrate their inner recesses, you will certainly recognize what a difference there is between our present discussion and those that are to follow, and how these latter excel, not only in the mental discernment required for their inquiry, but also in the lofty character and resplendent light of their truth. Only let us be religiously motivated so that God in His Providence may allow us to hold fast to the end the course we have embarked upon.

Ev. I accede to your will, and willingly concur with your judgment and wishes.

BOOK II

Chapter 1

Ev. Now explain to me, if that is possible, why God gave man free choice of the will since, if he had not received it, man would certainly be unable to sin.

Aug. Do you know for sure that God has given man something which you think should not have been given him?

Ev. From what I seem to gather from the previous book, we do have free choice of the will and this alone enables us to sin.

Aug. I also recall that this point was made clear. But I have asked you just now whether you know that it was God who gave us that very thing which we obviously possess and which enables us to sin.

Ev. I think it is none other, for it is from Him that we have our being and from Him that we merit reward or punishment, according as we live good or sinful lives.

Aug. I am also eager to know whether you see this clearly or whether you are willing to believe it on authority, even though you do not understand it.

Ev. I assure you that I first accepted this on authority; yet what could be truer than that everything good comes from God, that everything just is good, and that it is just that there should be punishment for sinners and rewards for the righteous? Hence the conclusion that God makes sinners unhappy and the righteous happy.

Aug. I agree, but I would raise this other question as to how you know that we have our being from God. For you did not now explain this, but only that it is from Him that we merit either punishment or reward.

Ev. I see that the only evidence for this point stems from our earlier conclusion that God punishes sins, since, in fact, all justice comes from Him. For while it is a mark of goodness to bestow benefits upon strangers, it is not in keeping with justice to inflict punishments upon them. Clearly, therefore, we belong to God, not only because He is most generous to us with His gifts, but also because He is most just in meting out punishment. Again, from the fact that every good comes from God, and here you agreed with my contention, we can understand that man too comes from God. For man himself, insofar as he is man, is something good because he can live an upright life whenever he so wishes.

Aug. Obviously, if this is so, the question you raised is already answered. If, indeed, man is something good and cannot do what is right unless he wills to, then he must have free will, without which he cannot do what is right. For we must not suppose that because a man can also sin by his free will that God gave it to him for this purpose. The fact that man cannot lead an upright life without it is sufficient reason why God should have given it. That it was given for this purpose can be seen from this, that when he has used it to commit sin, he is subject to divine punishment, which would be unjust if free will had been given him not only to live uprightly but also to commit sin. How could punishment be justly visited upon a man who used his will for the very purpose for which it was given him? But when God punishes a sinner, what does He seem to say but: "Why did you not use your free will for the purpose for which I gave it to you, namely, to do what is right?" Besides, if man were without free choice of the will, what would become of the good called justice whereby sins are punished and good deeds are honored? For, unless something is done by the will, it can be neither a sin nor a good deed. Consequently, punishments and rewards would be unjust if man did not possess free will. Moreover, there must be a place for justice both in punishments and rewards because it is one of those goods that come from God. It follows, therefore, that God should have given man free will.

Chapter 2

Ev. I admit now that God gave it. But let me ask you this: if it was given to do good, do you not think it should have been impossible to turn it to a sinful purpose? As with justice itself, which is given man to lead a good life, how could anyone lead a bad life by reason of his being just? So, too, if the will were given to do good, no one would be able to sin by his will.

Aug. I hope God will enable me to answer your question, or better, that He will enable you to answer it yourself, when you are enlightened by that truth within you, which is the greatest teacher of all.[3] I wish you would tell me shortly—provided you know for sure that God gave us free will, which was what I asked you—whether we should say that something should not have been given when we acknowledge that it was God who gave it. For, if it is not certain that He gave it, it is right for us to ask whether it was a good gift, so that if we find that it was, we will also have found that it was given by Him who has given all good things to man. Now if we find that it was not a good gift, we will realize that God did not give it, since it is blasphemous to charge Him with wrongdoing. But if it is certain that He Himself gave it, then, no matter how it was given, we must acknowledge that there is no reason why it either should not have been given or been given differently than it was given. For He gave it, who may never be rightly blamed for what He has done.

Ev. While I accept all this with a firm faith, yet, since I have no intellectual grasp of it, let us so conduct our inquiry as if it were all uncertain. As I see it, our uncertainty as to whether free will was given us to do good, since we can also sin by it, gives rise to the further uncertainty as to whether it should have been given at all. If it is uncertain that free will was given to do good, it is also uncertain whether it should have been given, and, consequently, also uncertain that God gave it to us. For, if it is uncertain whether it should have been given, it is uncertain that it was given by God since it would be impious to suppose that He has given anything which He should not have given.

Aug. You are certain, at least, that God exists.

Ev. This too I hold firmly, not from direct knowledge, but by faith.

Aug. Suppose, then, that one of these fools of whom it is related in the Scripture, "The fool has said in his heart, There is no God,"[4] should say this to you, and should be unwilling to go along with what you believe, but want to know whether what you believe is true. Would you abandon this man or would you think that he should somehow be convinced of what is a matter of firm belief for you, especially if he was not stubborn in his opposition but was eager in his desire to know?

Ev. What you just said clearly suggests how I should answer him. Even though he were utterly unreasonable, he would at least admit that no one should enter a discussion on any subject at all with a man who is insincere and obstinate, and, most of all, on a subject of such importance. Once this was admitted, he would first prevail upon me to believe that he is making this inquiry in good faith and that as far as the present problem is concerned, he harbors no hidden guile or obstinacy. I would then point out (and I think this would be a simple matter for anyone) that since he wishes another to believe the hidden thoughts of his own mind, thoughts known to him but unknown to the one who believes them, it is much more reasonable for him to believe in God's existence on the authority of the books of those great men who have left a written record testifying that they lived with the Son of God. They have also recorded certain things they witnessed which could not possibly have happened if there were no God. And it would be very foolish of him to reproach me for believing these men since he wished me to believe him. Now certainly he could find no good reason for not wanting to imitate what he is unable to reproach.

Aug. Now if you think it is enough to accept God's existence on the word of such great men without being rash, then what of those other questions which we undertook to explore, as if they were uncertain and completely unknown? Why, I ask, do you do not likewise think that we should also believe these things on the authority of these men to the extent that we need expend no further effort in investigating them?

Ev. But we are eager to know and understand what we believe.

Aug. Your memory serves you well. . . .

Chapter 3

Let us pursue our inquiry, if you will, according to this order: first, what evidence is there that God exists; next, do all things, insofar as they are good, come from God; lastly, should free will be numbered among things good. Once these questions have been answered, I think it will become clear enough whether it was right to give free will to man.

Hence, to begin with what is most evident, I will ask you whether you yourself exist. Possibly, you are afraid of being mistaken by this kind of a question when, actually, you could not be mistaken at all if you did not exist?

Ev. Go on instead to the other questions.

Aug. Then, since it is evident that you exist, and that this could not be so unless you were living, then the fact that you are living is also evident. Do you understand that these two points are absolutely true?

Ev. I understand that perfectly well.

Aug. Then this third point is also evident, namely, that you understand.

Ev. It is evident.

Aug. Which of these three, in your opinion, is the most excellent?

Ev. Understanding.

Aug. Why do you think so?

Ev. Because, while these are three in number, existence, life, and understanding, and though the stone exists and the animal lives, yet I do not think that the stone lives or that the animal understands, whereas it is absolutely certain that whoever understands also exists and is living. That is why I have no hesitation in concluding that the one which contains all three is more excellent than that which is lacking in one or both of these. Now whatever is living is certainly also existing, but it does not follow that it also understands. This kind of life, I think, is proper to animals. But it certainly does not follow that what exists must also live and understand, for I can admit that a corpse exists, but no one would say it lives. And still less can something understand if it is not living.

Aug. We maintain, then, that two of these three are lacking in a corpse, one in the animal, and none in man.

Ev. That is true.

Aug. We likewise maintain that the most excellent among the three is what man possesses together with the other two, namely, understanding, and that having this, he must also exist and live.

Ev. We do, indeed.

Aug. Now tell me whether you know you have these well-known senses of the body: sight, hearing, smell, taste, and touch.

Ev. I do.

Aug. What do you think is the function of sight, that is, what do we perceive when we see?

Ev. Anything corporeal.

Aug. When we see, we do not likewise perceive what is hard and soft, do we?

Ev. No.

Aug. What then is the proper[5] function of the eyes, that is, what do we perceive with them?

Ev. Color.

Aug. Of the ears?

Ev. Sound.

Aug. Of smell?

Ev. Odors.

Aug. Of taste?

Ev. Flavor.

Aug. Of touch?

Ev. Soft or hard, smooth or rough, and many such qualities.

Aug. And what of the shapes of bodies? Do we not perceive that they are large, small, square, round, and so on, both by touch and sight? Consequently, these qualities are not proper either to sight or vision alone, but belong to both.

Ev. I understand.

Aug. Then you further understand that each sense has its own proper object to report while some senses have certain objects in common.

Ev. I understand that also.

Aug. Can we, therefore, determine by any of these senses what is the proper object of each sense or what those objects are which some or all of them have in common?

Ev. Not at all. This is discerned by some power within.

Aug. Might not this be the reason itself, which is wanting in beasts? For, in my opinion, reason enables us to grasp these and to know just what they are.

Ev. I think it is rather reason that enables us to know that there is a kind of internal sense to which everything is referred by those well-known five senses. Now the power enabling the animal to see is one thing, that by which it shuns or seeks what it perceives by seeing is something else. The former is located in the eye, the latter within, in the soul itself. The inner sense enables the animal to seek and acquire things that delight and to repel and avoid things that are obnoxious, not only those that are perceived by sight and hearing, but all those which are grasped by the other bodily senses. But this power cannot be called either sight or hearing or smell or taste or touch, but is some other kind of power that presides over all of them together. Although, as I mentioned, we do grasp this power by our reason, yet we may not call it reason, since it is obviously present in beasts.

Aug. I acknowledge that this power, whatever it is, does exist, and I do not hesitate to call it the inner sense. . . .

Chapter 5

. . . Keep carefully in mind that when I asked whether you were existing, it was made clear that you knew not only this but also two other things.

Ev. I remember that too.

Aug. Now see which one of these three you think is that one to which pertains everything perceived by the bodily senses, that is, in what class of things you think we should locate whatever is perceived by our senses, by the eyes or by any other organ of the body. Should it be with things that merely exist, with those that also live, or with those that also understand?

Ev. With those that merely exist.

Aug. In which of the three classes do you think the sense power itself should be placed?

Ev. In the class of things living.

Aug. Which of these two do you think is better, the sense itself or its object?

Ev. The sense, of course.

Aug. Why is that?

Ev. Because whatever also has life is better than something which merely exists.

Aug. And what of that inner sense which we found was inferior to reason and which we still share in common with beasts? Would you hesitate to rank this sense above that by which we perceive a body, which you said should be ranked above the body itself?

Ev. I would have no hesitation whatever.

Aug. I should like you to tell me why you have no hesitation on this point. For you cannot say that this inner sense should be placed in that one of the three classes which also includes understanding, but rather in the class of things which exist and live, although they lack understanding. This inner sense is found also in beasts which are without understanding. If this is so, I would like to know why you rank the inner sense above that which perceives corporeal qualities, since both are found in the class of things that live. You ranked the sense which perceives bodies above bodies because the latter are in the class of things which only exist, while the former are in the class of things that also live. Since the inner sense is also found in this class, tell me why you think it is better.

If you say it is because the inner sense perceives the bodily sense, I do not believe you will find any rule that we could rely upon for holding that the subject perceiving is better than what it perceives. Otherwise, we might also be forced to conclude that the person understanding is better than what he understands. This, of course, is untrue because man understands wisdom but he is not better than wisdom itself. Consider, then, why you thought that the inner sense should be ranked above the sense by which we perceive things corporeal.

Ev. It is because I look upon the inner sense as a ruler and kind of judge of the latter. For if there is any shortcoming in the discharge of their function, the inner sense demands this service from the bodily senses as a kind of debt owed by its servant. . . . The sense of sight does not see that it is seeing or not seeing and, failing to do so, it cannot judge what is missing or what is sufficient. This is done by the inner sense which directs the soul of the beast to open its eyes when they are closed and to supply what it perceives is missing. There can be no doubt in anyone's mind that what judges is better than what is judged.

Aug. Do you understand then that even the bodily senses pass a kind of judgment on bodies? Pleasure and pain are theirs to experience whenever they come in contact gently or roughly with a body. Just as the inner sense judges as to what is missing or what is sufficient in visual perception, so the eyes themselves judge as to what is deficient or sufficient in the matter of color. So too in the case of hearing, just as the inner sense judges whether or not it is attentive enough, so the auditory sense judges concerning sounds, discerning those which either flow gently into the ear or which produce a harsh dissonance.

There is no need to continue with the rest of the bodily senses. I think you know already what I am trying to say, namely, that just as the inner sense judges the bodily senses, approving what is complete in them and requiring what is deficient, so too the bodily senses themselves judge bodies, admitting pleasurable sensations of touch found in them, while rejecting the opposite.

Ev. I see these points clearly and agree that they are perfectly true.

Chapter 6

Aug. See now whether reason also judges the inner sense. I am not asking whether you have any doubt that reason is better than the inner sense because I am sure that this is your judgment. Yet I feel that now we should not even have to ask whether reason passes judgment on the inner sense. For in the case of things inferior to it, namely, bodies, the bodily senses, and the inner sense, is it not, after all, reason itself that tells us how one is better than the other and how far superior reason itself is to all of them? This would not be possible at all unless reason were to judge them.

Ev. Obviously.

Aug. Consequently, that nature which not only exists but also lives, though it does not understand, such as the soul of beasts, is superior to one that merely exists and neither lives nor understands, such as the inanimate body. Again, that nature which at once exists and lives and understands, such as the rational mind in man, is superior to the animal nature. Do you think that anything can be found in us, namely, something among those elements which complete our nature and make us men, that is more excellent than that very thing which we made the third in those three classes of things? It is clear that we have a body and a kind of living principle which quickens the body itself and makes it grow, and we recognize that these two are also found in beasts. And it is also clear that there is a third something, the apex, so to speak, or eye of the soul, or whatever more appropriate term may be employed to designate reason and understanding, which the animal nature does not possess. So I ask you to consider whether there is anything in man's nature more excellent than reason.

Ev. I see nothing at all that is better.

Aug. But suppose we could find something which you are certain not only exists but is also superior to our reason, would you hesitate to call this reality, whatever it is, God?

Ev. If I were able to find something which is better than what is best in my nature, I would not immediately call it God. I do not like to call something God because my reason is inferior to it, but rather to call that reality God which has nothing superior to it.

Aug. That is perfectly true. For God Himself has given this reason of yours the power to think of Him with such reverence and truth. But I will ask you this: if you should find that there is nothing above our reason but an eternal and changeless reality, would you hesitate to say that this is God? You notice how bodies are subject to change, and it is clear that the living principle animating the body is not free from change but passes through various states. And reason itself is clearly shown to be changeable, seeing that at one time it endeavors to reach the truth, and at another time it does not, sometimes it arrives at the truth, sometimes it does not. If reason sees something eternal and changeless not by any bodily organ, neither by touch nor taste nor smell nor hearing nor sight, nor by any sense inferior to it, but sees this of itself, and sees at the same time its own inferiority, it will have to acknowledge that this being is its God.

Ev. I will openly acknowledge that to be God, if, as all agree, there is nothing higher existing.

Aug. Good! It will be enough for me to show that something of this kind exists. Either you will admit that *this* is God or, if there is something higher, you will admit that *it* is God. Accordingly, whether there exists something higher or not, it will become clear that God exists, when, with His assistance, I shall prove, as I promised, that there exists something above reason.

Ev. Prove then what you are promising. . . .

Chapter 8

Aug. . . . Tell me whether anything can be found which all thinking men perceive in common, each one making use of his own mind and reason. Something which is seen is present to everybody and is not changed into something else useful for those to whom it is present, like food and drink, but remains whole and entire, whether it is seen or not. Or do you think that perhaps no such thing exists?

Ev. On the contrary, I see there are many, but it is sufficient to single out one of them, the nature and truth of number which are present to all who make use of reason. Everyone engaged in computing them strives to grasp their nature with his own reason and intelligence. Some do this rather easily, others with more difficulty, while others cannot do it at all, though the truth makes itself equally available to all who can grasp it. And whenever someone experiences this, it is not altered or changed into a kind of nourishment for the one who perceives it. When anyone errs in judgment about it, the reality itself, which remains true and intact, is not at fault; rather, his own error is measured by his failure to behold the reality itself.

Aug. That is certainly true. I see you were quick to find an answer as becomes a man not unfamiliar with such matters. But suppose I were to tell you that these numbers have not been impressed upon our mind by any nature of their own but come from things which we grasp with the bodily senses and are a kind of sense-image of things visible, how would you reply? Or would you also be of the same opinion?

Ev. I could never think of such a thing. Even if I could perceive numbers by the bodily senses, I could not on this account also perceive the nature of numerical division and addition by the bodily sense. It is by the light of the mind that I show a man to be wrong whose computation indicates an incorrect total either in addition or subtraction. Besides, I cannot tell how long anything will endure which comes in contact with my bodily senses, such as the heavens and the earth, and all the other bodies which I see are contained in them. But seven and three are ten, not only now, but forever. And there has never been, nor will there ever be a time when seven and three were not ten. This is why I have said that the indestructible truth of number is common to me and to anyone at all who uses his reason.

Aug. I cannot gainsay the absolute truth and certainty of your answer. But you will readily see that even the numbers themselves have not been brought in through the bodily senses if you realize that all numbers are designated as multiples of the number one. For example, twice one is two, one tripled is three, and ten times one is ten. No matter what the number, it is so designated according to the number of times it contains the number one. But anyone with a true notion of "one" will doubtless discover that it cannot be perceived by the bodily senses. Whatever comes in contact with the bodily senses can be shown to be many, and not one, since, being a body, it also has numberless parts. . . . No matter how small the . . . body, it has one part on the right, another on the left, one above and another below, one to the far side and another on the near side, parts at the extremes and parts in between. We have to admit that such parts are found in any body, no matter how small it is. Accordingly, we acknowledge that no bodily reality is one, truly and simply, and yet it would be impossible to enumerate so many parts within the body unless these were differentiated by the concept of one. . . .

Chapter 12

You would in no way deny, then, that there exists unchangeable truth that embraces all things that are immutably true. You cannot call this truth mine or yours, or anyone else's. Rather, it is there to manifest itself as something common to all who behold immutable truths, as a light that in wondrous ways is both hidden and public. . . .

Ev. That is perfectly clear and true.

Aug. This truth, therefore, which we have discussed at length and in which, though it is one, we perceive so many things—do you think that compared to our minds it is more excellent, equally excellent, or inferior? Now if it were inferior, we would not be making judgments according to it, but about it. We do make judgments, for example, about bodies because they are lower, and we often state not only that they exist or do not exist this way, but also that they ought or ought not so to exist. So too with our souls; we not only know that our soul is in a certain state, but often know besides that this is the way it ought to be. We also make similar judgments about bodies, as when we say that a body is not so bright or so square as it ought to be, and so on, and also of souls, when we say the soul is not so well disposed as it ought to be, or that it is not so gentle or not so forceful, according to the dictates of our moral norms.

We make these judgments according to those rules of truth within us which we see in common, but no one ever passes judgment on the rules themselves. For whenever anyone affirms that the eternal ought to be valued above the things of time, or that seven and three are ten, no one judges that it ought to be so, but merely recognizes that it is so. He is not an examiner making corrections, but merely a discoverer, rejoicing over his discovery.

But if this truth were of equal standing with our minds, it would itself also be changeable. At times our minds see more of it, at other times less, thereby acknowledging that they are subject to change. But the truth which abides in itself, does not increase or decrease by our seeing more or less of it, but, remaining whole or inviolable, its light brings delight to those who have turned to it, and punishes with blindness those who have turned from it.

And what of the fact that we judge about our own minds in the light of this truth, though we are unable to judge at all about the truth itself? We say that our mind does not understand as well as it ought, or that it understands as much as it ought. But the mind's understanding should be in proportion to its ability to be drawn more closely and to cling to the unchangeable truth. Consequently, if truth is neither inferior nor equal to our minds, it has to be higher and more excellent.

Chapter 13

I had promised to show you, if you recall, that there is something higher than our mind and reason. There you have it—truth itself! Embrace it, if you can, and enjoy it; "find delight in the Lord and He will grant you the petitions of your heart."[6] For what more do you desire than to be happy? And who is happier than the man who finds joy in the firm, changeless, and most excellent truth?

Men proclaim they are happy when they embrace the beautiful bodies of their wives and even of harlots, which they desire so passionately, and shall we doubt that we are happy in the embrace of truth? Men proclaim they are happy when, suffering from parched throats, they come to a copious spring of healthful waters, or, when hungry, they come upon a big dinner or supper sumptuously prepared. Shall we deny we are happy when we are refreshed and nourished by truth? We often hear men proclaim they are happy if they recline amid roses and other flowers, or delight in the fragrance of ointments. But what is more fragrant, what more delightful, than the breath of truth? And shall we hesitate to say we are happy when we are filled with the breath of truth? Many decide that for them the happy life is found in vocal music and in the sounds of string instruments and flutes. Whenever these are absent, they account themselves unhappy, whereas when they are at hand, they are thrilled with joy. When truth steals into our minds with a kind of eloquent silence without, as it were, the noisy intrusion of words, shall we look for another happy life and not enjoy that which is so sure and intimately present to us? Men delight in the glitter of gold and silver, in the lustre of gems, and are delighted by the charm and splendor of light, whether it be the light in our own eyes, or that of fires on earth, or the light in the stars, the moon, or the sun. And they think themselves happy when they are not withdrawn from these enjoyments by some kind of trouble or penury, and they would like to go on living forever for the sake of those delights. And shall we be afraid to find our happiness in the light of truth? . . .

Chapter 14

Now no one is secure in the possession of goods which can be lost against his will. But no one loses truth or wisdom against his will, for he cannot be separated from them by spatial distances. What we call separation from truth and wisdom is a perverse will which makes inferior things the object of its love. But no one wills anything unwillingly.

In possessing truth, therefore, we have something which all of us can equally enjoy in common, for there is nothing wanting or defective in it. It welcomes all its lovers without any envy on their part; it is available to all, yet chaste with each. No one of them says to another: step back so I too may come close; take your hands away so I may also embrace it. All cling to it; all touch the selfsame thing. It is a food never divided into portions; you drink nothing from it that I cannot drink. By sharing in it, you make no part of it your personal possession. I do not have to wait for you to exhale its fragrance so that I too may draw it in. No part of it ever becomes the exclusive possession of any one man, or of a few, but is common to all at the same time in its entirety. . . .

Chapter 15

You granted that if I could prove that there was something above our minds, you would admit it was God, provided that there was still nothing higher. I agreed and stated that it would be enough for me to prove this point. For if there is anything more excellent, then this is God; if not, then truth itself is God. In either case, you cannot deny that God exists, which was the question we proposed to examine in our discussion. If you are uneasy because of what we have received on faith through the hallowed teaching of Christ, namely, that there is a Father of Wisdom, then remember that we have accepted this also on faith, namely, that the Wisdom begotten of the eternal Father is equal to Him. We are not to inquire further about this just now, but only to accept it with an unshaken faith.

God exists indeed, and He exists truly and most perfectly. As I see it, we not only hold this as certain by our faith, but we also arrive at it by a sure, though, as yet, very inadequate form of knowledge. But this is sufficient for the matter at hand and will enable us to explain the other points that have a bearing on the subject, unless, of course, you have some objections to raise.

Ev. I accept all this, overwhelmed as I am with an incredible joy which I am unable to express to you in words. I declare that it is absolutely certain. I do so, prompted by that inner voice which makes me want to hear the truth itself and to cling to it. I not only grant that this is good, but also that it is the highest good and the source of happiness. . . .

Chapter 17

Aug. Every changeable reality must also be capable of receiving form.[7] Just as we call something changeable which is capable of undergoing change, so I would call "formable" whatever is capable of receiving form. But nothing can impart form to itself, because nothing can give itself what it does not have, and, surely, a thing is given form so that it may have form. So if anything possesses form, there is no need for it to receive what it has. But if it does not have form, it cannot receive from itself what it does not have. Nothing, therefore, as we have said, can give itself form. Now what more can we say about the changing nature of body and soul, since enough has been said previously? We may conclude, then, that body and soul both receive forms from an immutable and everlasting form, with reference to which it was said: "Thou shalt change them, and they shall be changed. But Thou art forever the same, and thy years fail not."[8] The Prophet spoke of years that do not fail to indicate eternity. Of the same form it is likewise said that "abiding in itself, it renews all things."[9]

By this we may also understand that all things are ruled by providence. If everything in existence would become nothing, once form was entirely taken away, then this unchangeable form is itself their providence. Through it all changing realities subsist so as to achieve their perfection and movements by the numerical principles belonging to their forms. If this form did not exist, these would have no being. Accordingly, the man who is making his way toward wisdom will see, as he gazes thoughtfully upon the whole of creation, how wisdom reveals itself cheerfully to him along the way and comes to meet him with all providential care. And he will yearn all the more eagerly to complete this journey as the path itself is made more beautiful by that wisdom which he so ardently desires to reach.

If you are able to find some other class of creature besides that which exists without life, and that which exists with life but without understanding, and that which exists with life and understanding, then you might venture to affirm that there is something good which does not come from God. These three classes may even be expressed by two words, if we call them body and life. For that which has only life and no understanding, as animals, and that which has understanding, as man, are rightly said to have life. Now these two, namely, body and life, are reckoned among things created, since we also speak of life of the Creator Himself, and this is the highest form of life. Since these two, namely, body and life, are capable of receiving form, as our earlier remarks have shown, and since they would fall back into nothingness were all form to be taken away, they give sufficient indication that they owe their existence to that form which is always the same.

Consequently, all good things, however great or small, can only come from God. What can be greater among creatures than life endowed with understanding, or what can be less than body? No matter how far these deteriorate and tend towards nothingness, something of form remains in them to give them such existence as they have. Whatever form is left in anything undergoing such deterioration, comes to it from that form which knows no deterioration and which does not permit even the movements of things, whether towards progress or deterioration, to go beyond the limits imposed by their numbers. Consequently, whatever we find praiseworthy in nature, whether it be deemed worthy of great or of slight praise, must be referred to the highest and unspeakable praise of the Creator. But you may have something further to add.

Chapter 18

Ev. I am, I admit, sufficiently convinced that God exists and that all goods come from God, so far as such evidence is possible in the present life and for men like ourselves. All existing things come from God, whether they have understanding and life and existence, or have only life and existence, or have only existence. Now let us examine the third question to see whether it can be shown that free will should be reckoned among things that are good. Once this is proven, I will have no hesitation in granting that God gave it to us and that it is something that should have been given.

Aug. You recall very well the questions proposed, and you were quick to notice that the second question has already been cleared up. But you should have seen that the third was also settled. You gave it as your opinion that free will should not have been given because people commit sin by it. In opposition to your view, I retorted that moral conduct is only possible by free will and went on to assert that God had given it for this purpose. You replied that free will should have been given us in the same way as justice, which one can only use rightly. This reply of yours compelled us to embark upon these roundabout discussions to prove that good things, great and small, come from God alone. This point could only be clarified after we had refuted the wicked folly expressed by the fool who said in his heart, "There is no God."[10] Some kind of reasoning, suited to our feeble mentality, was undertaken on this important matter in order to give us something certain by way of conclusion, while God Himself was helping us along so perilous a course. Although these two truths, namely, that God exists, and that all good things come from Him, were at first held firmly by faith, they have now been examined in such a way that this third truth is manifestly evident, namely, that free will must be numbered among things that are good.

In an earlier discussion it was proven and agreed upon by us that a corporeal nature occupies a lower place in existence than does the nature of the soul, and that the soul is therefore a greater good than the body. If, then, among goods of the body we find some which man can misuse, we do not say that they should not therefore have been given, since we do acknowledge that these are good. We should not be surprised then if we also find in the soul some goods which we can also misuse. But because they are good, they could only be given by Him from whom all good things come.

You can see how a great good is wanting in a body having no hands; yet a man who perpetrates cruel and shameful deeds with them makes bad use of his hands. If you were to see someone with no feet, you would admit that an important good is wanting to the body's integrity, and yet you could not deny that a man who uses his feet to injure someone or to disgrace himself is making bad use of his feet.

With our eyes we can perceive light and distinguish bodily forms one from another. This power of sight is the noblest endowment of our body and for this reason these organs have been given a kind of exalted place of honor in our body. Our eyes also serve to protect health and furnish many other benefits to life. Yet, many men do much that is shameful with their eyes and enlist them to serve the cause of lust. You can see what a great good is wanting to a face having no eyes, but when we possess them, who else has given them but God, the Giver of all goods?

Just as you look favorably upon these goods in the body and praise Him who gave them, without regard to those who misuse them, so you should also grant that free will, without which no one can live right, is good and is given by God. You should further acknowledge that those who misuse this good should be condemned rather than admit that He who gave free will should not have given it.

Ev. I would like you to prove for me first that free will is a good, and then I would grant that God gave it to us, because I acknowledge that all things good come from God.

Aug. Have I failed then to prove this to you after so much effort in our earlier discussion? You granted at the time that the beauty and form of a body are wholly derived from the supreme form of all things, namely, the truth, and that these are good. Truth itself says in the Gospel that even the hairs of our head are numbered.[11] Have you forgotten what we said about the supremacy of number and how its power extends from end to end? What perversity to count the hairs of our head, small and lowly as they are, among things good, and fail to discover their cause and to see that God alone is the Creator of everything good, since all good things, great and small, derive from Him, from whom comes every good. Again, what perversity to doubt about free will, without which it is impossible to lead an upright life, as even they acknowledge who live wickedly.

In any case, please tell me now which you think is the higher good in us. Is it that without which we can live rightly, or that without which we cannot live rightly?

Ev. Please go easy on me, for I am ashamed that I could not see this. How could anyone doubt that that without which there can be no right living is the more excellent good by far?

Aug. Would you deny then that a man with one eye can live rightly?

Ev. May I never be guilty of such colossal folly!

Aug. Since you grant, then, that the eye is something good in the body, even though its loss is no hindrance to leading a good life, will you take the view that free will is not a good, when no one can live rightly without it?

Think of justice, which no one can put to bad use. It is reckoned among the greatest goods found in man and among all the virtues of the soul which make for a good and upright life. Nor does anyone put to bad use the virtues of prudence or courage or temperance. In all these virtues, as well as in justice itself, which you mentioned, it is right reason that prevails, and without it the virtues cannot exist. But no one can put right reason to a bad use. . . .

Chapter 20

Since the will undergoes movement when it turns from the unchangeable to the changeable good, you may perhaps ask how this movement originates. It is really evil, though free will must be reckoned as a good, since it is impossible to live rightly without it. For if this movement, namely, the turning away of the will from the Lord, is unquestionably sinful, we could not say, could we, that God is the cause of sin? If this movement, therefore, does not come from God, then where does it come from?

If I reply to your question by saying that I do not know, you may be distressed all the more. Yet, I would be answering you correctly, because what is nothing, cannot be known.

NOTES

1. the Manichaeans [D.C.A.]
2. Isaiah 7:9. The text of the Old Testament that Augustine used was a Latin translation of the Greek Septuagint version. Sometimes, as here, the Septuagint

rendering of the original Hebrew is inaccurate. The Hebrew of Isaiah 7:9 means: "Have firm faith, or you will not stand firm" (New English Bible). [D.C.A.]
3. Augustine held that we attain knowledge by divine illumination; God is the "inner teacher" who dwells within our mind. [D.C.A.]
4. Psalms 14:1 (13:1 in some versions); Psalms 53:1 (52:1) [D.C.A.]
5. *proper*: belonging characteristically or peculiarly to; distinctive [D.C.A.]
6. Psalms 37:4 (36:4) [D.C.A.]
7. *form*: pattern, archetype. According to Augustine, the forms of all creatures exist in the mind of God, and God makes a creature (e.g., a horse) by imparting a form (e.g., "horseness") to matter. It is due to its form that a thing exists. [D.C.A.]
8. Psalms 102:26–27 (101:26–27) [D.C.A.]
9. Wisdom 7:27 [D.C.A.]
10. Psalms 14:1 (13:1); Psalms 53:1 (52:1) [D.C.A.]
11. Matthew 10:30 [D.C.A.]

QUESTIONS FOR REFLECTION AND DISCUSSION

1. Does wrongdoing consist in preferring temporal things to eternal things?
2. Is evil a lack of 'being' (lack of form)?
3. Is God ultimately responsible for the evil we commit?
4. Does the will to live an upright life bring happiness?
5. Does the existence of truth prove that God exists?

SUGGESTIONS FOR FURTHER READING

I. Primary Sources

The Happy Life, in *Writings of Saint Augustine 1*, trans. Ludwig Schopp. New York: Cima, Fathers of the Church Ser., 1948, pp. 43–84.

A discussion of the universal human desire for happiness. Augustine argues that happiness lies in truth, which is God, the Supreme Good.

Divine Providence and the Problem of Evil, in *Writings of Saint Augustine 1*, trans. Robert P. Russell. New York: Cima, Fathers of the Church Ser., 1948, pp. 239–332.

An explanation of how the existence of evil can be reconciled with the universal order of God's providence.

The Nature of the Good Against the Manichees, in *Augustine: Earlier Writings*, ed. and trans. John H. S. Burleigh. Philadelphia: Westminster, Library of Christian Classics, 1953, pp. 326–348.

In the context of refuting the Manichaean doctrine of good and evil, Augustine argues that all things derive their being and goodness from God, the Supreme Good, and that evil is simply a lack of being and goodness.

Confessions, trans. R. S. Pine-Coffin. Harmondsworth, England: Penguin, 1961, 347 pp.

Augustine's renowned autobiography, centering on his dramatic conversion to Christianity. In the last part of the work, Augustine reflects on the nature of memory and time.

II. Secondary Sources

Brown, Peter. *Augustine of Hippo: A Biography.* Berkeley and Los Angeles: University of California Press, 1967, 463 pp.

A thorough and widely acclaimed study of Augustine's life. The work includes discussions of Augustine's principal doctrines in their historical context.

Chadwick, Henry. *Augustine.* Oxford, England: Oxford University Press, Past Masters Ser., 1986, 122 pp.

A lucid introduction to Augustine's main ideas, divided into ten brief chapters.

Evans, G. R. *Augustine on Evil.* Cambridge, England: Cambridge University Press, 1982, 188 pp.

A study of Augustine's quest to understand the nature and origin of evil and how its existence is compatible with an all-good and all-powerful God.

Gilson, Etienne. *The Christian Philosophy of St. Augustine,* trans. L. E. M. Lynch. 1960; reprint ed., New York: Octagon, 1983, 398 pp.

An exposition of Augustine's philosophy as a search for the happiness that can only be found in possessing God. Chap. 2 of the introductory section, "The Soul's Journey to God," pp. 11–24, discusses Augustine's proof for God's existence in *The Free Choice of the Will.*

Kirwan, Christopher. *Augustine.* London: Routledge, The Arguments of the Philosophers Ser., 1989, 247 pp.

A detailed analysis of Augustine's philosophical positions. See chap. 4, "Good and Bad," pp. 60–81, and chap. 5, "Defending Free Will," pp. 82–103. For more advanced students of Augustine.

6

Thomas Aquinas

Thomas Aquinas was born at Roccasecca, Italy, in about 1224. After receiving his initial schooling from the Benedictine monks at Monte Cassino, he went to study liberal arts at the University of Naples. There he encountered members of the newly formed (in 1216) Dominican order and joined it in 1244. His mother, distraught at his decision because she wanted him to become a Benedictine, had him abducted and detained him at home for a year before allowing him to return to the order.

Aquinas began his Dominican training in Paris, where he studied philosophy and theology under the Dominican Albert (later known as Albert the Great). When Albert was sent in 1248 to Cologne, Germany, to direct a new Dominican house of studies there, Aquinas went with him. A few years later Aquinas was ordained a priest. In 1252, upon Albert's recommendation, he went back to Paris to pursue an advanced degree in theology. After receiving his degree in 1256, he became a member of the faculty of one of the two Dominican schools in the University of Paris. While teaching at the university, he began his *Summa contra gentiles* ("Comprehensive Treatise Against the Gentiles"), written to serve as a manual for Dominican missionaries.

In 1259 Aquinas was assigned to the Dominican house at Naples. Two years later he was sent to the priory at Orvieto, Italy, where he completed the *Summa contra gentiles*. He went to Rome in 1265 to open a new Dominican house of studies and, two years after that, was assigned to the priory at Viterbo, Italy. While at Rome and Viterbo he wrote Part 1 of his principal work, the *Summa theologiae* ("Comprehensive Treatise on Theology"). This work (sometimes called the *Summa theologica*) is a systematic introduction to theology intended for beginners.

In November 1268 Aquinas was sent to Paris, where he resumed teaching at the University of Paris, wrote Part 2 of the *Summa theologiae*, and began writing commentaries on various works of the Greek philosopher Aristotle. In 1272 he went to Naples to set up a new Dominican house of studies at the University of Naples. At Naples he began to work on the third and final part of the *Summa theologiae* (which was never completed). In 1274 Aquinas was called by Pope Gregory X to serve as a consultant at the Second Council of Lyons. He died at Fossanova, Italy, while on his way to Lyons.

Aquinas's major intellectual achievement was to integrate principles of Aristotelian philosophy into Christian theology. For centuries, theology had been dominated by the ideas of Augustine, whose philosophical orientation was mainly Neoplatonic (see the introduction to Chapter 5). Aristotle's influence on Christian theology, and on medieval thought in general, was rather limited. In fact, except for certain treatises on logic, most of Aristotle's works were unknown to the West until the twelfth and thirteenth centuries, when they were rediscovered.

Aquinas had been exposed to the newly available works of Aristotle at the University of Naples and studied them in greater depth under Albert at Paris and Cologne. Despite outcries from Christians who abhorred the paganism of Aristotle (some of Aquinas's teachings were officially condemned by bishops and by the universities of Oxford and Paris), Aquinas proceeded to integrate, where possible, Aristotelian philosophy with the (largely Augustinian) Christian tradition. The influence of Aristotle—whom Aquinas calls simply "the Philosopher"—is especially evident in Aquinas's two *Summas* and his *Disputed Questions* (summaries of debates he conducted on various topics as a professor of theology).

Our selections are taken from the *Summa theologiae*. Although the work is primarily theological, it contains sections of philosophical argumentation, and it is from these sections that our three readings come. Our selection from the "Treatise on Man" (from Part 1 of the *Summa theologiae*) discusses the relation of the body and the soul. Aquinas rejects Plato's view that the body and the soul are two separate "things" and follows Aristotle's doctrine that body and soul are two principles, related to each other as matter ('stuff') to form (that which makes the 'stuff' what it is). The human soul, as form, is the inner principle that makes a potentially human body what it is (a human body). Aquinas diverges from Aristotle in arguing that the human soul—despite the fact that it is a principle and not a thing—is immortal.

In our selection from the "Treatise on Happiness" (from the first part of Part 2 of the *Summa theologiae*), Aquinas inquires about the ultimate end (goal) of human beings. He agrees with Aristotle that the end is happiness, which everyone desires, and that complete happiness is unattainable in this life. Unlike Aristotle, he holds that there is an afterlife and that complete happiness is possible through union with God in the next life.

In our final selection, taken from the "Treatise on Law" (also from the first part of Part 2 of the *Summa theologiae*), Aquinas develops a theory of 'natural law.' By 'natural law' he does not mean the laws of the physical world, such as the law of gravity, but the moral law that follows from the nature of human beings as rational animals.

A final note: Each main part of the *Summa theologiae* is divided into "questions," and each question is subdivided into "articles." Each article, in turn, has four sections: (1) a list of objections to the position Aquinas will defend, (2) a citation of an authority supporting Aquinas's position, (3) a presentation of Aquinas's own arguments, and (4) a response to the objections raised in (1). Our readings are taken entirely from the third sections of the articles selected; the other three sections have been omitted because of limitations of space and because of the considerable historical background required to understand many of the objections. Readers who seek a fuller understanding of Aquinas's arguments are encouraged to study the other three sections of the articles as well (see the bibliography).

SUMMA THEOLOGIAE

PART 1, "TREATISE ON MAN"

Question 75: On Man Who Is Composed of a Spiritual and a Corporeal Substance: and First, Concerning What Belongs to the Essence of the Soul

First Article: Whether the Soul Is a Body? . . . To seek the nature of the soul, we must premise that the soul is defined as the first principle[1] of life in those things in our world which live; for we call living things *animate*, and those things which have no life, *inanimate*.[2] Now life is shown principally by two activities, knowledge and movement. The philosophers of old, not being able to rise above their imagination, supposed that the principle of these actions was something corporeal; for they asserted that only bodies were real things, and that what is not corporeal is nothing. Hence they maintained that the soul is some sort of body. This opinion can be proved in many ways to be false; but we shall make use of only one proof, which shows quite universally and certainly that the soul is not a body.

It is manifest that not every principle of vital action is a soul, for then the eye would be a soul, as it is a principle of vision; and the same might be applied to the other instruments of the soul. But it is the *first* principle of life which we call the soul. Now, though a body may be a principle of life, as the heart is a principle of life in an animal, yet no body can be the first principle of life. For it is clear that to be a principle of life, or to be a living thing, does not belong to a body as a body, since, if that were the case, every body would be a living thing, or a principle of life. Therefore a body is competent to be a living thing, or even a principle of life, as *such* a body. Now that it is actually[3] such a body it owes to some principle which is called its act. Therefore the soul, which is the first principle of life, is not a body, but the act of a body; just as heat, which is the principle of calefaction,[4] is not a body, but an act of a body. . . .

Second Article: Whether the Human Soul Is Something Subsistent?[5] . . . It must necessarily be allowed that the principle of intellectual operation,[6] which we call the soul of man, is a principle both incorporeal and subsistent. For it is clear that by means of the intellect man can know all corporeal things. Now whatever knows certain things cannot have any of them in its own nature, because that which is in it naturally would impede the knowledge of anything else. Thus we observe that a sick man's tongue, being unbalanced by a feverish and bitter humor, is insensible to anything sweet, and everything seems bitter to it. Therefore, if the intellectual principle contained within itself the nature of any body, it would be unable to know all bodies. Now every body has its own determinate nature. Therefore it is impossible for the intellectual principle to be a body. It is also impossible for it to understand by means of a bodily organ, since the determinate nature of that organ would likewise impede knowledge of all bodies; as when a certain determinate color is not only in the pupil of the eye, but also in a glass vase, the liquid in the vase seems to be of that same color.

Therefore the intellectual principle, which we call the mind or the intellect, has essentially an operation in which the body does not share. Now only that which subsists in itself can have an operation in itself. For nothing can operate but what is actual, and so a thing operates according as it is; for which reason we do not say that heat imparts heat, but that what is hot gives heat. We must conclude, therefore, that the human soul, which is called intellect or mind, is something incorporeal and subsistent. . . .

Fourth Article: Whether the Soul Is Man? . . . The assertion, *the soul is a man,* can be taken in two senses. First, that man is a soul, though this particular man (Socrates, for instance) is not a soul, but composed of soul and body. I say this, because some held that the form alone belongs to the species, while matter is part of the individual, and not of the species.[7] This cannot be true, for to the nature of the species belongs what the definition signifies, and in natural things the definition does not signify the form only, but the form and the matter. Hence, in natural things the matter is part of the species. . . . Just as it belongs to the nature of this particular man to be composed of this soul, of this flesh, and of these bones, so it belongs to the nature of man to be composed of soul, flesh, and bones. . . .

That *the soul is a man* may also be understood in this sense, namely, that this soul is this man. Now this could be held if it were supposed that the operation of the sensitive soul[8] were proper to it without the body; because in that case all the operations which are attributed to man would belong only to the soul. But each thing is that which performs its own operations, and consequently that is man which performs the operations of a man.

But . . . sensation is not the operation of the soul alone.[9] Since, then, sensation is an operation of man, but not proper to the soul, it is clear that man is not only a soul, but something composed of soul and body. . . .

Fifth Article: Whether the Soul Is Composed of Matter and Form? . . . The soul has no matter. We may consider this question in two ways. First, from the notion of a soul in general, for it belongs to the notion of a soul to be the form of a body. Now, either it is a form in its entirety, or by virtue of some part of itself. If in its entirety, then it is impossible that any part of it should be matter, if by matter we understand something purely potential; for a form, as such, is an act, and that which is purely potential cannot be part of an act, since potentiality is repugnant to actuality as being its opposite. If, however, it be a form by virtue of a part of itself, then we shall call that part the soul, and that matter, which it actualizes first, we shall call the *primary animate*.

Secondly, we may proceed from the specific notion of the human soul, inasmuch as it is intellectual. For it is clear that whatever is received into something is received according to the condition of the recipient. Now a thing is known in as far as its form is in the knower.[10] But the intellectual soul knows a thing in its nature absolutely[11]: for instance, it knows a stone absolutely as a stone; and therefore the form of a stone absolutely, as to its proper formal notion,[12] is in the intellectual soul. Therefore the intellectual soul itself is an absolute form, and not something composed of matter and form. For if the intellectual soul were composed of matter and form, the forms of things would be received into it as individuals, and so it would only know the individual; just as it happens with the sensitive powers which receive forms in a corporeal organ. For matter is the principle by which forms are individuated.[13] It follows, therefore, that the intellectual soul, and every intellectual substance which has knowledge of forms absolutely, is exempt from composition of matter and form. . . .

Sixth Article: Whether the Human Soul Is Corruptible?[14] . . . We must assert that the intellectual principle which we call the human soul is incorruptible. For a thing may be corrupted in two ways—in itself and accidentally. Now it is impossible for any subsistent being to be generated or corrupted accidentally, that is, by the generation or corruption of something else. For generation and corruption belong to a thing in the same way that being belongs to it, which is acquired by generation and lost by corruption. Therefore, whatever has being in itself cannot be generated or corrupted except in itself; while things which do not subsist, such as accidents and material forms,[15] acquire being or lose it through the generation or corruption of composites. Now it was shown above that . . . the human soul [is subsistent; therefore it] could not be corrupted unless it were corrupted in itself. This is impossible, not only as regards the human soul, but also as regards anything subsistent that is a form alone. For it is clear that what belongs to a thing by virtue of the thing itself is inseparable from it. But being belongs to a form, which is an act, by virtue of itself. And thus, matter acquires actual being according as it acquires form; while it is corrupted so far as the form is separated from it. But it is impossible for a form to be separated from itself; and therefore it is impossible for a subsistent form to cease to exist. . . .

Question 76: The Union of Body and Soul

First Article: Whether the Intellectual Principle Is United to the Body as Its Form? . . . We must assert that the intellect which is the principle of intellectual operation is the form of the human body. For that whereby primarily anything acts is a form of the thing to which the act is attributed. For instance, that whereby a body is primarily healed is health, and that whereby the soul knows primarily is knowledge; hence health is a form of the body, and knowledge is a form of the soul. The reason for this is that nothing acts except so far as it is in act; and so, a thing acts by that whereby it is in act. Now it is clear that the first thing by which the body lives is the soul. And as life appears through various operations in different degrees of living things, that whereby we primarily perform each of all these vital actions is the soul. For the soul is the primary principle of our nourishment, sensation, and local movement; and likewise of our understanding. Therefore this principle by which primarily we understand, whether it be called the intellect or the intellectual soul, is the form of the body. This is the demonstration used by Aristotle.[16]

But if anyone says that the intellectual soul is not the form of the body, he must explain how it is that this action of understanding is the action of this particular man; for each one is conscious that it is he himself who understands. Now an action may be attributed to anyone in three ways, as is clear from the Philosopher.[17] For a thing is said to move or act, either by virtue of its whole self, for instance, as a physician heals; or by virtue of a part, as a man sees by his eye; or through an accidental quality, as when we say that something that is white builds, because it is accidental to the builder to be white. So when we say that Socrates or Plato understands, it is clear that this is not attributed to him accidentally, since it is ascribed to him as man, which is predicated of him essentially. We must therefore say either that Socrates understands by virtue of his whole self, as Plato maintained, holding that man is an intellectual soul;[18] or that the intellect is a part of Socrates. The first cannot stand . . . because it is one and the same man who is conscious both that he understands and that he senses. But one cannot sense without a body, and therefore the body must be some part of a man. It follows therefore that the intellect by which Socrates understands is a part of Socrates, so that it is in some way united to the body of Socrates. . . .

Third Article: Whether Besides the Intellectual Soul There Are in Man Other Souls Essentially Different from One Another? . . . If we suppose . . . that the soul is united to the body as its form, it is quite impossible for several essentially different souls to be in one body. . . .

An animal in which there were several souls would not be absolutely one. For nothing is absolutely one except by one form, by which a thing has being; because a thing has both being and unity from the same source, and therefore things which are denominated by various forms are not absolutely one; as, for instance, *a white man*. If, therefore, man were *living* by one form, the vegetative soul, and *animal* by another form, the sensitive soul, and *man* by another form, the intellectual soul, it would follow that man is not absolutely one. Thus Aristotle argues in *Metaphysics* 8.6, against Plato, that if the Idea[19] of an animal is distinct from the Idea of a biped, then a biped animal is not absolutely one. For this reason, against those who hold that there are several souls in the body, he asked, *what contains them?*—that is, what makes them one?[20] It cannot be said that they are united by the unity of the body; because it is rather the soul that contains the body and makes it one, than the reverse. . . .

We must therefore conclude that the sensitive soul, the intellectual soul and the nutritive soul are in man numerically one and the same soul. This can easily be explained, if we consider the differences of species and forms. For we observe that the species and forms of things differ from one another as the perfect and the less perfect; just as in the order of things, the animate are more perfect than the inanimate, animals more perfect than plants, and man more perfect than brute animals. . . . Thus the intellectual soul contains virtually[21] whatever belongs to the sensitive soul of brute animals, and to the nutritive soul of plants. Therefore, just as a surface which is of a pentagonal shape is not tetragonal by one shape, and pentagonal by another—since a tetragonal shape would be superfluous, as being contained in the pentagonal—so neither is Socrates a man by one soul, and an animal by another; but by one and the same soul he is both animal and man. . . .

Eighth Article: Whether the Whole Soul Is in Each Part of the Body? . . . Since the soul is united to the body as its form, it must necessarily be in the whole body, and in each part thereof. For it is not an accidental form, but the substantial form of the body.[22] Now the substantial form perfects not only the whole, but each part of the whole. For since a whole consists of parts, a form of the whole which does not give being to each of the parts of the body is a form consisting in composition and order, such as the form of a house; and such a form is accidental. But the soul is a substantial form, and therefore it must be the form and the act, not only of the whole, but also of each part. Therefore, on the withdrawal of the soul, just as we do not speak of an animal or a man unless equivocally (as we speak of a painted animal or a stone animal), so it is with the hand, the eye, the flesh and bones, as the Philosopher says.[23] A proof of which is that, on the withdrawal of the soul, no part of the body retains its proper work; although that which retains its species or form retains the action of the species. But act is in that of which it is the act, and therefore the soul must be in the whole body, and in each part thereof. . . .

PART 2, FIRST PART, "TREATISE ON HAPPINESS"

Question 1: Of Man's Last End[24]

First Article: Whether It Belongs to Man to Act for an End? . . . Of actions done by man those alone are properly called *human*, which are proper to man as man. Now man differs from irrational animals in this, that he is master of his actions. Wherefore those actions alone are properly called human, of which man is master. Now man is master of his actions through his reason and will; whence, too, the free-will is defined as *the faculty and will of reason*.[25] Therefore those actions are properly called human which proceed from a deliberate will. And if any other actions are found in man, they can be called actions *of a man*, but not properly *human* actions, since they are not proper to man as man.—Now it is clear that whatever actions proceed from a power, are caused by that power in accordance with the nature of its object. But the object of the will is the end and the good.[26] Therefore all human actions must be for an end. . . .

Fourth Article: Whether There Is One Last End of Human Life? . . . Absolutely speaking, it is not possible to proceed indefinitely in the matter of ends, from any point of view. For in whatsoever things there is an essential order of one to another, if the first be removed, those that are ordained to the first, must of necessity be removed also. Wherefore the Philosopher proves (*Physics* 8.5) that we cannot proceed to infinitude in causes of movement, because then there would be no first mover, without which neither can the others move, since they move only through being moved by the first mover. Now there is to be observed a twofold order in ends,—the order of intention, and the order of execution: and in either of these orders there must be something first. For that which is first in the order of intention, is the principle, as it were, moving the appetite; consequently, if you remove this principle, there will be nothing to move the appetite. On the other hand, the principle in execution is that wherein operation has its beginning; and if this principle be taken away, no one will begin to work.[27] Now the principle in the intention is the last end; while the principle in execution is the first of the things which are ordained to the end. Consequently, on neither side is it possible to go on to infinity; since if there were no last end, nothing would be desired, nor would any action have its term, nor would the intention of the agent be at rest; while if there is no first thing among those that are ordained to the end, none would begin to work at anything, and counsel would have no term, but would continue indefinitely. . . .

Sixth Article: Whether Man Wills All, Whatsoever He Wills, for the Last End? . . . Man must, of necessity, desire all, whatsoever he desires, for the last end. This is evident for two reasons. First, because whatever man desires, he desires it under the aspect of good. And if he desires it, not as his perfect good, which is the last end, he must, of necessity, desire it as tending to the perfect good, because the beginning of anything is always ordained to its completion; as is clearly the case in effects both of nature and of art. Wherefore every beginning of perfection is ordained to complete perfection which is achieved through the last end. Secondly, because the last end stands in the same relation in moving the appetite, as the first mover in other movements. Now it is clear that secondary moving causes do not move save inasmuch as they are moved by the first mover. Therefore secondary objects of the appetite do not move the appetite, except as ordained to the first object of the appetite, which is the last end. . . .

Seventh Article: Whether All Men Have the Same Last End? . . . We can speak of the last end in two ways: first, considering only the aspect of last end; secondly, considering the thing in which the aspect of last end is realized. So, then, as to the aspect of last end, all agree in desiring the last end: since all desire the fulfilment of their perfection, and it is precisely this fulfilment in which the last end consists. . . . But as to the thing in which this aspect is realized, all men are not agreed as to their last end: since some desire riches as their consummate good; some, pleasure; others, something else. Thus to every taste the sweet is pleasant; but to some, the sweetness of wine is most pleasant, to others, the sweetness of honey, or of something similar. Yet that sweet is absolutely the best of all pleasant things, in which he who has the best taste takes most pleasure. In like manner that good is most complete which the man with well-disposed affections desires for his last end. . . .

Question 2: Of Those Things in Which Man's Happiness Consists

First Article: Whether Man's Happiness Consists in Wealth? It is impossible for man's happiness to consist in wealth. For wealth is twofold, as the Philosopher says (*Politics* 1.3),[28] viz., natural and artificial. Natural wealth is that which serves man as a remedy for his natural wants, such as food, drink, clothing, cars, dwellings, and such like, while artificial wealth is that which is not a direct help to nature, as money, but is invented by the art of man, for the convenience of exchange, and as a measure of things salable.

Now it is evident that man's happiness cannot consist in natural wealth.

For wealth of this kind is sought for the sake of something else, viz., as a support of human nature: consequently it cannot be man's last end, rather is it ordained to man as to its end. . . .

And as to artificial wealth, it is not sought save for the sake of natural wealth; since man would not seek it except because, by its means, he procures for himself the necessaries of life. Consequently much less can it be considered in the light of the last end. Therefore it is impossible for happiness, which is the last end of man, to consist in wealth. . . .

Second Article: Whether Man's Happiness Consists in Honors? . . . It is impossible for happiness to consist in honor. For honor is given to a man on account of some excellence in him; and consequently it is a sign and attestation of the excellence that is in the person honored. Now a man's excellence is in proportion, especially, to his happiness, which is man's perfect good; and to its parts, i.e., those goods by which he has a certain share of happiness. And therefore honor can result from happiness, but happiness cannot principally consist therein. . . .

Fourth Article: Whether Man's Happiness Consists in Power? . . . It is impossible for happiness to consist in power; and this for two reasons. First, because power has the nature of principle, as is stated in [Aristotle's] *Metaphysics* 5.12, whereas happiness has the nature of last end. Secondly, because power has relation to good and evil, whereas happiness is man's proper and perfect good. Wherefore some happiness might consist in the good use of power, which is by virtue, rather than in power itself. . . .

Fifth Article: Whether Man's Happiness Consists in Any Bodily Good? . . . It is impossible for man's happiness to consist in the goods of the body; and this for two reasons. First, because, if a thing be ordained to another as to its end, its last end cannot consist in the preservation of its being. Hence a captain does not intend as a last end, the preservation of the ship entrusted to him, since a ship is ordained to something else as its end, viz., to navigation. Now just as the ship is entrusted to the captain that he may steer its course, so man is given over to his will and reason; according to Ecclesiasticus 15:14, *God made man from the beginning and left him in the hand of his own counsel.* Now it is evident that man is ordained to something as his end, since man is not the supreme good. Therefore the last end of man's reason and will cannot be the preservation of man's being.

Secondly, because, granted that the end of man's will and reason be the preservation of man's being, it could not be said that the end of man is some good of the body. For man's being consists in soul and body; and though the being of the body depends on the soul, yet the being of the human soul depends not on the body, as shown above [Part 1, Question 75, Second Article]; and the very body is for the soul, as matter for its form, and the instruments for the man that puts them into motion, that by their means he may do his work. Wherefore all goods of the body are ordained to the goods of the soul, as to their end. Consequently happiness, which is man's last end, cannot consist in goods of the body. . . .

Sixth Article: Whether Man's Happiness Consists in Pleasure? . . . Because bodily delights are more generally known, *the name of pleasure has been appropriated to them* ([*Nicomachean*] *Ethics* 7.13), although other delights excel them: and yet happiness does not consist in them. Because in every thing, that which pertains to its essence is distinct from its proper accident:[29] thus in man it is one thing that he is a mortal rational animal, and another that he is a risible animal. We must therefore consider that every delight is a proper accident resulting from happiness, or from some part of happiness; since the reason that a man is delighted is that he has some fitting good, either in reality, or in hope, or at least in memory. Now a fitting good, if indeed it be the perfect good, is precisely man's happiness: and if it is imperfect, it is a share of happiness, either proximate, or remote, or at least apparent. Therefore it is evident that neither is delight, which results from the perfect good, the very essence of happiness, but something resulting therefrom as its proper accident.

But bodily pleasure cannot result from the perfect good even in that way. For it results from a good apprehended by sense, which is a power of the soul, which power makes use of the body. Now, [a] good pertaining to the body, and apprehended by sense, cannot be man's perfect good. For since the rational soul excels the capacity of corporeal matter, that part of the soul which is independent of a corporeal organ has a certain infinity in regard to the body and those parts of the soul which are tied down to the body: just as immaterial things are in a way infinite as compared to material things, since a form is, after a fashion, contracted and bounded by matter, so that a form which is independent of matter is, in a way, infinite. Therefore sense, which is a power of the body, knows the singular, which is determinate through matter: whereas the intellect, which is a power independent of matter, knows the universal, which is abstracted from matter, and contains an infinite number of singulars. Consequently it is evident that [a] good which is fitting to the body, and which causes bodily delight through being apprehended by sense, is not man's perfect good, but is quite a trifle as compared with the good of the soul. . . .

Eighth Article: Whether Any Created Good Constitutes Man's Happiness? . . . It is impossible for any created good to constitute man's happiness. For happiness is the perfect good, which lulls the appetite altogether; else it would not be the last end, if something yet remained to be desired. Now the object of the will, i.e., of man's appetite, is the universal good; just as the object of the intellect is the universal true. Hence it is evident that naught can lull man's will, save the universal good. This is to be found, not in any creature, but in God alone; because every creature has goodness by participation.[30] Wherefore God alone can satisfy the will of man, according to the words of Psalms 102:5: *Who satisfieth thy desire with good things.* Therefore God alone constitutes man's happiness. . . .

Question 3: What Happiness Is

First Article: Whether Happiness Is Something Uncreated? . . . Our end is twofold. First, there is the thing itself which we desire to attain: thus for the miser, the end is money. Secondly, there is the attainment or possession, the use or enjoyment of the thing desired: thus we may say that the end of the miser is the possession of money, and the end of the intemperate man is to enjoy something pleasurable. In the first sense, then, man's last end is the uncreated good, namely, God, Who alone by His infinite goodness can perfectly satisfy man's will. But in the second way, man's last end is something created, existing in him, and this is nothing else than the attainment or enjoyment of the last end. Now the last end is called happiness. If, therefore, we consider man's happiness in its cause or object, then it is something uncreated; but if we consider it as to the very essence of happiness, then it is something created. . . .

Second Article: Whether Happiness Is an Operation? . . . In so far as man's happiness is something created, existing in him, we must needs say that it is an operation. For happiness is man's supreme perfection. Now each thing is perfect in so far as it is actual; since potentiality without act is imperfect. Consequently happiness must consist in man's last act. But it is evident that operation is the last act of the operator; wherefore the Philosopher calls it *second act* (*De anima* ["On the Soul"] 2.1):[31] because that which has a form can be potentially operating, just as he who knows is potentially considering. And hence it is that in other things, too, each one is said to be *for its operation* ([Aristotle] *De caelo* ["On the Heavens"] 2.3). Therefore man's happiness must of necessity consist in an operation. . . .

Third Article: Whether Happiness Is an Operation of the Sensitive Part, or of the Intellective Part Only? . . . A thing may belong to happiness in three ways: (1) essentially, (2) antecedently, (3) consequently. Now the operation of sense cannot belong to happiness essentially. For man's happiness consists essentially in his being united to the Uncreated Good, Which is his last end, as shown above (First Article); to Which man cannot be united by an operation of his senses. Again, in like manner, because, as shown above (Question 2, Fifth Article), man's happiness does not consist in goods of the body, which goods alone, however, we attain through the operation of the senses.

Nevertheless the operations of the senses can belong to happiness, both antecedently and consequently: antecedently, in respect of imperfect hapiness, such as can be had in this life, since the operation of the intellect demands a previous operation of the sense; [and] consequently, in that perfect happiness which we await in heaven; because at the resurrection, *from the very happiness of the soul*, as Augustine says (*Letter to Dioscorus* [Letter 118]), *the body and the bodily senses will receive a certain overflow, so as to be perfected in their operations*. . . . But then the operation whereby man's mind is united to God will not depend on the senses. . . .

Eighth Article: Whether Man's Happiness Consists in the Vision of the Divine Essence? . . . Final and perfect happiness can consist in nothing else than the vision of the Divine Essence. To make this clear, two points must be observed. First, that man is not perfectly happy, so long as something remains for him to desire and seek; secondly, that the perfection of any power is determined by the nature of its object. Now the object of the intellect is *what a thing is*, i.e., the essence of a thing, according to [Aristotle's] *De anima* ["*On the Soul*" 3.6]. Wherefore the intellect attains perfection, in so far as it knows the essence of a thing. If therefore an intellect know the essence of some effect, whereby it is not possible to know the essence of the cause, i.e., to know of the cause *what it is*; that intellect cannot be said to reach that cause simply, although it may be able to gather from the effect the knowledge that the cause is. Consequently, when man knows an effect, and knows that it has a cause, there naturally remains in man the desire to know about that cause, *what it is*. And this desire is one of wonder, and causes inquiry, as is stated in the beginning of [Aristotle's] *Metaphysics* (1.2). For instance, if a man, knowing the eclipse of the sun, considers that it must be due to some cause, and knows not what that cause is, he wonders about it, and from wondering proceeds to inquire. Nor does this inquiry cease until he arrives at a knowledge of the essence of the cause.

If therefore the human intellect, knowing the essence of some created effect, knows no more of God than *that He is*; the perfection of that intellect does not yet reach simply the First Cause,[32] but there remains in it the natural desire to seek the cause. Wherefore it is not yet perfectly happy. Consequently, for perfect happiness the intellect needs to reach the very Essence of the First Cause. And thus it will have its perfection through union with God as with that object, in which alone man's happiness consists, as stated above (First Article; also Question 2, Eighth Article). . . .

Question 4: Of Those Things That Are Required for Happiness

Fifth Article: Whether the Body Is Necessary for Man's Happiness? . . . Happiness is twofold; the one is imperfect and is had in this life; the other is perfect, consisting in the vision of God. Now it is evident that the body is necessary for the happiness of this life. For the happiness of this life consists in an operation of the intellect, either speculative or practical.[33] And the operation of the intellect in this life cannot be without a phantasm,[34] which is only in a bodily organ. . . . Consequently that happiness which can be had in this life, depends, in a way, on the body.

But as to perfect Happiness, which consists in the vision of God, some have maintained that it is not possible to the soul separated from the body; and have said that the souls of saints, when separated from their bodies, do not attain to that Happiness until the Day of Judgment, when they will receive their bodies back again. And this is shown to be false. . . . For the intellect needs not the body for its operation, save on account of the phantasms, wherein it looks on the intelligible truth. Now it is evident that the Divine Essence cannot be seen by means of phantasms. . . . Wherefore, since man's perfect Happiness consists in the vision of the Divine Essence, it does not depend on the body. Consequently, without the body the soul can be happy. . . .

Sixth Article: Whether Perfection of the Body Is Necessary for Happiness? . . . If we speak of that happiness which man can acquire in this life, it is evident that a well-disposed body is of necessity required for it. For this happiness consists, according to the Philosopher ([*Nicomachean*] *Ethics* 1.13) in *an operation according to perfect virtue;* and it is clear that man can be hindered, by indisposition of the body, from every operation of virtue.

But speaking of perfect Happiness, some have maintained that no disposition of body is necessary for Happiness; indeed, that it is necessary for the soul to be entirely separated from the body. Hence Augustine (*The City of God* 22.26) quotes the words of Porphyry[35] who said that *for the soul to be happy, it must be severed from everything corporeal.* But this is unreasonable. For since it is natural to the soul to be united to the body, it is not possible for the perfection of the soul to exclude its natural perfection.

Consequently, we must say that perfect disposition of the body is necessary, both antecedently and consequently, for that Happiness which is in all ways perfect.—Antecedently, because, as Augustine says (*The Literal Meaning of Genesis* 12.35), *if the body be such, that the governance thereof is difficult and burdensome, like unto flesh which is corruptible and weighs upon the soul, the mind is turned away from that vision of the highest heaven.* Whence he concludes that, *when this body will no longer be "natural," but "spiritual," then will it be equalled to the angels, and that will be its glory, which erstwhile was its burden.*— [And perfect disposition of the body is necessary] consequently, because from the Happiness of the soul there will be an overflow on to the body, so that this too will obtain its perfection. Hence Augustine says (*Letter to Dioscorus*) that *God gave the soul such a powerful nature that from its exceeding fulness of happiness the vigor of incorruption overflows into the lower nature.* . . .

Question 5: Of the Attainment of Happiness

Third Article: Whether One Can Be Happy in This Life? . . . A certain participation of Happiness can be had in this life, but perfect and true Happiness cannot be had in this life. This may be seen from a twofold consideration.

First, from the general notion of happiness. For since happiness is a *perfect and sufficient good*, it excludes every evil, and fulfils every desire. But in this life every evil cannot be excluded. For this present life is subject to many unavoidable evils, to ignorance on the part of the intellect; to inordinate affection on the part of the appetite, and to many penalties on the part of the body; as Augustine sets forth in *The City of God* 19.4. Likewise neither can the desire for good be satiated in this life. For man naturally desires the good, which he has, to be abiding. Now the goods of the present life pass away; since life itself passes away, which we naturally desire to have, and would wish to hold abidingly, for man naturally shrinks from death. Wherefore it is impossible to have true Happiness in this life.

Secondly, from a consideration of the specific nature of Happiness, viz., the vision of the Divine Essence, which man cannot obtain in this life. . . . Hence it is evident that none can attain true and perfect Happiness in this life. . . .

Eighth Article: Whether Every Man Desires Happiness? . . . Happiness can be considered in two ways. First, according to the general notion of happiness: and thus, of necessity, every man desires happiness. For the general notion of happiness consists in the perfect good, as stated above (Third Article). But since good is the object of the will, the perfect good of a man is that which entirely satisfies his will. Consequently to desire happiness is nothing else than to desire that one's will be satisfied. And this everyone desires. Secondly, we may speak of Happiness according to its specific notion, as to that in which it consists. And thus all do not know Happiness; because they know not in what thing the general notion of happiness is found. And consequently, in this respect, not all desire it. . . .

PART 2, FIRST PART, "TREATISE ON LAW"

Question 91: On the Various Kinds of Law

First Article: Whether There Is an Eternal Law? . . . Law is nothing else but a dictate of practical reason emanating from the ruler who governs a perfect community. Now it is evident, granted that the world is ruled by divine providence . . . that the whole community of the universe is governed by the divine reason. Therefore the very notion of the government of things in God, the ruler of the universe, has the nature of a law. And since the divine reason's conception of things is not subject to time, but is eternal, according to Proverbs 8:23, therefore it is that this kind of law must be called eternal. . . .

Second Article: Whether There Is in Us a Natural Law? . . . Law, being a rule and measure, can be in a person in two ways: in one way, as in him that rules and measures; in another way, as in that which is ruled and measured, since a thing is ruled and measured in so far as it partakes of the rule or measure. Therefore, since all things subject to divine providence are ruled and measured by the eternal law . . . it is evident that all things partake in some way in the eternal law, in so far as, namely, from its being imprinted on them, they derive their respective inclinations to their proper acts and ends. Now among all others, the rational creature is subject to divine providence in a more excellent way, in so far as it itself partakes of a share of providence, by being provident both for itself and for others. Therefore it has a share of the eternal reason, whereby it has a natural inclination to its proper act and end; and this participation of the eternal law in the rational creature is called the natural law. . . .

Question 94: The Natural Law

Second Article: Whether the Natural Law Contains Several Precepts, or Only One? . . . A certain order is to be found in those things that are apprehended by men. For that which first falls under apprehension is *being*, the understanding of which is included in all things whatsoever a man apprehends. Therefore the first indemonstrable principle is that *the same thing cannot be affirmed and denied at the same time*, which is based on the notion of *being* and *not-being*: and on this principle all others are based, as is stated in [Aristotle's] *Metaphysics* 4.3. Now as *being* is the first thing that falls under the apprehension absolutely, so *good* is the first thing that falls under the apprehension of the practical reason, which is directed to action (since every agent acts for an end, which has the nature of good). Consequently, the first principle in the practical reason is one founded on the nature of good, viz., that *good is that which all things seek after*.[36] Hence this is the first precept of law, that *good is to be done and promoted, and evil is to be avoided*. All other precepts of the natural law are based upon this; so that all the things which the practical reason naturally apprehends as man's good belong to the precepts of the natural law under the form of things to be done or avoided.

Since, however, good has the nature of an end, and evil, the nature of the contrary, hence it is that all those things to which man has a natural inclination are naturally apprehended by reason as being good, and consequently as objects of pursuit, and their contraries as evil, and objects of avoidance. Therefore, the order of the precepts of the natural law is according to the order of natural inclinations. For there is in man, first of all, an nclination to good in accordance with the nature which he has in common with all substances, inasmuch, namely, as every substance seeks the preservation of its own being, according to its nature; and by reason of this inclination, whatever is a means of preserving human life, and of warding off its obstacles, belongs to the natural law. Secondly, there is in man an inclination to things that pertain to him more specially, according to that nature which he has in common with other animals; and in virtue of this inclination, those things are said to belong to the natural law *which nature has taught to all animals*,[37] such as sexual intercourse, the education of offspring and so forth. Thirdly, there is in man an inclination to good according to the nature of his reason, which nature is proper to him. Thus man has a natural inclination to know the truth about God, and to live in society; and in this respect, whatever pertains to this inclination belongs to the natural law: e.g., to shun ignorance, to avoid offending those among whom one has to live, and other such things regarding the above inclination. . . .

Fourth Article: Whether the Natural Law Is the Same in All Men? . . . As we have stated above, to the natural law belong those things to which a man is inclined naturally; and among these it is proper to man to be inclined to act according to reason. Now it belongs to the reason to proceed from what is common to what is proper, as is stated in [Aristotle's] *Physics* 1.1. The speculative reason, however, is differently situated, in this matter, from the practical reason. For, since the speculative reason is concerned chiefly with necessary things, which cannot be otherwise than they are, its proper conclusions, like the universal principles, contain the truth without fail. The practical reason, on the other hand, is concerned with contingent matters, which is the domain of human actions; and, consequently, although there is necessity in the common principles, the more we descend towards the particular, the more frequently we encounter defects. Accordingly, then, in speculative matters truth is the same in all men, both as to principles and as to conclusions; although the truth is not known to all as regards the conclusions, but only as regards the principles which are called *common notions*.[38] But in matters of action, truth or practical rectitude is not the same for all as to what is particular, but only as to the common principles; and where there is the same rectitude in relation to particulars, it is not equally known to all.

It is therefore evident that, as regards the common principles whether of speculative or of practical reason, truth or rectitude is the same for all, and is equally known by all. But as to the proper conclusions of the speculative reason, the truth is the same for all, but it is not equally known to all. Thus, it is true for all that the three angles of a triangle are together equal to two right angles, although it is not known to all. But as to the proper conclusions of the practical reason, neither is the truth or rectitude the same for all, nor, where it is the same, is it equally known by all. Thus, it is right and true for all to act according to reason, and from this principle it follows, as a proper conclusion, that goods entrusted to another should be restored to their owner. Now this is true for the majority of cases. But it may happen in a particular case that it would be injurious, and therefore unreasonable, to restore goods held in trust; for instance, if they are claimed for the purpose of fighting against one's country. And this principle will be found to fail the more, according as we descend further towards the particular, e.g., if one were to say that goods held in trust should be restored with such and such a guarantee, or in such and such a way; because the greater the number of conditions added, the greater the number of ways in which the principle may fail, so that it be not right to restore or not to restore.

Consequently, we must say that the natural law, as to the first common principles, is the same for all, both as to rectitude and as to knowledge. But as to certain more particular aspects, which are conclusions, as it were, of those common principles, it is the same for all in the majority of cases, both as to rectitude and as to knowledge; and yet in some few cases it may fail, both as to rectitude, by reason of certain obstacles (just as natures subject to generation and corruption fail in some few cases because of some obstacle), and as to knowledge, since in some the reason is perverted by passion, or evil habit, or an evil disposition of nature. Thus at one time theft, although it is expressly contrary to the natural law, was not considered wrong among the Germans, as Julius Caesar relates[39]. . . .

Fifth Article: Whether the Natural Law Can Be Changed? . . . A change in the natural law may be understood in two ways. First, by way of addition. In this sense, nothing hinders the natural law from being changed, since many things for the benefit of human life have been added over and above the natural law, both by the divine law and by human laws.

Secondly, a change in the natural law may be understood by way of subtraction, so that what previously was according to the natural law, ceases to be so. In this sense, the natural law is altogether unchangeable in its first principles. But in its secondary principles, which, as we have said, are certain detailed proximate conclusions drawn from the first principles, the natural law is not changed so that what it prescribes be not right in most cases. But it may be changed in some particular cases of rare occurrence, through some special causes hindering the observance of such precepts, as was stated above. . . .

Sixth Article: Whether the Natural Law Can Be Abolished From the Heart of Man? . . . As we have stated above, there belong to the natural law, first, certain most common precepts that are known to all; and secondly, certain secondary and more particular precepts, which are, as it were, conclusions following closely from first principles. As to the common principles, the natural law, in its universal meaning, cannot in any way be blotted out from men's hearts. But it is blotted out in the case of a particular action, in so far as reason is hindered from applying the common principle to the particular action because of concupiscence[40] or some other passion. . . . But as to the other, i.e., the secondary precepts, the natural law can be blotted out from the human heart, either by evil persuasions, just as in speculative matters errors occur in respect of necessary conclusions; or by vicious customs and corrupt habits, as among some men, theft, and even unnatural vices, as the Apostle [Paul] states (Romans 1:24), were not esteemed sinful.

NOTES

1. *principle*: source, that from which something proceeds. The soul is the *first* principle of life because it is the primary inner source (God is the primary external source) of the life of a living being. As Aquinas explains, living beings also have other inner principles of activity; e.g., the eye is a source of seeing. These other principles are secondary to the soul because a being could not perform such activities if it were not alive. [D.C.A.]
2. The Latin adjectives *animatus* ("animate") and *inanimatus* ("inanimate") derive from the noun *anima* ("soul"). [D.C.A.]
3. In Aquinas's philosophy, the actual is contrasted to the potential. A being has a potency for something if it can be (or do) something but is not (or is not doing) it. A potency is actualized when the being becomes (or does) that of which it was capable of becoming (or doing). According to Aquinas, the soul is related to the body as act to potency; a body that is potentially alive is actually alive because of its soul. [D.C.A.]
4. *calefaction*: heating [D.C.A.]
5. *subsistent*: able to exist on its own (subsist). The question Aquinas asks here is whether the soul is able to exist without the body. [D.C.A.]
6. *operation*: activity [D.C.A.]
7. According to Aquinas, matter and form are principles that constitute every material thing. A thing's matter is the 'stuff' of which it is made; its form is that which makes the 'stuff' to be what it is. Matter is related to form as potency to act. In the case of a living being, the body is the matter and the form is the soul.
   Species here (and in Question 76, Third Article) means the kind of being a thing is, in contrast to individual beings of that kind. The human species is the category of human being, as distinct from individual human beings, such as Socrates. Aquinas argues here that the human species includes both the matter (the body) and the form (the soul). [D.C.A.]
8. *sensitive soul*: the inner principle by which a creature is able to sense. This sensitive soul is distinct from the vegetative (nutritive) soul, the principle by which a creature is able to live, and from the intellectual (rational) soul, the principle by which a creature is able to think. Strictly speaking, any living being has only one soul: An animal's sensitive soul includes its vegetative capacities, and a human being's intellectual soul includes its vegetative and sensitive capacities (see Question 76, Third Article). [D.C.A.]

9. Sensation is not the operation of the soul alone because the body is also required for sensation. [D.C.A.]

10. Aquinas holds that the human intellect is able to abstract (*abstrahere*, "draw away") the form of a material thing from its matter and that knowledge is the presence of the abstracted form in the intellect. To use Aquinas's example of a stone, we "know" a stone when our intellect abstracts the form 'stoneness' from the matter. [D.C.A.]

11. The intellect knows a thing "in its nature absolutely" because when it abstracts the form from the matter, it leaves behind all the characteristics peculiar to that particular thing. [D.C.A.]

12. *proper formal notion*: *Proper* here means "distinctive, belonging characteristically or peculiarly to"; *formal* means "pertaining to the form"; *notion* (*ratio*) means "meaning." The "proper formal notion" of a stone is the form 'stoneness' as the distinctive meaning of the stone, abstracted by the intellect. [D.C.A.]

13. According to Aquinas, matter "individuates" form because matter makes it possible for a form to be instantiated (represented) more than once. For example, there can be more than one carrot because although all carrots have the same form ('carrotness'), they have different matter. [D.C.A.]

14. *Corruptible* here means capable of being destroyed and ceasing to exist. To ask whether the human soul is corruptible, therefore, is to ask whether it is immortal. [D.C.A.]

15. Accidents are distinguished from substance: A *substance* is something that exists in itself (e.g., a rose), while an *accident* is a property of a substance that inheres in it and cannot exist apart from it (e.g., the redness of the rose).

    A *material form* is the form of a material thing. Just as an accident cannot exist without its substance, so a material form cannot exist without its matter. [D.C.A.]

16. in *De anima* ("On the Soul") 2.2. For more information on Aristotle, see the introduction to Chapter 2. [D.C.A.]

17. *the Philosopher*: Aristotle, in *Physics* 5.1 [D.C.A.]

18. See Plato, *Alcibiades I*, 130c. Scholars disagree as to whether Plato is actually the author of this dialogue. For more information on Plato, see the introduction to Chapter 1. [D.C.A.]

19. For Plato, 'Ideas' (Forms) were nonmaterial realities that existed in a separate world, outside space and time. [D.C.A.]

20. in *De anima* ("On the Soul") 1.5 [D.C.A.]

21. *virtually* (*in sua virtute*): in its capacity [D.C.A.]

22. *substantial form*: a form that causes the being as a whole (the *substance*) to be what it is; *accidental form*: a form that causes the being to have a property (an *accident*)
    See Note 15 above. [D.C.A.]

23. Aristotle, *De anima* ("On the Soul") 2.1 [D.C.A.]

24. *Last* here means "ultimate"; *end* means "goal." [D.C.A.]

25. by Peter Lombard in *Sentences* 2.24.3. Peter Lombard (about 1095–1160) was an Italian theologian. His *Sentences* is mostly a compilation of the opinions (*sententiae* in Latin) of authorities on various theological topics. [D.C.A.]

26. A *power* is an ability to perform a kind of activity; the *object of a power* is that to which the activity is directed. The *will* is a power whose object is the good as end (goal). [D.C.A.]

27. *work* (*operari*): engage in activity [D.C.A.]

28. Not all editions of the *Politics* have the same chapter divisions; in some editions the passage to which Aquinas refers is in 1.9. In the standard Greek edition by Immanuel Bekker, the passage appears on p. 1257a. [D.C.A.]
29. *proper accident*: a property that is specific to and naturally inheres in a substance. Aquinas's example here is *risibility* ("the ability to laugh"), which is specific to and naturally inheres in a human being. [D.C.A.]
30. To have goodness by participation means to receive it from God, who is Goodness itself. The Latin verb *participare* ("to participate") derives from *partem capere* ("to take a part"). [D.C.A.]
31. Aquinas refers to Aristotle's distinction between two senses of actuality, which Aristotle says are analogous to possessing knowledge (first act) and *considering* ("exercising") that knowledge (second act). First act can exist without second act, but second act is necessary for its completion. Aquinas argues that happiness must be an *operation* (an activity, the exercise of a first act) because happiness is the ultimate perfection (*perfectio*, "completion"), and therefore must be something complete. [D.C.A.]
32. Aquinas holds that it is possible to prove that finite beings have a First Cause and that this First Cause is God. (He presents five proofs for the existence of God in *Summa theologiae 1*, Question 2, Third Article.) Aquinas's point here is that to know God as First Cause is to know *that* God is, not *what* God is (the Divine Essence). [D.C.A.]
33. The *speculative intellect* seeks knowledge for its own sake; the *practical intellect* seeks knowledge as a means to performing some practical activity. These are not two separate intellects but one intellect directed toward two different ends. [D.C.A.]
34. *phantasm*: a sensory image. According to Aquinas, in this life all human intellectual activity begins with phantasms. [D.C.A.]
35. Porphyry (233–about 305), born of Syrian parents, was a scholar and philosopher. He was a disciple of the philosopher Plotinus (205–270), who was born in Egypt and taught in Rome. Both Plotinus and Porphyry wrote in Greek. [D.C.A.]
36. Aristotle, *Nicomachean Ethics* 1.1 [D.C.A.]
37. *Digest* 1. 1. 1. The *Digest* is a codification of the works of classical jurists published by the Roman emperor Justinian in 533. [D.C.A.]
38. *common notions*: notions (*conceptiones*, "conceptions") common to all human beings. The term comes from a theological treatise of Boethius called the *Hebdomads*. Boethius (about 480–524) was a Roman statesperson, philosopher, and theologian. [D.C.A.]
39. in *The Gallic War* 6.23 [D.C.A.]
40. *concupiscence*: the human tendency to let the desire for sensual pleasure overpower reason [D.C.A.]

QUESTIONS FOR REFLECTION AND DISCUSSION

1. Is the soul the 'form' of the body?
2. Can the soul exist without the body?
3. Does every human action aim at some good?

4. Does only union with God bring complete happiness?
5. Are all natural human inclinations good?

SUGGESTIONS FOR FURTHER READING

I. Primary Sources

Treatise on Man, trans. James F. Anderson. 1962; reprint ed., Westport, Conn.: Greenwood, 1981, 178 pp.

> Translation of Questions 75–88 of Part 1 of the *Summa theologiae*. This constitutes the entire "Treatise on Man" except for Question 89: The Knowledge of the Separated Soul.

Treatise on Happiness, trans. John A. Oesterle. 1964; reprint ed., University of Notre Dame Press, 1983, 208 pp.

> Translation of Questions 1–21 of the first part of Part 2 of the *Summa theologiae*. Since the book translates not only the "Treatise on Happiness" (Questions 1–5) but also the "Treatise on Human Acts" (Questions 6–21), the title is somewhat misleading.

Treatise on Law, translated by the Fathers of the English Dominican Province. Chicago: Regnery, 1963, 116 pp.

> Translation of Questions 90–97 of the first part of Part 2 of the *Summa theologiae*. The book omits Questions 98–108 of the "Treatise on Law," which discuss the Old Law and the New Law (the divine laws of the Old and New Testaments).

"Free Will," in *The Philosophy of Thomas Aquinas: Introductory Readings*, ed. and trans. Christopher Martin. London: Routledge, 1988, pp. 157–169.

> Translation of *Disputed Questions on Evil*, Question 6: On Human Choice, or Free Will. In addition to giving his own arguments, Aquinas states and responds to 24 objections against the position that human beings have free choice.

Questions on the Soul, trans. James H. Robb. Milwaukee: Marquette University Press, 1984, 275 pp.

> A difficult but important text covering 21 questions on the human soul. For more advanced students of Aquinas.

II. Secondary Sources

Chenu, M.-D. *Toward Understanding St. Thomas*, trans. A.-M. Landry and D. Hughes. Chicago: Regnery, Library of Living Catholic Thought, 1964, 386 pp.

> Chap. 11, "The *Summa Theologiae*," pp. 297–322, explains what a *summa* is and describes the overall structure and objectives of Aquinas's *Summa theologiae*.

Copleston, F. C. *Aquinas*. Harmondsworth, England: Penguin, 1955, 272 pp.

A clear exposition of the principal themes of Aquinas's philosophy. See especially chap. 4, "Man (1): Body and Soul," pp. 156–198. Copleston's extended introduction, which is largely a response to philosophical criticisms of Aquinas raised in the 1950s, can be skipped.

Gilson, Etienne. *The Christian Philosophy of St. Thomas Aquinas*, trans. L. K. Shook. 1956; reprint ed., New York: Octagon, 1983, 502 pp.

A classic and thorough exposition of three principal topics in Aquinas's philosophy: God (Aquinas's proofs for the existence of God and his discussion of the divine attributes), pp. 29–143; nature (including human nature), pp. 147–248; and morality, pp. 251–378. For more advanced students of Aquinas.

Kenny, Anthony. *Aquinas*. New York: Hill & Wang, Past Masters Ser., 1980, 81 pp.

A introductory work with chapters on Aquinas's life and works, his metaphysical doctrine, and his theory of the mind (intellect). Kenny relates Aquinas's views to those of contemporary philosophers.

McInerny, Ralph. *Ethica Thomistica: The Moral Philosophy of Thomas Aquinas*. Washington, D.C.: Catholic University of America Press, 1982, 129 pp.

A clear and accessible account of Aquinas's ethical theory, showing how it flows from his doctrine of human nature

7

René Descartes

René Descartes was born in La Haye (now called Descartes) in the region of Touraine in France in 1596. As a youth he was educated by the Jesuits at their college at La Flèche in the region of Anjou. In about 1614 he began studying at the University of Poitiers, receiving his law degree in 1616. Deciding to travel rather than practice law, he went to Holland in 1618 to serve in the army of the Dutch Prince Maurice of Nassau as a gentleman volunteer.

One day in November 1619, while on a military tour of Germany, Descartes sat alone in a small stove-heated room reflecting on a new philosophical system that would unify all branches of learning and give them the certainty of mathematics. That night he had three dreams, which he interpreted as a divine commission to construct this new system of knowledge. Shortly afterwards he left the army, never having engaged in active combat.

Uncertain how to work out the details of the new science he had glimpsed in broad outline in his vision, Descartes continued his travels for the next several years. In 1628 he began a major work (never finished) describing the proper method for attaining truth, *Rules for the Direction of the Mind*. The following year he moved to Holland, where he did research in mathematics, laying the foundations for analytic geometry (hence the term "Cartesian coordinates"). He also did work in physics, optics, physiology, and other sciences. In 1629 he began work on a comprehensive treatise that was to explain all natural phenomena. But in 1633, shortly before it was due to be published, he learned that Galileo had been condemned by the Inquisition for his theory that the earth rotates and moves around the sun. Being Catholic and wishing to avoid conflict with Rome, Descartes withdrew the work from publication. Two sections of it were published after his death, *The World; or, Treatise on Light* and *Treatise on Man*.

In 1637 Descartes published in a single volume treatises on optics, meteorology, and geometry, prefaced by a *Discourse on the Method of Rightly Conducting One's Reason and Seeking the Truth in the Sciences*. The *Discourse* is a brief statement of his new method, whose scientific fruitfulness is demonstrated in the three following treatises. (This work also presents autobiographical material and discusses certain philosophical issues.) From 1638 to 1640 Descartes expanded the ideas on method and philosophy set forth in the *Discourse* in his new work, *Meditations on First Philosophy in Which Are Demonstrated the Existence of God and the Immortality of the Soul*. He distributed the *Meditations* to friends for criticism, and in 1641 published the new treatise together with six sets of *Objections* his friends had raised and his *Replies to the Objections*. In the 1642 edition he added a seventh set of objections and replies and changed the last part of the title from "the immortality of the soul" to "the distinction between the human soul and the body." Descartes's later works include *Principles of Philosophy* (1644) and *The Passions of the Soul* (1649).

Meanwhile, Queen Christina of Sweden had been requesting that Descartes come to Stockholm to tutor her in philosophy. After much hesitation, he set sail for Sweden in the fall of 1649. The harsh winter of 1649–1650, together with the rigorous schedule imposed on him by the queen (e.g., philosophy lessons at five o'clock in the morning) took its toll on his health. In February 1650 he caught pneumonia and died. He was buried in Stockholm, but his remains were later brought back to France and buried in Paris.

Our selection is from *Meditations on First Philosophy*. By 'first philosophy' Descartes means truths about the basic topics of philosophy, which for him are God, the soul, and the external world. The term *meditations* is meant seriously: The reader is not simply to read the words Descartes has written but to accompany him on each step of his six-stage intellectual journey to indubitable philosophical truth.

Descartes begins by explaining his "method of doubt." He will not accept as true anything of which he cannot be absolutely certain. But practically everything seems open to doubt: Descartes reflects that he might even be deceived in his belief that there is an external world. He realizes, however, that he can be certain of at least one thing—that he exists. For even if he is deceived about the existence of the external world, he could not be deceived unless he existed. As he formulates this argument elsewhere, "I think, therefore I am." Proceeding from the certainty of his own existence, Descartes goes on to prove that God exists and then to prove that material things exist.

With regard to human nature, Descartes argues that a human being is essentially "a thing that thinks." The soul (mind) can exist without the body, but in this life it is, in some mysterious way, "very closely joined" to the body. Since the soul and the body are very different kinds of things, Descartes finds it difficult to explain how one can affect the other.

MEDITATIONS ON FIRST PHILOSOPHY

FIRST MEDITATION

What Can Be Called into Doubt

Some years ago I was struck by the large number of falsehoods that I had accepted as true in my childhood, and by the highly doubtful nature of the whole edifice that I had subsequently based on them. I realized that it was necessary, once in the course of my life, to demolish everything completely and start again right from the foundations if I wanted to establish anything at all in the sciences that was stable and likely to last. But the task looked an enormous one, and I began to wait until I should reach a mature enough age to ensure that no subsequent time of life would be more suitable for tackling such inquiries. This led me to put the project off for so long that I would now be to blame if by pondering over it any further I wasted the time still left for carrying it out. So today I have expressly rid my mind of all worries and arranged for myself a clear stretch of free time. I am here quite alone, and at last I will devote myself sincerely and without reservation to the general demolition of my opinions.

But to accomplish this, it will not be necessary for me to show that all my opinions are false, which is something I could perhaps never manage. Reason now leads me to think that I should hold back my assent from opinions which are not completely certain and indubitable just as carefully as I do from those which are patently false. So, for the purpose of rejecting all my opinions, it will be enough if I find in each of them at least some reason for doubt. And to do this I will not need to run through them all individually, which would be an endless task. Once the foundations of a building are undermined, anything built on them collapses of its own accord; so I will go straight for the basic principles on which all my former beliefs rested.

177

Whatever I have up till now accepted as most true I have acquired either from the senses or through the senses. But from time to time I have found that the senses deceive, and it is prudent never to trust completely those who have deceived us even once.

Yet although the senses occasionally deceive us with respect to objects which are very small or in the distance, there are many other beliefs about which doubt is quite impossible, even though they are derived from the senses—for example, that I am here, sitting by the fire, wearing a winter dressing-gown, holding this piece of paper in my hands, and so on. Again, how could it be denied that these hands or this whole body are mine? Unless perhaps I were to liken myself to madmen, whose brains are so damaged by the persistent vapours of melancholia that they firmly maintain they are kings when they are paupers, or say they are dressed in purple when they are naked, or that their heads are made of earthenware, or that they are pumpkins, or made of glass. But such people are insane, and I would be thought equally mad if I took anything from them as a model for myself.

A brilliant piece of reasoning! As if I were not a man who sleeps at night, and regularly has all the same experiences while asleep as madmen do when awake—indeed sometimes even more improbable ones. How often, asleep at night, am I convinced of just such familiar events—that I am here in my dressing-gown, sitting by the fire—when in fact I am lying undressed in bed! Yet at the moment my eyes are certainly wide awake when I look at this piece of paper; I shake my head and it is not asleep; as I stretch out and feel my hand I do so deliberately, and I know what I am doing. All this would not happen with such distinctness to someone asleep. Indeed! As if I did not remember other occasions when I have been tricked by exactly similar thoughts while asleep! As I think about this more carefully, I see plainly that there are never any sure signs by means of which being awake can be distinguished from being asleep. The result is that I begin to feel dazed, and this very feeling only reinforces the notion that I may be asleep. . . .

And yet firmly rooted in my mind is the long-standing opinion that there is an omnipotent God who made me the kind of creature that I am. How do I know that he has not brought it about that there is no earth, no sky, no extended thing, no shape, no size, no place, while at the same time ensuring that all these things appear to me to exist just as they do now? What is more, since I sometimes believe that others go astray in cases where they think they have the most perfect knowledge, may I not similarly go wrong every time I add two and three or count the sides of a square, or in some even simpler matter, if that is imaginable? But perhaps God would not have allowed me to be deceived in this way, since he is said to be supremely good. But if it were inconsistent with his goodness to have created me such that I am deceived all the time, it would seem equally foreign to his goodness to allow me to be deceived even occasionally; yet this last assertion cannot be made.

Perhaps there may be some who would prefer to deny the existence of so powerful a God rather than believe that everything else is uncertain. Let us not argue with them, but grant them that everything said about God is a fiction. According to their supposition, then, I have arrived at my present state by fate or chance or a continuous chain of events, or by some other means; yet since deception and error seem to be imperfections, the less powerful they make my original cause, the more likely it is that I am so imperfect as to be deceived all the time. I have no answer to these arguments, but am finally compelled to admit that there is not one of my former beliefs about which a doubt may not properly be raised; and this is not a flippant or ill-considered conclusion, but is based on powerful and well thought-out reasons. So in the future I must withhold my assent from these former beliefs just as carefully as I would from obvious falsehoods, if I want to discover any certainty. . . .

In the meantime, I know that no danger or error will result from my plan, and that I cannot possibly go too far in my distrustful attitude. This is because the task now in hand does not involve action but merely the acquisition of knowledge.

I will suppose therefore that not God, who is supremely good and the source of truth, but rather some malicious demon of the utmost power and cunning has employed all his energies in order to deceive me. I shall think that the sky, the air, the earth, colours, shapes, sounds and all external things are merely the delusions of dreams which he has devised to ensnare my judgement. I shall consider myself as not having hands or eyes, or flesh, or blood or senses, but as falsely believing that I have all these things. I shall stubbornly and firmly persist in this meditation; and, even if it is not in my power to know any truth, I shall at least do what is in my power, that is, resolutely guard against assenting to any falsehoods, so that the deceiver, however powerful and cunning he may be, will be unable to impose on me in the slightest degree. But this is an arduous undertaking, and a kind of laziness brings me back to normal life. I am like a prisoner who is enjoying an imaginary freedom while asleep; as he begins to suspect that he is asleep, he dreads being woken up, and goes along with the pleasant illusion as long as he can. In the same way, I happily slide back into my old opinions and dread being shaken out of them, for fear that my peaceful sleep may be followed by hard labour when I wake, and that I shall have to toil not in the light, but amid the inextricable darkness of the problems I have now raised.

SECOND MEDITATION

The Nature of the Human Mind, and How It Is Better Known Than the Body

So serious are the doubts into which I have been thrown as a result of yesterday's meditation that I can neither put them out of my mind nor see any way of resolving them. It feels as if I have fallen unexpectedly into a deep whirlpool which tumbles me around so that I can neither stand on the bottom nor swim up to the top. Nevertheless I will make an effort and once more attempt the same path which I started on yesterday. Anything which admits of the slightest doubt I will set aside just as if I had found it to be wholly false; and I will proceed in this way until I recognize something certain, or, if nothing else, until I at least recognize for certain that there is no certainty. Archimedes[1] used to demand just one firm and immovable point in order to shift the entire earth; so I too can hope for great things if I manage to find just one thing, however slight, that is certain and unshakeable.

I will suppose then, that everything I see is spurious. I will believe that my memory tells me lies, and that none of the things that it reports ever happened. I have no senses. Body, shape, extension, movement and place are chimeras. So what remains true? Perhaps just the one fact that nothing is certain.

Yet apart from everything I have just listed, how do I know that there is not something else which does not allow even the slightest occasion for doubt? Is there not a God, or whatever I may call him, who puts into me the thoughts I am now having? But why do I think this, since I myself may perhaps be the author of these thoughts? In that case am not I, at least, something? But I have just said that I have no senses and no body. This is the sticking point: what follows from this? Am I not so bound up with a body and with senses that I cannot exist without them? But I have convinced myself that there is absolutely nothing in the world, no sky, no earth, no minds, no bodies. Does it now follow that I too do not exist? No: if I convinced myself of something then I certainly existed. But there is a deceiver of supreme power and cunning who is deliberately and constantly deceiving me. In that case I too undoubtedly exist, if he is deceiving me; and let him deceive me as much as he can, he will never bring it about that I am nothing so long as I think that I am something. So after considering everything very thoroughly, I must finally conclude that this proposition, *I am, I exist*, is necessarily true whenever it is put forward by me or conceived in my mind.

But I do not yet have a sufficient understanding of what this 'I' is, that now necessarily exists. So I must be on my guard against carelessly taking something else to be this 'I', and so making a mistake in the very item of knowledge that I maintain is the most certain and evident of all. I will therefore go back and meditate on what I originally believed myself to be, before I embarked on this present train of thought. I will then subtract anything capable of being weakened, even minimally, by the arguments now introduced, so that what is left at the end may be exactly and only what is certain and unshakeable.

What then did I formerly think I was? A man. But what is a man? Shall I say 'a rational animal'? No; for then I should have to inquire what an animal is, what rationality is, and in this way one question would lead me down the slope to other harder ones, and I do not now have the time to waste on subtleties of this kind. Instead I propose to concentrate on what came into my thoughts spontaneously and quite naturally whenever I used to consider what I was. Well, the first thought to come to mind was that I had a face, hands, arms and the whole mechanical structure of limbs which can be seen in a corpse, and which I called the body. The next thought was that I was nourished, that I moved about, and that I engaged in sense-perception and thinking; and these actions I attributed to the soul. But as to the nature of this soul, either I did not think about this or else I imagined it to be something tenuous, like a wind or fire or ether, which permeated my more solid parts. As to the body, however, I had no doubts about it, but thought I knew its nature distinctly. If I had tried to describe the mental conception I had of it, I would have expressed it as follows: by a body I understand whatever has a determinable shape and a definable location and can occupy a space in such a way as to exclude any other body; it can be perceived by touch, sight, hearing, taste or smell, and can be moved in various ways, not by itself but by whatever else comes into contact with it. For, according to my judgement, the power of self-movement, like the power of sensation or of thought, was quite foreign to the nature of a body; indeed, it was a source of wonder to me that certain bodies were found to contain faculties of this kind.

But what shall I now say that I am, when I am supposing that there is some supremely powerful and, if it is permissible to say so, malicious deceiver, who is deliberately trying to trick me in every way he can? Can I now assert that I possess even the most insignificant of all the attributes which I have just said belong to the nature of a body? I scrutinize them, think about them, go over them again, but nothing suggests itself; it is tiresome and pointless to go through the list once more. But what about the attributes I assigned to the soul? Nutrition or movement? Since now I do not have a body, these are mere fabrications. Sense-perception? This surely does not occur without a body, and besides, when asleep I have appeared to perceive through the senses many things which I afterwards realized I did not perceive through the senses at all. Thinking? At last I have discovered it—thought; this alone is inseparable from me. I am, I exist—that is certain. But for how long? For as long as I am thinking. For it could be that were I totally to cease from thinking, I should totally cease to exist. At present I am not admitting anything except what is necessarily true. I am, then, in the strict sense only a thing that thinks; that is, I am a mind, or intelligence, or intellect, or reason— words whose meaning I have been ignorant of until now. But for all that I am a thing which is real and which truly exists. But what kind of a thing? As I have just said—a thinking thing.

What else am I? I will use my imagination. I am not that structure of limbs which is called a human body. I am not even some thin vapour which permeates the limbs—a wind, fire, air, breath, or whatever I depict in my imagination; for these are things which I have supposed to be nothing. Let this supposition stand; for all that I am still something. And yet may it not perhaps be the case that these very things which I am supposing to be nothing, because they are unknown to me, are in reality identical with the 'I' of which I am aware? I do not know, and for the moment I shall not argue the point, since I can make judgements only about things which are known to me. I know that I exist; the question is, what is this 'I' that I know? If the 'I' is understood strictly as we have been taking it, then it is quite certain that knowledge of it does not depend on things of whose existence I am as yet unaware; so it cannot depend on any of the things which I invent in my imagination. And this very word 'invent' shows me my mistake. It would indeed be a case of fictitious invention if I used my imagination to establish that I was something or other; for imagining is simply contemplating the shape or image of a corporeal thing. Yet now I know for certain both that I exist and at the same time that all such images and, in general, everything relating to the nature of body, could be mere dreams (and chimeras).[2] Once this point has been grasped, to say 'I will use my imagination to get to know more distinctly what I am' would seem to be as silly as saying 'I am now awake, and see some truth; but since my vision is not yet clear enough, I will deliberately fall asleep so that my dreams may provide a truer and clearer representation.' I thus realize that none of the things that the imagination enables me to grasp is at all relevant to this knowledge of myself which I possess, and that the mind must therefore be most carefully diverted from such things if it is to perceive its own nature as distinctly as possible.

But what then am I? A thing that thinks. What is that? A thing that doubts, understands, affirms, denies, is willing, is unwilling, and also imagines and has sensory perceptions.

This is a considerable list, if everything on it belongs to me. But does it? Is it not one and the same 'I' who is now doubting almost everything, who nonetheless understands some things, who affirms that this one thing is true, denies everything else, desires to know more, is unwilling to be deceived, imagines many things even involuntarily, and is aware of many things which apparently come from the senses? Are not all these things just as true as the fact that I exist, even if I am asleep all the time, and even if he who created me is doing all he can to deceive me? Which of all these activities is distinct from my thinking? Which of them can be said to be separate from myself? The fact that it is I who am doubting and understanding and willing is so evident that I see no way of making it any clearer. But it is also the case that the 'I' who imagines is the same 'I'. For even if, as I have supposed, none of the objects of imagination are real, the power of imagination is something which really exists and is part of my thinking. Lastly, it is also the same 'I' who has sensory perceptions, or is aware of bodily things as it were through the senses. For example, I am now seeing light, hearing a noise, feeling heat. But I am asleep, so all this is false. Yet I certainly *seem* to see, to hear, and to be warmed. This cannot be false; what is called 'having a sensory perception' is strictly just this, and in this restricted sense of the term it is simply thinking.

From all this I am beginning to have a rather better understanding of what I am. But it still appears—and I cannot stop thinking this—that the corporeal things of which images are formed in my thought, and which the senses investigate, are known with much more distinctness than this puzzling 'I' which cannot be pictured in the imagination. And yet it is surely surprising that I should have a more distinct grasp of things which I realize are doubtful, unknown and foreign to me, than I have of that which is true and known—my own self. But I see what it is: my mind enjoys wandering off and will not yet submit to being restrained within the bounds of truth. Very well then; just this once let us give it a completely free rein, so that after a while, when it is time to tighten the reins, it may more readily submit to being curbed.

Let us consider the things which people commonly think they understand most distinctly of all; that is, the bodies which we touch and see. I do not mean bodies in general—for general perceptions are apt to be somewhat more confused—but one particular body. Let us take, for example, this piece of wax. It has just been taken from the honeycomb; it has not yet quite lost the taste of the honey; it retains some of the scent of the flowers from which it was gathered; its colour, shape and size are plain to see; it is hard, cold and can be handled without difficulty; if you rap it with your knuckle it makes a sound. In short, it has everything which appears necessary to enable a body to be known as distinctly as possible. But even as I speak, I put the wax by the fire, and look: the residual taste is eliminated, the smell goes away, the colour changes, the shape is lost, the size increases; it becomes liquid and hot; you can hardly touch it, and if you strike it, it no longer makes a sound. But does the same wax remain? It must be admitted that it does; no one denies it, no one thinks otherwise. So what was it in the wax that I understood with such distinctness? Evidently none of the features which I arrived at by means of the senses; for whatever came under taste, smell, sight, touch or hearing has now altered—yet the wax remains.

Perhaps the answer lies in the thought which now comes to my mind; namely, the wax was not after all the sweetness of the honey, or the fragrance of the flowers, or the whiteness, or the shape, or the sound, but was rather a body which presented itself to me in these various forms a little while ago, but which now exhibits different ones. But what exactly is it that I am now imagining? Let us concentrate, take away everything which does not belong to the wax, and see what is left: merely something extended, flexible and changeable. But what is meant here by 'flexible' and 'changeable'? Is it what I picture in my imagination: that this piece of wax is capable of changing from a round shape to a square shape, or from a square shape to a triangular shape? Not at all; for I can grasp that the wax is capable of countless changes of this kind, yet I am unable to run through this immeasurable number of changes in my imagination, from which it follows that it is not the faculty of imagination that gives me my grasp of the wax as flexible and changeable. And what is meant by 'extended'? Is the extension of the wax also unknown? For it increases if the wax melts, increases again if it boils, and is greater still if the heat is increased. I would not be making a correct judgement about the nature of wax unless I believed it capable of being extended in many more different ways than I will ever encompass in my imagination. I must therefore admit that the nature of this piece of wax is in no way revealed by my imagination, but is perceived by the mind alone. (I am speaking of this particular piece of wax; the point is even clearer with regard to wax in general.) But what is this wax which is perceived by the mind alone? It is of course the same wax which I see, which I touch, which I picture in my imagination, in short the same wax which I thought it to be from the start. And yet, and here is the point, the perception I have of it is a case not of vision or touch or imagination—nor has it ever been, despite previous appearances—but of purely mental scrutiny; and this can be imperfect and confused, as it was before, or clear and distinct as it is now, depending on how carefully I concentrate on what the wax consists in. . . .

But what am I to say about this mind, or about myself? (So far, remember, I am not admitting that there is anything else in me except a mind.) What, I ask, is this 'I' which seems to perceive the wax so distinctly? Surely my awareness of my own self is not merely much truer and more certain than my awareness of the wax, but also much more distinct and evident. For if I judge that the wax exists from the fact that I see it, clearly this same fact entails much more evidently that I myself also exist. It is possible that what I see is not really the wax; it is possible that I do not even have eyes with which to see anything. But when I see, or think I see (I am not here distinguishing the two), it is simply not possible that I who am now thinking am not something. By the same token, if I judge that the wax exists from the fact that I touch it, the same result follows, namely that I exist. If I judge that it exists from the fact that I imagine it, or for any other reason, exactly the same thing follows. And the result that I have grasped in the case of the wax may be applied to everything else located outside me. Moreover, if my perception of the wax seemed more distinct after it was established not just by sight or touch but by many other considerations, it must be admitted that I now know myself even more distinctly. This is because every consideration whatsoever which contributes to my perception of the wax, or of any other body, cannot but establish even more effectively the nature of my own mind. But besides this, there is so much else in the mind itself which can serve to make my knowledge of it more distinct, that it scarcely seems worth going through the contributions made by considering bodily things.

I see that without any effort I have now finally got back to where I wanted. I now know that even bodies are not strictly perceived by the senses or the faculty of imagination but by the intellect alone, and that this perception derives not from their being touched or seen but from their being understood; and in view of this I know plainly that I can achieve an easier and more evident perception of my own mind than of anything else. But since the habit of holding on to old opinions cannot be set aside so quickly, I should like to stop here and meditate for some time on this new knowledge I have gained, so as to fix it more deeply in my memory.

THIRD MEDITATION

The Existence of God

I will now shut my eyes, stop my ears, and withdraw all my senses. I will eliminate from my thoughts all images of bodily things, or rather, since this is hardly possible, I will regard all such images as vacuous, false and worthless. I will converse with myself and scrutinize myself more deeply; and in this way I will attempt to achieve, little by little, a more intimate knowledge of myself. I am a thing that thinks: that is, a thing that doubts, affirms, denies, understands a few things, is ignorant of many things, is willing, is unwilling, and also which imagines and has sensory perceptions; for as I have noted before, even though the objects of my sensory experience and imagination may have no existence outside me, nonetheless the modes of thinking which I refer to as cases of sensory perception and imagination, in so far as they are simply modes of thinking, do exist within me—of that I am certain. . . .

But what about when I was considering something very simple and straightforward in arithmetic or geometry, for example that two and three added together make five, and so on? Did I not see at least these things clearly enough to affirm their truth? Indeed, the only reason for my later judgement that they were open to doubt was that it occurred to me that perhaps some God could have given me a nature such that I was deceived even in matters which seemed most evident. And whenever my preconceived belief in the supreme power of God comes to mind, I cannot but admit that it would be easy for him, if he so desired, to bring it about that I go wrong even in those matters which I think I see utterly clearly with my mind's eye. Yet when I turn to the things themselves which I think I perceive very clearly, I am so convinced by them that I spontaneously declare: let whoever can do so deceive me, he will never bring it about that I am nothing, so long as I continue to think I am something; or make it true at some future time that I have never existed, since it is now true that I exist; or bring it about that two and three added together are more or less than five, or anything of this kind in which I see a manifest contradiction. And since I have no cause to think that there is a deceiving God, and I do not yet even know for sure whether there is a God at all, any reason for doubt which depends simply on this supposition is a very slight and, so to speak, metaphysical one. But in order to remove even this slight reason for doubt, as soon as the opportunity arises I must examine whether there is a God, and, if there is, whether he can be a deceiver. For if I do not know this, it seems that I can never be quite certain about anything else. . . .

Now it is manifest by the natural light [of reason] that there must be at least as much ⟨reality⟩ in the efficient[3] and total cause as in the effect of that cause. For where, I ask, could the effect get its reality from, if not from the cause? And how could the cause give it to the effect unless it possessed it? It follows from this both that something cannot arise from nothing, and also that what is more perfect—that is, contains in itself more reality—cannot arise from what is less perfect. And this is transparently true not only in the case of effects which possess ⟨what the philosophers call⟩ actual or formal reality, but also in the case of ideas, where one is considering only ⟨what they call⟩ objective reality.[4] A stone, for example, which previously did not exist, cannot begin to exist unless it is produced by something which contains, either formally or eminently,[5] everything to be found in the stone; similarly, heat cannot be produced in an object which was not previously hot, except by something of at least the same order ⟨degree or kind⟩ of perfection as heat, and so on. But it is also true that the *idea* of heat, or of a stone, cannot exist in me unless it is put there by some cause which contains at least as much reality as I conceive to be in the heat or in the stone. For although this cause does not transfer any of its actual or formal reality to my idea, it should not on that account be supposed that it must be less real. The nature of an idea is such that of itself it requires no formal reality except what it derives from my thought, of which it is a mode. But in order for a given idea to contain such and such objective reality, it must surely derive it from some cause which contains at least as much formal reality as there is objective reality in the idea. For if we suppose that an idea contains something which was not in its cause, it must have got this from nothing; yet the mode of being by which a thing exists objectively ⟨or representatively⟩ in the intellect by way of an idea, imperfect though it may be, is certainly not nothing, and so it cannot come from nothing. . . .

The longer and more carefully I examine all these points, the more clearly and distinctly I recognize their truth. But what is my conclusion to be? If the objective reality of any of my ideas turns out to be so great that I am sure the same reality does not reside in me, either formally or eminently, and hence that I myself cannot be its cause, it will necessarily follow that I am not alone in the world, but that some other thing which is the cause of this idea also exists. But if no such idea is to be found in me, I shall have no argument to convince me of the existence of anything apart from myself. For despite a most careful and comprehensive survey, this is the only argument I have so far been able to find.

Among my ideas, apart from the idea which gives me a representation of myself, which cannot present any difficulty in this context, there are ideas which variously represent God, corporeal and inanimate things, angels, animals and finally other men like myself. . . .

I must consider whether there is anything in the idea [of God] which could not have originated in myself. By the word 'God' I understand a substance that is infinite, ⟨eternal, immutable,⟩ independent, supremely intelligent, supremely powerful, and which created both myself and everything else (if anything else there be) that exists. All these attributes are such that, the more carefully I concentrate on them, the less possible it seems that they could have originated from me alone. So from what has been said it must be concluded that God necessarily exists.

It is true that I have the idea of substance in me in virtue of the fact that I am a substance; but this would not account for my having the idea of an infinite substance, when I am finite, unless this idea proceeded from some substance which really was infinite.

And I must not think that, just as my conceptions of rest and darkness are arrived at by negating movement and light, so my perception of the infinite is arrived at not by means of a true idea but merely by negating the finite. On the contrary, I clearly understand that there is more reality in an infinite substance than in a finite one, and hence that my perception of the infinite, that is God, is in some way prior to my perception of the finite, that is myself. For how could I understand that I doubted or desired—that is, lacked something—and that I was not wholly perfect, unless there were in me some idea of a more perfect being which enabled me to recognize my own defects by comparison?

Nor can it be said that this idea of God is perhaps materially false[6] and so could have come from nothing, which [could happen] in the case of the ideas of heat and cold, and so on. On the contrary, it is utterly clear and distinct, and contains in itself more objective reality than any other idea; hence there is no idea which is in itself truer or less liable to be suspected of falsehood. This idea of a supremely perfect and infinite being is, I say, true in the highest degree; for although perhaps one may imagine that such a being does not exist, it cannot be supposed that the idea of such a being represents something unreal, as I said with regard to the idea of cold. The idea is, moreover, utterly clear and distinct; for whatever I clearly and distinctly perceive as being real and true, and implying any perfection, is wholly contained in it. It does not matter that I do not grasp the infinite, or that there are countless additional attributes of God which I cannot in any way grasp, and perhaps cannot even reach in my thought; for it is in the nature of the infinite not to be grasped by a finite being like myself. It is enough that I understand the infinite, and that I judge that all the attributes which I clearly perceive and know to imply some perfection—and perhaps countless others of which I am ignorant—are present in God either formally or eminently. This is enough to make the idea that I have of God the truest and most clear and distinct of all my ideas. . . .

It only remains for me to examine how I received this idea from God. For I did not acquire it from the senses; it has never come to me unexpectedly, as usually happens with the ideas of things that are perceivable by the senses, when these things present themselves to the external sense organs—or seem to do so. And it was not invented by me either; for I am plainly unable either to take away anything from it or to add anything to it. The only remaining alternative is that it is innate in me, just as the idea of myself is innate in me.

And indeed it is no surprise that God, in creating me, should have placed this idea in me to be, as it were, the mark of the craftsman stamped on his work—not that the mark need be anything distinct from the work itself. But the mere fact that God created me is a very strong basis for believing that I am somehow made in his image and likeness, and that I perceive that likeness, which includes the idea of God, by the same faculty which enables me to perceive myself. That is, when I turn my mind's eye upon myself, I understand that I am a thing which is incomplete and dependent on another and which aspires without limit to ever greater and better things; but I also understand at the same time that he on whom I depend has within him all those greater things, not just indefinitely and potentially but actually and infinitely, and hence that he is God. The whole force of the argument lies in this: I recognize that it would be impossible for me to exist with the kind of nature I have—that is, having within me the idea of God—were it not the case that God really existed. By 'God' I mean the very being the idea of whom is within me, that is, the possessor of all the perfections which I cannot grasp, but can somehow reach in my thought, who is subject to no defects whatsoever. It is clear enough from this that he cannot be a deceiver, since it is manifest by the natural light that all fraud and deception depend on some defect.

But before examining this point more carefully and investigating other truths which may be derived from it, I should like to pause here and spend some time in the contemplation of God; to reflect on his attributes, and to gaze with wonder and adoration on the beauty of this immense light, so far as the eye of my darkened intellect can bear it. For just as we believe through faith that the supreme happiness of the next life consists solely in the contemplation of the divine majesty, so experience tells us that this same contemplation, albeit much less perfect, enables us to know the greatest joy of which we are capable in this life. . . .

FIFTH MEDITATION

The Essence of Material Things, and the Existence of God Considered a Second Time

. . . If the mere fact that I can produce from my thought the idea of something entails that everything which I clearly and distinctly perceive to belong to that thing really does belong to it, is not this a possible basis for another argument to prove the existence of God? Certainly, the idea of God, or a supremely perfect being, is one which I find within me just as surely as the idea of any shape or number. And my understanding that it belongs to his nature that he always exists is no less clear and distinct than is the case when I prove of any shape or number that some property belongs to its nature. Hence, even if it turned out that not everything on which I have meditated in these past days is true, I ought still to regard the existence of God as having at least the same level of certainty as I have hitherto attributed to the truths of mathematics.

At first sight, however, this is not transparently clear, but has some appearance of being a sophism. Since I have been accustomed to distinguish between existence and essence in everything else, I find it easy to persuade myself that existence can also be separated from the essence of God, and hence that God can be thought of as not existing. But when I concentrate more carefully, it is quite evident that existence can no more be separated from the essence of God than the fact that its three angles equal two right angles can be separated from the essence of a triangle, or than the idea of a mountain can be separated from the idea of a valley. Hence it is just as much of a contradiction to think of God (that is, a supremely perfect being) lacking existence (that is, lacking a perfection), as it is to think of a mountain without a valley.

However, even granted that I cannot think of God except as existing, just as I cannot think of a mountain without a valley, it certainly does not follow from the fact that I think of a mountain with a valley that there is any mountain in the world; and similarly, it does not seem to follow from the fact that I think of God as existing that he does exist. For my thought does not impose any necessity on things; and just as I may imagine a winged horse even though no horse has wings, so I may be able to attach existence to God even though no God exists.

But there is a sophism concealed here. From the fact that I cannot think of a mountain without a valley, it does not follow that a mountain and valley exist anywhere, but simply that a mountain and a valley, whether they exist or not, are mutually inseparable. But from the fact that I cannot think of God except as existing, it follows that existence is inseparable from God, and hence that he really exists. It is not that my thought makes it so, or imposes any necessity on any thing; on the contrary, it is the necessity of the thing itself, namely the existence of God, which determines my thinking in this respect. For I am not free to think of God without existence (that is, a supremely perfect being without a supreme perfection) as I am free to imagine a horse with or without wings. . . .

SIXTH MEDITATION

The Existence of Material Things, and the Real Distinction Between Mind and Body

. . . I know that everything which I clearly and distinctly understand is capable of being created by God so as to correspond exactly with my understanding of it. Hence the fact that I can clearly and distinctly understand one thing apart from another is enough to make me certain that the two things are distinct, since they are capable of being separated, at least by God. The question of what kind of power is required to bring about such a separation does not affect the judgement that the two things are distinct. Thus, simply by knowing that I exist and seeing at the same time that absolutely nothing else belongs to my nature or essence except that I am a thinking thing, I can infer correctly that my essence consists solely in the fact that I am a thinking thing. It is true that I may have (or, to anticipate, that I certainly have) a body that is very closely joined to me. But nevertheless, on the one hand I have a clear and distinct idea of myself, in so far as I am simply a thinking, non-extended thing; and on the other hand I have a distinct idea of body, in so far as this is simply an extended, non-thinking thing. And accordingly, it is certain that I am really distinct from my body, and can exist without it. . . .

Since God is not a deceiver, it is quite clear that he does not transmit . . ideas [of corporeal things] to me either directly from himself, or indirectly, via some creature which contains the objective reality of the ideas not formally but only eminently. For God has given me no faculty at all for recognizing any such source for these ideas; on the contrary, he has given me a great propensity to believe that they are produced by corporeal things. So I do not see how God could be understood to be anything but a deceiver if the ideas were transmitted from a source other than corporeal things. It follows that corporeal things exist. They may not all exist in a way that exactly corresponds with my sensory grasp of them, for in many cases the grasp of the senses is very obscure and confused. But at least they possess all the properties which I clearly and distinctly understand, that is, all those which, viewed in general terms, are comprised within the subject-matter of pure mathematics. . . .

Nature also teaches me, by these sensations of pain, hunger, thirst and so on, that I am not merely present in my body as a sailor is present in a ship, but that I am very closely joined and, as it were, intermingled with it, so that I and the body form a unit. If this were not so, I, who am nothing but a thinking thing, would not feel pain when the body was hurt, but would perceive the damage purely by the intellect, just as a sailor perceives by sight if anything in his ship is broken. Similarly, when the body needed food or drink, I should have an explicit understanding of the fact, instead of having confused sensations of hunger and thirst. For these sensations of hunger, thirst, pain and so on are nothing but confused modes of thinking which arise from the union and, as it were, intermingling of the mind with the body. . . .

I should not have any further fears about the falsity of what my senses tell me every day; on the contrary, the exaggerated doubts of the last few days should be dismissed as laughable. This applies especially to the principal reason for doubt, namely my inability to distinguish between being asleep and being awake. For I now notice that there is a vast difference between the two, in that dreams are never linked by memory with all the other actions of life as waking experiences are. If, while I am awake, anyone were suddenly to appear to me and then disappear immediately, as happens in sleep, so that I could not see where he had come from or where he had gone to, it would not be unreasonable for me to judge that he was a ghost, or a vision created in my brain, rather than a real man. But when I distinctly see where things come from and where and when they come to me, and when I can connect my perceptions of them with the whole of the rest of my life without a break, then I am quite certain that when I encounter these things I am not asleep but awake. And I ought not to have even the slightest doubt of their reality if, after calling upon all the senses as well as my memory and my intellect in order to check them, I receive no conflicting reports from any of these sources. For from the fact that God is not a deceiver it follows that in cases like these I am completely free from error. But since the pressure of things to be done does not always allow us to stop and make such a meticulous check, it must be admitted that in this human life we are often liable to make mistakes about particular things, and we must acknowledge the weakness of our nature.

NOTES

1. Archimedes (about 287–212 B.C.E.) was a Greek mathematician and inventor. [D.C.A.]
2. Words placed in diamond brackets appear in the French version of *Meditations on First Philosophy* but not in the original Latin version. Several years after Descartes published his treatise in Latin, Louis-Charles d'Albert, Duc de Luynes (1620–1690), published a French translation that included some alterations from the original text. Descartes approved the translation, but scholars do not consider it as authoritative as the original Latin text. [D.C.A.]
3. *efficient cause*: the agent that brings a being into existence or brings about a change in some being [D.C.A.]
4. In Descartes's terminology, a thing has formal (actual) reality if it exists independently of its perception by a mind; it has objective reality if it exists as an object in the mind, i.e., as an idea (mental representation). [D.C.A.]
5. An efficient cause contains something formally if it possesses that thing in the *same form* as it produces in the effect; an efficient cause contains something eminently if it possesses that thing in a form *higher* than the one it produces in the effect. For example, a tree as an efficient cause of another tree contains 'treeness' formally, but God as an efficient cause of a tree contains 'treeness' eminently. [D.C.A.]
6. An idea is materially false if there is no reality outside the mind corresponding to it. [D.C.A.]

QUESTIONS FOR REFLECTION AND DISCUSSION

1. How can I be sure that I am not dreaming right now?
2. Am I basically "a thing that thinks"?

3. Is something necessarily true if I perceive it clearly and distinctly?
4. Would it be a contradiction for a supremely perfect being (God) not to exist?
5. If the body and the soul are very different kinds of things, how can they affect each other?

SUGGESTIONS FOR FURTHER READING

I. Primary Sources

Meditations on First Philosophy, With Selections from the Objections and Replies, trans. John Cottingham. Cambridge, England: Cambridge University Press, 1986, 120 pp.

Contains the complete text of *Meditations on First Philosophy* (pp. 3–62), along with excerpts from the seven sets of objections that Descartes's friends raised against his arguments in the *Meditations* and from his responses to their objections (pp. 63–115). This translation of the *Meditations,* along with a translation of all the *Objections* and *Replies,* was first published in *The Philosophical Writings of Descartes 2,* trans. John Cottingham, Robert Stoothoff, and Dugald Murdoch. Cambridge, England: Cambridge University Press, 1984, pp. 3–397.

Discourse on the Method of Rightly Conducting One's Reason and Seeking the Truth in the Sciences, trans. Robert Stoothoff, in *The Philosophical Writings of Descartes 1,* trans. John Cottingham, Robert Stoothoff, and Dugald Murdoch. Cambridge, England: Cambridge University Press, 1985, pp. 111–151.

Descartes wrote the *Discourse* as a preface to three scientific works (on optics, meteorology, and geometry) that he published together in 1637. The *Discourse* describes the method of doubt employed in these works and discusses several other philosophical issues—all topics that he developed more fully a few years later in *Meditations on First Philosophy.* In the *Discourse,* Descartes also talks about his life and examines topics in anatomy and physiology.

"The Passions in General and Incidentally the Whole Nature of Man," Part 1 of *The Passions of the Soul,* trans. Robert Stoothoff, in *The Philosophical Writings of Descartes 1,* pp. 328–348.

A discussion of the difficult problem of how the soul and body affect each other. Descartes argues that the site of interaction between body and soul is the pineal gland in the brain: The soul moves the body by acting directly on the pineal gland, and the body imparts sensations to the soul through this same gland.

II. Secondary Sources

Beck, L. J. *The Metaphysics of Descartes: A Study of the Meditations.* Oxford, England: Clarendon, 1965, 307 pp.

A scholarly study of the principal doctrines in Descartes's *Meditations on First Philosophy.* For more advanced students of Descartes.

Cottingham, John. *Descartes*. Oxford, England: Blackwell, 1986, 171 pp.

A general introduction to Descartes's philosophy that situates his ideas in their historical context and relates them to contemporary philosophical issues.

Kenny, Anthony. *Descartes: A Study of His Philosophy*. New York: Random House, Studies in Philosophy Ser., 1968, 242 pp.

An intermediate-level introduction to Descartes's philosophy that focuses on the topics discussed in *Meditations on First Philosophy*.

Sorell, Tom. *Descartes*. Oxford, England: Oxford University Press, Past Masters Ser., 1987, 120 pp.

A brief introduction to Descartes that presents him as primarily a scientist. Sorell sees Descartes's philosophical explorations as an attempt to ground his mathematical approach to physics.

Wilson, Margaret Dauler. *Descartes*. London: Routledge, The Arguments of the Philosophers Ser., 1978, 255 pp.

A detailed study of the arguments presented in *Meditations on First Philosophy*, with commentary on recent Cartesian scholarship. Wilson devotes a separate chapter to each of the six meditations.

8

David Hume

David Hume was born in Edinburgh, Scotland, in 1711. (He was born David Home but later changed the spelling of his last name to accord with its pronunciation.) His father died when he was an infant. The estate went to Hume's older brother, and the family decided that David should follow his father's profession and become a lawyer. Hume enrolled in the University of Edinburgh in 1723 to study liberal arts, but withdrew three years later to study law privately at home. He was not attracted to the legal profession, however—his real interests lay in literature, history, and philosophy—and so, abandoning law, he read extensively in his new areas of interest, becoming especially fascinated with philosophy. His intense study of these subjects took its toll on his health, and in 1729 he nearly had a nervous breakdown. He slowly recovered and, resolving to "lead a more active life," moved in 1734 to Bristol, England, to take a job as a clerk for a sugar company. But he disliked the life of commerce and resigned his job within four months.

He then decided to go to France to resume his study of philosophy. He lived there from 1734 to 1737, eventually settling in La Flèche in the region of Anjou. He made frequent use of the library at the Jesuit college at La Flèche—the school where the French philosopher René Descartes (1596–1650) had been educated over a hundred years earlier. While in France, Hume wrote *A Treatise of Human Nature: Being an Attempt to Introduce the Experimental Method of Reasoning into Moral Subjects*. His aim in this comprehensive work was to apply the scientific method employed by the English physicist Sir Isaac Newton (1642–1727) to the study of human nature. The *Treatise* was published after Hume returned to England, the first and second volumes in 1739 and the third volume in 1740.

To Hume's great disappointment, the *Treatise* generated little interest. To make his ideas more accessible, in 1740 he published *An Abstract of a Book Lately Published; Entituled, A Treatise of Human Nature, etc., Wherein the Chief Argument of That Book Is Farther Illustrated and Explained*, but this work was not well received either. He next published a two-volume work entitled *Essays, Moral and Political* (1741–1742), which did meet with some success.

In 1744 Hume applied for a position in moral philosophy at the University of Edinburgh. He was not chosen for the post, and during the next several years he took on various occupations in England and abroad. In 1748 he published *Philosophical Essays Concerning Human Understanding*, a reworking of the first volume of the *Treatise*. (This work is better known by the title of the 1758 revision, *An Enquiry Concerning Human Understanding*.) In 1751 Hume published *An Enquiry Concerning the Principles of Morals*, a recasting of the third volume of the *Treatise*.

For most of the period between 1751 and 1763, Hume lived in Edinburgh. Between the years 1754 and 1762, he published a comprehensive six-volume *History of England*. In 1763 he went to Paris, where he served for three years as secretary to the British embassy. Upon his return, he first lived in London but, in 1769, moved back to Edinburgh, where he lived until his death in 1776. His last major work, *Dialogues Concerning Natural Religion*, was published posthumously in 1779.

Hume's empirical, scientific approach to the philosophy of human nature is evident in *An Enquiry Concerning the Principles of Morals*, the work from which our selection is taken. This work (which Hume at the end of his life judged to be, of all his writings, "incomparably the best") attempts to find the basis for morality by examining the facts of ordinary human experience.

Hume argues that morality is based on sentiment rather than reason; more specifically, it is based on our approval of certain inner qualities and our disapproval of others. If we survey the various qualities of which we approve, such as benevolence and justice, we find that what they have in common is "public utility"—that is, their tendency to make people happy. The qualities that we censure have in common their tendency to make people unhappy. (Hume equates happiness with pleasure and unhappiness with pain.)

Why do we approve of utility? Why are we pleased when an action causes others to be happy? Hume's answer is that it is part of our human nature to feel sympathy: It is natural for us to rejoice when others are happy and to be sad when they are in pain. While some people possess greater sympathy than others, everyone has this feeling to some degree.

When using public utility as the criterion of morality, one should, strictly speaking, take into account one's own happiness as well as that of others. But Hume's moral doctrine of sympathy gives clear primacy to concern for the happiness of others. He rejects the view that we praise or censure qualities simply because of their potential effects on us personally. He admits—and emphasizes—that practicing the social virtues brings many personal benefits but denies that this makes morality selfish.

AN ENQUIRY CONCERNING THE PRINCIPLES OF MORALS

SECTION I: OF THE GENERAL PRINCIPLES OF MORALS

. . . There has been a controversy started of late . . . concerning the general foundation of Morals; whether they be derived from Reason, or from Sentiment; whether we attain the knowledge of them by a chain of argument and induction, or by an immediate feeling and finer internal sense; whether, like all sound judgement of truth and falsehood, they should be the same to every rational intelligent being; or whether, like the perception of beauty and deformity, they be founded entirely on the particular fabric and constitution of the human species.

The ancient philosophers, though they often affirm, that virtue is nothing but conformity to reason, yet, in general, seem to consider morals as deriving their existence from taste and sentiment. On the other hand, our modern enquirers, though they also talk much of the beauty of virtue, and deformity of vice, yet have commonly endeavoured to account for these distinctions by metaphysical reasonings, and by deductions from the most abstract principles of the understanding. Such confusion reigned in these subjects, that an opposition of the greatest consequence could prevail between one system and another, and even in the parts of almost each individual system; and yet nobody, till very lately, was ever sensible[1] of it. . . .

It must be acknowledged, that both sides of the question are susceptible of specious[2] arguments. Moral distinctions, it may be said, are discernible by pure *reason*: else, whence the many disputes that reign in common life, as well as in philosophy, with regard to this subject: the long chain of proofs often produced on both sides; the examples cited, the authorities appealed to, the analogies employed, the fallacies detected, the inferences drawn, and the several[3] conclusions adjusted to their proper principles. Truth is disputable; not taste: what exists in the nature of things is the standard of our judgement; what each man feels within himself is the standard of sentiment. Propositions

197

in geometry may be proved, systems in physics may be controverted; but the harmony of verse, the tenderness of passion, the brilliancy of wit, must give immediate pleasure. No man reasons concerning another's beauty; but frequently concerning the justice or injustice of his actions. In every criminal trial the first object of the prisoner is to disprove the facts alleged, and deny the actions imputed to him: the second to prove, that, even if these actions were real, they might be justified, as innocent and lawful. It is confessedly by deductions of the understanding, that the first point is ascertained: how can we suppose that a different faculty of the mind is employed in fixing the other?

On the other hand, those who would resolve all moral determinations into *sentiment*, may endeavour to show, that it is impossible for reason ever to draw conclusions of this nature. To virtue, say they, it belongs to be *amiable*, and vice *odious*. This forms their very nature or essence. But can reason or argumentation distribute these different epithets to any subjects, and pronounce beforehand, that this must produce love, and that hatred? Or what other reason can we ever assign for these affections, but the original fabric and formation of the human mind, which is naturally adapted to receive them?

The end of all moral speculations is to teach us our duty; and, by proper representations of the deformity of vice and beauty of virtue, beget correspondent habits, and engage us to avoid the one, and embrace the other. But is this ever to be expected from inferences and conclusions of the understanding, which of themselves have no hold of the affections nor set in motion the active powers of men? They discover truths: but where the truths which they discover are indifferent, and beget no desire or aversion, they can have no influence on conduct and behaviour. What is honourable, what is fair, what is becoming, what is noble, what is generous, takes possession of the heart, and animates us to embrace and maintain it. What is intelligible, what is evident, what is probable, what is true, procures only the cool assent of the understanding; and gratifying a speculative curiosity, puts an end to our researches.

Extinguish all the warm feelings and prepossessions in favour of virtue, and all disgust or aversion to vice: render men totally indifferent towards these distinctions; and morality is no longer a practical study, nor has any tendency to regulate our lives and actions.

These arguments on each side (and many more might be produced) are so plausible, that I am apt to suspect, they may, the one as well as the other, be solid and satisfactory, and that *reason* and *sentiment* concur in almost all moral determinations and conclusions. The final sentence,[4] it is probable, which pronounces characters and actions amiable or odious, praise-worthy or blameable; that which stamps on them the mark of honour or infamy, approbation or censure; that which renders morality an active principle and constitutes virtue our happiness, and vice our misery: it is probable, I say, that this final sentence depends on some internal sense or feeling, which nature has made universal in the whole species. For what else can have an influence of this nature? But in order to pave the way for such a sentiment, and give a proper discernment of its object, it is often necessary, we find, that much reasoning should precede, that nice distinctions be made, just conclusions drawn, distant comparisons formed, complicated relations examined, and general facts fixed and ascertained. Some species of beauty, especially the natural kinds, on their first appearance, command our affection and approbation; and where they fail of this effect, it is impossible for any reasoning to redress their influence, or adapt them better to our taste and sentiment. But in many orders of beauty, particularly those of the finer arts, it is requisite to employ much reasoning, in order to feel the proper sentiment; and a false relish may frequently be corrected by argument and reflection. There are just grounds to conclude, that moral beauty partakes much of this latter species, and demands the assistance of our intellectual faculties, in order to give it a suitable influence on the human mind.

But though this question, concerning the general principles of morals, be curious and important, it is needless for us, at present, to employ farther care in our researches concerning it. For if we can be so happy, in the course of this enquiry, as to discover the true origin of morals, it will then easily appear how far either sentiment or reason enters into all determinations of this nature. In order to attain this purpose, we shall endeavour to follow a very simple method: we shall analyse that complication[5] of mental qualities, which form what, in common life, we call Personal Merit: we shall consider every attribute of the mind, which renders a man an object either of esteem and affection, or of hatred and contempt; every habit or sentiment or faculty, which, if ascribed to any person, implies either praise or blame, and may enter into any panegyric or satire of his character and manners. The quick sensibility, which, on this head, is so universal among mankind, gives a philosopher sufficient assurance, that he can never be considerably mistaken in framing the catalogue, or incur any danger of misplacing the objects of his contemplation: he needs only enter into his own breast for a moment, and consider whether or not he should desire to have this or that quality ascribed to him, and whether such or such an imputation would proceed from a friend or an enemy. The very nature of language guides us almost infallibly in forming a judgement of this nature; and as every tongue possesses one set of words which are taken in a good sense, and another in the opposite, the least acquaintance with the idiom suffices, without any reasoning, to direct us in collecting and arranging the estimable or blameable qualities of men. The only object of reasoning is to discover the circumstances on both sides, which are common to these qualities; to observe that particular in which the estimable qualities agree on the one hand, and the blameable on the other; and thence to reach the foundation of ethics, and find those universal principles, from which all censure or approbation is ultimately derived. As this is a question of fact, not of abstract science, we can only expect success, by following the experimental method, and deducing general maxims from a comparison of particular instances. The other scientific method, where a general abstract principle is first established, and is afterwards branched out into a variety of inferences and conclusions, may be more perfect in itself, but suits less the imperfection of human nature, and is a common source of illusion and mistake in this as well as in other subjects. Men are now cured of their passion for hypotheses and systems in natural philosophy,[6] and will hearken to no arguments but those which are derived from experience. It is full time they should attempt a like reformation in all moral disquisitions; and reject every system of ethics, however subtle or ingenious, which is not founded on fact and observation.

We shall begin our enquiry on this head by the consideration of the social virtues, Benevolence and Justice. The explication of them will probably give us an opening by which the others may be accounted for.

SECTION II: OF BENEVOLENCE

Part I

It may be esteemed, perhaps, a superfluous task to prove, that the benevolent or softer affections are estimable; and wherever they appear, engage[7] the approbation and good-will of mankind. The epithets *sociable, good-natured, humane, merciful, grateful, friendly, generous, beneficent,* or their equivalents, are known in all languages, and universally express the highest merit, which *human nature* is capable of attaining. Where these amiable qualities are attended with birth and power and eminent abilities, and display themselves in the good government or useful instruction of mankind, they seem even to raise the possessors of them above the rank of *human nature,* and make them approach in some measure to the divine. Exalted capacity, undaunted courage, prosperous success; these may only expose a hero or politician to the envy and ill-will of the public: but as soon as the praises are added of humane and beneficent; when instances are displayed of lenity,[8] tenderness or friendship; envy itself is silent, or joins the general voice of approbation and applause. . . .

It is not my present business to recommend generosity and benevolence, or to paint, in their true colours, all the genuine charms of the social virtues. These, indeed, sufficiently engage every heart, on the first apprehension of them; and it is difficult to abstain from some sally of panegyric, as often as they occur in discourse or reasoning. But our object here being more the speculative, than the practical part of morals, it will suffice to remark, (what will readily, I believe, be allowed) that no qualities are more intitled[9] to the general good-will and approbation of mankind than beneficence and humanity, friendship and gratitude, natural affection and public spirit, or whatever proceeds from a tender sympathy with others, and a generous concern for our kind and species. These wherever they appear, seem to transfuse themselves, in a manner, into each beholder, and to call forth, in their own behalf, the same favourable and affectionate sentiments, which they exert on all around.

Part II

We may observe that, in displaying the praises of any humane, beneficent man, there is one circumstance which never fails to be amply insisted on, namely, the happiness and satisfaction, derived to[10] society from his intercourse and good offices.[11] To his parents, we are apt to say, he endears himself by his pious attachment and duteous care still more than by the connexions of nature. His children never feel his authority, but when employed for their advantage. With him, the ties of love are consolidated by beneficence and friendship. The ties of friendship approach, in a fond observance of each obliging office, to those of love and inclination. His domestics and dependants have in him a sure resource; and no longer dread the power of fortune, but so far as she exercises it over him. From him the hungry receive food, the naked clothing, the ignorant and slothful skill and industry. Like the sun, an inferior minister of providence he cheers, invigorates, and sustains the surrounding world.

If confined to private life, the sphere of his activity is narrower; but his influence is all benign and gentle. If exalted into a higher station, mankind and posterity reap the fruit of his labours.

As these topics[12] of praise never fail to be employed, and with success, where we would inspire esteem for any one; may it not thence be concluded, that the utility, resulting from the social virtues, forms, at least, a *part* of their merit, and is one source of that approbation and regard so universally paid to them?

When we recommend even an animal or a plant as *useful* and *beneficial*, we give it an applause and recommendation suited to its nature. As, on the other hand, reflection on the baneful influence of any of these inferior beings always inspires us with the sentiment of aversion. The eye is pleased with the prospect of corn-fields and loaded vineyards; horses grazing, and flocks pasturing: but flies the view of briars and brambles, affording shelter to wolves and serpents.

A machine, a piece of furniture, a vestment, a house well contrived for use and conveniency, is so far beautiful, and is contemplated with pleasure and approbation. An experienced eye is here sensible to[13] many excellencies, which escape persons ignorant and uninstructed.

Can anything stronger be said in praise of a profession, such as merchandize or manufacture, than to observe the advantages which it procures to society; and is not a monk and inquisitor[14] enraged when we treat his order as useless or pernicious to mankind?

The historian exults in displaying the benefit arising from his labours. The writer of romance[15] alleviates or denies the bad consequences ascribed to his manner of composition.

In general, what praise is implied in the simple epithet *useful*! What reproach in the contrary! . . .

In all determinations of morality, this circumstance of public utility is ever principally in view; and wherever disputes arise, either in philosophy or common life, concerning the bounds of duty, the question cannot, by any means, be decided with greater certainty, than by ascertaining, on any side, the true interests of mankind. If any false opinion, embraced from appearances, has been found to prevail; as soon as farther experience and sounder reasoning have given us juster notions of human affairs, we retract our first sentiment, and adjust anew the boundaries of moral good and evil.

Giving alms to common beggars is naturally praised; because it seems to carry relief to the distressed and indigent: but when we observe the encouragement thence arising to idleness and debauchery, we regard that species of charity rather as a weakness than a virtue.

Tyrannicide, or the assassination of usurpers and oppressive princes, was highly extolled in ancient times; because it both freed mankind from many of these monsters, and seemed to keep the others in awe, whom the sword or poinard[16] could not reach. But history and experience having since convinced us, that this practice increases the jealousy and cruelty of princes, a Timoleon and a Brutus,[17] though treated with indulgence on account of the prejudices of their times, are now considered as very improper models for imitation.

Liberality in princes is regarded as a mark of beneficence, but when it occurs, that the homely bread of the honest and industrious is often thereby converted into delicious cates[18] for the idle and the prodigal, we soon retract our heedless praises. The regrets of a prince, for having lost a day, were noble and generous: but had he intended to have spent it in acts of generosity to his greedy courtiers, it was better lost than misemployed after that manner.

Luxury, or a refinement on the pleasures and conveniencies of life, had long been supposed the source of every corruption in government, and the immediate cause of faction, sedition, civil wars, and the total loss of liberty. It was, therefore, universally regarded as a vice, and was an object of declamation to all satirists, and severe moralists. Those, who prove, or attempt to prove, that such refinements rather tend to the increase of industry, civility, and arts regulate anew our *moral* as well as *political* sentiments, and represent, as laudable or innocent, what had formerly been regarded as pernicious and blameable.

Upon the whole, then, it seems undeniable, *that* nothing can bestow more merit on any human creature than the sentiment of benevolence in an eminent degree; and *that* a *part*, at least, of its merit arises from its tendency to promote the interests of our species, and bestow happiness on human society. We carry our view into the salutary consequences of such a character and disposition; and whatever has so benign an influence, and forwards so desirable an end, is beheld with complacency[19] and pleasure. The social virtues are never regarded without their beneficial tendencies, nor viewed as barren and unfruitful. The happiness of mankind, the order of society, the harmony of families, the mutual support of friends, are always considered as the result of their gentle dominion over the breasts of men.

How considerable a *part* of their merit we ought to ascribe to their utility, will better appear from future disquisitions; as well as the reason, why this circumstance has such a command over our esteem and approbation.

SECTION III: OF JUSTICE

Part I

That Justice is useful to society, and consequently that *part* of its merit, at least, must arise from that consideration, it would be a superfluous undertaking to prove. That public utility is the *sole* origin of justice, and that reflections on the beneficial consequences of this virtue are the *sole* foundation of its merit; this proposition, being more curious and important, will better deserve our examination and enquiry.

Let us suppose that nature has bestowed on the human race such profuse *abundance* of all *external* conveniencies, that, without any uncertainty in the event, without any care or industry on our part, every individual finds himself fully provided with whatever his most voracious appetites can want, or luxurious imagination wish or desire. His natural beauty, we shall suppose, surpasses all acquired ornaments: the perpetual clemency of the seasons renders useless all clothes or covering: the raw herbage affords him the most delicious fare; the clear fountain, the richest beverage. No laborious occupation required: no tillage: no navigation. Music, poetry, and contemplation form his sole business: conversation, mirth, and friendship his sole amusement.

It seems evident that, in such a happy state, every other social virtue would flourish, and receive tenfold increase; but the cautious, jealous[20] virtue of justice would never once have been dreamed of. For what purpose make a partition of goods, where every one has already more than enough? Why give rise to property, where there cannot possibly be any injury? Why call this object *mine*, when upon the seizing of it by another, I need but stretch out my hand to possess myself of what is equally valuable? Justice, in that case, being totally useless, would be an idle ceremonial, and could never possibly have place in the catalogue of virtues.

We see, even in the present necessitous condition of mankind, that, wherever any benefit is bestowed by nature in an unlimited abundance, we leave it always in common among the whole human race, and make no subdivisions of right and property. Water and air, though the most necessary of all objects, are not challenged as the property of individuals; nor can any man commit injustice by the most lavish use and enjoyment of these blessings. In fertile extensive countries, with few inhabitants, land is regarded on the same footing. And no topic is so much insisted on by those, who defend the liberty of the seas, as the unexhausted use of them in navigation. Were the advantages, procured by navigation, as inexhaustible, these reasoners had never had any adversaries to refute; nor had any claims ever been advanced of a separate, exclusive dominion over the ocean. . . .

Again; suppose, that, though the necessities of human race continue the same as at present, yet the mind is so enlarged, and so replete with friendship and generosity, that every man has the utmost tenderness for every man, and feels no more concern for his own interest than for that of his fellows; it seems evident, that the use of justice would, in this case, be suspended by such an extensive benevolence, nor would the divisions and barriers of property and obligation have ever been thought of. Why should I bind another, by a deed or promise, to do me any good office, when I know that he is already prompted, by the strongest inclination, to seek my happiness, and would, of himself, perform the desired service; except the hurt, he thereby receives, be greater than the benefit accruing to me? in which case, he knows, that, from my innate humanity and friendship, I should be the first to oppose myself to his imprudent generosity. Why raise land-marks between my neighbour's field and mine, when my heart has made no division between our interests; but shares all his joys and sorrows with the same force and vivacity as if originally my own? Every man, upon this supposition, being a second self to another, would trust all his interests to the discretion of every man; without jealousy, without partition, without distinction. And the whole human race would form only one family; where all would lie in common, and be used freely, without regard to property; but cautiously too, with as entire regard to the necessities of each individual, as if our own interests were most intimately concerned.

In the present disposition of the human heart, it would, perhaps, be difficult to find complete instances of such enlarged affections; but still we may observe, that the case of families approaches towards it; and the stronger the mutual benevolence is among the individuals, the nearer it approaches; till all distinction of property be, in a great measure, lost and confounded among them. Between married persons, the cement of friendship is by the laws supposed so strong as to abolish all division of possessions; and has often, in reality, the force ascribed to it. And it is observable, that, during the ardour of new enthusiasms, when every principle is inflamed into extravagance, the community of goods has frequently been attempted; and nothing but experience of its inconveniencies, from the returning or disguised self-ishness of men, could make the imprudent fanatics adopt anew the ideas of justice and of separate property. So true is it, that this virtue derives its existence entirely from its necessary *use* to the intercourse and social state of mankind.

To make this truth more evident, let us reverse the foregoing suppositions; and carrying everything to the opposite extreme, consider what would be the effect of these new situations. Suppose a society to fall into such want of all common necessaries, that the utmost frugality and industry cannot preserve the greater number from perishing, and the whole from extreme misery; it will readily, I believe, be admitted, that the strict laws of justice are suspended, in such a pressing emergence,[21] and give place to the stronger motives of necessity and self-preservation. Is it any crime, after a shipwreck, to seize whatever means or instrument of safety one can lay hold of, without regard to former limitations of property? Or if a city besieged were perishing with hunger; can we imagine, that men will see any means of preservation before them, and lose their lives, from a scrupulous regard to what, in other situations, would be the rules of equity and justice? The use and tendency of that virtue is to procure happiness and security, by preserving order in society: but where the society is ready to perish from extreme necessity, no greater evil can be dreaded from violence and injustice; and every man may now provide for himself by all the means which prudence can dictate, or humanity permit. The public, even in less urgent necessities, opens granaries, without the consent of proprietors; as justly supposing, that the authority of magistracy may, consistent with equity, extend so far: but were any number of men to assemble, without the tie of laws or civil jurisdiction; would an equal partition of bread in a famine, though effected by power and even violence, be regarded as criminal or injurious?

Suppose likewise, that it should be a virtuous man's fate to fall into the society of ruffians, remote from the protection of laws and government; what conduct must he embrace in that melancholy situation? He sees such a desperate rapaciousness prevail; such a disregard to equity, such contempt of order, such stupid blindness to future consequences, as must immediately have the most tragical conclusion, and must terminate in destruction to the greater number, and in a total dissolution of society to the rest. He, meanwhile, can have no other expedient than to arm himself, to whomever the sword he seizes, or the buckler, may belong: To make provision of all means of defence and security: And his particular regard to justice being no longer of use to his own safety or that of others, he must consult the dictates of self-preservation alone, without concern for those who no longer merit his care and attention.

When any man, even in political society, renders himself by his crimes, obnoxious to the public, he is punished by the laws in his goods and person; that is, the ordinary rules of justice are, with regard to him, suspended for a moment, and it becomes equitable to inflict on him, for the *benefit* of society, what otherwise he could not suffer without wrong or injury.

The rage and violence of public war; what is it but a suspension of justice among the warring parties, who perceive, that this virtue is now no longer of any *use* or advantage to them? The laws of war, which then succeed to those of equity and justice, are rules calculated for the *advantage* and *utility* of that particular state, in which men are now placed. And were a civilized nation engaged with barbarians, who observed no rules even of war, the former must also suspend their observance of them, where they no longer serve to any purpose; and must render every action or rencounter[22] as bloody and pernicious as possible to the first aggressors.

Thus, the rules of equity or justice depend entirely on the particular state and condition in which men are placed, and owe their origin and existence to that utility, which results to the public from their strict and regular observance. Reverse, in any considerable circumstance, the condition of men: Produce extreme abundance or extreme necessity: Implant in the human breast perfect moderation and humanity, or perfect rapaciousness and malice: By rendering justice totally *useless*, you thereby totally destroy its essence, and suspend its obligation upon mankind.

The common situation of society is a medium amidst all these extremes. We are naturally partial to ourselves, and to our friends; but are capable of learning the advantage resulting from a more equitable conduct. Few enjoyments are given us from the open and liberal hand of nature; but by art, labour, and industry, we can extract them in great abundance. Hence the ideas of property become necessary in all civil society: Hence justice derives its usefulness to the public: And hence alone arises its merit and moral obligation. . . .

Were the human species so framed by nature as that each individual possessed within himself every faculty, requisite both for his own preservation and for the propagation of his kind: Were all society and intercourse cut off between man and man, by the primary intention of the supreme Creator: It seems evident, that so solitary a being would be as much incapable of justice, as of social discourse and conversation. Where mutual regards and forbearance serve to no manner of purpose, they would never direct the conduct of any reasonable man. The headlong course of the passions would be checked by no reflection on future consequences. And as each man is here supposed to love himself alone, and to depend only on himself and his own activity for safety and happiness, he would, on every occasion, to the utmost of his power, challenge the preference above every other being, to none of which he is bound by any ties, either of nature or of interest.

But suppose the conjunction of the sexes to be established in nature, a family immediately arises; and particular rules being found requisite for its subsistence, these are immediately embraced; though without comprehending the rest of mankind within their prescriptions. Suppose that several families unite together into one society, which is totally disjoined from all others, the rules, which preserve peace and order, enlarge themselves to the utmost extent of that society; but becoming then entirely useless, lose their force when carried one step farther. But again suppose, that several distinct societies maintain a kind of intercourse for mutual convenience and advantage, the boundaries of justice still[23] grow larger, in proportion to the largeness of men's views, and the force of their mutual connexions. History, experience, reason sufficiently instruct us in this natural progress of human sentiments, and in the gradual enlargement of our regards to justice, in proportion as we become acquainted with the extensive utility of that virtue.

Part II

If we examine the *particular* laws, by which justice is directed, and property determined; we shall still be presented with the same conclusion. The good of mankind is the only object of all these laws and regulations. Not only it is requisite, for the peace and interest of society, that men's possessions should be separated; but the rules, which we follow, in making the separation, are such as can best be contrived to serve farther the interests of society.

We shall suppose that a creature, possessed of reason, but unacquainted with human nature, deliberates with himself what rules of justice or property would best promote public interest, and establish peace and security among mankind: His most obvious thought would be, to assign the largest possessions to the most extensive virtue, and give every one the power of doing good, proportioned to his inclination. In a perfect theocracy, where a being, infinitely intelligent, governs by particular volitions, this rule would certainly have place, and might serve to the wisest purposes: But were mankind to execute such a law; so great is the uncertainty of merit, both from its natural obscurity, and from the self-conceit of each individual, that no determinate rule of conduct would ever result from it; and the total dissolution of society must be the immediate consequence. Fanatics may suppose, *that dominion is founded on grace*,[24] and *that saints alone inherit the earth*;[25] but the civil magistrate very justly puts these sublime theorists on the same footing with common robbers, and teaches them by the severest discipline, that a rule, which, in speculation, may seem the most advantageous to society, may yet be found, in practice, totally pernicious and destructive. . . .

We may conclude, therefore, that, in order to establish laws for the regulation of property, we must be acquainted with the nature and situation of man; must reject appearances, which may be false, though specious; and must search for those rules, which are, on the whole, most *useful* and *beneficial*. Vulgar[26] sense and slight experience are sufficient for this purpose; where men give not way to too selfish avidity, or too extensive enthusiasm.

Who sees not, for instance, that whatever is produced or improved by a man's art or industry ought, for ever, to be secured to him, in order to give encouragement to such *useful* habits and accomplishments? That the property ought also to descend to children and relations, for the same *useful* purpose?

That it may be alienated by consent, in order to beget that commerce and intercourse, which is so *beneficial* to human society? And that all contracts and promises ought carefully to be fulfilled, in order to secure mutual trust and confidence, by which the general *interest* of mankind is so much promoted?

Examine the writers on the laws of nature; and you will always find, that, whatever principles they set out with, they are sure to terminate here at last, and to assign, as the ultimate reason for every rule which they establish, the convenience and necessities of mankind. A concession thus extorted, in opposition to systems, has more authority than if it had been made in prosecution of them.

What other reason, indeed, could writers ever give, why this must be *mine* and that *yours*; since uninstructed nature surely never made any such distinction? The objects which receive those appellations are, of themselves, foreign to us; they are totally disjoined and separated from us; and nothing but the general interests of society can form the connexion. . . .

Does any one scruple, in extraordinary cases, to violate all regard to the private property of individuals, and sacrifice to public interest a distinction, which had been established for the sake of that interest? The safety of the people is the supreme law: All other particular laws are subordinate to it, and dependent on it: And if, in the *common* course of things, they be followed and regarded; it is only because the public safety and interest *commonly* demand so equal and impartial an administration. . . .

Thus we seem, upon the whole, to have attained a knowledge of the force of that principle here insisted on, and can determine what degree of esteem or moral approbation may result from reflections on public interest and utility. The necessity of justice to the support of society is the sole foundation of that virtue; and since no moral excellence is more highly esteemed, we may conclude that this circumstance of usefulness has, in general, the strongest energy, and most entire command over our sentiments. It must, therefore, be the source of a considerable part of the merit ascribed to humanity, benevolence, friendship, public spirit, and other social virtues of that stamp; as it is the sole source of the moral approbation paid to fidelity, justice, veracity, integrity, and those other estimable and useful qualities and principles. It is entirely agreeable to the rules of philosophy, and even of common reason; where any principle[27] has been found to have a great force and energy in one instance, to ascribe to it a like energy in all similar instances. . . .

SECTION V: WHY UTILITY PLEASES

Part I

. . The social virtues . . . have a natural beauty and amiableness, which, at first, antecedent to all precept or education, recommends them to the esteem of uninstructed mankind, and engages their affections. And as the public utility of these virtues is the chief circumstance, whence they derive their merit, it follows, that the end, which they have a tendency to promote, must be some way agreeable to us, and take hold of some natural affection. It must please, either from considerations of self-interest, or from more generous motives and regards.

It has often been asserted, that, as every man has a strong connexion with society, and perceives the impossibility of his solitary subsistence, he becomes, on that account, favourable to all those habits or principles, which promote order in society, and insure to him the quiet possession of so inestimable a blessing. As much as we value our own happiness and welfare, as much must we applaud the practice of justice and humanity, by which alone the social confederacy can be maintained, and every man reap the fruits of mutual protection and assistance. . . .

Usefulness is agreeable, and engages our approbation. This is a matter of fact, confirmed by daily observation. But, *useful*? For what? For somebody's interest, surely. Whose interest then? Not our own only: For our approbation frequently extends farther. It must, therefore, be the interest of those, who are served by the character or action approved of; and these we may conclude, however remote, are not totally indifferent to us. By opening up this principle, we shall discover one great source of moral distinctions.

Part II

Self-love is a principle in human nature of such extensive energy, and the interest of each individual is, in general, so closely connected with that of the community, that those philosophers were excusable, who fancied that all our concern for the public might be resolved into a concern for our own happiness and preservation. They saw every moment, instances of approbation or blame, satisfaction or displeasure towards characters and actions; they denominated the objects of these sentiments, *virtues*, or *vices*; they observed, that the former had a tendency to increase the happiness, and the latter the misery of mankind; they asked, whether it were possible that we could have any general concern for society, or any disinterested resentment of the welfare or injury of others; they found it simpler to consider all these sentiments as modifications of self-love; and they discovered a pretence, at least, for this unity of principle, in that close union of interest, which is so observable between the public and each individual.

But notwithstanding this frequent confusion of interests, it is easy to attain what natural philosophers, after Lord Bacon,[28] have affected to call the *experimentum crucis*,[29] or that experiment which points out the right way in any doubt or ambiguity. We have found instances, in which private interest was separate from public; in which it was even contrary: And yet we observed the moral sentiment to continue, notwithstanding this disjunction of interests. And wherever these distinct interests sensibly[30] concurred, we always found a sensible[31] increase of the sentiment, and a more warm affection to virtue, and detestation of vice, or what we properly call, *gratitude* and *revenge*. Compelled by these instances, we must renounce the theory, which accounts for every moral sentiment by the principle of self-love. We must adopt a more public affection, and allow, that the interests of society are not, even on their own account, entirely indifferent to us. Usefulness is only a tendency to a certain end; and it is a contradiction in terms, that anything pleases as means to an end, where the end itself no wise affects us. If usefulness, therefore, be a source of moral sentiment, and if this usefulness be not always considered with a reference to self; it follows, that everything, which contributes to the happiness of society, recommends itself directly to our approbation and good-will. Here is a principle, which accounts, in great part, for the origin of morality: And what need we seek for abstruse and remote systems, when there occurs one so obvious and natural?*

Have we any difficulty to comprehend the force of humanity[32] and benevolence? Or to conceive, that the very aspect[33] of happiness, joy, prosperity, gives pleasure; that of pain, suffering, sorrow, communicates uneasiness? The human countenance, says Horace,[34] borrows smiles or tears from the human countenance. Reduce a person to solitude, and he loses all enjoyment, except either of the sensual or speculative kind; and that because the movements of his heart are not forwarded[35] by correspondent movements in his fellow-creatures. The signs of sorrow and mourning, though arbitrary, affect us with melancholy; but the natural symptoms, tears and cries and groans, never fail to infuse compassion and uneasiness. And if the effects of misery touch us in so lively a manner; can we be supposed altogether insensible or indifferent towards its causes; when a malicious or treacherous character and behaviour are presented to us?

We enter, I shall suppose, into a convenient, warm, well-contrived apartment: We necessarily receive a pleasure from its very survey; because it presents us with the pleasing ideas of ease, satisfaction, and enjoyment. The hospitable, good-humoured, humane landlord appears. This circumstance surely must embellish the whole; nor can we easily forbear reflecting, with pleasure, on the satisfaction which results to every one from his intercourse and good-offices.

---

* It is needless to push our researches so far as to ask, why we have humanity or a fellow-feeling with others. It is sufficient, that this is experienced to be a principle in human nature. We must stop somewhere in our examination of causes: and there are, in every science, some general principles beyond which we cannot hope to find any principle more general. No man is absolutely indifferent to the happiness and misery of others. The first has a natural tendency to give pleasure; the second, pain. This every one may find in himself. It is not probable, that these principles can be resolved into principles more simple and universal, whatever attempts have been made to that purpose. But if it were possible, it belongs not to the present subject; and we may here safely consider these principles as original: happy, if we can render all the consequences sufficiently plain and perspicuous! [D.H.]

His whole family, by the freedom, ease, confidence, and calm enjoy-ment, diffused over their countenances, sufficiently express their happiness. I have a pleasing[36] sympathy in the prospect of so much joy, and can never consider the source of it, without the most agreeable emotions.

He tells me, that an oppressive and powerful neighbour had attempted to dispossess him of his inheritance, and had long disturbed all his innocent and social pleasures. I feel an immediate indignation arise in me against such violence and injury.

But it is no wonder, he adds, that a private wrong should proceed from a man, who had enslaved provinces, depopulated cities, and made the field and scaffold stream with human blood. I am struck with horror at the prospect of so much misery, and am actuated by the strongest antipathy against its author.

In general, it is certain, that, wherever we go, whatever we reflect on or converse about, everything still presents us with the view of human hap-piness or misery, and excites in our breast a sympathetic movement of pleasure or uneasiness. In our serious occupations, in our careless[37] amuse-ments, this principle still exerts its active energy. . . .

Let us suppose . . . a person ever so selfish; let private interest have ingrossed[38] ever so much his attention; yet in instances, where that is not concerned, he must unavoidably feel *some* propensity to the good of man-kind, and make it an object of choice, if everything else be equal. Would any man, who is walking along, tread as willingly on another's gouty toes, whom he has no quarrel with, as on the hard flint[39] and pavement? There is here surely a difference in the case. We surely take into consideration the hap-piness and misery of others, in weighing the several motives of action, and incline to the former, where no private regards draw us to seek our own promotion or advantage by the injury of our fellow-creatures. And if the principles of humanity are capable, in many instances, of influencing our actions, they must, at all times, have *some* authority over our sentiments, and give us a general approbation of what is useful to society, and blame of what is dangerous or pernicious. The degrees of these sentiments may be the subject of controversy; but the reality of their existence, one should think, must be admitted in every theory or system. . . .

If we consider the principles of the human make, such as they appear to daily experience and observation, we must, *a priori*, conclude it impossible for such a creature as man to be totally indifferent to the well or ill-being of his fellow-creatures, and not readily, of himself, to pronounce, where nothing gives him any particular bias, that what promotes their happiness is good, what tends to their misery is evil, without any farther regard or consideration. Here then are the faint rudiments, at least, or outlines, of a *general* distinction between actions; and in proportion as the humanity of the person is supposed to encrease,[40] his connexion with those who are injured or benefited, and his lively conception of their misery or happiness; his consequent censure or approbation acquires proportionable vigour. There is no necessity, that a generous action, barely mentioned in an old history or remote gazette, should communicate any strong feelings of applause and admiration. Virtue, placed at such a distance, is like a fixed star, which, though to the eye of reason it may appear as luminous as the sun in his meridian, is so infinitely removed as to affect the senses, neither with light nor heat. Bring this virtue nearer, by our acquaintance or connexion with the persons, or even by an eloquent recital of the case; our hearts are immediately caught, our sympathy enlivened, and our cool approbation converted into the warmest sentiments of friendship and regard. These seem necessary and infallible consequences of the general principles of human nature, as discovered in common life and practice.

Again; reverse these views and reasonings: Consider the matter *a posteriori*; and weighing the consequences, enquire if the merit of social virtue be not, in a great measure, derived from the feelings of humanity, with which it affects the spectators. It appears to be matter of fact, that the circumstance of *utility*, in all subjects, is a source of praise and approbation: That it is constantly appealed to in all moral decisions concerning the merit and demerit of actions: That it is the *sole* source of that high regard paid to justice, fidelity, honour, allegiance, and chastity: That it is inseparable from all the other social virtues, humanity, generosity, charity, affability, lenity, mercy, and moderation: And, in a word, that it is a foundation of the chief part of morals, which has a reference to mankind and our fellow-creatures.

It appears also, that, in our general approbation of characters and manners, the useful tendency of the social virtues moves us not by any regards to self-interest, but has an influence much more universal and extensive. It appears that a tendency to public good, and to the promoting of peace, harmony, and order in society, does always, by affecting the benevolent principles of our frame, engage us on the side of the social virtues. And it appears, as an additional confirmation, that these principles of humanity and sympathy enter so deeply into all our sentiments, and have so powerful an influence, as may enable them to excite the strongest censure and applause. The present theory is the simple result of all these inferences, each of which seems founded on uniform experience and observation.

Were it doubtful, whether there were any such principle in our nature as humanity or a concern for others, yet when we see, in numberless instances, that whatever has a tendency to promote the interests of society, is so highly approved of, we ought thence to learn the force of the benevolent principle; since it is impossible for anything to please as means to an end, where the end is totally indifferent. On the other hand, were it doubtful, whether there were, implanted in our nature, any general principle of moral blame and approbation, yet when we see, in numberless instances, the influence of humanity, we ought thence to conclude, that it is impossible, but that everything which promotes the interest of society must communicate pleasure, and what is pernicious give uneasiness. But when these different reflections and observations concur in establishing the same conclusion, must they not bestow an undisputed evidence upon it? . . .

SECTION IX: CONCLUSION

Part I

It may justly appear surprising that any man in so late an age, should find it requisite to prove, by elaborate reasoning, that Personal Merit consists altogether in the possession of mental qualities, *useful* or *agreeable* to the *person himself* or to *others*. It might be expected that this principle would have occurred even to the first rude,[41] unpractised enquirers concerning morals, and been received from its own evidence, without any argument or disputation. Whatever is valuable in any kind, so naturally classes itself under the division of *useful* or *agreeable*, the *utile* or the *dulce*,[42] that it is not easy to imagine why we should ever seek further, or consider the question as a matter of nice research or inquiry. And as every thing useful or agreeable must possess these qualities with regard either to the *person himself* or to *others*, the complete delineation or description of merit seems to be performed as naturally as a shadow is cast by the sun, or an image is reflected upon water. If the ground, on which the shadow is cast, be not broken and uneven; nor the surface from which the image is reflected, disturbed and confused; a just figure is immediately presented, without any art or attention. And it seems a reasonable presumption, that systems and hypotheses have perverted our natural understanding, when a theory, so simple and obvious, could so long have escaped the most elaborate examination.

But however the case may have fared with philosophy, in common life these principles are still implicitly[43] maintained; nor is any other topic[44] of praise or blame ever recurred to, when we employ any panegyric or satire, any applause or censure of human action and behaviour. If we observe men, in every intercourse of business or pleasure, in every discourse and conversation, we shall find them nowhere, except in the schools, at any loss upon this subject. What so natural, for instance, as the following dialogue? You are very happy, we shall suppose one to say, addressing himself to another, that you have given your daughter to Cleanthes. He is a man of honour and humanity. Every one, who has any intercourse with him, is sure of *fair* and *kind* treatment.* I congratulate you too, says another, on the promising expectations of this son-in-law; whose assiduous application to the study of the laws, whose quick penetration and early knowledge both of men and business, prognosti-

---

* Qualities useful to others [D.H.]

ate the greatest honours and advancement.* You surprise me, replies a
third, when you talk of Cleanthes as a man of business and application. I met
him lately in a circle of the gayest company, and he was the very life and soul
of our conversation: so much wit with good manners; so much gallantry
without affectation; so much ingenious knowledge so genteelly delivered, I
have never before observed in any one.† You would admire him still more,
says a fourth, if you knew him more familiarly. That cheerfulness, which you
might remark in him, is not a sudden flash struck out by company: it runs
through the whole tenor of his life, and preserves a perpetual serenity on his
countenance, and tranquillity in his soul. He has met with severe trials,
misfortunes as well as dangers; and by his greatness of mind, was still
superior to all of them.‡ . . . A philosopher might select this character as a
model of perfect virtue.

And as every quality which is useful or agreeable to ourselves or others
is, in common life, allowed to be a part of personal merit; so no other will ever
be received, where men judge of things by their natural, unprejudiced reason, without the delusive glosses[45] of superstition and false religion. Celi-
bacy, fasting, penance, mortification, self-denial, humility, silence, solitude,
and the whole train of monkish virtues; for what reason are they everywhere
rejected by men of sense, but because they serve to no manner of purpose;
neither advance a man's fortune in the world, nor render him a more valuable
member of society; neither qualify him for the entertainment of company, nor
increase his power of self-enjoyment? We observe, on the contrary, that they
cross all these desirable ends; stupify the understanding and harden the
heart, obscure the fancy and sour the temper. We justly, therefore, transfer
them to the opposite column, and place them in the catalogue of vices; nor
has any superstition force sufficient among men of the world, to pervert
entirely these natural sentiments. A gloomy, hair-brained[46] enthusiast, after
his death, may have a place in the calendar; but will scarcely ever be admitted, when alive, into intimacy and society, except by those who are as
delirious and dismal as himself.

It seems a happiness in the present theory, that it enters not into that
vulgar dispute concerning the *degrees* of benevolence or self-love, which
prevail in human nature; a dispute which is never likely to have any issue,
both because men, who have taken part, are not easily convinced, and
because the phenomena, which can be produced on either side, are so
dispersed,[47] so uncertain, and subject to so many interpretations, that it is
scarcely possible accurately to compare them, or draw from them any determinate inference or conclusion. It is sufficient for our present purpose, if it be
allowed, what surely, without the greatest absurdity cannot be disputed, that

Qualities useful to the person himself [D.H.]
Qualities immediately agreeable to others [D.H.]
Qualities immediately agreeable to the person himself [D.H.]

there is some benevolence, however small, infused into our bosom; some spark of friendship for human kind; some particle of the dove kneaded into our frame, along with the elements of the wolf and serpent. Let these generous sentiments be supposed ever so weak; let them be insufficient to move even a hand or finger of our body, they must still direct the determinations of our mind, and where everything else is equal, produce a cool preference of what is useful and serviceable to mankind, above what is pernicious and dangerous. . . .

When a man denominates another his *enemy*, his *rival*, his *antagonist*, his *adversary*, he is understood to speak the language of self-love, and to express sentiments, peculiar to himself, and arising from his particular circumstances and situation. But when he bestows on any man the epithets of *vicious* or *odious* or *depraved*, he then speaks another language, and expresses sentiments, in which he expects all his audience are to concur with him. He must here, therefore, depart from his private and particular situation, and must choose a point of view, common to him with others; he must move some universal principle of the human frame, and touch a string to which all mankind have an accord and symphony.[48] If he mean, therefore, to express that this man possesses qualities, whose tendency is pernicious to society, he has chosen this common point of view, and has touched the principle of humanity, in which every man, in some degree, concurs. While the human heart is compounded of the same elements as at present, it will never be wholly indifferent to public good, nor entirely unaffected with the tendency of characters and manners. And though this affection of humanity may not generally be esteemed so strong as vanity or ambition, yet, being common to all men, it can alone be the foundation of morals, or of any general system of blame or praise. One man's ambition is not another's ambition, nor will the same event or object satisfy both; but the humanity of one man is the humanity of every one, and the same object touches this passion in all human creatures. . . .

Part II

Having explained the moral *approbation* attending merit or virtue, there remains nothing but briefly to consider our interested *obligation* to it, and to inquire whether every man, who has any regard to his own happiness and welfare, will not best find his account[49] in the practice of every moral duty. If this can be clearly ascertained from the foregoing theory, we shall have the satisfaction to reflect, that we have advanced principles, which not only, it is hoped, will stand the test of reasoning and inquiry, but may contribute to the amendment of men's lives, and their improvement in morality and social virtue. And though the philosophical truth of any proposition by no means depends on its tendency to promote the interests of society; yet a man has but a bad grace, who delivers a theory, however true, which, he must confess,

eads to a practice dangerous and pernicious. Why rake into those corners of
nature which spread a nuisance all around? Why dig up the pestilence from
he pit in which it is buried? The ingenuity of your researches may be
admired, but your systems will be detested; and mankind will agree, if they
cannot refute them, to sink them, at least, in eternal silence and oblivion.
Truths which are *pernicious* to society, if any such there be, will yield to errors
which are salutary and *advantageous*.

But what philosophical truths can be more advantageous to society,
than those here delivered, which represent virtue in all her genuine and most
engaging charms, and make us approach her with ease, familiarity, and
affection? The dismal dress falls off, with which many divines, and some
philosophers, have covered her; and nothing appears but gentleness, human-
ty, beneficence, affability; nay, even at proper intervals, play, frolic, and
gaiety. She talks not of useless austerities and rigours, suffering and self-
denial. She declares that her sole purpose is to make her votaries and all
mankind, during every instant of their existence, if possible, cheerful and
happy; nor does she ever willingly part with any pleasure but in hopes of
ample compensation in some other period of their lives. The sole trouble
which she demands, is that of just calculation, and a steady preference of the
greater happiness. And if any austere pretenders approach her, enemies to
joy and pleasure, she either rejects them as hypocrites and deceivers; or, if
she admit them in her train, they are ranked, however, among the least
favoured of her votaries.

And, indeed, to drop all figurative expression, what hopes can we ever
have of engaging mankind to a practice which we confess full of austerity and
rigour? Or what theory of morals can ever serve any useful purpose, unless it
can show, by a particular detail, that all the duties which it recommends, are
also the true interest of each individual? The peculiar[50] advantage of the
foregoing system seems to be, that it furnishes proper mediums[51] for that
purpose.

That the virtues which are immediately *useful* or *agreeable* to the person
possessed of them, are desirable in a view to self-interest, it would surely be
superfluous to prove. Moralists, indeed, may spare themselves all the pains
which they often take in recommending these duties. To what purpose collect
arguments to evince that temperance is advantageous, and the excesses of
pleasure hurtful. When it appears that these excesses are only denominated
such, because they are hurtful; and that, if the unlimited use of strong liquors,
for instance, no more impaired health or the faculties of mind and body than
the use of air or water, it would not be a whit more vicious or blameable.

It seems equally superfluous to prove, that the *companionable* virtues of
good manners and wit, decency and genteelness, are more desirable than the
contrary qualities. Vanity alone, without any other consideration, is a sufficient motive to make us wish for the possession of these accomplishments.
No man was ever willingly deficient in this particular. All our failures here

proceed from bad education, want of capacity, or a perverse and unpliable disposition. Would you have your company coveted, admired, followed; rather than hated, despised, avoided? Can any one seriously deliberate in the case? As no enjoyment is sincere, without some reference to company and society; so no society can be agreeable, or even tolerable, where a man feels his presence unwelcome, and discovers all around him symptoms of disgust and aversion. . . .

Treating vice with the greatest candour, and making it all possible concessions, we must acknowledge that there is not, in any instance, the smallest pretext for giving it the preference above virtue, with a view to self-interest; except, perhaps, in the case of justice, where a man, taking things in a certain light, may often seem to be a loser by his integrity. And though it is allowed that, without a regard to property, no society could subsist; yet according to the imperfect way in which human affairs are conducted, a sensible knave, in particular incidents, may think that an act of iniquity or infidelity will make a considerable addition to his fortune, without causing any considerable breach in the social union and confederacy. That *honesty is the best policy*, may be a good general rule, but is liable to many exceptions; and he, it may perhaps be thought, conducts himself with most wisdom, who observes the general rule, and takes advantage of all the exceptions.

I must confess that, if a man think that this reasoning much requires an answer, it will be a little difficult to find any which will to him appear satisfactory and convincing. If his heart rebel not against such pernicious maxims, if he feel no reluctance to the thoughts of villainy or baseness, he has indeed lost a considerable motive to virtue; and we may expect that his practice will be answerable to his speculation. But in all ingenuous natures, the antipathy to treachery and roguery is too strong to be counterbalanced by any views of profit or pecuniary advantage. Inward peace of mind, consciousness of integrity, a satisfactory review of our own conduct; these are circumstances, very requisite to happiness, and will be cherished and cultivated by every honest man, who feels the importance of them.

Such a one has, besides, the frequent satisfaction of seeing knaves, with all their pretended cunning and abilities, betrayed by their own maxims; and while they purpose to cheat with moderation and secrecy, a tempting incident occurs, nature is frail, and they give into the snare; whence they can never extricate themselves, without a total loss of reputation, and the forfeiture of all future trust and confidence with mankind.

But were they ever so secret and successful, the honest man, if he has any tincture of philosophy, or even common observation and reflection, will discover that they themselves are, in the end, the greatest dupes, and have sacrificed the invaluable enjoyment of a character, with themselves at least, for the acquisition of worthless toys and gewgaws.[52] How little is requisite to supply the *necessities* of nature? And in a view to *pleasure*, what comparison between the unbought satisfaction of conversation, society, study, even

ealth and the common beauties of nature, but above all the peaceful reflec-
ion on one's own conduct; what comparison, I say, between these and the
everish, empty amusements of luxury and expense? These natural pleasures,
ndeed, are really without price; both because they are below all price in their
attainment, and above it in their enjoyment.

NOTES

1. *sensible*: aware [D.C.A.]
2. *specious*: plausible [P.H.N.]
3. *several*: various [P.H.N.]
4. *sentence*: judgement [P.H.N.]
5. *complication*: complex, combination [P.H.N.]
6. *natural philosophy*: philosophy of nature, i.e., natural science [D.C.A.]
7. *engage*: win, secure [P.H.N.]
8. *lenity*: mildness, mercifulness [P.H.N.]
9. *intitled*: entitled [D.C.A.]
10. *derived to*: imparted or communicated to [P.H.N.]
11. *offices*: attentions, services [P.H.N.]
12. *topics*: points [P.H.N.]
13. *sensible to*: sensitive to, aware of [P.H.N.]
14. *inquisitor*: member of the Inquisition, a former tribunal of the Roman Catholic Church for discovering and punishing heretics [D.C.A.]
15. *romance*: extravagant fiction [P.H.N.]
16. *poinard*: dagger [P.H.N.]
17. Timoleon (died about 334 B.C.E.) was a Corinthian general who fought against tyrants. Brutus (85–42 B.C.E.) was a leader of the conspiracy that resulted in the assassination of Julius Caesar in 44. [D.C.A.]
18. *cates*: delicate or dainty food [P.H.N.]
19. *complacency*: tranquil pleasure or satisfaction [P.H.N.]
20. *jealous*: scrupulously vigilant [P.H.N.]
21. *emergence*: emergency [D.C.A.]
22. *rencounter*: hostile encounter; conflict [P.H.N.]
23. *still*: continually [P.H.N.]
24. Romans 6:14 [D.C.A.]
25. Psalms 37:29 (36:29 in some versions); Matthew 5:5 [D.C.A.]
26. *vulgar*: ordinary, common [D.C.A.]
27. *principle*: cause [P.H.N.]
28. *Lord Bacon*: Francis Bacon (1561–1626), an English philosopher of science [D.C.A.]
29. *experimentum crucis*: a Latin phrase meaning "experiment of the cross," i.e., a "crucial" experiment that indicates which way to proceed at a crossroads [D.C.A.]
30. *sensibly*: perceptibly [D.C.A.]
31. *sensible*: perceptible [D.C.A.]
32. *humanity*: fellow-feeling [P.H.N.]
33. *aspect*: sight [P.H.N.]

34. Horace (65–8 B.C.E.) was a Roman poet and satirist. Hume's reference is to *The Art of Poetry*, lines 101–102. [D.C.A.]
35. *forwarded*: assisted, promoted [P.H.N.]
36. *pleasing*: i.e., pleasing to me [D.C.A.]
37. *careless*: carefree [P.H.N.]
38. *ingrossed*: engrossed [P.H.N.]
39. *flint*: stone [P.H.N.]
40. *encrease*: increase [D.C.A.]
41. *rude*: primitive, unsophisticated [P.H.N.]
42. *Utile* and *dulce* are the Latin words for "useful" and "agreeable," respectively. [D.C.A.]
43. *implicitly*: unquestioningly [P.H.N.]
44. *topic*: consideration, argument [P.H.N.]
45. *glosses*: intentionally misleading interpretations [D.C.A.]
46. *hair-brained*: harebrained [D.C.A.]
47. *dispersed*: diverse [P.H.N.]
48. *symphony*: harmony, agreement [P.H.N.]
49. *account*: advantage [D.C.A.]
50. *peculiar*: special, distinctive [P.H.N.]
51. *mediums*: means [P.H.N.]
52. *gewgaws*: trinkets [D.C.A.]

QUESTIONS FOR REFLECTION AND DISCUSSION

1. Is utility what makes an inner quality a moral virtue?
2. Is the ability to give pleasure the ultimate criterion for determining the utility of something?
3. If a rule of justice does not seem socially useful in a given situation, should we violate it?
4. Is sympathy an inborn, universal human trait?
5. Is it always ultimately in our own best self-interest to be moral?

SUGGESTIONS FOR FURTHER READING

I. Primary Sources

An Enquiry Concerning the Principles of Morals, in *Enquiries Concerning Human Understanding and Concerning the Principles of Morals*, 3d ed., ed. L. A. Selby-Bigge, rev by P. H. Nidditch. Oxford, England: Clarendon, 1975, pp. 169–323.

"Of Morals," Book 3 of *A Treatise of Human Nature: Being an Attempt to Introduce the Experimental Method of Reasoning into Moral Subjects*, 2d ed., ed. L. A. Selby-Bigge, rev. by P. H. Nidditch. Oxford, England: Clarendon, 1978, pp. 453–621.

This is Hume's initial presentation of his theory of morality, published in 1740. It presents in a more analytical and technical way the material covered in *An Enquiry Concerning the Principles of Morals*, which was published 11 years later.

"Concerning Moral Sentiment," Appendix I to *An Enquiry Concerning the Principles of Morals*, pp. 285–294.

Hume argues that the foundation of moral praise or blame is sentiment, not reason; while reason helps us determine utility, it is our positive feeling about utility that grounds moral judgments.

"Of Self-Love," Appendix II to *An Enquiry Concerning the Principles of Morals*, pp. 295–302.

Hume argues against the view that morality is ultimately selfish, rejecting the argument that we are concerned for the happiness of others only because this makes *us* happy.

An Abstract of a Book Lately Published; Entituled, A Treatise of Human Nature, etc., Wherein the Chief Argument of That Book Is Farther Illustrated and Explained, in *A Treatise of Human Nature*, pp. 641–662.

Hume's brief summary, published in 1740, of Books 1 and 2 of his *Treatise of Human Nature*. As Hume states in the preface, his intention is "to render a larger work more intelligible to ordinary capacities, by abridging it."

I. Secondary Sources

Ayer, A. J. *Hume*. New York: Hill & Wang, Past Masters Ser., 1980, 102 pp.

A brief study of Hume's philosophical method, theory of knowledge, doctrine of causation, and views on morality, politics, and religion.

Basson, A. H. (pseudonym of Anthony P. Cavendish). *David Hume*. 1958; reprint ed., Westport, Conn.: Greenwood, 1981, 183 pp.

A general introduction to Hume's philosophy. See especially chap. 5, "Reason and Morals," pp. 86–112.

Broad, C. D. *Five Types of Ethical Theory*. 1930; reprint ed., Paterson, N.J.: Littlefield, Adams & Co., 1959, 288 pp.

Chapter 4, "Hume," pp. 84–115, gives a lucid exposition and evaluation of Hume's principal doctrines in *An Enquiry Concerning the Principles of Morals*.

Mackie, J. L. *Hume's Moral Theory*. London: Routledge, International Library of Philosophy, 1980, 166 pp.

Examines Hume's moral theory in Book 3 of *A Treatise of Human Nature* and his psychology of action in Book 2. There are also chapters on Hume's predecessors and successors.

Stroud, Barry. *Hume*. London: Routledge, The Arguments of the Philosophers Ser., 1977, 280 pp.

A comprehensive study of Hume's philosophy that interprets him as primarily a philosopher of human nature. For more advanced students of Hume.

9

Karl Marx

Karl Marx was born in 1818 into a middle-class family in Trier, in the German state of Prussia. He began studying law at the University of Bonn at the age of seventeen. The next year he transferred to the University of Berlin, where he became interested in philosophy, especially the thought of Georg Wilhelm Friedrich Hegel (1770–1831), and associated with the politically radical Young Hegelians. In 1841 he received his doctorate in philosophy from the University of Jena, writing his dissertation on two ancient Greek philosophers, Democritus and Epicurus.

Unable to get a teaching position because of his political views, Marx in 1842 became editor of the *Rhenish Gazette*, a liberal newspaper in the Rhineland. The paper was closed down by the Prussian government the following year. Marx, who was becoming increasingly interested in socialism, moved to Paris to take a job as coeditor of a new socialist publication, the *German-French Annals*. There he met Friedrich Engels (1820–1895), a German socialist and fellow Young Hegelian who was to become his lifelong friend and collaborator. In the summer of 1844 Marx wrote a series of unfinished essays (not published until 1932) in which he criticized capitalism and espoused communism. These essays have become known as the *Economic and Philosophic Manuscripts of 1844* or, simply, the "Paris Manuscripts."

The *German-French Annals* was soon shut down by the authorities, and Marx was expelled from Paris in 1844. He moved to Brussels, Belgium, where he became involved in socialist organizations and studied economics. In 1845 he and Engels wrote *The German Ideology* (not published in full until 1932). Two years later Marx and Engels were asked by the Communist League to draw up a statement of its doctrines in simple language. The result was the *Communist Manifesto*, published in 1848.

Later that year, Marx moved to Paris and then to Prussia. He returned to Paris in 1849 but was once again expelled. He finally settled in London, where he studied capitalism, wrote articles for the New York *Tribune*, and helped to found the International Workingmen's Association (later known as the First International). In 1867 he published the first volume of *Capital*, his major work on economics, which he had begun in 1844.

In 1873 Marx suffered a stroke, but despite his impaired health he continued to work on the second and third volumes of *Capital*. In 1875 he wrote a criticism of German socialism entitled *Critique of the Gotha Program*. After Marx's death in London in 1883, Engels edited the unfinished portions of *Capital*, publishing the second volume in 1885 and the third volume in 1894.

Marx's writings often seem very abstract, but his aim is always concrete. As he states in his "Theses on Feuerbach" (the German philosopher Ludwig Feuerbach [1804–1872]): "Philosophers have only *interpreted* the world in various ways; the point is to *change* it." Marx wanted to change the world by replacing capitalism with communism, and his writings attempt to establish the intellectual basis for this revolution.

For Marx the fundamental human activity is labor. By *labor*, Marx means human activity that transforms the natural world in a way that makes possible and enhances human life. When we labor, we put part of ourselves into the products of our labor. Labor is by nature a creative and social human activity, but under capitalism (the economic system in which the means of production are privately owned), it becomes a source of alienation (estrangement). Workers in a capitalist system do not labor because they see it as a way to express themselves and to contribute to the human community; they are, instead, the paid slaves of the capitalist owner, working in order to get enough money to survive. Workers cannot keep or freely dispose of the products of their labor because the capitalist owner takes the products away. Thus the products, into which workers have put part of themselves, become alien (foreign, strange) to them. This alienation from the products of labor leads to the workers' alienation from their own human nature and from one another. The way to end this manifold alienation is to overthrow capitalism and establish a communist society—a society in which private ownership of the means of production is abolished and in which labor is a free expression of human creativity and an inherently social activity.

Our readings are excerpts from three of the essays in the *Economic and Philosophic Manuscripts of 1844*. In "Estranged Labor," Marx explains how capitalism (the theory of "political economy" set forth by writers such as Adam Smith [1723–1790], David Ricardo [1772–1823], and James Mill [1773–1836]) causes alienation. Marx distinguishes four aspects of alienation: alienation from the product of labor, alienation in the act of production, alienation from the human species, and alienation of human beings from one another.

"Private Property and Communism" describes the three stages in the process of overcoming (annulling) private property: first, a crude form of communism in which ownership of private property passes from individuals to the state (or smaller community), producing "universal private property" and making the state "the universal capitalist"; second, an intermediate stage in which there may or may not be a state, and in which society is less obviously influenced by the notion of private property but still remains captive to it; and third, true communism, in which there is no state and no vestige of private property, and in which human beings realize their genuinely social nature.

In "The Meaning of Human Requirements," Marx explains how capitalists create artificial human needs in order to sell products and thus profit from their fellow human beings. True human needs, meanwhile, go unfulfilled. Capitalism places value on what a person *has* rather than on what he or she *is*.

ECONOMIC AND PHILOSOPHIC MANUSCRIPTS OF 1844

ESTRANGED LABOR

We have proceeded from the premises of political economy. We have accepted its language and its laws. We presupposed private property,[1] the separation of labor, capital and land, and of wages, profit of capital and rent of land—likewise division of labor, competition, the concept of exchange-value, etc. On the basis of political economy itself, in its own words, we have shown that the worker sinks to the level of a commodity and becomes indeed the most wretched of commodities; that the wretchedness of the worker is in inverse proportion to the power and magnitude of his production; that the necessary result of competition is the accumulation of capital in a few hands, and thus the restoration of monopoly in a more terrible form; and that finally the distinction between capitalist and land rentier,[2] like that between the tiller of the soil and the factory worker, disappears and that the whole of society must fall apart into the two classes—the property *owners* and the propertyless *workers*.

Political economy starts with the fact of private property, but it does not explain it to us. It expresses in general, abstract formulas the *material* process through which private property actually passes, and these formulas it then takes for *laws*. It does not *comprehend* these laws, i.e., it does not demonstrate how they arise from the very nature of private property. Political economy does not disclose the source of the division between labor and capital, and between capital and land. When, for example, it defines the relationship of wages to profit, it takes the interest of the capitalists to be the ultimate cause, i.e., it takes for granted what it is supposed to explain. Similarly, competition comes in everywhere. It is explained from external circumstances. As to how far these external and apparently accidental circumstances are but the expression of a necessary course of development, political economy teaches us nothing. We have seen how exchange itself appears to it as an accidental fact. The only wheels which political economy sets in motion are *greed* and the war *amongst the greedy—competition*.

Precisely because political economy does not grasp the way the movement is connected, it was possible to oppose, for instance, the doctrine of competition to the doctrine of monopoly, the doctrine of the freedom of the crafts to the doctrine of the guild, the doctrine of the division of landed property to the doctrine of the big estate—for competition, freedom of the crafts, and the division of landed property were explained and comprehended only as accidental, premeditated, and violent consequences of monopoly, of the guild system, and of feudal property, not as their necessary, inevitable, and natural consequences.

Now, therefore, we have to grasp the essential connection between private property, greed, and the separation of labor, capital and landed property; between exchange and competition, value and the devaluation of men, monopoly and competition, etc.—the connection between this whole estrangement and the *money* system.

Do not let us go back to a fictitious primordial condition as the political economist does, when he tries to explain. Such a primordial condition explains nothing; it merely pushes the question away into a gray nebulous distance. It assumes in the form of a fact, of an event, what the economist is supposed to deduce—namely, the necessary relationship between two things—between, for example, division of labor and exchange. Theology in the same way explains the origin of evil by the fall of man; that is, it assumes as a fact, in historical form, what has to be explained.

We proceed from an economic fact *of the present*.

The worker becomes all the poorer the more wealth he produces, the more his production increases in power and size. The worker becomes an ever cheaper commodity the more commodities he creates. With the *increasing value* of the world of things proceeds in direct proportion the *devaluation* of the world of men. Labor produces not only commodities: it produces itself and the worker as a *commodity*—and this in the same general proportion in which it produces commodities.

This fact expresses merely that the object which labor produces—labor's product—confronts it as *something alien*, as a *power independent* of the producer. The product of labor is labor which has been embodied in an object, which has become material: it is the *objectification*[3] of labor. Labor's realization is its objectification. In the sphere of political economy this realization of labor appears as *loss of realization*[4] for the workers; objectification as *loss of the object* and *bondage to it*; appropriation as *estrangement*, as *alienation*.

So much does labor's realization appear as loss of realization that the worker loses realization to the point of starving to death. So much does objectification appear as loss of the object that the worker is robbed of the objects most necessary not only for his life but for his work. Indeed, labor self becomes an object which he can obtain only with the greatest effort and with the most irregular interruptions. So much does the appropriation of the object appear as estrangement that the more objects the worker produces, the less he can possess and the more he falls under the sway of his product, capital.

All these consequences result from the fact that the worker is related to the *product of his labor* as to an *alien* object. For on this premise it is clear that the more the worker spends himself, the more powerful becomes the alien world of objects which he creates over and against himself, the poorer he himself—his inner world—becomes, the less belongs to him as his own. It is the same in religion. The more man puts into God, the less he retains in himself. The worker puts his life into the object; but now his life no longer belongs to him but to the object. Hence, the greater this activity, the greater is the worker's lack of objects. Whatever the product of his labor is, he is not. Therefore the greater this product, the less is he himself. The *alienation* of the worker in his product means not only that his labor becomes an object, an *external* existence, but that it exists *outside him*, independently, as something alien to him, and that it becomes a power on its own confronting him. It means that the life which he has conferred on the object confronts him as something hostile and alien.

Let us now look more closely at the *objectification*, at the production of the worker; and in it at the *estrangement*, the *loss* of the object, of his product.

The worker can create nothing without *nature*, without the *sensuous*[5] *external world*. It is the material on which his labor is realized, in which it is active, from which and by means of which it produces.

But just as nature provides labor with the *means of life* in the sense that labor cannot *live* without objects on which to operate, on the other hand, it also provides the *means of life* in the more restricted sense, i.e., the means for the physical subsistence of the *worker* himself.

Thus the more the worker by his labor *appropriates* the external world, hence sensuous nature, the more he deprives himself of *means of life* in a double manner: first, in that the sensuous external world more and more ceases to be an object belonging to his labor—to be his labor's *means of life*; and secondly, in that it more and more ceases to be *means of life* in the immediate sense, means for the physical subsistence of the worker.

In both respects, therefore, the worker becomes a slave of his object, first, in that he receives an *object of labor*, i.e., in that he receives *work*; and secondly, in that he receives *means of subsistence*. Therefore, it enables him to exist, first, as a *worker*; and secondly as a *physical subject*. The height of this bondage is that it is only as a *worker* that he continues to maintain himself as a *physical subject*, and that it is only as a *physical subject* that he is a *worker*.

(The laws of political economy express the estrangement of the worker in his object thus: the more the worker produces, the less he has to consume; the more values he creates, the more valueless, the more unworthy he becomes; the better formed his product, the more deformed becomes the worker; the more civilized his object, the more barbarous becomes the worker; the more powerful labor becomes, the more powerless becomes the worker; the more ingenious labor becomes, the less ingenious becomes the worker and the more he becomes nature's bondsman.)

Political economy conceals the estrangement inherent in the nature of labor by not considering the direct relationship between the worker (labor) *and production.* It is true that labor produces for the rich wonderful things—but for the worker it produces privation. It produces palaces—but for the worker, hovels. It produces beauty—but for the worker, deformity. It replaces labor by machines, but it throws a section of the workers back to a barbarous type of labor, and it turns the other workers into machines. It produces intelligence—but for the worker stupidity, cretinism.

The direct relationship of labor to its products is the relationship of the worker to the objects of his production. The relationship of the man of means to the objects of production and to production itself is only a *consequence* of this first relationship—and confirms it. We shall consider this other aspect later.

When we ask, then, what is the essential relationship of labor, we are asking about the relationship of the *worker* to production.

Till now we have been considering the estrangement, the alienation, of the worker only in one of its aspects, i.e., the worker's *relationship to the products of his labor.* But the estrangement is manifested not only in the result but in the *act of production,* within the *producing activity* itself. How could the worker come to face the product of his activity as a stranger, were it not that in the very act of production he was estranging himself from himself? The product is after all but the summary of the activity, of production. If then the product of labor is alienation, production itself must be active alienation, the alienation of activity, the activity of alienation. In the estrangement of the object of labor is merely summarized the estrangement, the alienation, in the activity of labor itself.

What, then, constitutes the alienation of labor?

First, the fact that labor is *external* to the worker, i.e., it does not belong to his essential being; that in his work, therefore, he does not affirm himself but denies himself, does not feel content but unhappy, does not develop freely his physical and mental energy but mortifies his body and ruins his mind. The worker therefore only feels himself outside his work, and in his work feels outside himself. He is at home when he is not working, and when he is working he is not at home. His labor is therefore not voluntary, but coerced; it is *forced labor.* It is therefore not the satisfaction of a need; it is merely a *means* to satisfy needs external to it. Its alien character emerges clearly in the fact that as soon as no physical or other compulsion exists, labor is shunned like the plague. External labor, labor in which man alienates himself, is a labor of self-sacrifice, of mortification. Lastly, the external character of labor for the worker appears in the fact that it is not his own, but omeone else's, that it does not belong to him, that in it he belongs, not to himself, but to another. Just as in religion the spontaneous activity of the human imagination, of the human brain and the human heart, operates independently of the individual—that is, operates on him as an alien, divine or diabolical activity—so is the worker's activity not his spontaneous activity. It belongs to another; it is the loss of his self.

As a result, therefore, man (the worker) only feels himself freely active in his animal functions—eating, drinking, procreating, or at most in his dwelling and in dressing-up, etc.; and in his human functions he no longer feels himself to be anything but an animal. What is animal becomes human and what is human becomes animal.

Certainly eating, drinking, procreating, etc., are also genuinely human functions. But abstractly taken, separated from the sphere of all other human activity and turned into sole and ultimate ends, they are animal functions.

We have considered the act of estranging practical human activity, labor, in two of its aspects. (1) The relation of the worker to the *product of labor* as an alien object exercising power over him. This relation is at the same time the relation to the sensuous external world, to the objects of nature, as an alien world inimically opposed to him. (2) The relation of labor to the *act of production* within the *labor* process. This relation is the relation of the worker to his own activity as an alien activity not belonging to him; it is activity as suffering, strength as weakness, begetting as emasculating, the worker's *own* physical and mental energy, his personal life—indeed, what is life but activity?—as an activity which is turned against him, independent of him and not belonging to him. Here we have *self-estrangement*, as previously we had the estrangement of the *thing*.

We have still a third aspect of *estranged labor* to deduce from the two already considered.

Man is a species being,[6] not only because in practice and in theory he adopts the species as his object (his own as well as those of other things), but—and this is only another way of expressing it—also because he treats himself as the actual, living species; because he treats himself as a *universal* and therefore a free being.

The life of the species, both in man and in animals, consists physically in the fact that man (like the animal) lives on inorganic nature; and the more universal man is compared with an animal, the more universal is the sphere of inorganic nature on which he lives. Just as plants, animals, stones, air, light, etc., constitute theoretically a part of human consciousness, partly as objects of natural science, partly as objects of art—his spiritual inorganic nature, spiritual nourishment which he must first prepare to make palatable and digestible—so also in the realm of practice they constitute a part of human life and human activity. Physically man lives only on these products of nature, whether they appear in the form of food, heating, clothes, a dwelling, etc. The universality of man appears in practice precisely in the universality which makes all nature his *inorganic* body—both inasmuch as nature is (1) his direct means of life, and (2) the material, the object, and the instrument of his life activity. Nature is man's *inorganic body*—nature, that is, in so far as it is not itself the human body. Man *lives* on nature—means that nature is his *body*, with which he must remain in continuous interchange if he is not to die. That man's physical and spiritual life is linked to nature means simply that nature is linked to itself, for man is part of nature.

In estranging from man (1) nature, and (2) himself, his own active functions, his life activity, estranged labor estranges the *species* from man. It changes for him the *life of the species* into a means of individual life. First it estranges the life of the species and individual life, and secondly it makes individual life in its abstract form the purpose of the life of the species, likewise in its abstract and estranged form.

Indeed, labor, *life-activity*, *productive life* itself, appears in the first place merely as a *means* of satisfying a need—the need to maintain physical existence. Yet the productive life is the life of the species. It is life-engendering life. The whole character of a species—its species character—is contained in the character of its life activity; and free, conscious activity is man's species character. Life itself appears only as a *means to life*.

The animal is immediately one with its life activity. It does not distinguish itself from it. It is *its life activity*. Man makes his life activity itself the object of his will and of his consciousness. He has conscious life activity. It is not a determination with which he directly merges. Conscious life activity distinguishes man immediately from animal life activity. It is just because of this that he is a species being. Or rather, it is only because he is a species being that he is a conscious being, i.e., that his own life is an object for him. Only because of that is his activity free activity. Estranged labor reverses this relationship, so that it is just because man is a conscious being that he makes his life activity, his *essential* being, a mere means to his *existence*.

In creating a *world of objects* by his practical activity, in *his work upon* inorganic nature, man proves himself a conscious species being, i.e., as a being that treats the species as its own essential being, or that treats itself as a species being. Admittedly animals also produce. They build themselves nests, dwellings, like the bees, beavers, ants, etc. But an animal only produces what it immediately needs for itself or its young. It produces one-sidedly, whilst man produces universally. It produces only under the dominion of immediate physical need, whilst man produces even when he is free from physical need and only truly produces in freedom therefrom. An animal produces only itself, whilst man reproduces the whole of nature. An animal's product belongs immediately to its physical body, whilst man freely confronts his product. An animal forms things in accordance with the standard and the need of the species to which it belongs, whilst man knows how to produce in accordance with the standard of every species, and knows how to apply everywhere the inherent standard to the object. Man therefore also forms things in accordance with the laws of beauty.

It is just in his work upon the objective world, therefore, that man first really proves himself to be a *species being.* This production is his active species life. Through and because of this production, nature appears as *his* work and his reality. The object of labor is, therefore, the *objectification of man's species life:* for he duplicates himself not only, as in consciousness, intellectually, but also actively, in reality, and therefore he contemplates himself in a world that he has created. In tearing away from man the object of his production, therefore, estranged labor tears from him his *species life,* his real objectivity as a member of the species, and transforms his advantage over animals into the disadvantage that his inorganic body, nature, is taken away from him.

Similarly, in degrading spontaneous, free activity, to a means, estranged labor makes man's species life a means to his physical existence.

The consciousness which man has of his species is thus transformed by estrangement in such a way that species life becomes for him a means.

Estranged labor turns thus:

(3) *Man's species being,* both nature and his spiritual species property, into a being *alien* to him, into a *means* to his *individual existence.* It estranges from man his own body, as well as external nature and his spiritual essence, his *human* being.

(4) An immediate consequence of the fact that man is estranged from the product of his labor, from his life activity, from his species being, is the *estrangement of man* from *man.* When man confronts himself, he confronts the *other* man. What applies to a man's relation to his work, to the product of his labor and to himself, also holds of a man's relation to the other man, and to the other man's labor and object of labor.

In fact, the proposition that man's species nature is estranged from him means that one man is estranged from the other, as each of them is from man's essential nature.

The estrangement of man, and in fact every relationship in which man stands to himself, is first realized and expressed in the relationship in which a man stands to other men.

Hence within the relationship of estranged labor each man views the other in accordance with the standard and the relationship in which he finds himself as a worker.

We took our departure from a fact of political economy—the estrangement of the worker and his production. We have formulated this fact in conceptual terms as *estranged, alienated* labor. We have analyzed this concept—hence analyzing merely a fact of political economy.

Let us now see, further, how the concept of estranged, alienated labor must express and present itself in real life.

If the product of labor is alien to me, if it confronts me as an alien power, to whom, then, does it belong?

If my own activity does not belong to me, if it is an alien, a coerced activity, to whom, then, does it belong?

To a being *other* than myself.

Who is this being?

The *gods?* To be sure, in the earliest times the principal production (for example, the building of temples, etc., in Egypt, India, and Mexico) appears to be in the service of the gods, and the product belongs to the gods. However, the gods on their own were never the lords of labor. No more was *nature.* And what a contradiction it would be if, the more man subjugated nature by his labor and the more the miracles of the gods were rendered superfluous by the miracles of industry, the more man were to renounce the joy of production and the enjoyment of the product in favor of these powers.

The *alien* being, to whom labor and the product of labor belongs, in whose service labor is done and for whose benefit the product of labor is provided, can only be *man* himself.

If the product of labor does not belong to the worker, if it confronts him as an alien power, then this can only be because it belongs to some *man other than the worker.* If the worker's activity is a torment to him, to another it must be *delight* and his life's joy. Not the gods, not nature, but only man himself can be this alien power over man.

We must bear in mind the previous proposition that man's relation to himself only becomes for him *objective* and *actual* through his relation to the other man. Thus, if the product of his labor, his labor *objectified,* is for him an *alien,* hostile, powerful object independent of him, then his position towards it is such that someone else is master of this object, someone who is alien, hostile, powerful, and independent of him. If his own activity is to him related as an unfree activity, then he is related to it as an activity performed in the service, under the dominion, the coercion, and the yoke of another man.

Every self-estrangement of man, from himself and from nature, appears in the relation in which he places himself and nature to men other than and differentiated from himself. For this reason religious self-estrangement necessarily appears in the relationship of the layman to the priest, or again to a mediator, etc., since we are here dealing with the intellectual world. In the real practical world, self-estrangement can only become manifest through the real practical relationship to other men. The medium through which estrangement takes place is itself *practical.* Thus through estranged labor man not only creates his relationship to the object and to the act of production as to men that are alien and hostile to him; he also creates the relationship in which other men stand to his production and to his product, and the relationship in which he stands to these other men. Just as he creates his own production as the loss of his reality, as his punishment; his own product as a loss, as a product not belonging to him; so he creates the domination of the person who does not produce over production and over the product. Just as he estranges his own activity from himself, so he confers to the stranger an activity which is not his own.

We have until now only considered this relationship from the standpoint of the worker and later we shall be considering it also from the standpoint of the non-worker.

Through *estranged, alienated labor*, then, the worker produces the relationship to this labor of a man alien to labor and standing outside it. The relationship of the worker to labor creates the relation to it of the capitalist (or whatever one chooses to call the master of labor). *Private property* is thus the product, the result, the necessary consequence, of *alienated labor*, of the external relation of the worker to nature and to himself.

Private property thus results by analysis from the concept of *alienated labor*, i.e., of *alienated man*, of estranged labor, of estranged life, of *estranged* man.

True, it is as a result of the *movement of private property* that we have obtained the concept of *alienated labor (of alienated life)* from political economy. But on analysis of this concept it becomes clear that though private property appears to be the source, the cause of alienated labor, it is rather its consequence, just as the gods are *originally* not the cause but the effect of man's intellectual confusion. Later this relationship becomes reciprocal.

Only at the last culmination of the development of private property does this, its secret, appear again, namely, that on the one hand it is the *product* of alienated labor, and that on the other it is the *means* by which labor alienates itself, the *realization of this alienation*.

This exposition immediately sheds light on various hitherto unsolved conflicts.

(1) Political economy starts from labor as the real soul of production; yet to labor it gives nothing, and to private property everything. Confronting this contradiction, Proudhon[7] has decided in favor of labor against private property. We understand however, that this apparent contradiction is the contradiction of *estranged labor* with itself, and that political economy has merely formulated the laws of estranged labor.

We also understand, therefore, that *wages* and *private property* are identical: since the product, as the object of labor pays for labor itself, therefore the wage is but a necessary consequence of labor's estrangement. After all, in the wage of labor, labor does not appear as an end in itself but as the servant of the wage. We shall develop this point later, and meanwhile will only derive some conclusions.

An enforced increase of wages (disregarding all other difficulties, including the fact that it would only be by force, too, that higher wages, being an anomaly, could be maintained) would therefore be nothing but *better payment for the slave*, and would not win either for the worker or for labor their human status and dignity.

Indeed, even the *equality of wages* demanded by Proudhon only transforms the relationship of the present-day worker to his labor into the relationship of all men to labor. Society is then conceived as an abstract capitalist.

Wages are a direct consequence of estranged labor, and estranged labor
is the direct cause of private property. The downfall of the one must involve
the downfall of the other.

(2) From the relationship of estranged labor to private property it follows
further that the emancipation of society from private property, etc., from
servitude, is expressed in the *political* form of the *emancipation of the workers;*
not that *their* emancipation alone is at stake, but because the emancipation of
the workers contains universal human emancipation—and it contains this,
because the whole of human servitude is involved in the relation of the
worker to production, and every relation of servitude is but a modification
and consequence of this relation. . . .

PRIVATE PROPERTY AND COMMUNISM

. . . The antithesis between *lack of property* and *property*, so long as it is not
comprehended as the antithesis of *labor* and *capital*, still remains an indifferent
antithesis, not grasped in its *active connection*, with its *internal* relation—an
antithesis not yet grasped as a *contradiction*. It can find expression in this *first*
form even without the advanced development of private property (as in
ancient Rome, Turkey, etc.). It does not yet *appear* as having been established
by private property itself. But labor, the subjective essence of private property
as exclusion of property, and capital, objective labor as exclusion of labor,
constitute *private property* as its developed state of contradiction—hence a
dynamic relationship moving to its resolution. . . .

The transcendence[8] of self-estrangement follows the same course as self-
estrangement. *Private property* is first considered only in its objective aspect—
but nevertheless with labor as its essence. Its form of existence is therefore
capital, which is to be annulled "as such" (Proudhon). Or a *particular form* of
labor—labor leveled down, parceled, and therefore unfree—is conceived as
the source of private property's *perniciousness* and of its existence in estrangement from men. For instance, *Fourier*,[9] like the physiocrats,[10] conceives
agricultural labor to be at least the *exemplary* type, whilst *Saint-Simon*[11] declares
in contrast that *industrial labor* as such is the essence, and accordingly aspires
to the *exclusive* rule of the industrialists and the improvement of the workers'
condition. Finally, *communism* is the *positive* expression of annulled[12] private
property—at first as *universal* private property. By embracing this relation as a
whole, communism is:

(1) In its first form only a *generalization* and *consummation* of this relationship. As such it appears in a twofold form: on the one hand, the dominion
of *material* property bulks so large that it wants to destroy *everything* which is
not capable of being possessed by all as *private property*. It wants to do away *by*

orce with talent, etc. For it the sole purpose of life and existence is direct, physical *possession*. The task of the *laborer* is not done away with, but extended to all men. The relationship of private property persists as the relationship of the community to the world of things.

Finally, this movement of opposing universal private property to private property finds expression in the animal form of opposing to *marriage* (certainly a *form of exclusive private property*) the *community of women*, in which a woman becomes a piece of *communal* and *common* property. It may be said that this idea of the *community of women* gives away the *secret* of this as yet completely crude and thoughtless communism. Just as woman passes from marriage to general prostitution, so the entire world of wealth (that is, of man's objective substance) passes from the relationship of exclusive marriage with the owner of private property to a state of universal prostitution with the community. In negating the *personality* of man in every sphere, this type of communism is really nothing but the logical expression of private property, which is its negation. General *envy* constituting itself as a power is the disguise in which *greed* reestablishes itself and satisfies itself, only in *another way*. The thought of every piece of private property—inherent in each piece as such—is *at least* turned against all *wealthier* private property in the form of envy and the urge to reduce things to a common level, so that this envy and urge even constitute the essence of competition. The crude communism is only the culmination of this envy and of this leveling-down proceeding from the *preconceived* minimum. It has a *definite, limited* standard. How little this annulment of private property is really an appropriation is in fact proved by the abstract negation of the entire world of culture and civilization, the regression to the *unnatural* simplicity of the *poor and undemanding* man who has not only failed to go beyond private property, but has not yet even reached it.

The community is only a community of *labor*, and of equality of *wages* paid out by communal capital—the *community* as the universal capitalist. Both sides of the relationship are raised to an *imagined* universality—*labor* as a state in which every person is placed, and *capital* as the acknowledged universality and power of the community.

In the approach to *woman* as the spoil and handmaid of communal lust is expressed the infinite degradation in which man exists for himself, for the secret of this approach has its *unambiguous*, decisive, *plain* and undisguised expression in the relation of *man* to *woman* and in the manner in which the *direct* and *natural* species relationship is conceived. This direct, natural, and necessary relation of person to person is the *relation of man to woman*. In this *natural* species relationship man's relation to nature is immediately his relation to man, just as his relation to man is immediately his relation to nature— his own *natural* destination. In this relationship, therefore, is *sensuously manifested*, reduced to an observable *fact*, the extent to which the human essence has become nature to man, or to which nature to him has become the human essence of man. From this relationship one can therefore judge man's whole level of development. From the character of this relationship follows how much *man* as a *species being*, as *man*, has come to be himself and to comprehend himself; the relation of man to woman is *the most natural* relation of human being to human being. It therefore reveals the extent to which man's *natural* behavior has become *human*, or the extent to which the *human* essence in him has become a *natural* essence—the extent to which his *human nature* has come to be *nature to him*. In this relationship is revealed, too, the extent to which man's *need* has become a *human* need; the extent to which, therefore, the *other* person as a person has become for him a need—the extent to which he in his individual existence is at the same time a social being.

The first positive annulment of private property—*crude* communism—is thus merely one *form* in which the vileness of private property, which wants to set itself up as the *positive community, comes to the surface.*

(2) Communism (*a*) still political in nature—democratic or despotic; (*b*) with the abolition of the state, yet still incomplete and still being affected by private property (i.e., by the estrangement of man). In both forms communism already is aware of being reintegration or return of man to himself, the transcendence of human self-estrangement; but since it has not yet grasped the positive essence of private property, and just as little the *human* nature of need, it remains captive to it and infected by it. It has, indeed, grasped its concept, but not its essence.

(3) *Communism* as the *positive* transcendence of *private property*, as *human self-estrangement*, and therefore as the real *appropriation* of the *human* essence by and for man; communism therefore as the complete return of man to himself as a *social* (i.e., human) being—a return become conscious, and accomplished within the entire wealth of previous development. This communism, as fully developed naturalism, equals humanism, and as fully developed humanism equals naturalism; it is the *genuine* resolution of the conflict between man and nature and between man and man—the true resolution of the strife between existence and essence, between objectification and self-confirmation, between freedom and necessity, between the individual and the species. Communism is the riddle of history solved, and it knows itself to be this solution.

The entire movement of history is, therefore, both [communism's] *actual* act of genesis (the birth act of its empirical existence) and also for its thinking consciousness the *comprehended* and *known* process of its *becoming*. That other, still immature communism, meanwhile, seeks an *historical* proof for itself—a proof in the realm of what already exists—among disconnected historical phenomena opposed to private property, tearing single phases from the historical process and focusing attention on them as proofs of its historical pedigree (a hobbyhorse ridden hard especially by Cabet, Villegardelle, etc.).[13] By so doing it simply makes clear that by far the greater part of this process contradicts its own claim, and that, if it has ever existed, precisely its being in the *past* refutes its pretension to being *essential being*.

It is easy to see that the entire revolutionary movement necessarily finds both its empirical and its theoretical basis in the movement of *private property*—more precisely, in that of the economy.

This *material*, immediately perceptible private property is the material perceptible expression of *estranged human* life. Its movement—production and consumption—is the *perceptible* revelation of the movement of all production until now, i.e., the realization or the reality of man. Religion, family, state, law, morality, science, art, etc., are only *particular* modes of production, and fall under its general law. The positive transcendence of *private property*, as the appropriation of *human* life, is therefore the positive transcendence of all estrangement—that is to say, the return of man from religion, family, state, etc., to his *human*, i.e., *social* existence. Religious estrangement as such occurs only in the realm of *consciousness*, of man's inner life, but economic estrangement is that of *real life*; its transcendence therefore embraces both aspects. It is evident that the *initial* stage of the movement amongst the various peoples depends on whether the true and *authentic* life of the people manifests itself more in consciousness or in the external world—is more ideal or real. Communism begins from the outset with atheism; but atheism is at first far from being *communism*; indeed, it is still mostly an abstraction.

The philanthropy of atheism is therefore at first only *philosophical*, abstract, philanthropy, and that of communism is at once *real* and directly bent on *action*.

We have seen how on the assumption of positively annulled private property man produces man—himself and the other man; how the object, being the direct embodiment of his individuality, is simultaneously his own existence for the other man, the existence of the other man, and that existence for him. Likewise, however, both the material of labor and man as the subject, are the point of departure as well as the result of the movement (and precisely in this fact, that they must constitute the *point of departure*, lies the historical *necessity* of private property). Thus the *social* character is the general character of the whole movement: *just as* society itself produces *man as man*, so is society *produced* by him. Activity and mind, both in their content and in their *mode of existence*, are *social: social* activity and *social* mind. The *human* essence of nature first exists only for *social* man; for only here does nature exist for him as a *bond* with *man*—as his existence for the other and the other's existence for him—as the life-element of human reality. Only here does nature exist as the *foundation* of his own *human* existence. Only here has what is to him his *natural* existence become his *human* existence, and nature become man for him. Thus *society* is the unity of being of man with nature—the true resurrection of nature—the naturalism of man and the humanism of nature both brought to fulfillment.

Social activity and social mind exist by no means *only* in the form of some *directly* communal activity and directly *communal* mind, although *communal* activity and *communal* mind—i.e., activity and mind which are manifested and directly revealed in *real association* with other men—will occur wherever such a *direct* expression of sociability stems from the true character of the activity's content and is adequate to its nature.

But also when I am active *scientifically*, etc.,—when I am engaged in activity which I can seldom perform in direct community with others—then I am *social*, because I am active as a *man*. Not only is the material of my activity given to me as a social product (as is even the language in which the thinker is active): my *own* existence *is* social activity, and therefore that which I make of myself, I make of myself for society and with the consciousness of myself as a social being.

My *general* consciousness is only the *theoretical* shape of that of which the *living* shape is the *real* community, the social fabric, although at the present day *general* consciousness is an abstraction from real life and as such confronts it with hostility. The *activity* of my general consciousness, as an activity, is therefore also my *theoretical* existence as a social being.

Above all we must avoid postulating "society" again as an abstraction *vis-à-vis* the individual. The individual *is the social being.* His life, even if it may not appear in the direct form of a *communal* life in association with others—is therefore an expression and confirmation of *social life.* Man's individual and species life are not *different*, however much—and this is inevitable—the mode of existence of the individual is a more *particular* or more *general* mode of the life of the species, or the life of the species is a more *particular* or more *general* individual life.

In his *consciousness of species* man confirms his real *social life* and simply repeats his real existence in thought, just as conversely the being of the species confirms itself in species-consciousness and exists for *itself* in its generality as a thinking being.

Man, much as he may therefore be a *particular* individual (and it is precisely his particularity which makes him an individual, and a real *individual* social being), is just as much the *totality*—the ideal totality—the subjective existence of thought and experienced society for itself; just as he exists also in the real world as the awareness and the real mind of social existence, and as a totality of human manifestation of life.

Thinking and being are thus no doubt *distinct*, but at the same time they are in *unity* with each other.

Death seems to be a harsh victory of the species over the *definite* individual and to contradict their unity. But the particular individual is only a *particular species being,* and as such mortal. . . .

THE MEANING OF HUMAN REQUIREMENTS

We have seen what significance, given socialism, the *wealth* of human needs has, and what significance, therefore, both a *new mode of production* and a new *object* of production have: a new manifestation of the forces of *human* nature

and a new enrichment of *human* nature. Under private property their significance is reversed: every person speculates on creating a *new* need in another,
so as to drive him to a fresh sacrifice, to place him in a new dependence and to
seduce him into a new mode of *gratification* and therefore economic ruin. Each
tries to establish over the other an *alien power*, so as thereby to find satisfaction
of his own selfish need. The increase in the quantity of objects is accompanied
by an extension of the realm of the alien powers to which man is subjected,
and every new product represents a new *possibility* of mutual swindling and
mutual plundering. Man becomes ever poorer as man, his need for *money*
becomes ever greater if he wants to overpower hostile being. The power of his
money declines so to say in inverse proportion to the increase in the volume of
production: that is, his neediness grows as the *power* of money increases.

The need for money is therefore the true need produced by the modern
economic system, and it is the only need which the latter produces. The
quantity of money becomes to an ever greater degree its sole *effective* quality.
Just as it reduces everything to its abstract form, so it reduces itself in the
course of its own movement to *quantitative* entity. *Excess* and *intemperance*
come to be its true norm. Subjectively, this is partly manifested in that the
extension of products and needs falls into *contriving* and ever-*calculating*
subservience to inhuman, unnatural and *imaginary* appetites. Private property does not know how to change crude need into *human* need. Its *idealism* is
fantasy, *caprice* and *whim*; and no eunuch flatters his despot more basely or
uses more despicable means to stimulate his dulled capacity for pleasure in
order to sneak a favor for himself than does the industrial eunuch—the
producer—in order to sneak for himself a few pennies—in order to charm the
golden birds out of the pockets of his dearly beloved neighbors in Christ. He
puts himself at the service of the other's most depraved fancies, plays the
pimp between him and his need, excites in him morbid appetites, lies in wait
for each of his weaknesses—all so that he can then demand the cash for this
service of love. (Every product is a bait with which to seduce away the other's
very being, his money; every real and possible need is a weakness which will
lead the fly to the gluepot. General exploitation of communal human nature,
just as every imperfection in man, is a bond with heaven—an avenue giving
the priest access to his heart; every need is an opportunity to approach one's
neighbor under the guise of the utmost amiability and to say to him: Dear
friend, I give you what you need, but you know the *conditio sine qua non*;[14] you
know the ink in which you have to sign yourself over to me; in providing for
your pleasure, I fleece you.)

This estrangement manifests itself in part in that it produces sophistica-
tion of needs and of their means on the one hand, and a bestial barbarization,
a complete, unrefined, abstract simplicity of need, on the other; or rather in
that it merely resurrects itself in its opposite. Even the need for fresh air
ceases for the worker. Man returns to a cave dwelling, which is now, however, contaminated with the pestilential breath of civilization, and which he

continues to occupy only *precariously*, it being for him an alien habitation which can be withdrawn from him any day—a place from which, if he does not pay, he can be thrown out any day. For this mortuary he has to *pay*. A dwelling in the *light*, which Prometheus in Aeschylus designated as one of the greatest boons, by means of which he made the savage into a human being,[15] ceases to exist for the worker. Light, air, etc.—the simplest *animal* cleanliness—ceases to be a need for man. *Filth*, this stagnation and putrefaction of man—the *sewage* of civilization (speaking quite literally)—comes to be the *element of life* for him. Utter, *unnatural* neglect, putrefied nature, comes to be his *life-element*. None of his senses exists any longer, and not only in his human fashion, but in an *inhuman* fashion, and therefore not even in an animal fashion. The crudest *methods* (and *instruments*) of human labor are coming back: the *treadmill* of the Roman slaves, for instance, is the means of production, the means of existence, of many English workers. It is not only that man has no human needs—even his *animal* needs cease to exist. The Irishman no longer knows any need now but the need to *eat*, and indeed only the need to eat *potatoes*—and *scabby potatoes* at that, the worst kind of potatoes. But in each of their industrial towns England and France have already a *little* Ireland. The savage and the animal have at least the need to hunt, to roam, etc.—the need of companionship. Machine labor is simplified in order to make a worker out of the human being still in the making, the completely immature human being, the *child*—whilst the worker has become a neglected child. The machine accommodates itself to the *weakness* of the human being in order to make the *weak* human being into a machine.

How the multiplication of needs and of the means of their satisfaction breeds the absence of needs and of means is demonstrated by the political economist (and the capitalist: it should be noted that it is always *empirical* businessmen we are talking about when we refer to political economists, their *scientific* confession and existence). This he shows:

(1) By reducing the worker's need to the barest and most miserable level of physical subsistence, and by reducing his activity to the most abstract mechanical movement. He says: Man has no other need either of activity or of enjoyment. For he calls *even* this life *human* life and existence.

(2) By *counting* the *lowest* possible level of life (existence) as the standard, indeed, as the general standard—general because it is applicable to the mass of men. He changes the worker into an insensible being lacking all needs, just as he changes his activity into a pure abstraction from all activity. To him, therefore, every *luxury* of the worker seems to be reprehensible, and everything that goes beyond the most abstract need—be it in the realm of passive enjoyment, or a manifestation of activity—seems to him a luxury. Political economy, this science of *wealth*, is therefore simultaneously the science of renunciation, of want, of *saving*—and it actually reaches the point where it *spares* man the *need* of either fresh *air* or physical *exercise*. This science of marvelous industry is simultaneously the science of *asceticism*, and its true

deal is the *ascetic* but *extortionate* miser and the *ascetic* but *productive* slave. Its moral ideal is the *worker* who takes part of his wages to the savings-bank, and it has even found ready-made an abject *art* in which to embody this pet idea: they have presented it, bathed in sentimentality, on the stage. Thus political economy—despite its worldly and wanton appearance—is a true moral science, the most moral of all the sciences. Self-renunciation, the renunciation of life and of all human needs, is its principal thesis. The less you eat, drink, and buy books; the less you go to the theater, the dance hall, the public house; the less you think, love, theorize, sing, paint, fence, etc.; the more you *save*—the greater becomes your treasure which neither moths nor rust will devour—your *capital*. The less you *are*, the less you express your own life, the greater is your *alienated* life, the more you *have*, the greater is the store of your estranged being. Everything which the political economist takes from you in life and in humanity, he replaces for you in *money* and in *wealth;* and all the things which you cannot do, your money can do. It can eat and drink, go to the dance hall and the theater; it can travel, it can appropriate art, learning, the treasures of the past, political power—all this it *can* appropriate for you—it can buy all this for you: it is the true *endowment.* Yet being all this, it is *inclined* to do nothing but create itself, buy itself; for everything else is after all its servant. And when I have the master I have the servant and do not need his servant. All passions and all activity must therefore be submerged in *greed.* The worker may only have enough for him to want to live, and may only want to live in order to have that. . . .

And you must not only stint the immediate gratification of your senses, as by stinting yourself on food, etc.: you must also spare yourself all sharing of general interest, all sympathy, all trust, etc.; if you want to be economical, if you do not want to be ruined by illusions.

You must make everything that is yours *saleable,* i.e., useful. If I ask the political economist: Do I obey economic laws if I extract money by offering my body for sale, by surrendering it to another's lust? (The factory workers in France call the prostitution of their wives and daughters the nth working hour, which is literally correct.)—Or am I not acting in keeping with political economy if I sell my friend to the Moroccans? (And the direct sale of men in the form of a trade in conscripts, etc., takes place in all civilized countries.)—Then the political economist replies to me: You do not transgress my laws; but see what Cousin Ethics and Cousin Religion have to say about it. My *political economic* ethics and religion have nothing to reproach you with, but—But whom am I now to believe, political economy or ethics? The ethics of political economy is *acquisition*, work, thrift, sobriety—but political economy promises to satisfy my needs. The political economy of ethics is the opulence of a good conscience, of virtue, etc.; but how can I live virtuously if I do not live? And how can I have a good conscience if I am not conscious of anything?

It stems from the very nature of estrangement that each sphere applies to me a different and opposite yardstick—ethics one and political economy another; for each is a specific estrangement of many and focuses attention on a particular round of estranged essential activity, and each stands in an estranged relation to the other. Thus M. *Michel Chevalier*[16] reproaches Ricardo with having abstracted from ethics. But Ricardo is allowing political economy to speak its own language, and if it does not speak ethically, this is not Ricardo's fault. M. Chevalier abstracts from political economy in so far as he moralizes, but he really and necessarily abstracts from ethics in so far as he practices politial economy. The relationship of political economy to ethics, if it is other than an arbitrary, contingent and therefore unfounded and unscientific relationship, if it is not being put up as a *sham* but is meant to be *essential*, can only be the relationship of the laws of political economy to ethics. If there is no such connection, or if the contrary is rather the case, can Ricardo help it? Moreover, the opposition between political economy and ethics is only a *sham* opposition and just as much no opposition as it is an opposition. All that happens is that political economy expresses moral laws *in its own way*.

Needlessness as the principle of political economy is *most brilliantly* shown in its *theory of population*. There are *too many* people. Even the existence of men is a pure luxury; and if the worker is *"ethical,"* he will be *sparing* in procreation. (Mill suggests public acclaim for those who prove themselves continent in their sexual relations, and public rebuke for those who sin against such barrenness of marriage. . . . Is not this the ethics, the teaching of asceticism?) The production of people appears as public misery.

The meaning which production has in relation to the rich is seen *revealed* in the meaning which it has for the poor. At the top the manifestation is always refined, veiled, ambiguous—a sham; lower, it is rough, straightforward, frank—the real thing. The worker's *crude* need is a far greater source of gain than the *refined* need of the rich. The cellar dwellings in London bring more to those who let them than do the palaces; that is to say, with reference to the landlord they constitute *greater wealth*, and thus (to speak the language of political economy) greater *social* wealth.

Industry speculates on the refinement of needs, but it speculates just as much on their *crudeness*, but on their artificially produced crudeness, whose true enjoyment, therefore, is *self-stupefaction*—this *illusory* satisfaction of need—this civilization contained *within* the crude barbarism of need; the English gin shops are therefore the *symbolical representations* of private property. Their *luxury* reveals the true relation of industrial luxury and wealth to man. They are therefore rightly the only Sunday pleasures of the people, treated mildly at least by the English police.

We have already seen how the political economist establishes the unity of labor and capital in a variety of ways: (1) Capital is *accumulated labor*. (2) The purpose of capital within production—partly, reproduction of capital with profit, partly, capital as raw material (material of labor), and partly, as itself a *working instrument* (the machine is capital directly equated with labor)—is *productive labor*. (3) The worker is a capital. (4) Wages belong to costs of capital. (5) In relation to the worker, labor is the reproduction of his life-capital. (6) In relation to the capitalist, labor is an aspect of his capital's activity.

Finally, (7) the political economist postulates the original unity of capital and labor as the unity of the capitalist and the worker; this is the original state of paradise. The way in which these two aspects, as two persons, leap at each other's throats is for the political economist an *accidental* event, and hence only to be explained by reference to external factors. . . .

In order to abolish the *idea* of private property, the *idea* of communism is completely sufficient. It takes *actual* communist action to abolish *actual* private property. History will come to it; and this movement, which in *theory* we already know to be a self-transcending movement, will constitute *in actual fact* a very severe and protracted process. But we must regard it as a real advance to have gained beforehand a consciousness of the limited character as well as of the goal of this historical movement—and a consciousness which reaches out beyond it.

When communist *artisans* associate with one another, theory, propaganda, etc., is their first end. But at the same time, as a result of this association, they acquire a new need—the need for society—and what appears as a means becomes an end. In this practical process the most splendid results are to be observed whenever French socialist workers are seen together. Such things as smoking, drinking, eating, etc., are no longer means of contact or means that bring together. Company, association, and conversation, which again has society as its end, are enough for them; the brotherhood of man is no mere phrase with them, but a fact of life, and the nobility of man shines upon us from their work-hardened bodies.

When political economy claims that demand and supply always balance each other, it immediately forgets that according to its own claim (theory of population) the supply of *people* always exceeds the demand, and that, therefore, in the essential result of the whole production process—the existence of man—the disparity between demand and supply gets its most striking expression.

The extent to which money, which appears as a means, constitutes true power and the sole *end*—in general *that* means which gives me essence, which gives me possession of alien objective essence, is an *end in itself*—can be clearly seen from the fact that landed property, wherever land is the source of life, and *horse* and *sword*, wherever these are the *true means of life*, are also acknowledged as the true political powers in life. In the Middle Ages a social class is emancipated as soon as it is allowed to carry the *sword*. Amongst nomadic peoples it is the *horse* which makes me a free man and a participant in the life of the community.

We have said above that man is regressing to the *cave dwelling*, etc.—but that he is regressing to it in an estranged, malignant form. The savage in his cave—a natural element which freely offers itself for his use and protection—feels himself no more a stranger, or rather feels himself to be just as much at home as a *fish* in water. But the cellar dwelling of the poor man is a hostile dwelling, "an alien, restraining power which only gives itself up to him in so far as he gives up to it his blood and sweat"—a dwelling which he cannot regard as his own home where he might at last exclaim, "Here I am at home," but where instead he finds himself in *someone else's* house, in the house of a *stranger* who daily lies in wait for him and throws him out if he does not pay his rent. He is also aware of the contrast in quality between his dwelling and a human dwelling—a residence in that *other* world, the heaven of wealth.

Estrangement is manifested not only in the fact that *my* means of life belong to *someone else*, that *my* desire is the inaccessible possession of *another*, but also in the fact that everything is itself something *different* from itself—that my activity is *something else* and that, finally (and this applies also to the capitalist), all is under the sway of *inhuman* power.

There is a form of inactive, extravagant wealth given over wholly to pleasure, the enjoyer of which on the one hand *behaves* as a mere *ephemeral* individual frantically spending himself to no purpose, and also regards the slave-labor of others (human *sweat and blood*) as the prey of his cupidity. Therefore knows man himself, and hence also his own self, as a sacrificed and empty being. With such wealth, contempt of man makes its appearance, partly as arrogance and as squandering of what can give sustenance to a hundred human lives, and partly as the infamous illusion that his own unbridled extravagance and ceaseless, unproductive consumption is the condition of the other's *labor* and therefore of his *subsistence*. He knows the realization of the *essential powers* of many only as the realization of his own excesses, his whims and capricious, bizarre notions. This wealth which, on the other hand, again knows wealth as a mere means, as something that is good for nothing but to be annihilated and which is therefore at once slave and master, at once generous and mean, capricious, presumptuous, conceited, refined, cultured and witty—this wealth has not yet experienced *wealth* as an utterly *alien power* over itself: it sees in it, rather, only its own power, and not wealth but *gratification* [is its] final aim and end.

NOTES

1. *private property*: private ownership of the means of producing goods [D.C.A.]
2. *land rentier*: a person who receives income from land [D.C.A.]
3. *objectification*: the process of becoming an object [D.J.S./M.M.]
4. *loss of realization (Entwirklichung)* : the loss of reality; diminishment [D.C.A.]
5. *sensuous*: able to be sensed [D.C.A.]
6. *species being*: a being that is conscious of itself not only as an individual but also as a member of a particular species. In being conscious of its own species, a species

being is also conscious of other species. A species being is also conscious of the distinction between itself and its activity and can freely pursue its own ends. Only human beings are species beings. [D.C.A.]
7. Pierre-Joseph Proudhon (1809–1865) was a French socialist writer. [D.C.A.]
8. *transcendence (Aufhebung)*: an annulling or overcoming that takes something up into new and higher reality [D.C.A.]
9. Charles Fourier (1772–1837) was a French socialist reformer. [D.C.A.]
10. *physiocrats*: a school of eighteenth-century French political economists [D.C.A.]
11. Comte de Saint-Simon (Claude Henri de Rouvroy) (1760–1825) was a French social philosopher. [D.C.A.]
12. *annulled (aufgehoben)*: transcended, overcome [D.C.A.]
13. Étienne Cabet (1788–1856) and François Villegardelle (1810–1856) were French communists. [D.C.A.]
14. *conditio sine qua non*: an indispensable condition. The Latin phrase means, literally, "a condition without which not." [D.C.A.]
15. The reference is to *Prometheus Bound*, a play by the Greek dramatist Aeschylus (525–456 B.C.E.). In Greek mythology, Prometheus was a demigod who stole fire from the gods and gave it to the human race. [D.C.A.]
16. Michel Chevalier (1806–1879) was a French economist. (The "M." before Chevalier's name stands for *Monsieur*, French for "Mr.") [D.C.A.]

QUESTIONS FOR REFLECTION AND DISCUSSION

1. Does capitalism necessarily cause alienation?
2. Does the institution of private property go against the social nature of human beings?
3. Is it possible for everyone's work to be personally fulfilling?
4. Is it possible to have a society in which all labor is done voluntarily?
5. Is capitalism based on the creation of false needs?

SUGGESTIONS FOR FURTHER READING

Primary Sources

The Power of Money in Bourgeois Society," in *Economic and Philosophic Manuscripts of 1844*, ed. Dirk J. Struik, trans. Martin Milligan. New York: International Publishers, 1964, pp. 165–169.

A brief essay on the alienating role of money in capitalist society. Marx argues that in capitalism, what I can buy is what I *am*. This essay also appears in most anthologies of Marx's early writings, including *Karl Marx: Early Texts*.

On the Jewish Question," in *Karl Marx: Early Texts*, ed. and trans. David McLellan. New York: Barnes & Noble, 1971, pp. 85–114. Reprinted in *Karl Marx: Selected Writings*, ed. David McLellan. Oxford, England: Oxford University Press, 1977, pp. 39–62.

An 1843 article by Marx responding to two essays by Bruno Bauer, his former teacher. Bauer had argued that Jewish emancipation required the abolition of Christianity as a state religion; the state must be secular. Marx criticizes Bauer for not going far enough: The state itself, even if secular, prevents true human emancipation. Marx presents his general views on the relation of the political state to civil society.

The Communist Manifesto, coauthored with Friedrich Engels, trans. Samuel Moore. 1888; reprint ed., Harmondsworth, England: Penguin, 1967, 124 pp. (This 1888 English translation was supervised by Engels.)

Marx and Engels's classic popular exposition of the main tenets of communism. It presents their interpretation of the modern class struggle, ending with the famous exhortation: "The proletarians have nothing to lose but their chains. They have a world to win. Working men of all countries, unite!" The *Manifesto* is included in many anthologies of Marx's writings.

II. Secondary Sources

Koren, Henry. *Marx and the Authentic Man: A First Introduction to the Philosophy of Karl Marx*. Pittsburgh: Duquesne University Press, 1967, 150 pp.

A study of Marx's theory of human nature that relates it to the existentialist concept of authenticity.

McLellan, David. *Karl Marx*. Harmondsworth, England: Penguin, Modern Masters Ser., 1975, 110 pp.

The three chapters of this brief book examine the life, thought, and reputation of Marx. McLellan focuses on Marx's attempt to understand the economic revolutions of his time.

Ollman, Bertell. *Alienation: Marx's Conception of Man in Capitalist Society*, 2d ed. Cambridge, England: Cambridge University Press, Cambridge Studies in the History and Theory of Politics, 1976, 338 pp.

A detailed study of Marx's theory of alienation and the concept of human nature underlying it, focusing on the *Economic and Philosophic Manuscripts of 1844*. For more advanced students of Marx.

Singer, Peter. *Marx*. Oxford, England: Oxford University Press, Past Masters Ser., 1980, 82 pp.

A brief and accessible overview of Marx's philosophy. Singer sees human freedom as Marx's primary concern.

Wood, Allen W. *Karl Marx*. London: Routledge, The Arguments of the Philosophers Ser., 1981, 282 pp.

Part 1, "Alienation," pp. 1–59, is a scholarly discussion of the meaning of this concept in Marx's early writings and the role it plays in his later thought.

10

Friedrich Nietzsche

Friedrich Nietzsche was born in Röcken, in the German state of Prussia, in 1844. His father, a Lutheran minister, died when he was four, and the following year the family moved to Naumburg. Nietzsche attended the Lutheran boarding school at Pforta, where he received extensive training in Latin and Greek. After graduation in 1864, he studied theology for a year at the University of Bonn, where he began to have doubts about his Christian faith. When he came home to Naumburg for the Easter holidays in 1865, he refused to attend church services. He later became an atheist and a harsh critic of Christianity: He felt that its doctrines calling for the acceptance of suffering, repentance for sin, and focus on happiness in the next life rather than this one were life denying rather than life affirming.

In 1865 Nietzsche transferred to the University of Leipzig to study classical philology (Greek and Latin language and literature) and music. There he happened upon a copy of *The World as Will and Representation* by the German philosopher Arthur Schopenhauer (1788–1860). He was strongly influenced by Schopenhauer's ideas that the universe is irrational, that human beings are driven more by will than intellect, and that suffering is inevitable because one person's will conflicts with others'.

In 1867 Nietzsche enlisted in the Prussian army, continuing to study classical philology in the evenings. But the following year, while mounting a horse, he sustained a chest injury from which he did not fully recover. He was consequently discharged from the military, and he returned to Leipzig to resume his studies. Nietzsche was soon recognized as a brilliant student of philology, and at the age of twenty-four, before he had even finished his doctorate, he was offered the chair of classical philology at the University of Basel in Switzerland. The University of Leipzig quickly awarded Nietzsche his degree (without requiring examinations or a dissertation), and in 1869 Nietzsche received the appointment at Basel.

Soon after arriving at Basel, he called on the German composer Richard Wagner (1813–1883) at his villa at Tribschen, Switzerland. The two men, who had first met in Leipzig in 1868, became close friends.

In 1870 Nietzsche took a leave of absence from the University of Basel to serve as a medic in the Prussian army in the Franco-Prussian war. He soon contracted dysentery and diphtheria—and would remain in poor health the rest of his life. Nietzsche was once again discharged from the army, and he resumed his post at Basel. In 1872 he published his first book, *The Birth of Tragedy out of the Spirit of Music*. In it he argues that Greek tragedy arose as an integration of Apollonian and Dionysian artistic impulses (Apollo, the god of light, symbolizes harmony, measure, and form; Dionysus, the god of wine, represents frenzy, excess, and defiance of limitation) and that tragedy had been reborn in Wagner's music.

Nietzsche's continuing poor health led him to take sick leave from the University of Basel in 1876. By this time, his friendship with Wagner had become so strained by Wagner's nationalism, anti-Semitism, and exploitation of Christian beliefs that Nietzsche broke off the relationship. In 1878 Nietzsche published *Human, All Too Human: A Book for Free Spirits*, in which he criticizes common assumptions about metaphysics, morality, religion, and art, describes the role of a "free spirit" in society, and makes various psychological observations about society and the individual.

Persistent illness caused Nietzsche to resign his professorship in 1879. For the next ten years, half-blind and in unremitting pain, he wandered through Switzerland, Germany, and Italy, searching for a cure while continuing to write and publish. His publications during this period include *Thus Spoke Zarathustra* (in four parts, 1883–1885), *Beyond Good and Evil* (1886), and *On the Genealogy of Morals* (1887).

Nietzsche's mental health also began to deteriorate. The reason is unclear; it is possible that he had contracted syphilis early in his life and that the disease was infecting his brain. At any rate, in 1889 he collapsed on the streets of Turin, Italy, completely insane. He was taken at first to an asylum in Basel and, later, was cared for by his mother and, after his mother's death in 1897, by his sister. He died in Weimar in 1900.

The central concern of Nietzsche's philosophy is values—how they arise and how they function in our lives. Rejecting the idea that values are grounded in God ("God is dead") or in anything else external to human beings, Nietzsche concludes that we create our own values. This means that it is possible for us to replace our conventionally accepted values with new ones based on how we honestly think and feel: We can undertake a "revaluation of all values."

Our reading is from the second section of *Human, All Too Human*, entitled "On the History of Moral Feelings." Nietzsche here presents, in a series of aphorisms, psychological observations on the origin and subsequent history of our notions of good and evil. Placing human nature on "the psychological operating table," Nietzsche argues that all of our actions—both "good" and "evil"—are rooted in the desire to gain pleasure (including the pleasure of exercising power) and avoid pain. Since we are driven by this desire, we have neither free will nor moral responsibility.

HUMAN, ALL TOO HUMAN

SECTION TWO: ON THE HISTORY OF MORAL FEELINGS

35

The Advantages of Psychological Observation That meditating on things human, all too human (or, as the learned phrase goes, "psychological observation") is one of the means by which man can ease life's burden; that by exercising this art, one can secure presence of mind in difficult situations and entertainment amid boring surroundings; indeed, that from the thorniest and unhappiest phases of one's own life one can pluck maxims and feel a bit better thereby: this was believed, known—in earlier centuries. Why has it been forgotten in this century, when many signs point, in Germany at least, if not throughout Europe, to the dearth of psychological observation? Not particularly in novels, short stories, and philosophical meditations, for these are the work of exceptional men; but more in the judging of public events and personalities; most of all we lack the art of psychological dissection and calculation in all classes of society, where one hears a lot of talk about men, but none at all *about man*. Why do people let the richest and most harmless source of entertainment get away from them? Why do they not even read the great masters of the psychological maxim any more? For it is no exaggeration to say that it is hard to find the cultured European who has read La Rochefoucauld[1] and his spiritual and artistic cousins. Even more uncommon is the man who knows them and does not despise them. . . .

36

Objection Or might there be a counterargument to the thesis that psychological observation is one of life's best stimulants, remedies, and palliatives? Might one be so persuaded of the unpleasant consequences of this art as to

251

intentionally divert the student's gaze from it? Indeed, a certain blind faith in the goodness of human nature, an inculcated aversion to dissecting human behavior, a kind of shame with respect to the naked soul, may really be more desirable for a man's overall happiness than the trait of psychological sharp-sightedness, which is helpful in isolated instances. And perhaps the belief in goodness, in virtuous men and actions, in an abundance of impersonal goodwill in the world, has made men better, in that it has made them less distrustful. If one imitates Plutarch's[2] heroes with enthusiasm and feels an aversion toward tracing skeptically the motives for their actions, then the welfare of human society has benefited (even if the truth of human society has not). Psychological error, and dullness in this area generally, help humanity forward; but knowledge of the truth might gain more from the stimulating power of an hypothesis like the one La Rochefoucauld places at the beginning of the first edition of his *Sentences et maximes morales:* "Ce que le monde nomme vertu n'est d'ordinaire qu'un fantôme formé par nos passions, à qui on donne un nom honnête pour faire impunément ce qu'on veut."[3] La Rochefoucauld and those other French masters of soul searching . . . are like accurately aimed arrows, which hit the mark again and again, the black mark of man's nature. Their skill inspires amazement, but the spectator who is guided not by the scientific spirit, but by the humane spirit, will eventually curse an art which seems to implant in the souls of men a predilection for belittling and doubt.

37

Nevertheless However the argument and counterargument stand, the present condition of one certain, single science has made necessary the awakening of moral observation, and mankind cannot be spared the horrible sight of the psychological operating table, with its knives and forceps. For now that science rules which asks after the origin and history of moral feelings and which tries as it progresses to pose and solve the complicated sociological problems; the old philosophy doesn't even acknowledge such problems and has always used meager excuses to avoid investigating the origin and history of moral feelings. We can survey the consequences very clearly, many examples having proven how the errors of the greatest philosophers usually start from a false explanation of certain human actions and feelings, how an erroneous analysis of so-called selfless behavior, for example, can be the basis for false ethics, for whose sake religion and mythological confusion are then drawn in, and finally how the shadows of these sad spirits also fall upon physics and the entire contemplation of the world. But if it is a fact that the superficiality of psychological observation has laid the most dangerous traps for human judgment and conclusions, and continues to lay them anew, then what we need now is a persistence in work that does not tire of piling stone upon stone, pebble upon pebble; we need a sober courage to do such humble work without shame and to defy any who disdain it. It is true that countless individual remarks about things human and all too human were first detected and stated in those social circles which would make every sort of sacrifice not for scientific knowledge, but for a witty coquetry. And because the scent of that old homeland (a very seductive scent) has attached itself almost inextricably to the whole genre of the moral maxim, the scientific man instinctively shows some suspicion towards this genre and its seriousness. . . .

39

The Fable of Intelligible Freedom The history of those feelings, by virtue of which we consider a person responsible, the so-called moral feelings, is divided into the following main phases. At first we call particular acts good or evil without any consideration of their motives, but simply on the basis of their beneficial or harmful consequences. Soon, however, we forget the origin of these terms and imagine that the quality "good" or "evil" is inherent in the actions themselves, without consideration of their consequences; this is the same error language makes when calling the stone itself hard, the tree itself green—that is, we take the effect to be the cause. Then we assign the goodness or evil to the motives, and regard the acts themselves as morally ambiguous. We go even further and cease to give to the particular motive the predicate good or evil, but give it rather to the whole nature of a man; the motive grows out of him as a plant grows out of the earth. So we make man responsible in turn for the effects of his actions, then for his actions, then for his motives and finally for his nature. Ultimately we discover that his nature cannot be responsible either, in that it is itself an inevitable consequence, an outgrowth of the elements and influences of past and present things; that is, man cannot be made responsible for anything, neither for his nature, nor his motives, nor his actions, nor the effects of his actions. And thus we come to understand that the history of moral feelings is the history of an error, an error called "responsibility," which in turn rests on an error called "freedom of the will."

Schopenhauer, on the other hand, concluded as follows: because certain actions produce *displeasure* ("sense of guilt"), a responsibility must exist. For there would be *no reason* for this displeasure if not only all human actions occurred out of necessity (as they actually do, according to this philosopher's insight), but if man himself also acquired his entire *nature* out of the same necessity (which Schopenhauer denies). From the fact of man's displeasure, Schopenhauer thinks he can prove that man somehow must have had a freedom, a freedom which did not determine his actions but rather determined his nature: freedom, that is, *to be* this way or the other, not *to act* this way or the other. According to Schopenhauer, *operari* (doing), the sphere of strict causality, necessity, and lack of responsibility, follows from *esse* (being), the sphere of freedom and responsibility. The displeasure man feels

eems to refer to *operari* (to this extent it is erroneous), but in truth it refers
o *esse*, which is the act of a free will, the primary cause of an individual's
existence. Man becomes that which he *wants* to be; his volition precedes his
existence.

In this case, we are concluding falsely that we can deduce the justifica-
ion, the rational *admissibility* of this displeasure, from the fact that it exists;
nd from this false deduction Schopenhauer arrives at his fantastic conclusion
of so-called intelligible freedom. But displeasure after the deed need not be
ational at all: in fact, it certainly is not rational, for it rests on the erroneous
ssumption that the deed did *not* have to follow necessarily. Thus, because he
hinks he is free (but not because he is free), man feels remorse and the pangs
of conscience.

Furthermore, this displeasure is a habit that can be given up; many men
do not feel it at all, even after the same actions that cause many other men to
eel it. Tied to the development of custom and culture, it is a very changeable
hing, and present perhaps only within a relatively short period of world
iistory.

No one is responsible for his deeds, no one for his nature; to judge is to
e unjust. This is also true when the individual judges himself. The tenet is as
right as sunlight, and yet everyone prefers to walk back into the shadow and
untruth—for fear of the consequences.

0

he Super-Animal   The beast in us wants to be lied to; morality is a white lie,
o keep it from tearing us apart. Without the errors inherent in the postulates
of morality, man would have remained an animal. But as it is he has taken
iimself to be something higher and has imposed stricter laws upon himself.
Ie therefore has a hatred of those stages of man that remain closer to the
nimal state, which explains why the slave used to be disdained as a non-
iuman, a thing. . . .

2

Morality and the Ordering of the Good   The accepted hierarchy of the good,
based on how a low, higher, or a most high egoism desires that thing or the
ther, decides today about morality or immorality. To prefer a low good
sensual pleasure, for example) to one esteemed higher (health, for example)
s taken for immoral, likewise to prefer comfort to freedom. The hierarchy of
he good, however, is not fixed and identical at all times. If someone prefers
evenge to justice, he is moral by the standard of an earlier culture, yet by the
tandard of the present culture he is immoral. "Immoral" then indicates that
omeone has not felt, or not felt strongly enough, the higher, finer, more
piritual motives which the new culture of the time has brought with it. It
ndicates a backward nature, but only in degree.

The hierarchy itself is not established or changed from the point of view of morality; nevertheless an action is judged moral or immoral according to the prevailing determination.

43

Cruel Men as Backward We must think of men who are cruel today as stages of *earlier cultures*, which have been left over; in their case, the mountain range of humanity shows openly its deeper formations, which otherwise lie hidden. They are backward men whose brains, because of various possible accidents of heredity, have not yet developed much delicacy or versatility. They show us what we *all* were, and frighten us. But they themselves are as little responsible as a piece of granite for being granite. In our brain, too, there must be grooves and bends which correspond to that state of mind, just as there are said to be reminders of the fish state in the form of certain human organs. But these grooves and bends are no longer the bed in which the river of our feeling courses.

44

Gratitude and Revenge The powerful man feels gratitude for the following reason: through his good deed, his benefactor has, as it were, violated the powerful man's sphere and penetrated it. Now through his act of gratitude the powerful man requites himself by violating the sphere of the benefactor. It is a milder form of revenge. Without the satisfaction of gratitude, the powerful man would have shown himself to be unpowerful and henceforth would be considered such. For that reason, every society of good men (that is, originally, of powerful men) places gratitude among its first duties. . . .

45

Double Prehistory of Good and Evil The concept of good and evil has a double prehistory: namely, first of all, in the soul of the ruling clans and castes. The man who has the power to requite goodness with goodness, evil with evil, and really does practice requital by being grateful and vengeful, is called "good." The man who is unpowerful and cannot requite is taken for bad. As a good man, one belongs to the "good," a community that has a communal feeling, because all the individuals are entwined together by their feeling for requital. As a bad man, one belongs to the "bad," to a mass of abject, powerless men who have no communal feeling. The good men are a caste; the bad men are a multitude, like particles of dust. Good and bad are for a time equivalent to noble and base, master and slave. Conversely, one does not regard the enemy as evil: he can requite. In Homer,[5] both the Trojan and the Greek are good. Not the man who inflicts harm on us, but the man who is contemptible, is bad. In the community of the good, goodness is hereditary; it s impossible for a bad man to grow out of such good soil. Should one of the good men nevertheless do something unworthy of good men, one resorts to excuses; one blames God, for example, saying that he struck the good man with blindness and madness.

Then, in the souls of oppressed, powerless men, every *other* man is taken for hostile, inconsiderate, exploitative, cruel, sly, whether he be noble or base. "Evil" is their epithet for man, indeed for every possible living being, even, for example, for a god; "human," "divine" mean the same as "devilish," "evil." Signs of goodness, helpfulness, pity are taken anxiously for malice, the prelude to a terrible outcome, bewilderment, and deception, in short, for refined evil. With such a state of mind in the individual, a community can scarcely come about at all—or at most in the crudest form; so that wherever this concept of good and evil predominates, the downfall of individuals, their clans and races, is near at hand.

Our present morality has grown up on the ground of the *ruling* clans and castes.

46

Pity More Intense than Suffering There are cases where pity is more intense than actual suffering. When one of our friends is guilty of something ignominious, for example, we feel it more painfully than when we ourselves do it. For we believe in the purity of his character more than he does. Thus our love for him (probably because of this very belief) is more intense than his own love for himself. Even if his egoism suffers more than our egoism, in that he has to feel the bad consequences of his fault more intensely, our selflessness (this word must never be taken literally, but only as a euphemism) is touched more intensely by his guilt than is his selflessness. . . .

49

Goodwill Among the small but endlessly abundant and therefore very effective things that science ought to heed more than the great, rare things, is goodwill. I mean those expressions of a friendly disposition in interactions, that smile of the eye, those handclasps, that ease which usually envelops nearly all human actions. Every teacher, every official brings this ingredient to what he considers his duty. It is the continual manifestation of our humanity, its rays of light, so to speak, in which everything grows. Especially within the narrowest circle, in the family, life sprouts and blossoms only by this goodwill. Good nature, friendliness, and courtesy of the heart are everflowing tributaries of the selfless drive and have made much greater contributions to culture than those much more famous expressions of this drive, called pity, charity, and self-sacrifice. But we tend to underestimate them, and in fact there really is not much about them that is selfless. The *sum* of these small doses is nevertheless mighty; its cumulative force is among the strongest of forces.

Similarly, there is much more happiness to be found in the world than dim eyes can see, if one calculates correctly and does not forget all those moments of ease which are so plentiful in every day of every human life, even the most oppressed.

50

Desire to Arouse Pity In the most noteworthy passage of his self-portrait (first published in 1658), La Rochefoucauld certainly hits the mark when he warns all reasonable men against pity, when he advises them to leave it to those common people who need passions (because they are not directed by reason) to bring them to the point of helping the sufferer and intervening energetically in a misfortune. For pity, in his (and Plato's)[5] judgment, weakens the soul. Of course one ought to *express* pity, but one ought to guard against *having* it; for unfortunate people are so *stupid* that they count the expression of pity as the greatest good on earth.

Perhaps one can warn even more strongly against having pity for the unfortunate if one does not think of their need for pity as stupidity and intellectual deficiency, a kind of mental disorder resulting from their misfortune (this is how La Rochefoucauld seems to regard it), but rather as something quite different and more dubious. Observe how children weep and cry *so that* they will be pitied, how they wait for the moment when their condition will be noticed. Or live among the ill and depressed, and question whether their eloquent laments and whimpering, the spectacle of their misfortune, is not basically aimed at *hurting* those present. The pity that the spectators then express consoles the weak and suffering, inasmuch as they see that, despite all their weakness, they still *have* at least one *power: the power to hurt.* When expressions of pity make the unfortunate man aware of this feeling of superiority, he gets a kind of pleasure from it; his self-image revives; he is still important enough to inflict pain on the world. Thus the thirst for pity is a thirst for self-enjoyment, and at the expense of one's fellow men. It reveals man in the complete inconsideration of his most intimate dear self, but not precisely in his "stupidity," as La Rochefoucauld thinks.

In social dialogue, three-quarters of all questions and answers are framed in order to hurt the participants a little bit; this is why many men thirst after society so much: it gives them a feeling of their strength. In these countless, but very small doses, malevolence takes effect as one of life's powerful stimulants, just as goodwill, dispensed in the same way throughout the human world, is the perennially ready cure.

But will there be many people honest enough to admit that it is a pleasure to inflict pain? That not infrequently one amuses himself (and well) by offending other men (at least in his thoughts) and by shooting pellets of petty malice at them? Most people are too dishonest, and a few men are too good, to know anything about this source of shame. So they may try to deny that Prosper Merimée is right when he says, "Sachez aussi qu'il n'y a rien de plus commun que de faire le mal pour le plaisir de le faire."[6]

51

How Seeming Becomes Being Ultimately, not even the deepest pain can keep the actor from thinking of the impression of his part and the overall theatrical effect, not even, for example, at his child's funeral. He will be his own audience, and cry about his own pain as he expresses it. The hypocrite who always plays one and the same role finally ceases to be a hypocrite. Priests, for example, who are usually conscious or unconscious hypocrites when they are young men, finally end by becoming natural, and then they really are priests, with no affectation. Or if the father does not get that far, perhaps the son, using his father's headway, inherits the habit. If someone wants to *seem* to be something, stubbornly and for a long time, he eventually finds it hard to *be* anything else. The profession of almost every man, even the artist, begins with hypocrisy, as he imitates from the outside, copies what is effective. The man who always wears the mask of a friendly countenance eventually has to gain power over benevolent moods without which the expression of friendliness cannot be forced—and eventually then these moods gain power over him, and he *is* benevolent.

52

The Point of Honesty in Deception In all great deceivers there occurs a noteworthy process to which they owe their power. In the actual act of deception, among all the preparations, the horror in the voice, expression, gestures, amid the striking scenery, the *belief in themselves* overcomes them. It is this that speaks so miraculously and convincingly to the onlookers. The founders of religions are distinguished from those other great deceivers by the fact that they do not come out of this condition of self-deception: or, very infrequently, they do have those clearer moments, when doubt overwhelms them; but they usually comfort themselves by foisting these clearer moments off on the evil adversary. Self-deception must be present, so that both kinds of deceivers can have a grand *effect*. For men will believe something is true, if it is evident that others believe in it firmly.

53

Alleged Levels of Truth One common false conclusion is that because someone is truthful and upright toward us he is speaking the truth. Thus the child believes his parents' judgments, the Christian believes the claims of the

church's founders. Likewise, people do not want to admit that all those
things which men have defended with the sacrifice of their lives and happiness in earlier centuries were nothing but errors. Perhaps one calls them
levels of truth. Basically, however, one thinks that if someone honestly
believed in something and fought for his belief and died it would be too *unfair*
if he had actually been inspired by a mere error. Such an occurrence seems to
contradict eternal justice. Therefore the hearts of sensitive men always decree
in opposition to their heads that there must be a necessary connection between moral actions and intellectual insights. Unfortunately, it is otherwise,
for there is no eternal justice.

54

The Lie Why do men usually tell the truth in daily life? Certainly not because
a god has forbidden lying. Rather it is because, first, it is more convenient: for
lies demand imagination, dissembling, and memory (which is why Swift[7]
says that the man who tells a lie seldom perceives the heavy burden he is
assuming: namely, he must invent twenty other lies to make good the first).
Then, it is because it is advantageous in ordinary circumstances to say directly: I want this, I did that, and so on; that is, because the path of obligation
and authority is safer than that of cunning.

If a child has been raised in complicated domestic circumstances, however, he will employ the lie naturally, and will always say instinctively that
which corresponds to his interests. A feeling for truth, a distaste for lying in
and of itself, is alien to him and inaccessible; and so he lies in complete
innocence.

55

To Suspect Morality Because of Belief No power can maintain itself if only
hypocrites represent it. However many "worldly" elements the Catholic
Church may have, its strength rests on those priestly natures, still numerous,
who make life deep and difficult for themselves, and whose eye and emaci-
ated body speak of nightly vigils, fasting, fervent prayers, perhaps even
flagellation. These men shock others and worry them: what if it were *necessary*
to live like that?—this is the horrible question that the sight of them brings to
the tongue. By spreading this doubt they keep reestablishing a pillar of their
power. Not even the most free-minded dare to resist so selfless a man with
the hard sense for truth, and say: "You who are deceived, do not deceive
others."

Only a difference of insight separates them from this man, by no means
a difference of goodness or badness; but if one does not like a thing, one
generally tends to treat it unjustly, too. Thus one speaks of the Jesuits'[8]
cunning and their infamous art, but overlooks what self-conquest each single

esuit imposes upon himself, and how that lighter regimen preached in Jesuit extbooks is certainly not for their own benefit, but rather for the layman's. ndeed, one might ask if we the enlightened, using their tactics and organiza- ion, would be such good instruments, so admirably self-mastering, untiring, nd devoted.

6

riumph of Knowledge Over Radical Evil The man who wants to gain visdom profits greatly from having thought for a time that man is basically vil and degenerate: this idea is wrong, like its opposite, but for whole •eriods of time it was predominant and its roots have sunk deep into us and nto our world. To understand ourselves we must understand *it*; but to climb ligher, we must then climb over and beyond it. We recognize that there are 10 sins in the metaphysical sense; but, in the same sense, neither are there ny virtues; we recognize that this entire realm of moral ideas is in a continual tate of fluctuation, that there are higher and deeper concepts of good and vil, moral and immoral. A man who desires no more from things than to nderstand them easily makes peace with his soul and will err (or "sin," as he world calls it) at the most out of ignorance, but hardly out of desire. He vill no longer want to condemn and root out his desires; but his single goal, overning him completely, to *understand* as well as he can at all times, will ool him down and soften all the wildness in his disposition. In addition, he as rid himself of a number of tormenting ideas; he no longer feels anything t the words "pains of hell," "sinfulness," "incapacity for the good": for him hey are only the evanescent silhouettes of erroneous thoughts about life and he world.

7

Morality as Man's Dividing Himself A good author, who really cares about is subject, wishes that someone would come and destroy him by represent- ıg the same subject more clearly and by answering every last question ontained in it. The girl in love wishes that she might prove the devoted aithfulness of her love through her lover's faithlessness. The soldier wishes nat he might fall on the battlefield for his victorious fatherland, for in the ictory of his fatherland his greatest desire is also victorious. The mother ives the child what she takes from herself: sleep, the best food, in some 1stances even her health, her wealth.

Are all these really selfless states, however? Are these acts of morality iiracles because they are, to use Schopenhauer's phrase, "impossible and yet eal"? Isn't it clear that, in all these cases, man is loving *something of himself*, a 10ught, a longing, an off-spring, more than *something else of himself*; that he is 1us *dividing up* his being and sacrificing one part for the other? Is it something *essentially* different when a pigheaded man says, "I would rather be shot at once than move an inch to get out of that man's way"?

The *inclination towards something* (a wish, a drive, a longing) is present in all the above-mentioned cases; to yield to it, with all its consequences, is in any case not "selfless." In morality, man treats himself not as an "individuum," but as a "dividuum."[9] . . .

65

Where Honesty May Lead Someone had the unfortunate habit of speaking out from time to time quite honestly about the motives for his actions, motives which were as good and as bad as those of all other men. At first he gave offense, then he awoke suspicion, and at length he was virtually ostracized and banished. Finally, justice remembered this depraved creature on occasions when it otherwise averted or winked its eye. His want of silence about the universal secret, and his irresponsible inclination to see what no one wants to see—his own self—brought him to prison and an untimely death. . . .

68

Morality and Success It is not only the witnesses of a deed who often measure its moral or immoral nature by its success. No, the author of a deed does so, too. For motives and intentions are seldom sufficiently clear and simple, and sometimes even memory seems to be dimmed by the success of a deed, so that one attributes false motives to his deed, or treats inessential motives as essential. Often it is success that gives to a deed the full, honest lustre of a good conscience; failure lays the shadow of an uneasy conscience upon the most estimable action. This leads to the politician's well-known practice of thinking: "Just grant me success; with it I will bring all honest souls to my side—and make myself honest in my own sight."

In a similar way, success can take the place of more substantial arguments. Even now, many educated people think that the victory of Christianity over Greek philosophy is a proof of the greater truth of the former—although in this case it is only that something more crude and violent has triumphed over something more spiritual and delicate. We can determine which of them has the greater truth by noting that the awakening sciences have carried on point for point with the philosophy of Epicurus,[10] but have rejected Christianity point for point.

69

Love and Justice Why do we overestimate love to the disadvantage of justice, saying the nicest things about it, as if it were a far higher essence than justice?

sn't love obviously more foolish? Of course, but for just that reason so much
more pleasant for everyone. Love is foolish, and possesses a rich horn of
plenty; from it she dispenses her gifts to everyone, even if he does not
deserve them, indeed, even if he does not thank her for them. She is as
nonpartisan as rain, which (according to the Bible[11] and to experience) rains
not only upon the unjust, but sometimes soaks the just man to the skin, too.

70

Executions How is it that every execution offends us more than a murder? It
is the coldness of the judges, the painful preparations, the understanding that
a man is here being used as a means to deter others. For guilt is not being
punished, even if there were guilt; guilt lies in the educators, the parents, the
environment, in us, not in the murderer—I am talking about the motivating
circumstances.

71

Hope Pandora[12] brought the jar with the evils and opened it. It was the gods'
gift to man, on the outside a beautiful, enticing gift, called the "lucky jar."
Then all the evils, those lively, winged beings, flew out of it. Since that time,
they roam around and do harm to men by day and night. One single evil had
not yet slipped out of the jar. As Zeus had wished, Pandora slammed the top
down and it remained inside. So now man has the lucky jar in his house
forever and thinks the world of the treasure. It is at his service; he reaches for
it when he fancies it. For he does not know that that jar which Pandora
brought was the jar of evils, and he takes the remaining evil for the greatest
worldly good—it is hope, for Zeus did not want man to throw his life away,
no matter how much the other evils might torment him, but rather to go on
letting himself be tormented anew. To that end, he gives man hope. In truth,
it is the most evil of evils because it prolongs man's torment.

72

Degree of Moral Inflammability Unknown Whether or not our passions
reach the point of red heat and guide our whole life depends on whether or
not we have been exposed to certain shocking sights or impressions—for
example, a father falsely executed, killed or tortured; an unfaithful wife; a
cruel ambush by an enemy. No one knows how far circumstances, pity, or
indignation may drive him; he does not know the degree of his inflammability. Miserable, mean conditions make one miserable; it is usually not the
quality of the experiences but rather the quantity that determines the lower
and the higher man, in good and in evil.

73

The Martyr Against His Will In one party, there was a man who was too anxious and cowardly ever to contradict his comrades. They used him for every service; they demanded everything of him, because he was more afraid of the bad opinions of his companions than of death itself. His was a miserable, weak soul. They recognized this and on the basis of those qualities they made him first into a hero and finally into a martyr. Although the cowardly man always said "no" inwardly, he always said "yes" with his lips, even on the scaffold, when he died for the views of his party. Next to him stood one of his old comrades, who tyrannized him so by word and glance that he really did suffer death in the most seemly way, and has since been celebrated as a martyr and a man of great character.

74

Everyday Rule-of-Thumb One will seldom go wrong to attribute extreme actions to vanity, moderate ones to habit, and petty ones to fear.

75

Misunderstanding About Virtue The man who has come to know vice in connection with pleasure, like the man who has a pleasure-seeking youth behind him, imagines that virtue must be associated with displeasure. On the other hand, the man who has been greatly plagued by his passions and vices longs to find peace and his soul's happiness in virtue. Thus it is possible that two virtuous people will not understand each other at all. . . .

80

The Old Man and Death One may well ask why, aside from the demands of religion, it is more praiseworthy for a man grown old, who feels his powers decrease, to await his slow exhaustion and disintegration, rather than to put a term to his life with complete consciousness. In this case, suicide is quite natural, obvious, and should by rights awaken respect for the triumph of reason. This it did in those times when the leading Greek philosophers and the doughtiest Roman patriots used to die by suicide. Conversely, the compulsion to prolong life from day to day, anxiously consulting doctors and accepting the most painful, humiliating conditions, without the strength to come nearer the actual goal of one's life: this is far less worthy of respect. Religions provide abundant excuses to escape the need to kill oneself: this is how they insinuate themselves with those who are in love with life.

31

Misunderstanding Between the Sufferer and the Perpetrator When a rich man takes a possession from a poor man (for example, when a prince robs a plebeian of his sweetheart), the poor man misunderstands. He thinks that the rich man must be a villain to take from him the little he has. But the rich man does not feel the value of a *particular* possession so deeply because he is accustomed to having many. So he cannot put himself in the place of the poor man, and he is by no means doing as great an injustice as the poor man believes. Each has a false idea of the other. The injustice of the mighty, which enrages us most in history, is by no means as great as it appears. Simply the inherited feeling of being a higher being, with higher pretensions, makes one rather cold, and leaves the conscience at peace. Indeed, none of us feels anything like injustice when there is a great difference between ourselves and some other being, and we kill a gnat, for example, without any twinge of conscience. So it is no sign of wickedness in Xerxes[13] (whom even all the Greeks portray as exceptionally noble) when he takes a son from his father and has him cut to pieces, because the father had expressed an anxious and doubtful distrust of their entire campaign. In this case the individual man is eliminated like an unpleasant insect; he stands too low to be allowed to keep on arousing bothersome feelings in a world ruler. Indeed, no cruel man is cruel to the extent that the mistreated man believes. The idea of pain is not the same as the suffering of it. It is the same with an unjust judge, with a journalist who misleads public opinion by little dishonesties. In each of these cases, cause and effect are experienced in quite different categories of thought and feeling; nevertheless, it is automatically assumed that the perpetrator and sufferer think and feel the same, and the guilt of the one is therefore measured by the pain of the other.

32

The Skin of the Soul Just as the bones, flesh, intestines, and blood vessels are enclosed by skin, which makes the sight of a man bearable, so the stirrings and passions of the soul are covered up by vanity: it is the skin of the soul.

33

Sleep of Virtue When virtue has slept, it will arise refreshed.

34

Refinement of Shame Men are not ashamed to think something dirty, but they are ashamed when they imagine that others might believe them capable of these dirty thoughts.

85

Malice Is Rare Most men are much too concerned with themselves to be malicious.

86

Tipping the Scales We praise or find fault, depending on which of the two provides more opportunity for our powers of judgment to shine.

87

Luke 18:14,[14] Improved He who humbleth himself wants to be exalted.

88

Prevention of Suicide There is a justice according to which we take a man's life, but no justice according to which we take his death: that is nothing but cruelty.

89

Vanity We care about the good opinion of others first because it is profitable, and then because we want to give others joy (children want to give joy to their parents, pupils to their teachers, men of goodwill to all other men). Only when someone holds the good opinion of others to be important without regard to his interests or his wish to give joy, do we speak of vanity. In this case, the man wants to give joy to himself, but at the expense of his fellow men, in that he either misleads them to a false opinion about himself or aims at a degree of "good opinion" that would have to cause them all pain (by arousing their envy). Usually the individual wants to confirm the opinion he has of himself through the opinion of others and strengthen it in his own eyes; but the mighty habituation to authority (which is as old as man) also leads many to base their own belief in themselves upon authority, to accept it only from the hand of others. They trust other people's powers of judgment more than their own.

In the vain man, interest in himself, his wish to please himself, reaches such a peak that he misleads others to assess him wrongly, to overvalue him greatly, and then he adheres to their authority; that is, he brings about the error and then believes in it.

One must admit, then, that vain men want to please not only others, but also themselves, and that they go so far as to neglect their own interests thereby; for they are often concerned to make their fellow men ill-disposed,

ostile, envious, and thus destructive toward them, only for the sake of
aving pleasure in themselves, self-enjoyment.

0

Limit of Human Love Any man who has once declared the other man to be
fool, a bad fellow, is annoyed when that man ends by showing that he is
ot. . . .

2

Origin of Justice Justice (fairness) originates among approximately *equal
powers*, as Thucydides (in the horrifying conversation between the Athenian
nd Melian envoys)[15] rightly understood. When there is no clearly recogniz-
ble supreme power and a battle would lead to fruitless and mutual injury,
one begins to think of reaching an understanding and negotiating the claims
n both sides: the initial character of justice is *barter*. Each satisfies the other in
hat each gets what he values more than the other. Each man gives the other
what he wants, to keep henceforth, and receives in turn that which he
wishes. Thus, justice is requital and exchange on the assumption of approx-
mately equal positions of strength. For this reason, revenge belongs initially
o the realm of justice: it is an exchange. Likewise gratitude.
  Justice naturally goes back to the viewpoint of an insightful self-preser-
ation, that is, to the egoism of this consideration: "Why should I uselessly
njure myself and perhaps not reach my good anyway?"
  So much about the *origin* of justice. Because men, in line with their
intellectual habits, have *forgotten* the original purpose of so-called just, fair
ctions, and particularly because children have been taught for centuries to
dmire and imitate such actions, it has gradually come to appear that a just
ction is a selfless one. The high esteem of these actions rests upon this
ppearance, an esteem which, like all estimations, is also always in a state of
rowth: for men strive after, imitate, and reproduce with their own sacrifices
hat which is highly esteemed, and it grows because its worth is increased by
he worth of the effort and exertion made by each individual.
  How slight the morality of the world would seem without forgetfulness!
A poet could say that God had stationed forgetfulness as a guardian at the
loor to the temple of human dignity.

3

The Right of the Weaker If one party, a city under siege, for example, submits under certain conditions to a greater power, its reciprocal condition is
hat this first party can destroy itself, burn the city, and thus make the power

suffer a great loss. Thus there is a kind of *equalization*, on the basis of which rights can be established. Preservation is to the enemy's advantage.

Rights exist between slaves and masters to the same extent, exactly insofar as the possession of his slave is profitable and important to the master. The *right* originally extends *as far* as the one *appears* to the other to be valuable, essential, permanent, invincible, and the like. In this regard even the weaker of the two has rights, though they are more modest. Thus the famous dictum: "unusquisque tantum juris habet, quantum potentia valet"[16] (or, more exactly, "quantum potentia valere creditur"[17]).

94

The Three Phases of Morality Until Now The first sign that an animal has become human is that his behavior is no longer directed to his momentary comfort, but rather to his enduring comfort, that is, when man becomes useful, *expedient*: then for the first time the free rule of reason bursts forth. A still higher state is reached when man acts according to the principle of *honor*, by means of which he finds his place in society, submitting to commonly held feelings; that raises him high above the phase in which he is guided only by personal usefulness. Now he shows—and wants to be shown—respect; that is, he understands his advantage as dependent on his opinion of others and their opinion of him. Finally, at the highest stage of morality *until now*, he acts according to *his* standard of things and men; he himself determines for himself and others what is honorable, what is profitable. He has become the lawgiver of opinions, in accordance with the ever more refined concept of usefulness and honor. Knowledge enables him to prefer what is most useful, that is, general usefulness to personal usefulness, and the respectful recognition of what has common, enduring value to things of momentary value. He lives and acts as a collective-individual.

95

Morality of the Mature Individual Until now man has taken the true sign of a moral act to be its impersonal nature; and it has been shown that in the beginning all impersonal acts were praised and distinguished in respect to the common good. Might not a significant transformation of these views be at hand, now when we see with ever greater clarity that precisely in the most *personal* respect the common good is also greatest; so that now it is precisely the strictly personal action which corresponds to the current concept of morality (as a common profit)? To make a whole *person* of oneself and keep in mind that person's *greatest good* in everything one does—this takes us further than any pitying impulses and actions for the sake of others. To be sure, we all still suffer from too slight a regard for our own personal needs; it has been poorly developed. Let us admit that our mind has instead been forcibly diverted from it and offered in sacrifice to the state, to science, to the needy, as if it were something bad which had to be sacrificed. Now too we wish to work for our fellow men, but only insofar as we find our own highest advantage in this work; no more, no less. It depends only on what one understands by his *advantage*. The immature, undeveloped, crude individual will also understand it most crudely.

96

Mores and Morality To be moral, correct, ethical means to obey an age-old law or tradition. Whether one submits to it gladly or with difficulty makes no difference; enough that one submits. We call "good" the man who does the moral thing as if by nature, after a long history of inheritance—that is, easily, and gladly, whatever it is (he will, for example, practice revenge when that is considered moral, as in the older Greek culture). He is called good because he is good "for" something. But because, as mores changed, goodwill, pity, and the like were always felt to be "good for" something, useful, it is primarily the man of goodwill, the helpful man, who is called "good." To be evil is to be "not moral" (immoral), to practice bad habits, go against tradition, however reasonable or stupid it may be. To harm one's fellow, however, has been felt primarily as injurious in all moral codes of different times, so that when we hear the word "bad" now, we think particularly of voluntary injury to one's fellow. When men determine between moral and immoral, good and evil, the basic opposition is not "egoism" and "selflessness," but rather adherence to a tradition or law, and release from it. The *origin* of the tradition makes no difference, at least concerning good and evil, or an immanent categorical imperative;[18] but is rather above all for the purpose of maintaining *a community*, a people. Every superstitious custom, originating in a coincidence that is interpreted falsely, forces a tradition that it is moral to follow. To release oneself from it is dangerous, even more injurious for the *community* than for the individual (because the divinity punishes the whole community for sacrilege and violation of its rights, and the individual only as a part of that community). Now, each tradition grows more venerable the farther its origin lies in the past, the more it is forgotten; the respect paid to the tradition accumulates from generation to generation; finally the origin becomes sacred and awakens awe; and thus the morality of piety is in any case much older than that morality which requires selfless acts.

97

Pleasure in Custom An important type of pleasure, and thus an important source of morality, grows out of habit. One does habitual things more easily, skillfully, gladly; one feels a pleasure at them, knowing from experience that the habit has stood the test and is useful. A morality one can live with has been proved salutary, effective, in contrast to all the as yet unproven new experiments. Accordingly, custom is the union of the pleasant and the useful; in addition, it requires no thought. As soon as man can exercise force, he exercises it to introduce and enforce his mores, for to him they represent proven wisdom. Likewise, a community will force each individual in it to the same mores. Here is the error: because one feels good with one custom, or at least because he lives his life by means of it, this custom is necessary, for he holds it to be the *only* possibility by which one can feel good; the enjoyment of life seems to grow out of it alone. This idea of habit as a condition of existence is carried right into the smallest details of custom: since lower peoples and cultures have only very slight insight into the real causality, they make sure, with superstitious fear, that everything takes the same course; even where a custom is difficult, harsh, burdensome, it is preserved because it seems to be highly useful. They do not know that the same degree of comfort can also exist with other customs and that even higher degrees of comfort can be attained. But they do perceive that all customs, even the harshest, become more pleasant and mild with time, and that even the severest way of life can become a habit and thus a pleasure.

98

Pleasure and Social Instinct From his relationship to other men, man gains a new kind of pleasure, in addition to those pleasurable feelings which he gets from himself. In this way he widens significantly the scope of his pleasurable feelings. Perhaps some of these feelings have come down to him from the animals, who visibly feel pleasure when playing with each other, particularly mothers playing with their young. Next one might think of sexual relations, which make virtually every lass seem interesting to every lad (and vice versa) in view of potential pleasure. Pleasurable feeling based on human relations generally makes man better; shared joy, pleasure taken together, heightens this feeling; it gives the individual security, makes him better-natured, dissolves distrust and envy: one feels good oneself and can see the other man feel good in the same way. *Analogous expressions of pleasure* awaken the fantasy of empathy, the feeling of being alike. Shared sorrows do it, too: the same storms, dangers, enemies. Upon this basis man has built the oldest covenant, whose purpose is to eliminate and resist communally any threatening unpleasure, for the good of each individual. And thus social instinct grows out of pleasure.

99

Innocence of So-called Evil Actions All "evil" actions are motivated by the drive for preservation, or, more exactly, by the individual's intention to gain

leasure and avoid unpleasure; thus they are motivated, but they are not evil.
Giving pain in and of itself" *does not exist*, except in the brain of philoso-
hers, nor does "giving pleasure in and of itself" (pity, in the
chopenhauerian sense). In conditions *preceding* organized states, we kill any
eing, be it ape or man, that wants to take a fruit off a tree before we do, just
'hen we are hungry and running up to the tree. We would treat the animal
ie same way today, if we were hiking through inhospitable territory.

Those evil actions which outrage us most today are based on the error
aat that man who harms us has free will, that is, that he had the *choice* not to
o this bad thing to us. This belief in his choice arouses hatred, thirst for
:venge, spite, the whole deterioration of our imagination; whereas we get
uch less angry at an animal because we consider it irresponsible. To do
arm not out of a drive for preservation, but for requital—that is the result of
n erroneous judgment, and is therefore likewise innocent. The individual
an, in conditions preceding the organized state, treat others harshly and
ruelly to *intimidate* them, to secure his existence through such intimidating
emonstrations of his power. This is how the brutal, powerful man acts, the
riginal founder of a state, who subjects to himself those who are weaker. He
as the right to do it, just as the state now takes the right. Or rather, there is
o right that can prevent it. The ground for all morality can only be prepared
'hen a greater individual or collective-individual, as, for example, society or
ie state, subjects the individuals in it, that is, when it draws them out of their
olatedness and integrates them into a union. *Force* precedes morality; in-
eed, for a time morality itself is force, to which others acquiesce to avoid
npleasure. Later it becomes custom, and still later free obedience, and finally
lmost instinct: then it is coupled to pleasure, like all habitual and natural
iings, and is now called *virtue*. . . .

01

idge Not[19] When we consider earlier periods, we must be careful not to fall
ito unjust abuse. The injustice of slavery, the cruelty in subjugating persons
id peoples, cannot be measured by our standards. For the instinct for justice
'as not so widely developed then. Who has the right to reproach Calvin of
eneva[20] for burning Dr. Servet?[21] His was a consistent act, flowing out of his
>nvictions, and the Inquisition[22] likewise had its reasons; it is just that the
iews dominant then were wrong and resulted in a consistency that we find
arsh, because we now find those views so alien. Besides, what is the
urning of one man compared to the eternal pains of hell for nearly everyone!
nd yet this much more terrible idea used to dominate the whole world
ithout doing any essential damage to the idea of a god. In our own time, we
eat political heretics harshly and cruelly, but because we have learned to
elieve in the necessity of the state we are not as sensitive to this cruelty as we
:e to that cruelty whose justification we reject. Cruelty to animals, by

children and Italians, stems from ignorance; namely, in the interests of its teachings, the church has placed the animal too far beneath man.

Likewise, in history much that is frightful and inhuman, which one would almost like not to believe, is mitigated by the observation that the commander and the executor are different people: the former does not witness his cruelty and therefore has no strong impression of it in his imagination; the latter is obeying a superior and feels no responsibility. Because of a lack of imagination, most princes and military leaders can easily appear to be harsh and cruel, without being so.

Egoism is not evil, for the idea of one's "neighbor" (the word has a Christian origin[23] and does not reflect the truth) is very weak in us; and we feel toward him almost as free and irresponsible as toward plants and stones. That the other suffers *must be learned*; and it can never be learned completely.

102

"Man Always Acts for the Good"[24] We don't accuse nature of immorality when it sends us a thunderstorm, and makes us wet: why do we call the injurious man immoral? Because in the first case, we assume necessity, and in the second a voluntarily governing free will. But this distinction is in error. Furthermore, even intentional injury is not called immoral in all circumstances: without hesitating, we intentionally kill a gnat, for example, simply because we do not like its buzz; we intentionally punish the criminal and do him harm, to protect ourselves and society. In the first case it is the individual who does harm intentionally, for self-preservation or simply to avoid discomfort; in the second case the state does the harm. All morality allows the intentional infliction of harm *for self-defense*; that is, when it is a matter of *self-preservation*! But these two points of view are *sufficient* to explain all evil acts which men practice against other men; man wants to get pleasure or resist unpleasure; in some sense it is always a matter of self-preservation. Socrates and Plato are right: whatever man does, he always acts for the good; that is, in a way that seems to him good (useful) according to the degree of his intellect, the prevailing measure of his rationality.

103

Harmlessness of Malice Malice does not aim at the suffering of the other in and of itself, but rather at our own enjoyment, for example, a feeling of revenge or a strong nervous excitement. Every instance of teasing shows that it gives us pleasure to release our power on the other person and experience an enjoyable feeling of superiority. Is the *immoral* thing about it, then, to have *pleasure on the basis of other people's unpleasure*? Is *Schadenfreude*[25] devilish, as Schopenhauer says? Now, in nature, we take pleasure in breaking up twigs, loosening stones, fighting with wild animals, in order to gain awareness of ur own strength. Is the *knowledge*, then, that another person is suffering ecause of us supposed to make immoral the same thing about which we therwise feel no responsibility? But if one did not have this knowledge, one vould not have that pleasure in his own superiority, which can *be discovered* nly in the suffering of the other, in teasing, for example. All joy in oneself is either good nor bad; where should the determination come from that to ave pleasure in oneself one may not cause unpleasure in others? Solely from he point of view of advantage, that is, from consideration of the *consequences*, f possible unpleasure, when the injured party or the state representing him eads us to expect requital and revenge; this alone can have been the original asis for denying oneself these actions.

Pity does not aim at the pleasure of others any more than malice (as we aid above) aims at the pain of others, per se. For in pity, at least two (maybe nany more) elements of personal pleasure are contained, and it is to that xtent self-enjoyment: first of all, it is the pleasure of the emotion (the kind of ity we find in tragedy) and second, when it drives us to act, it is the pleasure f our satisfaction in the exercise of power. If, in addition, a suffering person s very close to us, we reduce our own suffering by our acts of pity.

Aside from a few philosophers, men have always placed pity rather low n the hierarchy of moral feelings—and rightly so.

04

elf-Defense If we accept self-defense as moral, then we must also accept early all expressions of so-called immoral egoism; we inflict harm, rob or kill, o preserve or protect ourselves, to prevent personal disaster; where cunning nd dissimulation are the correct means of self-preservation, we lie. *To do jury intentionally*, when it is a matter of our existence or security (preserva-on of our well-being) is conceded to be moral; the state itself injures from his point of view when it imposes punishment. Of course, there can be no nmorality in unintentional injury; there coincidence governs. Can there be a ind of intentional injury where it is *not* a matter of our existence, the reservation of our well-being? Can there be an injury out of pure *malice*, in ruelty, for example? If one does not know how painful an action is, it cannot e malicious; thus the child is not malicious or evil to an animal: he examines nd destroys it like a toy. But do we ever completely *know* how painful an ction is to the other person? As far as our nervous system extends, we rotect ourselves from pain; if it extended further, right into our fellow men, ve would not do harm to anyone (except in such cases where we do it to urselves, that is, where we cut ourselves in order to cure ourselves, exert nd strain ourselves to be healthy). We *conclude* by analogy that something urts another, and through our memory and power of imagination we our-elves can feel ill at such a thought. But what difference remains between a oothache and the ache (pity) evoked by the sight of a toothache? That is, hen we injure out of so-called malice, the *degree* of pain produced is in any case unknown to us; but in that we feel *pleasure* in the action (feeling of our own power, our own strong excitement), the action takes place to preserve the well-being of the individual and thus falls within a point of view similar to that of self-defense or a white lie. No life without pleasure; the struggle for pleasure is the struggle for life. Whether the individual fights this battle in ways such that men call him *good* or such that they call him *evil* is determined by the measure and makeup of his intellect.

105

A Rewarding Justice The man who has fully understood the theory of complete irresponsibility can no longer include the so-called justice that punishes and rewards within the concept of justice, if that consists in giving each his due. For the man who is punished does not deserve the punishment: he is only being used as the means to frighten others away from certain future actions; likewise, the man who is rewarded does not deserve this reward; he could not act other than as he did. Thus a reward means only an encouragement, for him and others, to provide a motive for subsequent actions: praise is shouted to the runner on the track, not to the one who has reached the finish line. Neither punishment nor reward are due to anyone as *his*; they are given to him because it is useful, without his justly having any claims on them. One must say, "The wise man rewards not because men have acted rightly," just as it was said, "The wise man punishes not because men have acted badly, but so they will not act badly." If we were to dispense with punishment and reward, we would lose the strongest motives driving men away from certain actions and toward other actions; the advantage of man requires that they continue; and in that punishment and reward, blame and praise, affect vanity most acutely, the same advantage also requires that vanity continue.

106

At the Waterfall When we see a waterfall, we think we see freedom of will and choice in the innumerable turnings, windings, breakings of the waves; but everything is necessary; each movement can be calculated mathematically. Thus it is with human actions; if one were omniscient, one would be able to calculate each individual action in advance, each step in the progress of knowledge, each error, each act of malice. To be sure, the acting man is caught in his illusion of violition; if the wheel of the world were to stand still for a moment and an omniscient, calculating mind were there to take advantage of this interruption, he would be able to tell into the farthest future of each being and describe every rut that wheel will roll upon. The acting man's delusion about himself, his assumption that free will exists, is also part of the calculable mechanism.

07

Irresponsibility and Innocence Man's complete lack of responsibility, for his behavior and for his nature, is the bitterest drop which the man of knowledge must swallow, if he had been in the habit of seeing responsibility and duty as humanity's claim to nobility. All his judgments, distinctions, dislikes have hereby become worthless and wrong: the deepest feeling he had offered a victim or a hero was misdirected; he may no longer praise, no longer blame, for it is nonsensical to praise and blame nature and necessity. Just as he loves a good work of art, but does not praise it, because it can do nothing about itself, just as he regards a plant, so he must regard the actions of men and his own actions. He can admire their strength, beauty, abundance, but he may not find any earned merit in them: chemical processes, and the clash of elements, the agony of the sick man who yearns for recovery, these have no more earned merit than do those inner struggles and crises in which a man is torn back and forth by various motives until he finally decides for the most powerful—as is said (in truth, until the most powerful motive decides about us). But all these motives, whatever great names we give them, have grown out of the same roots which are thought to hold the evil poisons. Between good and evil actions there is no difference in type; at most, a difference in degree. Good actions are sublimated evil actions; evil actions are good actions become coarse and stupid. The individual's only demand, for self-enjoyment (along with the fear of losing it), is satisfied in all circumstances: man may act as he can, that is, as he must, whether in deeds of vanity, revenge, pleasure, usefulness, malice, cunning, or in deeds of sacrifice, pity, knowledge. His powers of judgment determine where a man will let this demand for self-enjoyment take him. In each society, in each individual, a hierarchy of the good is always present, by which man determines his own actions and judges other people's actions. But this standard is continually in flux; many actions are called evil, and are only stupid, because the degree of intelligence which chose them was very low. Indeed, in a certain sense *all* actions are stupid even now, for the highest degree of human intelligence which can now be attained will surely be surpassed. And then, in hindsight, all *our* behavior and judgments will appear as inadequate and rash as the behavior and judgments of backward savage tribes now seem to us inadequate and rash.

To understand all this can cause great pain, but afterwards there is consolation. These pains are birth pangs. The butterfly wants to break through his cocoon; he tears at it, he rends it: then he is blinded and confused by the unknown light, the realm of freedom. Men who are *capable* of that sorrow (how few they will be!) will make the first attempt to see if mankind *can transform itself* from a *moral* into a *wise* mankind. In those individuals, the sun of a new gospel is casting its first ray onto the highest mountaintop of the soul; the fog is condensing more thickly than ever, and the brightest light and cloudiest dusk lie next to each other. Everything is necessity: this is the new knowledge, and this knowledge itself is necessity. Everything is innocence:

and knowledge is the way to insight into this innocence. If pleasure, egoism, vanity are *necessary* for the generation of moral phenomena and their greatest flower, the sense for true and just knowledge; if error and confusion of imagination were the only means by which mankind could raise itself gradually to this degree of self-illumination and self-redemption—who could scorn those means? Who could be sad when he perceives the goal to which those paths lead? Everything in the sphere of morality has evolved; changeable, fluctuating, everything is fluid, it is true: but *everything is also streaming onward*—to one goal. Even if the inherited habit of erroneous esteeming, loving, hating continues to govern us, it will grow weaker under the influence of growing knowledge: a new habit, that of understanding, non-loving, non-hating, surveying is gradually being implanted in us on the same ground, and in thousands of years will be powerful enough perhaps to give mankind the strength to produce wise, innocent (conscious of their innocence) men as regularly as it now produces unwise, unfair men, conscious of their guilt—*these men are the necessary first stage, but not the opposite of those to come.*

NOTES

1. Duc François de La Rochefoucauld (1613–1680) was a French moralist and writer of aphorisms. [D.C.A.]
2. Plutarch of Chaeronea (about 46–120) was a Greek biographer and philosopher. [D.C.A.]
3. "That which men call virtue is usually no more than a phantom formed by our passions, to which one gives an honest name in order to do with impunity whatever one wishes." [M.F.]
4. Homer (8th or 9th century B.C.E.) is the Greek poet to whom the epics the *Iliad* and the *Odyssey* are attributed. The *Iliad* deals with the war between the Greeks and the Trojans. [D.C.A.]
5. Nietzsche may be referring to Plato *Republic* 3.387–388. For more information on Plato, see the introduction to Chapter 1. [D.C.A.]
6. Prosper Merimée (1803–1870), *Lettres à une inconnue* ["Letters to an Unknown"], 1.8. "Know that nothing is more common than to do harm for the pleasure of doing it." [M.F.]
7. Jonathan Swift (1667–1745) was an English satirist. [D.C.A.]
8. *Jesuits*: members of the Society of Jesus, a Roman Catholic religious order [D.C.A.]
9. *Individuum* is Latin for "an undivided thing"; *dividuum* means "a divided thing." [D.C.A.]
10. Epicurus (341–270 B.C.E.) was a Greek philosopher. [D.C.A.]
11. Matthew 5:45. "His sun rises on the bad and the good, he rains on the just and the unjust." [M.F.]
12. *Pandora*: in Greek mythology, first woman on earth. She was sent by Zeus to the human race with a jar (or box) that contained every evil. [D.C.A.]
13. Xerxes I (about 519–465 B.C.E.) was king of ancient Persia from 486 to 465. He led an invasion against the Greeks. [D.C.A.]
14. Luke 18:14. "He who humbleth himself shall be exalted." [M.F.]

5. Thucydides (about 460–400 B.C.E.) was a Greek historian. His account of the conversation between the envoys of Athens and Melos appears in Thucydides *History of the Peloponnesian War* 5.84–113. The Athenians enslaved the Melians in 416. [D.C.A.]
6. "Each has as much right as his power is worth." Benedict (Baruch) Spinoza, *Political Treatise* 2.8. Spinoza (1632–1677) was a Dutch philosopher. [D.C.A., after M.F.]
7. "as his power is assessed to be" [M.F.]
8. *categorical imperative*: an unconditionally binding moral obligation [D.C.A.]
9. Matthew 7:1 [M.F.]
10. John Calvin (1509–1564) was a French religious reformer and theologian of the Reformation who settled in Geneva, Switzerland. [D.C.A.]
11. Michael Servet (Servetus) (1511–1553) was a Spanish physician and theologian. In Geneva, Calvin had him arrested and, after a long trial, he was burned for his heretical views on the Trinity. [D.C.A., after M.F.]
12. *Inquisition*: a former tribunal of the Roman Catholic Church for discovering and punishing heretics [D.C.A.]
13. Nietzsche is probably referring to Luke 10:25–37, the parable of the Good Samaritan. [M.F.]
14. A paraphrase of the view defended by Socrates in Plato *Gorgias* 468. Socrates (about 470–399 B.C.E.) was a Greek philosopher who greatly influenced Plato. See the introduction to Chapter 1. [D.C.A.]
15. *Schadenfreude*: enjoyment derived from the misfortune of others [D.C.A.]

QUESTIONS FOR REFLECTION AND DISCUSSION

1. Are all of our actions, good and evil, motivated by our desire to gain pleasure and avoid pain?
2. Is free will an illusion?
3. If we are not morally responsible for our actions, are reward and punishment justified?
4. Does being moral mean following tradition?
5. Is human nature neither good nor evil?

SUGGESTIONS FOR FURTHER READING

Primary Sources

Human, All Too Human: A Book for Free Spirits, trans. Marion Faber with Stephen Lehmann. Lincoln: University of Nebraska Press, 1984, 275 pp.

"'Good and Evil,' 'Good and Bad,'" first essay in *On the Genealogy of Morals: A Polemic*, trans. Walter Kaufmann and R. J. Hollingdale, in *On the Genealogy of Morals [and] Ecce Homo*, ed. Walter Kaufmann, New York: Vintage, 1969, pp. 24–56.

Developing some ideas set forth in our selection from *Human, All Too Human* (especially 45, "Double Prehistory of Good and Evil"), Nietzsche argues that "good and bad" derive from "master morality" whereas "good and evil" derive from "slave morality."

Thus Spoke Zarathustra: A Book for Everyone and No One, trans. R. J. Hollingdale. 1961; reprint ed. with new introduction, Harmondsworth, England: Penguin, 1969, 343 pp. Also *Thus Spoke Zarathustra: A Book for All and None*, trans. Walter Kaufmann. 1954; reprint ed., Harmondsworth, England: Penguin, 1978, 327 pp.

Nietzsche's most famous work, in which he introduces his doctrines of the will to power; the superhuman being (*Übermensch*), who embodies what Nietzsche considers the highest level of human development; and the eternal recurrence of the same events.

Twilight of the Idols; or, How to Philosophize with a Hammer, in *Twilight of the Idols [and] The Anti-Christ*, trans. R. J. Hollingdale. 1968; reprint ed. with new introduction, Harmondsworth, England: Penguin, 1990, pp. 29–122. Also *Twilight of the Idols; or, How One Philosophizes with a Hammer*, in *The Portable Nietzsche*, ed. and trans. Walter Kaufmann. New York: Viking, 1954, pp. 465–563.

In this work, written in 1888, the year before his breakdown, Nietzsche gives a brief summary of his philosophy. The original title was *A Psychologist's Leisure; or, The Idle Hours of a Psychologist* but, at the urging of an admirer, Nietzsche came up with a wittier title—one that parodies Wagner's opera *Twilight of the Gods.*

II. Secondary Sources

Danto, Arthur C. *Nietzsche as Philosopher*. 1965; reprint ed., New York: Columbia University Press, 1980, 250 pp.

A general study of Nietzsche's philosophical views. Danto sees Nietzsche, in part, as a precursor of contemporary analytic philosophy.

Hollingdale, R. J. *Nietzsche*. London: Routledge, Routledge Author Guides, 1973, 225 pp.

An accessible introduction to Nietzsche that focuses on exposition rather than interpretation, quoting extensively from Nietzsche's works.

Kaufmann, Walter. *Nietzsche: Philosopher, Psychologist, Antichrist*. 1950; 4th ed., Princeton, N.J.: Princeton University Press, 1974, 532 pp.

This comprehensive study of Nietzsche, which stresses the notion of the will to power, helped bring Nietzsche into the philosophical mainstream. Kaufmann dissociates Nietzsche from Nazism, with which his philosophy has been commonly linked.

Morgan, George Allen. *What Nietzsche Means*. 1941; reprint ed., New York: Harper & Row, 1965, 400 pp.

A thorough and sympathetic study of Nietzsche, with a detailed analytic table of contents. See chap. 6, "The Genealogy of Modern Morals," pp. 141–167.

tern, J. P. *Friedrich Nietzsche*. Harmondsworth, England: Penguin, Modern Masters
     Ser., 1979, 175 pp.

An accessible introduction to Nietzsche's philosophy that points out connections to the thought of Marx and Freud.

11

Sigmund Freud

Sigmund Freud was born in 1856 in Freiberg, Moravia, formerly of Austria, now of Czechoslovakia. When he was four, his family moved to Vienna, where he lived until he was eighty-two. In 1873 he enrolled in the medical school at the University of Vienna and received his degree eight years later. Freud preferred scientific research to the practice of medicine, but because he was Jewish it was difficult for him to obtain an academic appointment. So, in 1882, he began working as a resident physician at Vienna's general hospital, where he continued his studies of the brain.

Freud's special interest was neurology—specifically, neurotic disorders such as hysteria. When his research led him to believe that the physical symptoms from which neurotics suffered, such as paralysis or vision impairment, had psychological rather than physiological causes, he shifted the focus of his research from physiology to psychology.

In 1885 he went to Paris to study under the French neurologist Jean-Martin Charcot (1825–1893), who had been successfully treating hysterical patients through hypnosis. He returned to Vienna the following year and opened a private practice in neurology.

Freud began collaborating in research with Josef Breuer (1842–1925), a physician who had developed a method of freeing hysterical patients from their symptoms by having them talk about certain past experiences while in a hypnotic state ("the talking cure," as Breuer's most famous patient, Anna O., termed it). In 1895 Freud and Breuer published *Studies on Hysteria*, in which they describe the treatment of Anna O. and other patients.

Convinced that neurotic symptoms were caused by unconscious forces, Freud concluded that to cure neurosis the physician must explore the dark realm of the patient's unconscious mind. He found that the best technique for this was to analyze a patient's dreams, and in 1900 he published a comprehensive study entitled *The Interpretation of Dreams*. Freud believed that neurotic symptoms were always caused ultimately by some kind of sexual problem, and in 1905 he set forth his findings in *Three Essays on the Theory of Sexuality*. Meanwhile, in 1902, he had been able to obtain an appointment as professor of neurology at the University of Vienna—a post he held until 1938.

Freud's research and clinical experience led him to develop a new theory of the structure and workings of the mind, a theory he called *psychoanalysis*. He used the same term to designate the psychotherapeutic method based on his theory.) Freud's reputation spread to the United States, and in 1909 he was awarded an honorary degree by Clark University in Worcester, Massachusetts. There Freud gave a series of public lectures setting forth the main ideas of psychoanalysis, later published under the title *Five Lectures on Psychoanalysis*.

As the years passed, Freud focused more and more of his attention on the broad social applications of psychoanalysis, examining group psychology (*Group Psychology and the Analysis of the Ego*, 1921), religious belief (*The Future of an Illusion*, 1927), the conflict between the individual and society (*Civilization and Its Discontents*, 1930), and the origins of Judaism (*Moses and Monotheism*, completed in 1938, published in 1939). When the Nazis occupied Austria in 1938, it was imperative that Freud leave Vienna. So, at the age of eighty-two, he emigrated to London. He died there the following year.

Our selection is from *Five Lectures on Psychoanalysis*. Speaking to a public audience, Freud assumes no prior acquaintance with his views. He gives a historical account of psychoanalytic theory, beginning with Breuer's successful use of hypnosis to treat his hysterical patient Anna O. He tells how Breuer used hypnosis to release powerful emotions that had been buried in her mind—in the part of the mind Freud would term the *unconscious*.

Freud explains that at first he adopted Breuer's technique of hypnosis to explore his patients' unconscious mind, but then abandoned hypnosis in favor of other methods: (1) simply insisting to his patients that they could recall past traumatic experiences if they really tried, (2) having his patients say whatever came into their mind (*free association*), (3) interpreting their dreams, and (4) analyzing their faulty utterances and actions ("Freudian slips"). Freud goes on to present his theory of the origin of neurotic symptoms, arguing that these symptoms invariably go back to traumatic sexual experiences during childhood. He also asserts his belief in the complete determination of psychic life: There is always a cause for what a person thinks or feels—a psychic event never "just happens."

At the time of the *Five Lectures*, Freud had not yet formulated an overall principle explaining what motivates psychic events. He later proposed the "pleasure principle" as the explanation: Every psychic event is motivated by a desire (conscious or unconscious) to gain pleasure or avoid pain. Although we can be mistaken about what will bring us the most pleasure (the neurotic, for example, ends up with more pain than pleasure), the fact remains that what we seek is pleasure. An important implication of the pleasure principle is that we are not free because we must, by our very nature, choose what we believe will bring us the most pleasure. One can see foreshadowed in the *Five Lectures* both the pleasure principle and its corollary that human beings are not free.

FIVE LECTURES ON PSYCHOANALYSIS

FIRST LECTURE

Ladies and Gentlemen,—It is with novel and bewildering feelings that I find myself in the New World, lecturing before an audience of expectant enquirers. No doubt I owe this honour only to the fact that my name is linked with the topic of psychoanalysis; and it is of psychoanalysis, therefore, that I intend to speak to you. I shall attempt to give you, as succinctly as possible, a survey of the history and subsequent development of this new method of examination and treatment.

If it is a merit to have brought psychoanalysis into being, that merit is not mine. I had no share in its earliest beginnings. I was a student and working for my final examinations at the time when another Viennese physician, Dr. Josef Breuer, first (in 1880-1882) made use of this procedure on a girl who was suffering from hysteria. Let us turn our attention straightaway to the history of this case and its treatment, which you will find set out in detail in the *Studies on Hysteria* which were published later by Breuer and myself.[1]

But I should like to make one preliminary remark. It is not without satisfaction that I have learnt that the majority of my audience are not members of the medical profession. You have no need to be afraid that any special medical knowledge will be required for following what I have to say. It is true that we shall go along with the doctors on the first stage of our journey, but we shall soon part company with them and, with Dr. Breuer, shall pursue a quite individual path.

Dr. Breuer's patient was a girl of twenty-one, of high intellectual gifts. Her illness lasted for over two years, and in the course of it she developed a series of physical and psychological disturbances which decidedly deserved to be taken seriously. She suffered from a rigid paralysis, accompanied by loss of sensation, of both extremities on the right side of her body; and the same

283

trouble from time to time affected her on her left side. Her eye movements were disturbed and her power of vision was subject to numerous restrictions. She had difficulties over the posture of her head; she had a severe nervous cough. She had an aversion to taking nourishment, and on one occasion she was for several weeks unable to drink in spite of a tormenting thirst. Her powers of speech were reduced, even to the point of her being unable to speak or understand her native language. Finally, she was subject to conditions of *"absence,"*[2] of confusion, of delirium, and of alteration of her whole personality, to which we shall have presently to turn our attention.

When you hear such an enumeration of symptoms, you will be inclined to think it safe to assume, even though you are not doctors, that what we have before us is a severe illness, probably affecting the brain, that it offers small prospect of recovery and will probably lead to the patient's early decease. You must be prepared to learn from the doctors, however, that, in a number of cases which display severe symptoms such as these, it is justifiable to take a different and far more favourable view. If a picture of this kind is presented by a young patient of the female sex, whose vital internal organs (heart, kidneys, etc.) are shown on objective examination to be normal, but who has been subjected to violent *emotional* shocks—if, moreover, her various symptoms differ in certain matters of detail from what would have been expected—then doctors are not inclined to take the case too seriously. They decide that what they have before them is not an organic disease of the brain, but the enigmatic condition which, from the time of ancient Greek medicine, has been known as "hysteria" and which has the power of producing illusory pictures of a whole number of serious diseases. They consider that there is then no risk to life but that a return to health—even a complete one—is probable. It is not always quite easy to distinguish a hysteria like this from a severe organic illness. There is no need for us to know, however, how a differential diagnosis of that kind is made; it will suffice to have an assurance that the case of Breuer's patient was precisely of a kind in which no competent physician could fail to make a diagnosis of hysteria. And here we may quote from the report of the patient's illness the further fact that it made its appearance at a time when she was nursing her father, of whom she was devotedly fond, through the grave illness which led to his death, and that, as a result of her own illness, she was obliged to give up nursing him.

So far it has been an advantage to us to accompany the doctors; but the moment of parting is at hand. For you must not suppose that a patient's prospects of medical assistance are improved in essentials by the fact that a diagnosis of hysteria has been substituted for one of severe organic disease of the brain. Medical skill is in most cases powerless against severe diseases of the brain; but neither can the doctor do anything against hysterical disorders. He must leave it to kindly Nature to decide when and how his optimistic prognosis shall be fulfilled.

Thus the recognition of the illness as hysteria makes little difference to the patient; but to the doctor quite the reverse. It is noticeable that his attitude towards hysterical patients is quite other than towards sufferers from organic diseases. He does not have the same sympathy for the former as for the latter: for the hysteric's ailment is in fact far less serious and yet it seems to claim to be regarded as equally so. And there is a further factor at work. Through his studies, the doctor has learnt many things that remain a sealed book to the layman: he has been able to form ideas on the causes of illness and on the changes it brings about—e.g. in the brain of a person suffering from apoplexy or from a malignant growth—ideas which must to some degree meet the case, since they allow him to understand the details of the illness. But all his knowledge—his training in anatomy, in physiology and in pathology— leaves him in the lurch when he is confronted by the details of hysterical phenomena. He cannot understand hysteria, and in the face of it he is himself a layman. This is not a pleasant situation for anyone who as a rule sets so much store by his knowledge. So it comes about that hysterical patients forfeit his sympathy. He regards them as people who are transgressing the laws of his science—like heretics in the eyes of the orthodox. He attributes every kind of wickedness to them, accuses them of exaggeration, of deliberate deceit, of malingering. And he punishes them by withdrawing his interest from them.

Dr. Breuer's attitude towards his patient deserved no such reproach. He gave her both sympathy and interest, even though, to begin with, he did not know how to help her. It seems likely that she herself made his task easier by the admirable qualities of intellect and character to which he has testified in her case history. Soon, moreover, his benevolent scrutiny showed him the means of bringing her a first instalment of help.

It was observed that, while the patient was in her states of *"absence"* (altered personality accompanied by confusion), she was in the habit of muttering a few words to herself which seemed as though they arose from some train of thought that was occupying her mind. The doctor, after getting a report of these words, used to put her into a kind of hypnosis and then repeat them to her so as to induce her to use them as a starting-point. The patient complied with the plan, and in this way reproduced in his presence the mental creations which had been occupying her mind during the *"absences"* and which had betrayed their existence by the fragmentary words which she had uttered. They were profoundly melancholy phantasies— "daydreams" we should call them—sometimes characterized by poetic beauty, and their starting-point was as a rule the position of a girl at her father's sick bed. When she had related a number of these phantasies, she was as if set free, and she was brought back to normal mental life. The improvement in her condition, which would last for several hours, would be succeeded next day by a further attack of *"absence"*; and this in turn would be removed in the same way by getting her to put into words her freshly constructed phantasies. It was impossible to escape the conclusion that the alteration in her mental state which was expressed in the *"absences"* was a result of the stimulus proceeding from these highly emotional phantasies. The patient herself, who, strange to say, could at this time only speak and

nderstand English, christened this novel kind of treatment the "talking
ure" or used to refer to it jokingly as "chimney-sweeping."

It soon emerged, as though by chance, that this process of sweeping the
mind clean could accomplish more than the merely temporary relief of her
ever-recurring mental confusion. It was actually possible to bring about the
disappearance of the painful symptoms of her illness, if she could be brought
to remember under hypnosis, with an accompanying expression of affect, on
what occasion and in what connection the symptoms had first appeared. "It
was in the summer during a period of extreme heat, and the patient was
suffering very badly from thirst; for, without being able to account for it in
any way, she suddenly found it impossible to drink. She would take up the
glass of water that she longed for, but as soon as it touched her lips she would
push it away like someone suffering from hydrophobia. As she did this, she
was obviously in an *absence* for a couple of seconds. She lived only on fruit,
such as melons, etc., so as to lessen her tormenting thirst. This had lasted for
some six weeks, when one day during hypnosis she grumbled about her
English 'lady-companion,' whom she did not care for, and went on to describe, with every sign of disgust, how she had once gone into this lady's
room and how her little dog—horrid creature!—had drunk out of a glass
there. The patient had said nothing, as she had wanted to be polite. After
giving further energetic expression to the anger she had held back, she asked
for something to drink, drank a large quantity of water without any difficulty,
and awoke from her hypnosis with the glass at her lips; and thereupon the
disturbance vanished, never to return."[3]

With your permission, I should like to pause a moment over this event.
Never before had anyone removed a hysterical symptom by such a method or
had thus gained so deep an insight into its causation. It could not fail to prove
a momentous discovery if the expectation were confirmed that others of the
patient's symptoms—perhaps the majority of them— had arisen and could
be removed in this same manner. Breuer spared no pains in convincing
himself that this was so, and he proceeded to a systematic investigation of the
pathogenesis of the other and more serious symptoms of the patient's illness.
And it really *was* so. Almost all the symptoms had arisen in this way as
residues—"precipitates" they might be called—of emotional experiences. To
these experiences, therefore, we later gave the name of "psychical traumas,"[4]
while the particular nature of the symptoms was explained by their relation to
the traumatic scenes which were their cause. They were, to use a technical
term, "determined" by the scenes of whose recollection they represented
residues, and it was no longer necessary to describe them as capricious or
enigmatic products of the neurosis. One unexpected point, however, must be
noticed. What left the symptom behind was not always a *single* experience.
On the contrary, the result was usually brought about by the convergence of
several traumas, and often by the repetition of a great number of similar ones.
Thus it was necessary to reproduce the whole chain of pathogenic memories
in chronological order, or rather in reversed order, the latest ones first and the

earliest ones last; and it was quite impossible to jump over the later traumas in order to get back more quickly to the first, which was often the most potent one.

No doubt you will now ask me for some further instances of the causation of hysterical symptoms besides the one I have already given you of a fear of water produced by disgust at a dog drinking out of a glass. But if I am to keep to my programme I shall have to restrict myself to very few examples. In regard to the patient's disturbances of vision, for instance, Breuer describes how they were traced back to occasions such as one on which, "when she was sitting by her father's bedside with tears in her eyes, he suddenly asked her what time it was. She could not see clearly; she made a great effort, and brought her watch near to her eyes. The face of the watch now seemed very big—thus accounting for her macropsia and convergent squint.[5] Or again, she tried hard to suppress her tears so that the sick man should not see them." Moreover, all of the pathogenic impressions came from the period during which she was helping to nurse her sick father. "She once woke up during the night in great anxiety about the patient, who was in a high fever; and she was under the strain of expecting the arrival of a surgeon from Vienna who was to operate. Her mother had gone away for a short time and Anna was sitting at the bedside with her right arm over the back of her chair. She fell into a waking dream and saw a black snake coming towards the sick man from the wall to bite him. (It is most likely that there were in fact snakes in the field behind the house and that these had previously given the girl a fright; they would thus have provided the material for her hallucination.) She tried to keep the snake off, but it was as though she was paralysed. Her right arm, over the back of the chair, had gone to sleep, and had become anaesthetic and paretic; and when she looked at it the fingers turned into little snakes with death's heads (the nails). (It seems probable that she had tried to use her paralysed right hand to drive off the snake and that its anaesthesia and paralysis had consequently become associated with the hallucination of the snake.) When the snake vanished, in her terror she tried to pray. But language failed her: she could find no tongue in which to speak, till at last she thought of some children's verses in English and then found herself able to think and pray in that language." When the patient had recollected this scene in hypnosis, the rigid paralysis of her left arm, which had persisted since the beginning of her illness, disappeared, and the treatment was brought to an end. . . .

If I may be allowed to generalize—which is unavoidable in so condensed an account as this—I should like to formulate what we have learned so far as follows: *our hysterical patients suffer from reminiscences.* Their symptoms are residues and mnemic symbols of particular (traumatic) experiences. We may perhaps obtain a deeper understanding of this kind of symbolism if we compare them with other mnemic symbols in other fields. The monuments and memorials with which large cities are adorned are also mnemic

ymbols. If you take a walk through the streets of London, you will find, in
ont of one of the great railway termini, a richly carved Gothic column—
Charing Cross. One of the old Plantagenet kings of the thirteenth century
rdered the body of his beloved Queen Eleanor to be carried to Westminster;
nd at every stage at which the coffin rested he erected a Gothic cross.[6]
Charing Cross is the last of the monuments that commemorate the funeral
ortège. At another point in the same town, not far from London Bridge, you
vill find a towering, and more modern, column, which is simply known as
'The Monument.'' It was designed as a memorial of the Great Fire, which
roke out in that neighbourhood in 1666 and destroyed a large part of the city.
These monuments, then, resemble hysterical symptoms in being mnemic
ymbols; up to that point the comparison seems justifiable. But what should
ve think of a Londoner who paused today in deep melancholy before the
nemorial of Queen Eleanor's funeral instead of going about his business in
he hurry that modern working conditions demand or instead of feeling joy
ver the youthful queen of his own heart? Or again what should we think of a
Londoner who shed tears before the Monument that commemorates the
eduction of his beloved metropolis to ashes although it has long since risen
gain in far greater brilliance? Yet every single hysteric and neurotic behaves
ke these two unpractical Londoners. Not only do they remember painful
xperiences of the remote past, but they still cling to them emotionally; they
annot get free of the past and for its sake they neglect what is real and
nmediate. This fixation of mental life to pathogenic traumas is one of the
nost significant and practically important characteristics of neurosis.

I am quite ready to allow the justice of an objection that you are probably
aising at this moment on the basis of the case history of Breuer's patient. It is
uite true that all her traumas dated from the period when she was nursing
er sick father and that her symptoms can only be regarded as mnemic signs
f his illness and death. Thus they correspond to a display of mourning, and
here is certainly nothing pathological in being fixated to the memory of a
ead person so short a time after his decease; on the contrary, it would be a
ormal emotional process. I grant you that in the case of Breuer's patient
here is nothing striking in her fixation to her trauma. But in other
ases . . . the feature of an abnormal attachment to the past is very clear; and
seems likely that Breuer's patient would have developed a similar feature if
he had not received cathartic treatment[7] so soon after experiencing the
raumas and developing the symptoms.

So far we have only been discussing the relations between a patient's
ysterical symptoms and the events of her life. There are, however, two
urther factors in Breuer's observation which enable us to form some notion of
ow the processes of falling ill and of recovering occur.

In the first place, it must be emphasized that Breuer's patient, in almost
ll her pathogenic situations, was obliged to *suppress* a powerful emotion

instead of allowing its discharge in the appropriate signs of emotion, words or actions. In the episode of her lady-companion's dog, she suppressed any manifestation of her very intense disgust, out of consideration for the woman's feelings; while she watched at her father's bedside she was constantly on the alert to prevent the sick man from observing her anxiety and her painful depression. When subsequently she reproduced these scenes in her doctor's presence, the affect which had been inhibited at the time emerged with peculiar violence, as though it had been saved up for a long time. Indeed, the symptom which was left over from one of these scenes would reach its highest pitch of intensity at the time when its determining cause was being approached, only to vanish when that cause had been fully ventilated. On the other hand, it was found that no result was produced by the recollection of a scene in the doctor's presence if for some reason the recollection took place without any generation of affect. Thus it was what happened to these affects, which might be regarded as displaceable magnitudes, that was the decisive factor both for the onset of illness and for recovery. One was driven to assume that the illness occurred because the affects generated in the pathogenic situations had their normal outlet blocked, and that the essence of the illness lay in the fact that these "strangulated" affects were then put to an abnormal use. In part they remained as a permanent burden upon the patient's mental life and a source of constant excitation for it; and in part they underwent a transformation into unusual somatic innervations and inhibitions,[8] which manifested themselves as the physical symptoms of the case. For this latter process we coined the term "hysterical conversion." Quite apart from this, a certain portion of our mental excitation is normally directed along the paths of somatic innervation and produces what we know as an "expression of the emotions." Hysterical conversion exaggerates this portion of the discharge of an emotionally cathected mental process;[9] it represents a far more intense expression of the emotions, which has entered upon a new path. When the bed of a stream is divided into two channels, then, if the current in one of them is brought up against an obstacle, the other will at once be overfilled. As you see, we are on the point of arriving at a purely psychological theory of hysteria, with affective processes in the front rank.

SECOND LECTURE

Ladies and Gentlemen,—. . . When, later on, I set about continuing on my own account the investigations that had been begun by Breuer, I soon arrived at another view of the origin of hysterical dissociation (the splitting of consciousness). . . .

I was driven forward above all by practical necessity. The cathartic procedure, as carried out by Breuer, presupposed putting the patient into a tate of deep hypnosis; for it was only in a state of hypnosis that he attained a nowledge of the pathogenic connections which escaped him in his normal tate. But I soon came to dislike hypnosis, for it was a temperamental and, ne might almost say, a mystical ally. When I found that, in spite of all my fforts, I could not succeed in bringing more than a fraction of my patients nto a hypnotic state, I determined to give up hypnosis and to make the athartic procedure independent of it. Since I was not able at will to alter the nental state of the majority of my patients, I set about working with them in heir *normal* state. At first, I must confess, this seemed a senseless and opeless undertaking. I was set the task of learning from the patient something that I did not know and that he did not know himself. How could one ope to elicit it? But there came to my help a recollection of a most remarkable nd instructive experiment which I had witnessed when I was with ernheim[10] at Nancy [in 1889]. Bernheim showed us that people whom he ad put into a state of hypnotic somnambulism, and who had had all kinds of xperiences while they were in that state, only *appeared* to have lost the nemory of what they had experienced during somnambulism; it was possible o revive these memories in their normal state. It is true that, when he uestioned them about their somnambulistic experiences, they began by naintaining that they knew nothing about them; but if he refused to give vay, and insisted, and assured them that they *did* know about them, the orgotten experiences always reappeared.

So I did the same thing with my patients. When I reached a point with hem at which they maintained that they knew nothing more, I assured them hat they *did* know it all the same, and that they had only to say it; and I entured to declare that the right memory would occur to them at the noment at which I laid my hand on their forehead. In that way I succeeded, vithout using hypnosis, in obtaining from the patients whatever was required for establishing the connection between the pathogenic scenes they ad forgotten and the symptoms left over from those scenes. But it was a aborious procedure, and in the long run an exhausting one; and it was nsuited to serve as a permanent technique.

I did not abandon it, however, before the observations I made during ny use of it afforded me decisive evidence. I found confirmation of the fact hat the forgotten memories were not lost. They were in the patient's possesion and were ready to emerge in association to what was still known by him; ut there was some force that prevented them from becoming conscious and ompelled them to remain unconscious. The existence of this force could be ssumed with certainty, since one became aware of an effort corresponding to if, in opposition to it, one tried to introduce the unconscious memories into he patient's consciousness. The force which was maintaining the pathological condition became apparent in the form of *resistance* on the part of the atient.

It was on this idea of resistance, then, that I based my view of the course of psychical events in hysteria. In order to effect a recovery, it had proved necessary to remove these resistances. Starting out from the mechanism of cure, it now became possible to construct quite definite ideas of the origin of the illness. The same forces which, in the form of resistance, were now offering opposition to the forgotten material's being made conscious, must formerly have brought about the forgetting and must have pushed the pathogenic experiences in question out of consciousness. I gave the name of *"repression"* to this hypothetical process, and I considered that it was proved by the undeniable existence of resistance.

The further question could then be raised as to what these forces were and what the determinants were of the repression in which we now recognized the pathogenic mechanism of hysteria. A comparative study of the pathogenic situations which we had come to know through the cathartic procedure made it possible to answer this question. All these experiences had involved the emergence of a wishful impulse which was in sharp contrast to the subject's other wishes and which proved incompatible with the ethical and aesthetic standards of his personality. There had been a short conflict, and the end of this internal struggle was that the idea which had appeared before consciousness as the vehicle of this irreconcilable wish fell a victim to repression, was pushed out of consciousness with all its attached memories, and was forgotten. Thus the incompatibility of the wish in question with the patient's ego[11] was the motive for the repression; the subject's ethical and other standards were the repressing forces. An acceptance of the incompatible wishful impulse or a prolongation of the conflict would have produced a high degree of unpleasure; this unpleasure was avoided by means of repression, which was thus revealed as one of the devices serving to protect the mental personality.

To take the place of a number of instances, I will relate a single one of my cases, in which the determinants and advantages of repression are sufficiently evident. For my present purpose I shall have once again to abridge the case history and omit some important underlying material. The patient was a girl who had lost her beloved father after she had taken a share in nursing him—a situation analogous to that of Breuer's patient. Soon afterwards her elder sister married, and her new brother-in-law aroused in her a peculiar feeling of sympathy which was easily masked under a disguise of family affection. Not long afterwards her sister fell ill and died, in the absence of the patient and her mother. They were summoned in all haste without being given any definite information of the tragic event. When the girl reached the bedside of her dead sister, there came to her for a brief moment an idea that might be expressed in these words: "Now he is free and can marry me." We may assume with certainty that this idea, which betrayed to her consciousness the intense love for her brother-in-law of which she had not herself been conscious, was surrendered to repression a moment later, owing

ɔ the revolt of her feelings. The girl fell ill with severe hysterical symptoms;
nd while she was under my treatment it turned out that she had completely
ɔrgotten the scene by her sister's bedside and the odious egoistic impulse
hat had emerged in her. She remembered it during the treatment and
eproduced the pathogenic moment with signs of the most violent emotion,
nd, as a result of the treatment, she became healthy once more.

Perhaps I may give you a more vivid picture of repression and of its
ecessary relation to resistance, by a rough analogy derived from our actual
ituation at the present moment. Let us suppose that in this lecture-room and
mong this audience, whose exemplary quiet and attentiveness I cannot
ufficiently commend, there is nevertheless someone who is causing a distur-
ance and whose ill-mannered laughter, chattering and shuffling with his feet
re distracting my attention from my task. I have to announce that I cannot
roceed with my lecture; and thereupon three or four of you who are strong
nen stand up and, after a short struggle, put the interrupter outside the door.
o now he is "repressed," and I can continue my lecture. But in order that the
nterruption shall not be repeated, in case the individual who has been
xpelled should try to enter the room once more, the gentlemen who have
ut my will into effect place their chairs up against the door and thus establish
"resistance" after the repression has been accomplished. If you will now
ranslate the two localities concerned into psychical terms as the "conscious"
nd the "unconscious," you will have before you a fairly good picture of the
rocess of repression. . . .

We must not omit now to consider . . . from the standpoint of the
heory of repression [the discoveries of Breuer about the relation between
ymptoms and psychical traumas]. At first sight it really seems impossible to
race a path from repression to the formation of symptoms. Instead of giving a
omplicated theoretical account, I will return here to the analogy which I
mployed earlier for my explanation of repression. If you come to think of it,
he removal of the interrupter and the posting of the guardians at the door
nay not mean the end of the story. It may very well be that the individual
vho has been expelled, and who has now become embittered and reckless,
vill cause us further trouble. It is true that he is no longer among us; we are
ree from his presence, from his insulting laughter and his *sotto voce*[12] com-
nents. But in some respects, nevertheless, the repression has been unsuc-
essful; for now he is making an intolerable exhibition of himself outside the
oom, and his shouting and banging on the door with his fists interfere with
ny lecture even more than his bad behaviour did before. In these circum-
tances we could not fail to be delighted if our respected president, Dr.
tanley Hall,[13] should be willing to assume the role of the mediator and
eacemaker. He would have a talk with the unruly person outside and would
hen come to us with a request that he should be re-admitted after all: he
imself would guarantee that the man would now behave better. On Dr.

Hall's authority we decide to lift the repression, and peace and quiet are restored. This presents what is really no bad picture of the physician's task in the psychoanalytic treatment of the neuroses.

To put the matter more directly. The investigation of hysterical patients and of other neurotics leads us to the conclusion that their repression of the idea to which the intolerable wish is attached has been a *failure*. It is true that they have driven it out of consciousness and out of memory and have apparently saved themselves a large amount of unpleasure. *But the repressed wishful impulse continues to exist in the unconscious.* It is on the lookout for an opportunity of being activated, and when that happens it succeeds in sending into consciousness a disguised and unrecognizable *substitute* for what had been repressed, and to this there soon become attached the same feelings of unpleasure which it was hoped had been saved by the repression. This substitute for the repressed idea—the *symptom*—is proof against further attacks from the defensive ego; and in place of the short conflict an ailment now appears which is not brought to an end by the passage of time. Alongside the indication of distortion in the symptom, we can trace in it the remains of some kind of indirect resemblance to the idea that was originally repressed. The paths along which the substitution was effected can be traced in the course of the patient's psychoanalytic treatment; and in order to bring about recovery, the symptom must be led back along the same paths and once more turned into the repressed idea. If what was repressed is brought back again into conscious mental activity—a process which presupposes the overcoming of considerable resistances—the resulting psychical conflict, which the patient had tried to avoid, can, under the physician's guidance, reach a better outcome than was offered by repression. There are a number of such opportune solutions, which may bring the conflict and the neurosis to a happy end, and which may in certain instances be combined. The patient's personality may be convinced that it has been wrong in rejecting the pathogenic wish and may be directed to a higher and consequently unobjectionable aim (this is what we call its "sublimation"); or the rejection of the wish may be recognized as a justifiable one, but the automatic and therefore inefficient mechanism of repression may be replaced by a condemning judgement with the help of the highest human mental functions—conscious control of the wish is attained. . . .

THIRD LECTURE

Ladies and Gentlemen,—It is not always easy to tell the truth, especially when one has to be concise; and I am thus today obliged to correct a wrong statement that I made in my last lecture. I said to you that, having dispensed with hypnosis, I insisted on my patients nevertheless telling me what occurred to them in connection with the subject under discussion, and assured

em that they really knew everything that they had ostensibly forgotten and
at the idea that occurred to them would infallibly contain what we were in
earch of; and I went on to say to you that I found that the first idea occurring
o my patients did in fact produce the right thing and turned out to be the
orgotten continuation of the memory. This, however, is not in general the
ase, and I only put the matter so simply for the sake of brevity. Actually it
as only for the first few times that the right thing which had been forgotten
urned up as a result of simple insistence on my part. When the procedure
as carried further, ideas kept on emerging that could not be the right ones,
nce they were not appropriate and were rejected as being wrong by the
atients themselves. Insistence was of no further help at this point, and I
ound myself once more regretting my abandonment of hypnosis.

While I was thus at a loss, I clung to a prejudice the scientific justification
or which was proved years later by my friend C. G. Jung[14] and his pupils in
urich. I am bound to say that it is sometimes most useful to have prejudices.
cherished a high opinion of the strictness with which mental processes are
etermined, and I found it impossible to believe that an idea produced by a
atient while his attention was on the stretch could be an arbitrary one and
nrelated to the idea we were in search of. The fact that the two ideas were
ot identical could be satisfactorily explained from the postulated psychologi-
al state of affairs. In the patient under treatment two forces were in operation
gainst each other: on the one hand, his conscious endeavour to bring into
onsciousness the forgotten idea in his unconscious, and on the other hand,
e resistance we already know about, which was striving to prevent what
as repressed or its derivatives from thus becoming conscious. If this re-
istance amounted to little or nothing, what had been forgotten became
onscious without distortion. It was accordingly plausible to suppose that the
reater the resistance against what we were in search of becoming conscious,
e greater would be its distortion. The idea which occurred to the patient in
ace of what we were in search of had thus itself originated like a symptom:
was a new, artificial and ephemeral substitute for what had been repressed,
nd was dissimilar to it in proportion to the degree of distortion it had
ndergone under the influence of the resistance. But, owing to its nature as a
ymptom, it must nevertheless have a certain similarity to what we were in
earch of; and if the resistance were not too great, we ought to be able to
uess the latter from the former. The idea occurring to the patient must be in
e nature of an *allusion* to the repressed element, like a representation of it in
ndirect speech.

We know cases in the field of normal mental life in which situations
nalogous to the one we have just assumed produce similar results. One such
ase is that of jokes. The problems of psychoanalytic technique have com-
elled me to investigate the technique of making jokes. I will give you one
xample of this—incidentally, a joke in English.

This is the anecdote. Two not particularly scrupulous business men had succeeded, by dint of a series of highly risky enterprises, in amassing a large fortune, and they were now making efforts to push their way into good society. One method, which struck them as a likely one, was to have their portraits painted by the most celebrated and highly-paid artist in the city, whose pictures had an immense reputation. The precious canvases were shown for the first time at a large evening party, and the two hosts themselves led the most influential connoisseur and art critic up to the wall on which the portraits were hanging side by side. He studied the works for a long time, and then, shaking his head, as though there was something he had missed, pointed to the gap between the pictures and asked quietly: "But where's the Saviour?" I see you are all much amused at this joke. Let us now proceed to examine it. Clearly what the connoisseur meant to say was: "You are a couple of rogues, like the two thieves between whom the Saviour was crucified." But he did not say this. Instead he made a remark which seems at first sight strangely inappropriate and irrelevant, but which we recognize a moment later as an *allusion* to the insult that he had in mind and as a perfect substitute for it. We cannot expect to find in jokes *all* the characteristics that we have attributed to the ideas occurring to our patients, but we must stress the identity of the *motive* for the joke and for the idea. Why did the critic not tell the rogues straight out what he wanted to say? Because he had excellent counter-motives working against his desire to say it to their faces. There are risks attendant upon insulting people who are one's hosts and who have at their command the fists of a large domestic staff. One might easily meet with the fate which I suggested in my last lecture as an analogy for repression. That was the reason why the critic did not express the insult he had in mind directly but in the form of an "allusion accompanied by omission"; and the same state of things is responsible for our patients' producing a more or less distorted *substitute* instead of the forgotten idea we are in search of.

It is highly convenient, Ladies and Gentlemen, to follow the Zurich school (Bleuler,[15] Jung, etc.) in describing a group of interdependent ideational elements cathected with affect as a "complex." We see, then, that if in our search for a repressed complex in one of our patients we start out from the last thing he remembers, we shall have every prospect of discovering the complex, provided that the patient puts a sufficient number of his free associations[16] at our disposal. Accordingly, we allow the patient to say whatever he likes, and hold fast to the postulate that nothing can occur to him which is not in an indirect fashion dependent on the complex we are in search of. If this method of discovering what is repressed strikes you as unduly circumstantial, I can at least assure you that it is the only practicable one.

When we come to putting this procedure into effect, we are subject to yet another interference. For the patient will often pause and come to a stop, and assert that he can think of nothing to say, and that nothing whatever occurs to his mind. If this were so and if the patient were right, then our procedure would once again have proved ineffective. But closer observation shows that such a stoppage of the flow of ideas never in fact occurs. It *appears* to happen only because the patient holds back or gets rid of the idea that he has become aware of, under the influence of the resistances which disguise themselves as various critical judgements about the value of the idea that has occurred to him. We can protect ourselves against this by warning him beforehand of this behaviour and requiring him to take no notice of such criticisms. He must, we tell him, entirely renounce any critical selection of this kind and say whatever comes into his head, even if he considers it incorrect or irrelevant or nonsensical, and above all if he finds it disagreeable to let himself think about what has occurred to him. So long as this ordinance is carried out, we are certain of obtaining the material which will put us on the track of the repressed complexes.

This associative material, which the patient contemptuously rejects when he is under the influence of the resistance instead of under the doctor's, serves the psychoanalyst, as it were, as ore from which, with the help of some simple interpretative devices, he extracts its content of precious metal. . . .

Working over the ideas that occur to patients when they submit to the main rule of psychoanalysis is not our only technical method of discovering the unconscious. The same purpose is served by two other procedures: the interpretation of patients' dreams and the exploitation of their faulty and haphazard actions.

I must admit, Ladies and Gentlemen, that I hesitated for a long time whether, instead of giving you this condensed general survey of the whole field of psychoanalysis, it might not be better to present you with a detailed account of dream-interpretation. I was held back by a purely subjective and seemingly secondary motive. It seemed to me almost indecent in a country which is devoted to practical aims to make my appearance as a "dream-interpreter," before you could possibly know the importance that can attach to that antiquated and derided art. The interpretation of dreams is in fact the royal road to a knowledge of the unconscious; it is the securest foundation of psychoanalysis and the field in which every worker must acquire his convictions and seek his training. If I am asked how one can become a psychoanalyst, I reply: "By studying one's own dreams." Every opponent of psychoanalysis hitherto has, with a nice discrimination, either evaded any consideration of *The Interpretation of Dreams*,[17] or has sought to skirt over it with the most superficial objections. If, on the contrary, you can accept the solutions of the problems of dream-life, the novelties with which psychoanalysis confronts your minds will offer you no further difficulties.

You should bear in mind that the dreams which we produce at night have, on the one hand, the greatest external similarity and internal kinship with the creations of insanity, and are, on the other hand, compatible with complete health in waking life. There is nothing paradoxical in the assertion that no one who regards these "normal" illusions, delusions and character-changes with astonishment instead of comprehension has the slightest prospect of understanding the abnormal structures of pathological mental states otherwise than as a layman. You may comfortably count almost all psychiatrists among such laymen.

I invite you now to follow me on a brief excursion through the region of dream-problems. When we are awake we are in the habit of treating dreams with the same contempt with which patients regard the associations that are demanded of them by the psychoanalyst. We dismiss them, too, by forgetting them as a rule, quickly and completely. Our low opinion of them is based on the strange character even of those dreams that are not confused and meaningless, and on the obvious absurdity and nonsensicalness of other dreams. Our dismissal of them is related to the uninhibited shamelessness and immorality of the tendencies openly exhibited in some dreams. . . .

In the first place, not all dreams are alien to the dreamer, incomprehensible and confused. If you inspect the dreams of very young children, from eighteen months upwards, you will find them perfectly simple and easy to explain. Small children always dream of the fulfilment of wishes that were aroused in them the day before but not satisfied. You will need no interpretative art in order to find this simple solution; all you need do is to enquire into the child's experiences on the previous day (the "dream-day"). Certainly the most satisfactory solution of the riddle of dreams would be to find that adults' dreams too were like those of children—fulfilments of wishful impulses that had come to them on the dream-day. And such in fact is the case. The difficulties in the way of this solution can be overcome step by step if dreams are analysed more closely.

The first and most serious objection is that the content of adults' dreams is as a rule unintelligible and could not look more unlike the fulfilment of a wish. And here is the answer. Such dreams have been subjected to distortion, the psychical process underlying them might originally have been expressed in words quite differently. You must distinguish the *manifest content of the dream*, as you vaguely recollect it in the morning and laboriously (and, as it seems, arbitrarily) clothe it in words, and the *latent dream-thoughts*, which you must suppose were present in the unconscious. This distortion in dreams is the same process that you have already come to know in investigating the formation of hysterical symptoms. It indicates, too, that the same interplay of mental forces is at work in the formation of dreams as in that of symptoms. The manifest content of the dream is the distorted substitute for the unconscious dream-thoughts and this distortion is the work of the ego's forces of defence—of resistances. In waking life these resistances altogether prevent the repressed wishes of the unconscious from entering consciousness; and during the lowered state of sleep they are at least strong enough to oblige them to adopt a veil of disguise. Thereafter, the dreamer can no more

nderstand the meaning of his dreams than the hysteric can understand the
onnection and significance of his symptoms.

You can convince yourself that there are such things as latent dream-
houghts and that the relation between them and the manifest content of the
ream is really as I have described it, if you carry out an analysis of dreams,
ie technique of which is the same as that of psychoanalysis. You entirely
isregard the apparent connections between the elements in the manifest
ream and collect the ideas that occur to you in connection with each separate
lement of the dream by free association according to the psychoanalytic rule
f procedure. From this material you arrive at the latent dream-thoughts, just
s you arrived at the patient's hidden complexes from his associations to his
ymptoms and memories. The latent dream-thoughts which have been
eached in this way will at once show you how completely justified we have
een in tracing back adults' dreams to children's dreams. The true meaning of
ie dream, which has now taken the place of its manifest content, is always
learly intelligible; it has its starting-point in experiences of the previous day,
nd proves to be a fulfilment of unsatisfied wishes. The manifest dream,
vhich you know from your memory when you wake up, can therefore only
e described as a *disguised* fulfilment of *repressed* wishes. . . .

I can now pass on to the third group of mental phenomena whose study
as become one of the technical instruments of psychoanalysis.

The phenomena in question are the small faulty actions performed by
oth normal and neurotic people, to which as a rule no importance is at-
iched: forgetting things that might be known and sometimes in fact *are*
nown (e.g. the occasional difficulty in recalling proper names), slips of the
ingue in talking, by which we ourselves are so often affected, analogous
ips of the pen and misreadings, bungling the performance of actions, losing
bjects or breaking them. All of these are things for which as a rule no
sychological determinants are sought and which are allowed to pass without
riticism as consequences of distraction or inattention or similar causes. Be-
des these there are the actions and gestures which people carry out without
oticing them at all, to say nothing of attributing any psychological impor-
ince to them: playing about and fiddling with things, humming tunes,
ngering parts of one's own body or one's clothing and so on. These small
iings, faulty actions and symptomatic or haphazard actions alike, are not so
isignificant as people, by a sort of conspiracy of silence, are ready to sup-
ose. They always have a meaning, which can usually be interpreted with
ase and certainty from the situation in which they occur. And it turns out
iat once again they give expression to impulses and intentions which have to
e kept back and hidden from one's own consciousness, or that they are
ctually derived from the same repressed wishful impulses and complexes
vhich we have already come to know as the creators of symptoms and the
onstructors of dreams. They therefore deserve to be rated as symptoms, and
they are examined they may lead, just as dreams do, to the uncovering of

the hidden part of the mind. A man's most intimate secrets are as a rule betrayed by their help. If they occur particularly easily and frequently even in healthy people in whom the repression of unconscious impulses has on the whole been quite successful, they have their triviality and inconspicuousness to thank for it. But they can claim a high theoretical value, since they prove that repression and the formation of substitutes occur even under healthy conditions.

As you already see, psychoanalysts are marked by a particularly strict belief in the determination of mental life. For them there is nothing trivial, nothing arbitrary or haphazard. They expect in every case to find sufficient motives where, as a rule, no such expectation is raised. Indeed, they are prepared to find *several* motives for one and the same mental occurrence, whereas what seems to be our innate craving for causality declares itself satisfied with a *single* psychical cause. . . .

FOURTH LECTURE

Ladies and Gentlemen,—You will want to know now what we have found out about the pathogenic complexes and repressed wishful impulses of neurotics with the help of the technical methods I have described.

First and foremost we have found out one thing. Psychoanalytic research traces back the symptoms of patients' illnesses with really surprising regularity to impressions from their *erotic life*. It shows us that the pathogenic wishful impulses are in the nature of erotic instinctual components; and it forces us to suppose that among the influences leading to the illness the predominant significance must be assigned to erotic disturbances, and that this is the case in both sexes.

I am aware that this assertion of mine will not be willingly believed. Even workers who are ready to follow my psychological studies are inclined to think that I overestimate the part played by sexual factors; they meet me with the question why *other* mental excitations should not lead to the phenomena I have described of repression and the formation of substitutes. I can only answer that I do not know why they should not, and that I should have no objection to their doing so; but experience shows that they do not carry this weight, that at most they *support* the operation of the sexual factors but cannot replace them. Far from this position having been postulated by me theoretically, at the time of the joint publication of the *Studies [on Hysteria]* with Dr. Breuer in 1895 I had not yet adopted it; and I was only converted to it when my experiences became more numerous and penetrated into the subject more deeply. . . .

A conviction of the correctness of this thesis was not precisely made easier by the behavior of patients. Instead of willingly presenting us with information about their sexual life, they try to conceal it by every means in

heir power. People are in general not candid over sexual matters. They do
ot show their sexuality freely, but to conceal it they wear a heavy overcoat
voven of a tissue of lies, as though the weather were bad in the world of
exuality. Nor are they mistaken. It is a fact that sun and wind are not
avourable to sexual activity in this civilized world of ours; none of us can
eveal his erotism freely to others. But when your patients discover that they
an feel quite easy about it while they are under your treatment, they discard
his veil of lies, and only then are you in a position to form a judgement on
his debatable question. Unluckily even doctors are not preferred above other
uman creatures in their personal relation to questions of sexual life, and
nany of them are under the spell of the combination of prudery and pru-
ience which governs the attitude of most "civilized people" in matters of
exuality.

Let me now proceed with my account of our findings. In another set of
ases psychoanalytic investigation traces the symptoms back, it is true, not to
exual experiences but to commonplace traumatic ones. But this distinction
ses its significance owing to another circumstance. For the work of analysis
equired for the thorough explanation and complete recovery of a case never
omes to a stop at events that occurred at the time of the onset of the illness,
ut invariably goes back to the patient's puberty and early childhood; and it is
nly there that it comes upon the impressions and events which determined
he later onset of the illness. It is only experiences in childhood that explain
usceptibility to later traumas and it is only by uncovering these almost
nvariably forgotten memory-traces and by making them conscious that we
cquire the power to get rid of the symptoms. And here we reach the same
onclusion as in our investigation of dreams: the imperishable, repressed
vishful impulses of childhood have alone provided the power for the con-
truction of symptoms, and without them the reaction to later traumas would
ave taken a normal course. But these powerful wishful impulses of child-
ood may without exception be described as sexual.

And now at last I am quite certain that I have surprised you. "Is there
uch a thing, then, as infantile sexuality?" you will ask "Is not childhood on
he contrary the period of life that is marked by the absence of the sexual
nstinct?" No, Gentlemen, it is certainly not the case that the sexual instinct
nters into children at the age of puberty in the way in which, in the Gospel,
he devil entered into the swine.[18] A child has its sexual instincts and ac-
ivities from the first; it comes into the world with them; and, after an
mportant course of development passing through many stages, they lead to
vhat is known as the normal sexuality of the adult. There is even no difficulty
n observing the manifestations of these sexual activities in children; on the
ontrary, it calls for some skill to overlook them or explain them away. . . .

Put away your doubts, then, and join me in a consideration of infantile
exuality from the earliest age. A child's sexual instinct turns out to be put

together out of a number of factors; it is capable of being divided up into numerous components which originate from various sources. Above all, it is still independent of the reproductive function, into the service of which it will later be brought. It serves for the acquisition of different kinds of pleasurable feeling, which, basing ourselves on analogies and connections, we bring together under the idea of sexual pleasure. The chief source of infantile sexual pleasure is the appropriate excitation of certain parts of the body that are especially susceptible to stimulus: apart from the genitals, these are the oral, anal and urethral orifices, as well as the skin and other sensory surfaces. Since at this first phase of infantile sexual life satisfaction is obtained from the subject's own body and extraneous objects are disregarded, we term this phase (from a word coined by Havelock Ellis[19]) that of *auto-erotism*. We call the parts of the body that are important in the acquisition of sexual pleasure "erotogenic zones." Thumb-sucking (or sensual sucking) in the youngest infants is a good example of this auto-erotic satisfaction from an erotogenic zone. . . .

We have . . . paid more attention to the somatic than to the mental phenomena of sexual life. The child's first choice of an object, which derives from its need for help, claims our further interest. Its choice is directed in the first instance to all those who look after it, but these soon give place to its parents. Children's relations to their parents, as we learn alike from direct observations of children and from later analytic examination of adults, are by no means free from elements of accompanying sexual excitation. The child takes both of its parents, and more particularly one of them, as the object of its erotic wishes. In so doing, it usually follows some indication from its parents, whose affection bears the clearest characteristics of a sexual activity, even though of one that is inhibited in its aims. As a rule a father prefers his daughter and a mother her son; the child reacts to this by wishing, if he is a son, to take his father's place, and, if she is a daughter, her mother's. The feelings which are aroused in these relations between parents and children and in the resulting ones between brothers and sisters are not only of a positive or affectionate kind but also of a negative or hostile one. The complex which is thus formed is doomed to early repression; but it continues to exercise a great and lasting influence from the unconscious. It is to be suspected that, together with its extensions, it constitutes the *nuclear complex* of every neurosis, and we may expect to find it no less actively at work in other regions of mental life. The myth of King Oedipus, who killed his father and took his mother to wife, reveals, with little modification, the infantile wish, which is later opposed and repudiated by the *barrier against incest*. Shakespeare's *Hamlet* is equally rooted in the soil of the incest-complex, but under a better disguise.[20] . . .

It is inevitable and perfectly normal that a child should take his parents as the first objects of his love. But his libido[21] should not remain fixated to hese first objects; later on, it should merely take them as a model, and should make a gradual transition from them on to extraneous people when the time or the final choice of an object arrives. The detachment of the child from his parents is thus a task that cannot be evaded if the young individual's social tness is not to be endangered. During the time at which repression is making its selection among the component instincts,[22] and later, when there hould be a slackening of the parents' influence, which is essentially responsible for the expenditure of energy on these repressions, the task of education meets with great problems, which at the present time are certainly not always dealt with in an understanding and unobjectionable manner. . . .

IFTH LECTURE

adies and Gentlemen,—With the discovery of infantile sexuality and the racing back of neurotic symptoms to erotic instinctual components we have arrived at some unexpected formulas concerning the nature and purposes of eurotic illnesses. We see that human beings fall ill when, as a result of xternal obstacles or of an internal lack of adaptation, the satisfaction of their rotic needs *in reality* is frustrated. We see that they then take flight into *illness* a order that by its help they may find a satisfaction to take the place of what as been frustrated. We recognize that the pathological symptoms constitute portion of the subject's sexual activity or even the whole of his sexual life, nd we find that the withdrawal from reality is the main purpose of the illness ut also the main damage caused by it. We suspect that our patients' resistance to recovery is no simple one, but compounded of several motives. Not only does the patient's ego rebel against giving up the repressions by means of which it has risen above its original disposition, but the sexual instincts are unwilling to renounce their substitutive satisfaction so long as it s uncertain whether reality will offer them anything better.

The flight from unsatisfactory reality into what, on account of the biological damage involved, we call illness (though it is never without an immediate ield of pleasure to the patient) takes place along the path of involution, of regression, of a return to earlier phases of sexual life, phases from which at ne time satisfaction was not withheld. This regression appears to be a wofold one: a *temporal* one, in so far as the libido, the erotic needs, hark back o stages of development that are earlier in time, and a *formal* one, in that the riginal and primitive methods of psychical expression are employed in manifesting those needs. Both these kinds of regression, however, lead back o childhood and unite in bringing about an infantile condition of sexual life.

The deeper you penetrate into the pathogenesis of nervous illness, the more you will find revealed the connection between the neuroses and other roductions of the human mind, including the most valuable. You will be aught that we humans, with the high standards of our civilization and under the pressure of our internal repressions, find reality unsatisfying quite generally, and for that reason entertain a life of phantasy in which we like to make up for the insufficiencies of reality by the production of wish-fulfilments. These phantasies include a great deal of the true constitutional essence of the subject's personality as well as of those of his impulses which are repressed where reality is concerned. The energetic and successful man is one who succeeds by his efforts in turning his wishful phantasies into reality. Where this fails, as a result of the resistances of the external world and of the subject's own weakness, he begins to turn away from reality and withdraws into his more satisfying world of phantasy, the content of which is transformed into symptoms should he fall ill. In certain favourable circumstances, it still remains possible for him to find another path leading from these phantasies to reality, instead of becoming permanently estranged from it by regressing to infancy. If a person who is at loggerheads with reality possesses an *artistic gift* (a thing that is still a psychological mystery to us), he can transform his phantasies into artistic creations instead of into symptoms. In this manner he can escape the doom of neurosis and by this roundabout path regain his contact with reality. . . . If there is persistent rebellion against the real world and if this precious gift is absent or insufficient, it is almost inevitable that the libido, keeping to the sources of the phantasies, will follow the path of regression, and will revive infantile wishes and end in neurosis. Today neurosis takes the place of the monasteries which used to be the refuge of all whom life had disappointed or who felt too weak to face it.

Let me at this point state the principal finding to which we have been led by the psychoanalytic investigation of neurotics. The neuroses have no psychical content that is peculiar to them and that might not equally be found in healthy people. Or, as Jung has expressed it, neurotics fall ill of the same complexes against which we healthy people struggle as well. Whether that struggle ends in health, in neurosis, or in a countervailing superiority of achievement, depends on *quantitative* considerations, on the relative strength of the conflicting forces. . . .

From the intellectual point of view we must, I think, take into account two special obstacles to recognizing psychoanalytic trains of thought. In the first place, people are unaccustomed to reckoning with a strict and universal application of determinism to mental life; and in the second place, they are ignorant of the peculiarities which distinguish unconscious mental processes from the conscious ones that are familiar to us. One of the most widespread resistances to psychoanalytic work, in the sick and healthy alike, can be traced to the second of these two factors. People are afraid of doing harm by psychoanalysis; they are afraid of bringing the repressed sexual instincts into the patient's consciousness, as though that involved a danger of their overwhelming his higher ethical trends and of their robbing him of his cultural acquisitions. People notice that the patient has sore spots in his mind, but

hrink from touching them for fear of increasing his sufferings. We can accept
his analogy. It is no doubt kinder not to touch diseased spots if it can do
othing else but cause pain. But, as we know, a surgeon does not refrain from
xamining and handling a focus of disease, if he is intending to take active
measures which he believes will lead to a permanent cure. No one thinks of
blaming him for the inevitable suffering caused by the examination or for the
reactions to the operation, if only it gains its end and the patient achieves a
asting recovery as a result of the temporary worsening of his state. The case
s similar with psychoanalysis. It may make the same claims as surgery: the
increase in suffering which it causes the patient during treatment is incomparably less than what a surgeon causes, and is quite negligible in proportion
o the severity of the underlying ailment. On the other hand, the final
outcome that is so much dreaded—the destruction of the patient's cultural
character by the instincts which have been set free from repression—is totally
mpossible. For alarm on this score takes no account of what our experiences
have taught us with certainty—namely that the mental and somatic power of
a wishful impulse, when once its repression has failed, is far stronger if it is
unconscious than if it is conscious; so that to make it conscious can only be to
weaken it. An unconscious wish cannot be influenced and it is independent
of any contrary tendencies, whereas a conscious one is inhibited by whatever
else is conscious and opposed to it. Thus the work of psychoanalysis puts
itself at the orders of precisely the highest and most valuable cultural trends,
as a better substitute for the unsuccessful repression.

What, then, becomes of the unconscious wishes which have been set
free by psychoanalysis? Along what paths do we succeed in making them
harmless to the subject's life? There are several such paths. The most frequent
outcome is that, while the work is actually going on, these wishes are
destroyed by the rational mental activity of the better impulses that are
opposed to them. *Repression* is replaced by a *condemning judgement* carried out
along the best lines. That is possible because what we have to get rid of is to a
great extent only the consequences arising from earlier stages of the ego's
development. The subject only succeeded in the past in repressing the unserviceable instinct because he himself was at that time imperfectly organized
and feeble. In his present-day maturity and strength, he will perhaps be able
to master what is hostile to him with complete success.

A second outcome of the work of psychoanalysis is that it then becomes
possible for the unconscious instincts revealed by it to be employed for the
useful purposes which they would have found earlier if development had not
been interrupted. For the extirpation of the infantile wishful impulses is by no
means the ideal aim of development. Owing to their repressions, neurotics
have sacrificed many sources of mental energy whose contributions would
have been of great value in the formation of their character and in their
activity in life. We know of a far more expedient process of development,
called *"sublimation,"* in which the energy of the infantile wishful impulses is
not cut off but remains ready for use—the unserviceable aim of the various

impulses being replaced by one that is higher, and perhaps no longer sexual. It happens to be precisely the components of the *sexual* instinct that are specially marked by a capacity of this kind for sublimation, for exchanging their sexual aim for another one which is comparatively remote and socially valuable. It is probable that we owe our highest cultural successes to the contributions of energy made in this way to our mental functions. Premature repression makes the sublimation of the repressed instinct impossible; when the repression is lifted, the path to sublimation becomes free once more.

We must not omit to consider the third of the possible outcomes of the work of psychoanalysis. A certain portion of the repressed libidinal impulses has a claim to direct satisfaction and ought to find it in life. Our civilized standards make life too difficult for the majority of human organizations. Those standards consequently encourage the retreat from reality and the generating of neuroses, without achieving any surplus of cultural gain by this excess of sexual repression. We ought not to exalt ourselves so high as completely to neglect what was originally animal in our nature. Nor should we forget that the satisfaction of the individual's happiness cannot be erased from among the aims of our civilization. The plasticity of the components of sexuality, shown by their capacity for sublimation, may indeed offer a great temptation to strive for still greater cultural achievements by still further sublimation. But, just as we do not count on our machines converting more than a certain fraction of the heat consumed into useful mechanical work, we ought not to seek to alienate the whole amount of the energy of the sexual instinct from its proper ends. We cannot succeed in doing so; and if the restriction upon sexuality were to be carried too far it would inevitably bring with it all the evils of soil-exhaustion.

It may be that you for your part will regard the warning with which I close as an exaggeration. I shall only venture on an indirect picture of my conviction by telling you an old story and leaving you to make what use you like of it. German literature is familiar with a little town called Schilda, to whose inhabitants clever tricks of every possible sort are attributed. The citizens of Schilda, so we are told, possessed a horse with whose feats of strength they were highly pleased and against which they had only one objection—that it consumed such a large quantity of expensive oats. They determined to break it of this bad habit very gently by reducing its ration by a few stalks every day, till they had accustomed it to complete abstinence. For a time things went excellently: the horse was weaned to the point of eating only one stalk a day, and on the succeeding day it was at last to work without any oats at all. On the morning of that day the spiteful animal was found dead; and the citizens of Schilda could not make out what it had died of.

We should be inclined to think that the horse was starved and that no work at all could be expected of an animal without a certain modicum of oats.

I must thank you for your invitation and for the attention with which you have listened to me.

NOTES

1. Josef Breuer and Sigmund Freud, *Studien über Hysterie*, Leipzig and Vienna, Deuticke, 1895 [D.C.A.]
2. *absence*: a French term meaning (as Freud states later on) "altered personality accompanied by confusion" [D.C.A.]
3. This and the two subsequent quotations describing the symptoms of Breuer's patient (Anna O.) are from *Studies on Hysteria*. [D.C.A.]
4. In Greek, *trauma* is, literally, a "physical wound." Freud's concept of "psychical trauma" extends this notion of wound to the mind. [D.C.A.]
5. *macropsia*: a condition of the eye in which objects appear larger than they are *convergent squint*: a condition in which the eyes are crossed and squint [D.C.A.]
6. The Plantagenet king of England to whom Freud refers is Edward I (1239–1307); his queen was Eleanor of Castile (1246–1290). Edward had Gothic crosses erected at each of the 12 places where Eleanor's funeral procession paused on its way from Harby, Nottinghamshire, to Westminster Abbey in London. [D.C.A.]
7. *cathartic treatment*: treatment of neurotic symptoms by bringing the patient's repressed feelings to consciousness and having the patient vent them. The Greek noun *katharsis* means "cleansing, purification." [D.C.A.]
8. *somatic innervations and inhibitions*: bodily actions and inabilities of the body to act [D.C.A.]
9. *emotionally cathected mental process*: a mental process invested with energy from one's emotions. *Cathect* is a psychoanalytic term meaning "attach energy to, invest with energy." [D.C.A.]
10. Hippolyte Bernheim (1837–1919) was a French physician. [D.C.A.]
11. *ego*: in psychoanalytic theory, the conscious part of the psyche, by which a person deals with external reality [D.C.A.]
12. *sotto voce*: under the breath (an Italian phrase meaning, literally, "under the voice") [D.C.A.]
13. Granville Stanley Hall (1844–1924) was an American psychologist who, as president of Clark University in Worcester, Massachusetts, invited Freud to visit the university to receive an honorary degree and to give this series of lectures on psychoanalysis. [D.C.A.]
14. Carl Gustav Jung (1875–1961) was a Swiss psychologist. [D.C.A.]
15. Eugen Bleuler (1857–1939) was a Swiss psychologist and neurologist. [D.C.A.]
16. *free associations*: words, ideas, and images that result from the psychoanalytic technique of *free association*, in which a patient says, in the presence of the psychoanalyst, whatever "falls into" his or her mind. "Association" translates the German word *Einfall*, which means, literally, "a falling in, an invasion." [D.C.A.]
17. *The Interpretation of Dreams*: Freud's detailed study of dreams, published in 1900 [D.C.A.]
18. Matthew 8:28–32; Mark 5:1–13; Luke 8:26–33 [D.C.A.]
19. Havelock Ellis (1859–1939) was an English psychologist and writer. [D.C.A.]
20. Freud adopted the term "Oedipus complex" for the first time shortly after these lectures were delivered. [J.S.]
21. *libido*: sexual energy [D.C.A.]
22. *component instincts*: the various components of the sexual instinct [D.C.A.]

QUESTIONS FOR REFLECTION AND DISCUSSION

1. Are human beings motivated primarily by unconscious wishes and desires?
2. Does the mind have conscious and unconscious "parts"?
3. Is every neurotic symptom caused by the repression of a painful experience?
4. Is every psychic event automatically determined by the desire to gain pleasure or avoid pain?
5. In what sense can a child's desires and activities be called *sexual*?

SUGGESTIONS FOR FURTHER READING

I. Primary Sources

Five Lectures on Psychoanalysis, ed. and trans. James Strachey. 1961; reprint ed. with new introduction, New York: Norton, 1989, 77 pp.

The Question of Lay Analysis: Conversations with an Impartial Person, ed. and trans. James Strachey. 1969; reprint ed. with new introduction, New York: Norton, 1989, 106 pp.

> Freud's main goal in this book is to argue that one does not need a medical degree to be a good practitioner of psychoanalytic therapy. In the course of his conversation with an imaginary "impartial person," he gives a lucid, nontechnical explanation of psychoanalytic therapy. Composed in 1927, the book makes use of id, ego, and superego—concepts Freud introduced in 1923.

Civilization and Its Discontents, ed. and trans. James Strachey. 1961; reprint ed. with new introduction, New York: Norton, 1989, 127 pp.

> This essay, published in 1930, examines the conflict between the individual's desire for instinctual satisfaction and the restrictions imposed by society. Freud discusses the relation between Eros, a cosmic force that aims at unity, and the death instinct, the destructive force he postulated in 1920 in *Beyond the Pleasure Principle.*

Introductory Lectures on Psychoanalysis, ed. and trans. James Strachey. 1966; reprint ed. with new introduction, New York: Norton, 1989, 621 pp.

> A series of 28 lectures delivered by Freud at the University of Vienna between 1915 and 1917, in which he gave a detailed account of psychoanalytic theory.

II. Secondary Sources

Abel, Donald C. *Freud on Instinct and Morality.* Albany: State University of New York Press, 1989, 123 pp.

> An examination of Freud's views on the nature and classification of human instincts, and the moral theory implied by these views.

ilman, Ilham. *Freud and Human Nature*. Oxford, England: Blackwell, Values and
    Philosophical Inquiry Ser., 1983, 207 pp.

    A discussion of Freud's conceptions of sexuality, love, and morality. Dilman
    argues that certain common criticisms of Freud are superficially valid but fail to
    appreciate what Freud was actually trying to say. For more advanced students of
    Freud.

all, Calvin S. *A Primer of Freudian Psychology*. 1954; reprint ed. New York: Octagon,
    1985, 127 pp.

    A brief and very clear exposition of Freud's theory of the structure, dynamics,
    and development of personality.

torr, Anthony. *Freud*. Oxford, England: Oxford University Press, Past Masters Ser.,
    1989, 135 pp.

    An accessible overview of Freud's principal ideas, including those on art, liter-
    ature, and religion. Includes a chapter on the current status of psychoanalysis.

ollheim, Richard. *Sigmund Freud*. 1971; reprint ed. with new preface, Cambridge,
    England: Cambridge University Press, 1990, 290 pp.

    A comprehensive study of Freud's thought, written in the form of an intellectual
    biography. Wollheim stresses Freud's quest for an overall theory of the mind.

12

Jean-Paul Sartre

Jean-Paul Sartre was born in Paris in 1905. His father died when he was two, and Sartre was raised in his grandfather's home at La Rochelle. At the age of nineteen, he began studying philosophy at the École Normale Supérieure in Paris. There he met fellow philosophy student Simone de Beauvoir (1908–1986) and began what turned out to be a lifelong friendship and intellectual and sexual relationship. After receiving his graduate degree in 1929, he served in the military for a little over a year. In 1931 he began teaching philosophy at Le Havre.

Sartre did research at the Institut Français in Berlin during the 1933–1934 academic year, focusing on the work of the German philosophers Edmund Husserl (1859–1938) and Martin Heidegger (1889–1976). He then taught at Le Havre for two more years and later took posts at other French schools.

Sartre began exploring the field of philosophical psychology, publishing *The Transcendence of the Ego* in 1937, *The Emotions: Outline of a Theory* in 1939, and *The Psychology of Imagination* in 1940. During this same period he also published two literary works (he had been writing fiction since his student days): *Nausea*, a philosophical novel (1938), and *The Wall*, a collection of short stories (1939).

Sartre was drafted by the French army in 1939 to fight in World War II. He was captured by the Germans in 1940, but escaped the following year. Sartre then went to Paris, where he resumed teaching and writing while also participating in the resistance movement against the Nazi occupation of France. During the occupation he wrote his main philosophical work, *Being and Nothingness: An Essay on Phenomenological Ontology*, and his first plays, *The Flies* and *No Exit*.

In 1944, together with Simone de Beauvoir, philosopher Maurice Merleau-Ponty (1908–1961), and others, he founded the leftist literary and political review *Les Temps modernes* ("Modern Times," named after the Charlie Chaplin film), and the first issue appeared in 1945. After the war Sartre gave up teaching to devote himself entirely to writing. He became known as an

existentialist" thinker, and in 1945 he gave a public lecture entitled "Existen-
alism Is a Humanism" in which he set forth some basic tenets of this
hilosophy.

Politically, Sartre was leftist, and became more so as the years passed. In
960 he published the first volume of his *Critique of Dialectical Reason* (a project
ever completed), which argued for the compatibility of existentialism and
Marxism. He and Beauvoir traveled to a number of Communist countries,
ften meeting with the heads of state.

In 1964 Sartre published his autobiography, *The Words*. Later that year
e was named winner of the Nobel Prize in Literature but refused the award
or both personal and political reasons. His last major work was *The Family
Idiot*, a three-volume biography of the French novelist Gustave Flaubert
(821–1880), which was published in 1971 and 1972. Sartre died in 1980; his
uneral was attended by 25,000 people.

Our selection is from Sartre's 1945 lecture "Existentialism Is a Human-
sm." Because the lecture was intended for the general public, it is not as
etailed or developed as Sartre's other philosophical works, but it is a good
ntroduction to Sartre's philosophy of human nature.

The lecture is structured as a response to certain objections that had
een raised against existentialism. Sartre believed the objections arose from a
misunderstanding of what existentialism is, and so his lecture is mostly an
xposition of (his version of) that philosophy. Sartre explains that the central
otion in his philosophy is human freedom. We are radically free, and
hrough our choices we create our own "essence," making ourselves into the
ind of person we are. There is no preexistent pattern of human nature to
uide us in making our choices; each of us is utterly free to fashion our
ssence in any way we wish. This freedom brings with it a burdensome
esponsibility: We alone are responsible for who we are. Sartre expresses
reat disdain for people who contrive to escape responsibility by blaming
enetic, psychological, or environmental influences.

How should we use our freedom? What should we choose? We want to
hoose what is valuable, but things receive value only from the fact that we
hoose them. Sartre is an atheist, and therefore he rejects any theory that
rounds value in God's will. Our human predicament is that while we must
hoose, there is no ultimate basis on which to make our choices. We may
ttempt to avoid exercising our freedom by refusing to choose, but this in
self is a choice. We are, in short, "condemned to be free."

Sartre believes that despite the distress it creates, freedom is still some
hing fundamentally positive because it gives human beings a dignity that sets
hem apart from everything else in the world: Existentialism is a humanism.

EXISTENTIALISM IS A HUMANISM

I should like on this occasion to defend existentialism against some charges which have been brought against it.

First, it has been charged with inviting people to remain in a kind of desperate quietism[1] because, since no solutions are possible, we should have to consider action in this world as quite impossible. We should then end up in a philosophy of contemplation; and since contemplation is a luxury, we come in the end to a bourgeois philosophy. The communists in particular have made these charges.

On the other hand, we have been charged with dwelling on human degradation, with pointing up everywhere the sordid, shady, and slimy, and neglecting the gracious and beautiful, the bright side of human nature; for example, according to Mlle. Mercier, a Catholic critic, with forgetting the smile of the child. Both sides charge us with having ignored human solidarity, with considering man as an isolated being. The communists say that the main reason for this is that we take pure subjectivity, the *Cartesian I think,*[2] as our starting point. . . .

From the Christian standpoint, we are charged with denying the reality and seriousness of human undertakings, since, if we reject God's commandments and the eternal verities, there no longer remains anything but pure caprice, with everyone permitted to do as he pleases and incapable, from his own point of view, of condemning the points of view and acts of others.

I shall try today to answer these different charges. . . . What can be said from the very beginning is that by existentialism we mean a doctrine which makes human life possible and, in addition, declares that every truth and every action implies a human setting and a human subjectivity.

As is generally known, the basic charge against us is that we put the emphasis on the dark side of human life. Someone recently told me of a lady who, when she let slip a vulgar word in a moment of irritation, excused herself by saying, "I guess I'm becoming an existentialist." Consequently,

xistentialism is regarded as something ugly; that is why we are said to be
aturalists; and if we are, it is rather surprising that in this day and age we
ause so much more alarm and scandal than does naturalism, properly so
alled. The kind of person who can take in his stride such a novel as Zola's[3]
he Earth is disgusted as soon as he starts reading an existentialist novel; the
ind of person who is resigned to the wisdom of the ages—which is pretty
ad—finds us even sadder. Yet, what can be more disillusioning than saying
"true charity begins at home" or "a scoundrel will always return evil for
ood"?

We know the commonplace remarks made when this subject comes up,
emarks which always add up to the same thing: we shouldn't struggle
gainst the powers-that-be; we shouldn't resist authority; we shouldn't try to
ise above our station; any action which doesn't conform to authority is
omantic; any effort not based on past experience is doomed to failure;
xperience shows that man's bent is always toward trouble, that there must
e a strong hand to hold him in check, if not, there will be anarchy. There are
till people who go on mumbling these melancholy old saws, the people who
ay, "It's only human!" whenever a more or less repugnant act is pointed out
o them, the people who glut themselves on *chansons réalistes*;[4] these are the
eople who accuse existentialism of being too gloomy, and to such an extent
hat I wonder whether they are complaining about it, not for its pessimism,
ut much rather its optimism. Can it be that what really scares them in the
octrine I shall try to present here is that it leaves to man a possibility of
hoice? To answer this question, we must reexamine it on a strictly philosoph-
al plane. What is meant by the term *existentialism*?

Most people who use the word would be rather embarrassed if they had
o explain it, since, now that the word is all the rage, even the work of a
usician or painter is being called existentialist. A gossip columnist in *Clartés*
igns himself *The Existentialist*, so that by this time the word has been so
tretched and has taken on so broad a meaning, that it no longer means
nything at all. It seems that for want of an advance-guard doctrine analogous
o surrealism, the kind of people who are eager for scandal and flurry turn to
his philosophy which in other respects does not at all serve their purposes in
his sphere.

Actually, it is the least scandalous, the most austere of doctrines. It is
ntended strictly for specialists and philosophers. Yet it can be defined easily.
Vhat complicates matters is that there are two kinds of existentialist; first,
hose who are Christian, among whom I would include Jaspers and Gabriel
Marcel,[5] both Catholic; and on the other hand the atheistic existentialists,
mong whom I class Heidegger,[6] and then the French existentialists and
nyself. What they have in common is that they think that existence precedes
ssence, or, if you prefer, that subjectivity must be the starting point.

Just what does that mean? Let us consider some object that is manufac-
ured, for example, a book or a paper-cutter: here is an object which has been

made by an artisan whose inspiration came from a concept. He referred to the concept of what a paper-cutter is and likewise to a known method of production, which is part of the concept, something which is, by and large, a routine. Thus, the paper-cutter is at once an object produced in a certain way and, on the other hand, one having a specific use; and one can not postulate a man who produces a paper-cutter but does not know what it is used for. Therefore, let us say that, for the paper-cutter, essence—that is, the ensemble of both the production routines and the properties which enable it to be both produced and defined—precedes existence. Thus, the presence of the paper-cutter or book in front of me is determined. Therefore, we have here a technical view of the world whereby it can be said that production precedes existence.

When we conceive God as the Creator, He is generally thought of as a superior sort of artisan. Whatever doctrine we may be considering, whether one like that of Descartes or that of Leibniz,[7] we always grant that will more or less follows understanding or, at the very least, accompanies it, and that when God creates He knows exactly what He is creating. Thus, the concept of man in the mind of God is comparable to the concept of paper-cutter in the mind of the manufacturer, and, following certain techniques and a conception, God produces man, just as the artisan, following a definition and a technique, makes a paper-cutter. Thus, the individual man is the realization of a certain concept in the divine intelligence. . . .

Atheistic existentialism, which I represent . . . states that if God does not exist, there is at least one being in whom existence precedes essence, a being who exists before he can be defined by any concept, and that this being is man, or, as Heidegger says, human reality. What is meant here by saying that existence precedes essence? It means that, first of all, man exists, turns up, appears on the scene, and, only afterwards, defines himself. If man, as the existentialist conceives him, is indefinable, it is because at first he is nothing. Only afterward will he be something, and he himself will have made what he will be. Thus, there is no human nature, since there is no God to conceive it. Not only is man what he conceives himself to be, but he is also only what he wills himself to be after this thrust toward existence.

Man is nothing else but what he makes of himself. Such is the first principle of existentialism. It is also what is called subjectivity, the name we are labeled with when charges are brought against us. But what do we mean by this, if not that man has a greater dignity than a stone or table? For we mean that man first exists, that is, that man first of all is the being who hurls himself toward a future and who is conscious of imagining himself as being in the future. Man is at the start a plan which is aware of itself, rather than a patch of moss, a piece of garbage, or a cauliflower; nothing exists prior to this plan; there is nothing in heaven; man will be what he will have planned to be—not what he will want to be, because by the word "want" we generally mean a conscious decision, which is subsequent to what we have already ıade of ourselves. I may want to belong to a political party, write a book, get ıarried; but all that is only a manifestation of an earlier, more spontaneous hoice that is called "will." But if existence really does precede essence, man ; responsible for what he is. Thus, existentialism's first move is to make very man aware of what he is and to make the full responsibility of his xistence rest on him. And when we say that a man is responsible for himself, ʻe do not only mean that he is responsible for his own individuality, but that e is responsible for all men.

The word subjectivism has two meanings, and our opponents play on ıe two. Subjectivism means, on the one hand, that an individual chooses nd makes himself; and, on the other, that it is impossible for man to ʻanscend human subjectivity. The second of these is the essential meaning of xistentialism. When we say that man chooses his own self, we mean that very one of us does likewise; but we also mean by that that in making this hoice he also chooses all men. In fact, in creating the man that we want to be, ıere is not a single one of our acts which does not at the same time create an ınage of man as we think he ought to be. To choose to be this or that is to ffirm at the same time the value of what we choose, because we can never hoose evil. We always choose the good, and nothing can be good for us ʻithout being good for all.

If, on the other hand, existence precedes essence, and if we grant that ʻe exist and fashion our image at one and the same time, the image is valid ɔr everybody and for our whole age. Thus, our responsibility is much greater ıan we might have supposed, because it involves all mankind. If I am a ʻorkingman and choose to join a Christian trade-union rather than be a ommunist, and if by being a member I want to show that the best thing for ıan is resignation, that the kingdom of man is not of this world, I am not ıly involving my own case—I want to be resigned for everyone. As a result, ıy action has involved all humanity. To take a more individual matter, if I ʻant to marry, to have children; even if this marriage depends solely on my ʻwn circumstances or passion or wish, I am involving all humanity in monog- my and not merely myself. Therefore, I am responsible for myself and for veryone else. I am creating a certain image of man of my own choosing. In hoosing myself, I choose man.

This helps us understand what the actual content is of such rather randiloquent words as anguish, forlornness, despair. As you will see, it's all ùite simple.

First, what is meant by anguish? The existentialists say at once that man ; anguish. What that means is this: the man who involves himself and who ealizes that he is not only the person he chooses to be, but also a lawmaker ʻho is, at the same time, choosing all mankind as well as himself, cannot help scape the feeling of his total and deep responsibility. Of course, there are ıany people who are not anxious; but we claim that they are hiding their nxiety, that they are fleeing from it. Certainly, many people believe that when they do something, they themselves are the only ones involved, and when someone says to them, "What if everyone acted that way?" they shrug their shoulders and answer, "Everyone doesn't act that way." But really, one should always ask himself, "What would happen if everybody looked at things that way?" There is no escaping this disturbing thought except by a kind of double-dealing. A man who lies and makes excuses for himself by saying "not everybody does that," is someone with an uneasy conscience, because the act of lying implies that a universal value is conferred upon the lie.

Anguish is evident even when it conceals itself. This is the anguish that Kierkegaard[8] called the anguish of Abraham. You know the story: an angel has ordered Abraham to sacrifice his son; if it really were an angel who has come and said, "You are Abraham, you shall sacrifice your son," everything would be all right. But everyone might first wonder, "Is it really an angel, and am I really Abraham? What proof do I have?"

There was a madwoman who had hallucinations; someone used to speak to her on the telephone and give her orders. Her doctor asked her, "Who is it who talks to you?" She answered, "He says it's God." What proof did she really have that it was God? If an angel comes to me, what proof is there that it's an angel? And if I hear voices, what proof is there that they come from heaven and not from hell, or from the subconscious, or a pathological condition? What proves that they are addressed to me? What proof is there that I have been appointed to impose my choice and my conception of man on humanity? I'll never find any proof or sign to convince me of that. If a voice addresses me, it is always for me to decide that this is the angel's voice; if I consider that such an act is a good one, it is I who will choose to say that it is good rather than bad.

Now, I'm not being singled out as an Abraham, and yet at every moment I'm obliged to perform exemplary acts. For every man, everything happens as if all mankind had its eyes fixed on him and were guiding itself by what he does. And every man ought to say to himself, "Am I really the kind of man who has the right to act in such a way that humanity might guide itself by my actions?" And if he does not say that to himself, he is masking his anguish.

There is no question here of the kind of anguish which would lead to quietism, to inaction. It is a matter of a simple sort of anguish that anybody who has had responsibilities is familiar with. For example, when a military officer takes the responsibility for an attack and sends a certain number of men to death, he chooses to do so, and in the main he alone makes the choice. Doubtless, orders come from above, but they are too broad; he interprets them, and on this interpretation depend the lives of ten or fourteen or twenty men. In making a decision he can not help having a certain anguish. All leaders know this anguish. That doesn't keep them from acting; on the contrary, it is the very condition of their action. For it implies that they

nvisage a number of possibilities, and when they choose one, they realize
1at it has value only because it is chosen. We shall see that this kind of
nguish, which is the kind that existentialism describes, is explained, in
ddition, by a direct responsibility to the other men whom it involves. It is not
 curtain separating us from action, but is part of action itself.

   When we speak of forlornness, a term Heidegger was fond of, we mean
nly that God does not exist and that we have to face all the consequences of
1is. The existentialist is strongly opposed to a certain kind of secular ethics
/hich would like to abolish God with the least possible expense. About 1880,
ome French teachers tried to set up a secular ethics which went something
ke this: God is a useless and costly hypothesis; we are discarding it; but,
1eanwhile, in order for there to be an ethics, a society, a civilization, it is
ssential that certain values be taken seriously and that they be considered as
aving an *a priori* existence. It must be obligatory, *a priori*, to be honest, not to
e, not to beat your wife, to have children, etc., etc. So we're going to try a
ttle device which will make it possible to show that values exist all the same,
ascribed in a heaven of ideas, though otherwise God does not exist. In other
/ords—and this, I believe, is the tendency of everything called reformism in
rance—nothing will be changed if God does not exist. We shall find our-
elves with the same norms of honesty, progress, and humanism, and we
hall have made of God an outdated hypothesis which will peacefully die off
y itself.

   The existentialist, on the contrary, thinks it very distressing that God
oes not exist, because all possibility of finding values in a heaven of ideas
isappears along with Him; there can no longer be an *a priori* Good, since
1ere is no infinite and perfect consciousness to think it. Nowhere is it written
1at the Good exists, that we must be honest, that we must not lie; because
1e fact is we are on a plane where there are only men. Dostoievsky[9] said, "If
;od didn't exist, everything would be possible." That is the very starting
oint of existentialism. Indeed, everything is permissible if God does not
xist, and as a result man is forlorn, because neither within him nor without
oes he find anything to cling to. He can't start making excuses for himself.

   If existence really does precede essence, there is no explaining things
way by reference to a fixed and given human nature. In other words, there is
o determinism, man is free, man is freedom. On the other hand, if God does
ot exist, we find no values or commands to turn to which legitimize our
onduct. So, in the bright realm of values, we have no excuse behind us, nor
istification before us. We are alone, with no excuses.

   That is the idea I shall try to convey when I say that man is condemned
) be free: condemned, because he did not create himself, yet, in other
espects is free; because, once thrown into the world, he is responsible for
verything he does. The existentialist does not believe in the power of pas-
ion. He will never agree that a sweeping passion is a ravaging torrent which
atally leads a man to certain acts and is therefore an excuse. He thinks that
1an is responsible for his passion.

The existentialist does not think that man is going to help himself by finding in the world some omen by which to orient himself. Because he thinks that man will interpret the omen to suit himself. Therefore, he thinks that man, with no support and no aid, is condemned every moment to invent man. Ponge,[10] in a very fine article, has said, "Man is the future of man." That's exactly it. But if it is taken to mean that this future is recorded in heaven, that God sees it, then it is false, because it would really no longer be a future. If it is taken to mean that, whatever a man may be, there is a future to be forged, a virgin future before him, then this remark is sound. But then we are forlorn.

To give you an example which will enable you to understand forlornness better, I shall cite the case of one of my students who came to see me under the following circumstances: his father was on bad terms with his mother, and, moreover, was inclined to be a collaborationist;[11] his older brother had been killed in the German offensive in 1940, and the young man, with somewhat immature but generous feelings, wanted to avenge him. His mother lived alone with him, very much upset by the half-treason of her husband and the death of her older son; the boy was her only consolation.

The boy was faced with the choice of leaving for England and joining the Free French Forces—that is, leaving his mother behind—or remaining with his mother and helping her to carry on. He was fully aware that the woman lived only for him and that his going-off—and perhaps his death—would plunge her into despair. He was also aware that every act that he did for his mother's sake was a sure thing, in the sense that it was helping her to carry on, whereas every effort he made toward going off and fighting was an uncertain move which might run aground and prove completely useless; for example, on his way to England he might, while passing through Spain, be detained indefinitely in a Spanish camp; he might reach England or Algiers and be stuck in an office at a desk job. As a result, he was faced with two very different kinds of action: one, concrete, immediate, but concerning only one individual; the other concerned an incomparably vaster group, a national collectivity, but for that very reason was dubious, and might be interrupted en route. And, at the same time, he was wavering between two kinds of ethics: on the one hand, an ethics of sympathy, of personal devotion; on the other, a broader ethics, but one whose efficacy was more dubious. He had to choose between the two.

Who could help him choose? Christian doctrine? No. Christian doctrine says, "Be charitable, love your neighbor, take the more rugged path, etc., etc." But which is the more rugged path? Whom should he love as a brother, the fighting man or his mother? Which does the greater good, the vague act of fighting in a group, or the concrete one of helping a particular human being to go on living? Who can decide *a priori*? Nobody. No book of ethics can tell him. The Kantian ethics[12] says, "Never treat any person as a means, but as an end." Very well, if I stay with my mother, I'll treat her as an end and not as a means; but by virtue of this very fact, I'm running the risk of treating the

eople around me who are fighting, as a means; and, conversely, if I go to
in those who are fighting, I'll be treating them as an end, and, by doing
at, I run the risk of treating my mother as a means.

If values are vague, and if they are always too broad for the concrete and
ecific case that we are considering, the only thing left for us is to trust our
stincts. That's what this young man tried to do; and when I saw him, he
id, "In the end, feeling is what counts. I ought to choose whichever pushes
e in one direction. If I feel that I love my mother enough to sacrifice
verything else for her—my desire for vengeance, for action, for adventure—
en I'll stay with her. If, on the contrary, I feel that my love for my mother
n't enough, I'll leave."

But how is the value of a feeling determined? What gives his feeling for
s mother value? Precisely the fact that he remained with her. I may say that
like so-and-so well enough to sacrifice a certain amount of money for him,
ut I may say so only if I've done it. I may say "I love my mother well enough
remain with her" if I have remained with her. The only way to determine
e value of this affection is, precisely, to perform an act which confirms and
efines it. But, since I require this affection to justify my act, I find myself
ught in a vicious circle.

On the other hand, Gide[13] has well said that a mock feeling and a true
eling are almost indistinguishable; to decide that I love my mother and will
:main with her, or to remain with her by putting on an act, amount some-
hat to the same thing. In other words, the feeling is formed by the acts one
erforms; so, I cannot refer to it in order to act upon it. This means that I can
either seek within myself the true condition which will impel me to act, nor
pply to a system of ethics for concepts which will permit me to act. You will
ıy, "At least, he did go to a teacher for advice." But if you seek advice from a
riest, for example, you have chosen this priest; you already knew, more or
:ss, just about what advice he was going to give you. In other words,
hoosing your adviser is involving yourself. The proof of this is that if you are
 Christian, you will say, "Consult a priest." But some priests are collaborat-
ıg, some are just marking time, some are resisting. Which to choose? If the
oung man chooses a priest who is resisting or collaborating, he has already
ecided on the kind of advice he's going to get. Therefore, in coming to see
ıe he knew the answer I was going to give him, and I had only one answer to
ive: "You're free, choose, that is, invent." No general ethics can show you
hat is to be done; there are no omens in the world. The Catholics will reply,
But there are." Granted—but, in any case, I myself choose the meaning they
ave.

When I was a prisoner, I knew a rather remarkable young man who was
 Jesuit.[14] He had entered the Jesuit order in the following way: he had had a
umber of very bad breaks; in childhood, his father died, leaving him in
overty, and he was a scholarship student at a religious institution where he
as constantly made to feel that he was being kept out of charity; then, he

failed to get any of the honors and distinctions that children like; later on, at about eighteen, he bungled a love affair; finally, at twenty-two, he failed in military training, a childish enough matter, but it was the last straw.

This young fellow might well have felt that he had botched everything. It was a sign of something, but of what? He might have taken refuge in bitterness or despair. But he very wisely looked upon all this as a sign that he was not made for secular triumphs, and that only the triumphs of religion, holiness, and faith were open to him. He saw the hand of God in all this, and so he entered the order. Who can help seeing that he alone decided what the sign meant?

Some other interpretation might have been drawn from this series of setbacks; for example, that he might have done better to turn carpenter or revolutionist. Therefore, he is fully responsible for the interpretation. Forlornness implies that we ourselves choose our being. Forlornness and anguish go together.

As for despair, the term has a very simple meaning. It means that we shall confine ourselves to reckoning only with what depends upon our will, or on the ensemble of probabilities which make our action possible. When we want something, we always have to reckon with probabilities. I may be counting on the arrival of a friend. The friend is coming by rail or streetcar; this supposes that the train will arrive on schedule, or that the streetcar will not jump the track. I am left in the realm of possibility; but possibilities are to be reckoned with only to the point where my action comports with the ensemble of these possibilities, and no further. The moment the possibilities I am considering are not rigorously involved by my action, I ought to disengage myself from them, because no God, no scheme, can adapt the world and its possibilities to my will. When Descartes said, "Conquer yourself rather than the world," he meant essentially the same thing.

The Marxists[15] to whom I have spoken reply, "You can rely on the support of others in your action, which obviously has certain limits because you're not going to live forever. That means: rely on both what others are doing elsewhere to help you, in China, in Russia, and what they will do later on, after your death, to carry on the action and lead it to its fulfillment, which will be the revolution. You even *have* to rely upon that, otherwise you're immoral." I reply at once that I will always rely on fellow-fighters insofar as these comrades are involved with me in a common struggle, in the unity of a party or a group in which I can more or less make my weight felt; that is, one whose ranks I am in as a fighter and whose movements I am aware of at every moment. In such a situation, relying on the unity and will of the party is exactly like counting on the fact that the train will arrive on time or that the car won't jump the track. But, given that man is free and that there is no human nature for me to depend on, I cannot count on men whom I do not know by relying on human goodness or man's concern for the good of society. I don't know what will become of the Russian revolution; I may make an example of

t to the extent that at the present it is apparent that the proletariat plays a part
n Russia that it plays in no other nation. But I can't swear that this will
nevitably lead to a triumph of the proletariat. I've got to limit myself to what I
ee.

Given that men are free and that tomorrow they will freely decide what
man will be, I can not be sure that, after my death, fellow-fighters will carry
•n my work to bring it to its maximum perfection. Tomorrow, after my death,
ome men may decide to set up Fascism, and the others may be cowardly and
nuddled enough to let them do it. Facism will then be the human reality, so
nuch the worse for us.

Actually, things will be as man will have decided they are to be. Does
hat mean that I should abandon myself to quietism? No. First, I should
nvolve myself; then, act on the old saw, "Nothing ventured, nothing
gained." Nor does it mean that I shouldn't belong to a party, but rather that I
hall have no illusions and shall do what I can. For example, suppose I ask
myself, "Will socialization, as such, ever come about?" I know nothing about
t. All I know is that I'm going to do everything in my power to bring it about.
Beyond that, I can't count on anything. Quietism is the attitude of people
who say, "Let others do what I can't do." The doctrine I am presenting is the
very opposite of quietism, since it declares, "There is no reality except in
ction." Moreover, it goes further, since it adds, "Man is nothing else than his
•lan; he exists only to the extent that he fulfills himself; he is therefore
nothing else than the ensemble of his acts, nothing else than his life."

According to this, we can understand why our doctrine horrifies certain
•eople, because often the only way they can bear their wretchedness is to
hink, "Circumstances have been against me. What I've been and done
doesn't show my true worth. To be sure, I've had no great love, no great
riendship, but that's because I haven't met a man or woman who was
worthy. The books I've written haven't been very good because I haven't had
he proper leisure. I haven't had children to devote myself to because I didn't
ind a man with whom I could have spent my life. So there remains within
me, unused and quite viable, a host of propensities, inclinations, possibilities,
hat one wouldn't guess from the mere series of things I've done."

Now, for the existentialist there is really no love other than one which
manifests itself in a person's being in love. There is no genius other than one
which is expressed in works of art; the genius of Proust[16] is the sum of
Proust's works; the genius of Racine[17] is his series of tragedies. Outside of
hat, there is nothing. Why say that Racine could have written another
ragedy, when he didn't write it? A man is involved in life, leaves his impress
•n it, and outside of that there is nothing. To be sure, this may seem a harsh
hought to someone whose life hasn't been a success. But, on the other hand,
t prompts people to understand that reality alone is what counts, that
dreams, expectations, and hopes warrant no more than to define a man as a
disappointed dream, as miscarried hopes, as vain expectations—in other

words, to define him negatively and not positively. However, when we say, "You are nothing else than your life," that does not imply that the artist will be judged solely on the basis of his works of art; a thousand other things will contribute toward summing him up. What we mean is that a man is nothing else than a series of undertakings, that he is the sum, the organization, the ensemble of the relationships which make up these undertakings.

When all is said and done, what we are accused of, at bottom, is not our pessimism, but an optimistic toughness. If people throw up to us our works of fiction in which we write about people who are soft, weak, cowardly, and sometimes even downright bad, it's not because these people are soft, weak, cowardly, or bad; because if we were to say, as Zola did, that they are that way because of heredity, the workings of environment, society, because of biological or psychological determinism, people would be reassured. They would say, "Well, that's what we're like, no one can do anything about it." But when the existentialist writes about a coward, he says that this coward is responsible for his cowardice. He's not like that because he has a cowardly heart or lung or brain; he's not like that on account of his physiological make-up; but he's like that because he has made himself a coward by his acts. There's no such thing as a cowardly constitution; there are nervous constitutions; there is poor blood, as the common people say, or strong constitutions. But the man whose blood is poor is not a coward on that account, for what makes cowardice is the act of renouncing or yielding. A constitution is not an act; the coward is defined on the basis of the acts he performs. People feel, in a vague sort of way, that this coward we're talking about is guilty of being a coward, and the thought frightens them. What people would like is that a coward or a hero be born that way.

One of the complaints most frequently made about *The Ways of Freedom*[18] can be summed up as follows: "After all, these people are so spineless, how are you going to make heroes out of them?" This objection almost makes me laugh, for it assumes that people are born heroes. That's what people really want to think. If you're born cowardly, you may set your mind perfectly at rest; there's nothing you can do about it; you'll be cowardly all your life, whatever you may do. If you're born a hero, you may set your mind just as much at rest; you'll be a hero all your life; you'll drink like a hero and eat like a hero. What the existentialist says is that the coward makes himself cowardly, that the hero makes himself heroic. There's always a possibility for the coward not to be cowardly any more and for the hero to stop being heroic. What counts is total involvement; some one particular action or set of circumstances is not total involvement.

Thus, I think we have answered a number of the charges concerning existentialism. You see that it cannot be taken for a philosophy of quietism, since it defines man in terms of action; nor for a pessimistic description of man—there is no doctrine more optimistic, since man's destiny is within himself; nor for an attempt to discourage man from acting, since it tells him hat the only hope is in his acting and that action is the only thing that enables man to live. Consequently, we are dealing here with an ethics of action and involvement.

Nevertheless, on the basis of a few notions like these, we are still harged with immuring man in his private subjectivity. There again we're very much misunderstood. Subjectivity of the individual is indeed our point of departure, and this for strictly philosophic reasons—not because we are bourgeois, but because we want a doctrine based on truth and not a lot of fine theories, full of hope but with no real basis. There can be no other truth to ake off from than this: *I think; therefore, I exist.* There we have the absolute truth of consciousness becoming aware of itself. Every theory which takes man out of the moment in which he becomes aware of himself is, at its very beginning, a theory which confounds truth, for outside the Cartesian *cogito*,[19] all views are only probable, and a doctrine of probability which is not bound to a truth dissolves into thin air. In order to describe the probable, you must have a firm hold on the true. Therefore, before there can be any truth whatsoever, there must be an absolute truth; and this one is simple and easily arrived at; it's on everyone's doorstep; it's a matter of grasping it directly.

Secondly, this theory is the only one which gives man dignity, the only one which does not reduce him to an object. The effect of all materialism is to treat all men, including the one philosophizing, as objects, that is, as an ensemble of determined reactions in no way distinguished from the ensemble of qualities and phenomena[20] which constitute a table or a chair or a stone. We definitely wish to establish the human realm as an ensemble of values distinct from the material realm. But the subjectivity that we have thus arrived at, and which we have claimed to be truth, is not a strictly individual subjectivity, for we have demonstrated that one discovers in the *cogito* not only himself, but others as well.

The philosophies of Descartes and Kant to the contrary, through the *I think* we reach our own self in the presence of others, and the others are just as real to us as our own self. Thus, the man who becomes aware of himself through the *cogito* also perceives all others, and he perceives them as the condition of his own existence. He realizes that he can not be anything (in the sense that we say that someone is witty or nasty or jealous) unless others recognize it as such. In order to get any truth about myself, I must have contact with another person. The other is indispensable to my own existence, as well as to my knowledge about myself. This being so, in discovering my inner being I discover the other person at the same time, like a freedom placed in front of me which thinks and wills only for or against me. Hence, let us at once announce the discovery of a world which we shall call intersubjectivity; this is the world in which man decides what he is and what others are.

Besides, if it is impossible to find in every man some universal essence which would be human nature, yet there does exist a universal human condition. It's not by chance that today's thinkers speak more readily of man's condition than of his nature. By condition they mean, more or less definitely, the *a priori* limits which outline man's fundamental situation in the universe. Historical situations vary; a man may be born a slave in a pagan society or a feudal lord or a proletarian. What does not vary is the necessity for him to exist in the world, to be at work there, to be there in the midst of other people, and to be mortal there. The limits are neither subjective nor objective, or, rather, they have an objective and a subjective side: objective because they are to be found everywhere and are recognizable everywhere; subjective because they are *lived* and are nothing if man does not live them, that is, freely determine his existence with reference to them. And though the configurations may differ, at least none of them is completely strange to me, because they all appear as attempts either to pass beyond these limits or recede from them or deny them or adapt to them. Consequently, every configuration, however individual it may be, has a universal value. . . .

This does not entirely settle the objection to subjectivism. In fact, the objection still takes several forms. First, there is the following: we are told, "So you're able to do anything, no matter what!" This is expressed in various ways. First we are accused of anarchy; then they say, "You're unable to pass judgment on others, because there's no reason to prefer one configuration to another"; finally they tell us, "Everything is arbitrary in this choosing of yours. You take something from one pocket and pretend you're putting it into the other."

These three objections aren't very serious. Take the first objection. "You're able to do anything, no matter what" is not to the point. In one sense choice is possible, but what is not possible is not to choose. I can always choose, but I ought to know that if I do not choose, I am still choosing. Though this may seem purely formal, it is highly important for keeping fantasy and caprice within bounds. If it is true that in facing a situation, for example, one in which, as a person capable of having sexual relations, of having children, I am obliged to choose an attitude, and if I in any way assume responsibility for a choice which, in involving myself, also involves all mankind, this has nothing to do with caprice, even if no *a priori* value determines my choice. . . .

Man is in an organized situation in which he himself is involved. Through his choice, he involves all mankind, and he cannot avoid making a choice: either he will remain chaste, or he will marry without having children, or he will marry and have children; anyhow, whatever he may do, it is impossible for him not to take full responsibility for the way he handles this problem. Doubtless, he chooses without referring to preestablished values, but it is unfair to accuse him of caprice. Instead, let us say that moral choice is to be compared to the making of a work of art. And before going any further, let it be said at once that we are not dealing here with an aesthetic ethics, because our opponents are so dishonest that they even accuse us of that. The example I've chosen is a comparison only.

Having said that, may I ask whether anyone has ever accused an artist
who has painted a picture of not having drawn his inspiration from rules set
up *a priori*? Has anyone ever asked, "What painting ought he to make?" It is
clearly understood that there is no definite painting to be made, that the artist
is engaged in the making of his painting, and that the painting to be made is
precisely the painting he will have made. It is clearly understood that there
are no *a priori* aesthetic values, but that there are values which appear
subsequently in the coherence of the painting, in the correspondence between what the artist intended and the result. Nobody can tell what the
painting of tomorrow will be like. Painting can be judged only after it has
once been made. What connection does that have with ethics? We are in the
same creative situation. We never say that a work of art is arbitrary. When we
speak of a canvas of Picasso,[21] we never say that it is arbitrary; we understand
quite well that he was making himself what he is at the very time he was
painting, that the ensemble of his work is embodied in his life.

The same holds on the ethical plane. What art and ethics have in
common is that we have creation and invention in both cases. We can not
decide *a priori* what there is to be done. I think that I pointed that out quite
sufficiently when I mentioned the case of the student who came to see me,
and who might have applied to all the ethical systems, Kantian or otherwise,
without getting any sort of guidance. He was obliged to devise his law
himself. Never let it be said by us that this man—who, taking affection,
individual action, and kind-heartedness toward a specific person as his ethical first principle, chooses to remain with his mother, or who, preferring to
make a sacrifice, chooses to go to England—has made an arbitrary choice.
Man makes himself. He isn't ready made at the start. In choosing his ethics,
he makes himself, and force of circumstances is such that he can not abstain
from choosing one. We define man only in relationship to involvement. It is
therefore absurd to charge us with arbitrariness of choice.

In the second place, it is said that we are unable to pass judgment on
others. In a way this is true, and in another way, false. It is true in this sense,
that, whenever a man sanely and sincerely involves himself and chooses his
configuration, it is impossible for him to prefer another configuration, regardless of what his own may be in other respects. It is true in this sense, that
we do not believe in progress. Progress is betterment. Man is always the
same. The situation confronting him varies. Choice always remains a choice
in a situation. The problem has not changed since the time one could choose
between those for and those against slavery, for example, at the time of the
Civil War, and the present time, when one can side with the Maquis Resistance Party, or with the Communists.

But, nevertheless, one can still pass judgment, for, as I have said, one
makes a choice in relationship to others. First, one can judge (and this is
perhaps not a judgment of value, but a logical judgment) that certain choices
are based on error and others on truth. If we have defined man's situation as a

free choice, with no excuses and no recourse, every man who takes refuge behind the excuse of his passions, every man who sets up a determinism, is a dishonest man.

The objection may be raised, "But why mayn't he choose himself dishonestly?" I reply that I am not obliged to pass moral judgment on him, but that I do define his dishonesty as an error. One can not help considering the truth of the matter. Dishonesty is obviously a falsehood because it belies the complete freedom of involvement. On the same grounds, I maintain that there is also dishonesty if I choose to state that certain values exist prior to me; it is self-contradictory for me to want them and at the same state that they are imposed on me. Suppose someone says to me, "What if I want to be dishonest?" I'll answer, "There's no reason for you not to be, but I'm saying that that's what you are, and that the strictly coherent attitude is that of honesty."

Besides, I can bring moral judgment to bear. When I declare that freedom in every concrete circumstance can have no other aim than to want itself, if man has once become aware that in his forlornness he imposes values, he can no longer want but one thing, and that is freedom, as the basis of all values. That doesn't mean that he wants it in the abstract. It means simply that the ultimate meaning of the acts of honest men is the quest for freedom as such. A man who belongs to a communist or revolutionary union wants concrete goals; these goals imply an abstract desire for freedom; but this freedom is wanted in something concrete. We want freedom for freedom's sake and in every particular circumstance. And in wanting freedom we discover that it depends entirely on the freedom of others, and that the freedom of others depends on ours. Of course, freedom as the definition of man does not depend on others, but as soon as there is involvement, I am obliged to want others to have freedom at the same time that I want my own freedom. I can take freedom as my goal only if I take that of others as a goal as well. Consequently, when, in all honesty, I've recognized that man is a being in whom existence precedes essence, that he is a free being who, in various circumstances, can want only his freedom, I have at the same time recognized that I can want only the freedom of others.

Therefore, in the name of this will for freedom, which freedom itself implies, I may pass judgment on those who seek to hide from themselves the complete arbitrariness and the complete freedom of their existence. Those who hide their complete freedom from themselves out of a spirit of seriousness or by means of deterministic excuses, I shall call cowards; those who try to show that their existence was necessary, when it is the very contingency of man's appearance on earth, I shall call stinkers. But cowards or stinkers can be judged only from a strictly unbiased point of view. . . .

The third objection is the following: "You take something from one pocket and put it into the other. That is, fundamentally, values aren't serious, since you choose them." My answer to this is that I'm quite vexed that that's the way it is; but if I've discarded God the Father, there has to be someone to nvent values. You've got to take things as they are. Moreover, to say that we invent values means nothing else but this: life has no meaning *a priori*. Before you come alive, life is nothing; it's up to you to give it a meaning, and value is nothing else but the meaning that you choose. In that way, you see, there is a possibility of creating a human community. . . .

From these few reflections it is evident that nothing is more unjust than the objections that have been raised against us. Existentialism is nothing else than an attempt to draw all the consequences of a coherent atheistic position. It isn't trying to plunge man into despair at all. But if one calls every attitude of unbelief despair, like the Christians, then the word is not being used in its original sense. Existentialism isn't so atheistic that it wears itself out showing that God doesn't exist. Rather, it declares that even if God did exist, that would change nothing. There you've got our point of view. Not that we believe that God exists, but we think that the problem of His existence is not the issue. In this sense existentialism is optimistic, a doctrine of action, and it is plain dishonesty for Christians to make no distinction between their own despair and ours and then to call us despairing.

NOTES

1. *quietism*: the attitude of being passive, of not getting involved [D.C.A.]
2. *Cartesian I think*: the statement of the French philosopher René Descartes (1596–1650) that "I think, therefore I am" (see the introduction to Chapter 7). Sartre accepts Descartes's doctrine that the starting point of philosophy is the indubitable truth: "I exist." This is a "subjective" starting point because it begins with the subject (*I*) without presupposing the reality of objects in the external world. [D.C.A.]
3. Émile Zola (1840–1902) was a French novelist. [D.C.A.]
4. *chansons réalistes*: cabaret songs [D.C.A.]
5. Karl Jaspers (1883–1969) was a German philosopher; Gabriel Marcel (1889–1973) was a French philosopher. [D.C.A.]
6. Martin Heidegger (1889–1976) was a German philosopher. [D.C.A.]
7. Gottfried Wilhelm Leibniz (1646–1716) was a German philosopher and mathematician. [D.C.A.]
8. Søren Kierkegaard (1813–1855) was a Danish philosopher and theologian. Sartre is referring to Kierkegaard's discussion, in *Fear and Trembling*, of God's testing Abraham by commanding him to sacrifice his son Isaac (Genesis 22:1–19). [D.C.A.]
9. Fyodor Dostoievsky (Dostoyevski) (1821–1881) was a Russian novelist. [D.C.A.]
10. Francis Ponge (1889–1988) was a French poet and essayist. [D.C.A.]
11. Sartre is referring to collaboration with the Nazis, who occupied France during World War II. [D.C.A]
12. *Kantian ethics*: the ethical theory of the German philosopher Immanuel Kant (1724–1804) [D.C.A.]
13. André Gide (1859–1951) was a French novelist, essayist, and critic. [D.C.A.]

14. *Jesuit*: a member of the Society of Jesus, a Roman Catholic religious order [D.C.A.]
15. For more information on the German social philosopher Karl Marx (1818–1883), see the introduction to Chapter 9. [D.C.A.]
16. Marcel Proust (1871–1922) was a French novelist. [D.C.A.]
17. Jean Racine (1639–1699) was a French dramatist. [D.C.A.]
18. *The Ways of Freedom*: Sartre's 3-volume novel about World War II. At the time of this lecture, Sartre had published the first 2 volumes, *The Age of Reason* and *The Reprieve* (both 1945). The third volume, *Troubled Sleep*, appeared in 1949. Sartre wrote a draft of a fourth volume, to have been entitled *The Last Chance*, but never published it. [D.C.A.]
19. *Cartesian cogito*: a reference to Descartes's statement that "I think, therefore I am" (see Note 2). *Cogito* is the first word of Descartes's Latin sentence, *Cogito ergo sum*. [D.C.A.]
20. *phenomena*: appearances [D.C.A.]
21. Pablo Picasso (1881–1973) was a Spanish painter and sculptor. He settled in France in 1904. [D.C.A.]

QUESTIONS FOR REFLECTION AND DISCUSSION

1. Do we determine who we are through our choices?
2. Does the value of something derive wholly from the fact that we choose it?
3. When I make a choice (e.g., marriage), am I saying that all human beings should choose this?
4. If there is no God, is there any basis for judging whether our choices are right or wrong?
5. Is it being inconsistent to use one's freedom to restrict the freedom of others?

SUGGESTIONS FOR FURTHER READING

I. Primary Sources

"Bad Faith," in *Being and Nothingness: An Essay on Phenomenological Ontology*, trans. Hazel E. Barnes. 1956; reprint ed., New York: Washington Square, 1966, Part 1, Chap. 2, pp. 86–116.

Sartre explains the notion of "bad faith" as an attempt to flee from what one is, to adopt the pretense that one is not free. He distinguishes bad faith from lying, which involves an awareness of the truth one conceals.

The Emotions: Outline of a Theory, trans. Bernard Frechtman. New York: Philosophical Library, 1948, 94 pp.

In this 1939 essay, Sartre examines the psychological phenomena of emotions. He criticizes classical and psychoanalytic views of the emotions and presents a sketch of his own phenomenological theory. He argues that emotions are a way of relating to the world.

ausea, trans. Lloyd Alexander. 1949; reprint ed., Cambridge, Mass.: Robert Bentley, 1979, 178 pp.

Sartre's 1938 novel about a writer named Antoine Roquentin, presented in the form of entries in a diary. Roquentin is nauseated by the world, by other people—and by his own body. Aspects of Sartre's philosophy are seen in his portrayal of Roquentin's attempts to come to terms with life.

The Wall," in *Intimacy and Other Stories*, trans. Lloyd Alexander. 1948; reprint ed., as *The Wall and Other Stories*, New York: New Directions, 1969, pp. 1–17.

A short story written in 1939 about a political prisoner sentenced to be executed by a firing squad. Sartre's depiction of how the man prepares himself psychologically for death, along with the story's ironic ending, reveals Sartre's philosophical view on living in a way that anticipates one's death.

I. Secondary Sources

nderson, Thomas C. *The Foundation and Structure of Sartrean Ethics*. Lawrence: Regents Press of Kansas, 1979, 184 pp.

A study of Sartre's attempt to construct a moral theory in the absence of any objective values. Anderson shows how Sartre's metaphysics grounds his ethics.

arnes, Hazel E. *Sartre*. Philadelphia: Lippincott, Portraits Ser., 1973, 194 pp.

An accessible introduction to Sartre that outlines his development and shows the unity of his thoughts. Barnes did the English translation of Sartre's *Being and Nothingness*.

anto, Arthur C. *Jean-Paul Sartre*. New York: Viking, Modern Masters Ser., 1975, 175 pp.

A clear presentation of Sartre's main ideas. Danto's book is intended, in part, as a response to those who have strongly criticized Sartre from the perspective of contemporary analytic philosophy.

etmer, David. *Freedom as a Value: A Critique of the Ethical Theory of Jean-Paul Sartre*. La Salle, Ill.: Open Court, 1988, 262 pp.

A thorough and sympathetic examination of Sartre's ethical doctrine that freedom is the highest value. Detmer clarifies some ambiguities found in Sartre's various statements about freedom.

rene, Marjorie. *Sartre*. New York: New Viewpoints, 1973, 300 pp.

Grene's 2 chapters on "Sartre and His Predecessors" (chaps. 4 and 5, pp. 31–104) explain the influence of René Descartes, Edmund Husserl, Martin Heidegger, Georg Wilhelm Friedrich Hegel, Søren Kierkegaard, and Karl Marx on Sartre's thought.

13

Simone de Beauvoir

Simone de Beauvoir was born in Paris in 1908. At the age of fifteen she decided to become a writer. She completed her secondary education in 1926 and earned a certificate of letters and philosophy in 1927 by taking courses at the Institut Catholique in Paris, the Institut Sainte-Marie in Neuilly (a suburb of Paris), and the Sorbonne in Paris. The following year she began graduate studies in philosophy at the Sorbonne and at the École Normale Supérieure, also in Paris. In 1929, at the age of twenty-one, Beauvoir received her graduate degree—the youngest person in France ever to earn this degree in philosophy.

Beauvoir's fellow students at the École Normale included philosophers Jean-Paul Sartre (1905–1980) and Maurice Merleau-Ponty (1908–1961). Beauvoir and Sartre quickly became friends, entering into a personal, intellectual, and sexual relationship that was to continue until Sartre's death fifty-one years later.

Beauvoir began teaching at Marseilles in 1931 and was appointed to a post in Rouen in 1933. Five years later she began teaching in Paris. When the Nazis were approaching Paris in 1940, Beauvoir fled the city, but two weeks later she returned to Nazi-occupied Paris and resumed her teaching post. In 1941 she joined a political group of writers and intellectuals that Sartre was organizing as part of the resistance movement against the Nazis. (The group dissolved after several months.)

In 1943 she was dismissed from her teaching post on the grounds of being a bad moral influence on a student. Beauvoir then devoted herself entirely to writing, an activity she had engaged in for many years. Between 1943 and 1946 she published her first three novels, *She Came to Stay*, *The Blood of Others*, and *All Men Are Mortal*. In 1944, along with Sartre, Merleau-Ponty, and others, she founded the leftist literary and political journal *Les Temps modernes* ("Modern Times").

Beauvoir's fiction emphasizes the importance of human freedom and our ability to create who we are by our choices—an idea central to the philosophical movement that was becoming known as *existentialism*. Beauvoir's writing was not restricted to fiction: She also wrote explicitly philosophical

orks expounding existentialist themes. In *Pyrrhus et Cinéas* (1944; never
anslated into English), she defines human beings as creatures who strive for
oals beyond themselves and are free to choose how to relate to the world.
he *Ethics of Ambiguity* (1947) explores the ethical implications of the human
ituation that Sartre delineated in *Being and Nothingness* (1943): We are radi-
ally different from mere objects because we have consciousness, but we
onstantly strive toward the impossible goal of becoming an object while still
etaining our consciousness of objects. The collection of essays entitled *L'Exis-
entialisme et la sagesse des nations* (1948; never translated into English) analyzes
arious topics from an existentialist viewpoint.

Prompted in part by the fact that she had been living in ways then
nconventional for a woman—pursuing a career, remaining unmarried and
hildless, maintaining a permanent but nonexclusive liaison—Beauvoir be-
ame increasingly interested in the question of what it meant to be a woman.
his led to the publication, in 1949, of her most famous book, *The Second Sex*,
n examination of the notion of femininity from the perspectives of several
isciplines. Rejecting the notion of an "eternal feminine" (a set of qualities
iat constitutes a specifically female human nature), Beauvoir argues that the
ubordinate role of women in society is a product of culture, not of nature,
nd that subordination can be overcome.

In 1954 Beauvoir published a novel entitled *The Mandarins*, for which she
eceived the prestigious French literary award, the Prix Goncourt. Subse-
uent works included a four-volume autobiography: *Memoirs of a Dutiful
>aughter*, *The Prime of Life*, *Force of Circumstance*, and *All Said and Done*, all
ublished between 1958 and 1972.

Beauvoir, like Sartre, was sympathetic to communism and socialism.
ogether they visited China (in 1955), Brazil and Cuba (in 1960), and then the
oviet Union (four times). Beauvoir also worked for the liberation of Algeria
om French rule and actively protested the military intervention of the
Inited States in Vietnam. In the 1970s she became politically involved in the
eminist movement; she was named president of the newly formed League of
Vomen's Rights in 1974. She died in Paris in 1986.

Our selection is from Chapter 2 of *The Ethics of Ambiguity*. Beauvoir
egins by discussing the existentialist theme of the "anguish of freedom."
he explains that we escape this anguish when we are children but begin to
onfront it during adolescence. She then divides people into five character
ypes based on the way they respond (all with some dishonesty) to their
reedom: (1) the subhuman person, (2) the serious person, (3) the nihilist, (4)
ie adventurer, and (5) the passionate person. At the end of the selection she
rgues that morality requires that we respect the freedom of others.

THE ETHICS OF AMBIGUITY

CHAPTER 2. PERSONAL FREEDOM AND OTHERS

Man's unhappiness, says Descartes,[1] is due to his having first been a child. And indeed the unfortunate choices which most men make can only be explained by the fact that they have taken place on the basis of childhood. The child's situation is characterized by his finding himself cast into a universe which he has not helped to establish, which has been fashioned without him, and which appears to him as an absolute to which he can only submit. In his eyes, human inventions, words, customs, and values are given facts, as inevitable as the sky and the trees. This means that the world in which he lives is a serious world, since the characteristic of the spirit of seriousness is to consider values as ready-made things. That does not mean that the child himself is serious. On the contrary, he is allowed to play, to expend his existence freely. In his child's circle he feels that he can passionately pursue and joyfully attain goals which he has set up for himself. But if he fulfills this experience in all tranquillity, it is precisely because the domain open to his subjectivity seems insignificant and puerile in his own eyes. He feels himself happily irresponsible. The real world is that of adults where he is allowed only to respect and obey. The naive victim of the mirage of the for-others, he believes in the *being* of his parents and teachers.[2] He takes them for the divinities which they vainly try to be[3] and whose appearance they like to borrow before his ingenuous eyes. Rewards, punishments, prizes, words of praise or blame instill in him the conviction that there exist a good and an evil which, like a sun and a moon, exist as ends in themselves. In his universe of definite and substantial things, beneath the sovereign eyes of grown-up persons, he thinks that he too has *being* in a definite and substantial way. He is a good little boy or a scamp; he enjoys being it. If something deep inside him belies his conviction, he conceals this imperfection. He consoles himself for an inconsistency which he attributes to his young age by pinning his opes on the future. Later on he too will become a big imposing statue. While waiting, he plays at being: at being a saint, a hero, a guttersnipe. He feels himself like those models whose images are sketched out in his books in broad, unequivocal strokes: explorer, brigand, sister of charity. This game of being serious can take on such an importance in the child's life that he himself actually becomes serious. We know such children who are caricatures of adults. Even when the joy of existing is strongest, when the child abandons himself to it, he feels himself protected against the risk of existence by the ceiling which human generations have built over his head. And it is by virtue of this that the child's condition (although it can be unhappy in other respects) is metaphysically privileged. Normally the child escapes the anguish of freedom. He can, if he likes, be recalcitrant, lazy; his whims and his faults concern only him. They do not weigh upon the earth. They cannot make a dent in the serene order of a world which existed before him, without him, where he is in a state of security by virtue of his very insignificance. He can do with impunity whatever he likes. He knows that nothing can ever happen through him; everything is already given; his acts engage nothing, not even himself.

There are beings whose life slips by in an infantile world because, having been kept in a state of servitude and ignorance, they have no means of breaking the ceiling which is stretched over their heads. Like the child, they can exercise their freedom, but only within this universe which has been set up before them, without them. This is the case, for example, of slaves who have not raised themselves to the consciousness of their slavery. The southern planters were not altogether in the wrong in considering the Negroes who docilely submitted to their paternalism as "grown-up children." To the extent that they respected the world of the whites, the situation of the black slaves was exactly an infantile situation. This is also the situation of women in many civilizations; they can only submit to the laws, the gods, the customs, and the truths created by the males. Even today in Western countries, among women who have not had in their work an apprenticeship of freedom, there are still many who take shelter in the shadow of men; they adopt without discussion the opinions and values recognized by their husband or their lover, and that allows them to develop childish qualities which are forbidden to adults because they are based on a feeling of irresponsibility. If what is called women's futility often has so much charm and grace, if it sometimes has a genuinely moving character, it is because it manifests a pure and gratuitous taste for existence, like the games of children; it is the absence of the serious. The unfortunate thing is that in many cases this thoughtlessness, this gaiety, these charming inventions imply a deep complicity with the world of men which they seem so graciously to be contesting, and it is a mistake to be astonished, once the structure which shelters them seems to be in danger, to see sensitive, ingenuous, and light-minded women show themselves harder, more bitter, and even more furious or cruel than their masters. It is then that we discover the difference which distinguishes them from an actual child: the child's situation is imposed upon him, whereas the woman (I mean the Western woman of today) chooses it or at least consents to it. Ignorance and error are facts as inescapable as prison walls. The Negro slave of the eighteenth century, the Mohammedan woman enclosed in a harem have no instrument, be it in thought or by astonishment or anger, which permits them to attack the civilization which oppresses them. Their behavior is defined and can be judged only within this given situation, and it is possible that in this situation, limited like every human situation, they realize a perfect assertion of their freedom. But once there appears a possibility of liberation, it is resignation of freedom not to exploit the possibility, a resignation which implies dishonesty and which is a positive fault.

The fact is that it is very rare for the infantile world to maintain itself beyond adolescence. From childhood on, flaws begin to be revealed in it. With astonishment, revolt and disrespect the child little by little asks himself, "Why must I act that way? What good is it? And what will happen if I act in another way?" He discovers his subjectivity;[4] he discovers that of others. And when he arrives at the age of adolescence he begins to vacillate because he notices the contradictions among adults as well as their hesitations and weakness. Men stop appearing as if they were gods, and at the same time the adolescent discovers the human character of the reality about him. Language, customs, ethics, and values have their source in these uncertain creatures. The moment has come when he too is going to be called upon to participate in their operation; his acts weigh upon the earth as much as those of other men. He will have to choose and decide. It is comprehensible that it is hard for him to live this moment of his history, and this is doubtless the deepest reason for the crisis of adolescence; the individual must at last assume his subjectivity.

From one point of view, the collapsing of the serious world is a deliverance. Although he was irresponsible, the child also felt himself defenseless before obscure powers which directed the course of things. But whatever the joy of this liberation may be, it is not without great confusion that the adolescent finds himself cast into a world which is no longer ready-made, which has to be made; he is abandoned, unjustified, the prey of a freedom that is no longer chained up by anything. What will he do in the face of this new situation? This is the moment when he decides. If what might be called the natural history of an individual, his affective complexes, etc. depend above all upon his childhood, it is adolescence which appears as the moment of moral choice. Freedom is then revealed and he must decide upon his attitude in the face of it. Doubtless, this decision can always be reconsidered, but the fact is that conversions are difficult because the world reflects back upon us a choice which is confirmed through this world which it has fashioned. Thus, a more and more rigorous circle is formed from which one is more and more unlikely to escape. Therefore, the misfortune which comes to man as a result of the fact that he was a child is that his freedom was first oncealed from him and that all his life he will be nostalgic for the time when he did not know its exigencies.

This misfortune has still another aspect. Moral choice is free, and therefore unforeseeable. The child does not contain the man he will become. Yet, it is always on the basis of what he has been that a man decides upon what he wants to be. He draws the motivations of his moral attitude from within the character which he has given himself and from within the universe which is its correlative. Now, the child set up this character and this universe little by little, without foreseeing its development. He was ignorant of the disturbing aspect of this freedom which he was heedlessly exercising. He tranquilly abandoned himself to whims, laughter, tears, and anger which seemed to him to have no morrow and no danger, and yet which left ineffaceable imprints about him. The drama of original choice is that it goes on moment by moment for an entire lifetime, that it occurs without reason, before any reason, that freedom is there as if it were present only in the form of contingency. . . .

To exist is to *make oneself* a lack of being; it is to *cast* oneself into the world.[5] Those who occupy themselves in restraining this original movement can be considered as sub-men. They have eyes and ears, but from their childhood on they make themselves blind and deaf, without love and without desire. This apathy manifests a fundamental fear in the face of existence, in the face of the risks and tensions which it implies. The sub-man rejects this "passion" which is his human condition, the laceration and the failure of that drive toward being which always misses its goal, but which thereby is the very existence which he rejects.

Such a choice immediately confirms itself. Just as a bad painter, by a single movement, paints bad paintings and is satisfied with them, whereas in a work of value the artist immediately recognizes the demand of a higher sort of work, in like fashion the original poverty of his project exempts the sub-man from seeking to legitimize it. He discovers around him only an insignificant and dull world. How could this naked world arouse within him any desire to feel, to understand, to live? The less he exists, the less is there reason for him to exist, since these reasons are created only by existing.

Yet, he exists. By the fact of transcending himself he indicates certain goals, he circumscribes certain values. But he at once effaces these uncertain shadows. His whole behavior tends toward an elimination of their ends. By the incoherence of his plans, by his haphazard whims, or by his indifference, he reduces to nothingness the meaning of his surpassing. His acts are never positive choices, only flights. He cannot prevent himself from being a presence in the world, but he maintains this presence on the plane of bare facticity.[6]

However, if a man were permitted to be a brute fact, he would merge with the trees and pebbles which are not aware that they exist; we would consider these opaque lives with indifference. But the sub-man arouses contempt; that is, one recognizes him to be responsible for himself at the moment that one accuses him of not willing himself. The fact is that no man is a datum which is passively suffered; the rejection of existence is still another way of existing; nobody can know the peace of the tomb while he is alive. There we have the defeat of the sub-man. He would like to forget himself, to be ignorant of himself, but the nothingness which is at the heart of man[7] is also the consciousness that he has of himself. His negativity is revealed positively as anguish, desire, appeal, laceration, but as for the genuine return to the positive, the sub-man eludes it. He is afraid of engaging himself in a project as he is afraid of being disengaged and thereby of being in a state of danger before the future, in the midst of its possibilities. He is thereby led to take refuge in the ready-made values of the serious world. He will proclaim certain opinions; he will take shelter behind a label; and to hide his indifference he will readily abandon himself to verbal outbursts or even physical violence. One day a monarchist, the next day, an anarchist, he is more readily anti-Semitic, anti-clerical, or anti-republican. Thus, though we have defined him as a denial and a flight, the sub-man is not a harmless creature. He realizes himself in the world as a blind uncontrolled force which anybody can get control of. In lynchings, in pogroms, in all the great bloody movements organized by the fanaticism of seriousness and passion, movements where there is no risk, those who do the actual dirty work are recruited from among the sub-men. That is why every man who wills himself free within a human world fashioned by free men will be so disgusted by the sub-men. Ethics is the triumph of freedom over facticity, and the sub-man feels only the facticity of his existence. Instead of aggrandizing the reign of the human, he opposes his inert resistence to the projects of other men. . . .

Fundamental as a man's fear in the face of existence may be, though he has chosen from his earliest years to deny his presence in the world, he can not keep himself from existing, he can not efface the agonizing evidence of his freedom. That is why, as we have just seen, in order to get rid of his freedom, he is led to engage it positively. The attitude of the sub-man passes logically over into that of the serious man; he forces himself to submerge his freedom in the content which the latter accepts from society. He loses himself in the object in order to annihilate his subjectivity. . . . The serious man gets rid of his freedom by claiming to subordinate it to values which would be unconditioned. He imagines that the accession to these values likewise permanently confers values upon himself. Shielded with "rights," he fulfills himself as a *being* who is escaping from the stress of existence. The serious is not defined by the nature of the ends pursued. A frivolous lady of fashion can have this mentality of the serious as well as an engineer. There is the serious from the moment that freedom denies itself to the advantage of ends which one claims are absolute.

Since all of this is well known, I should like to make only a few remarks in this place. It is easily understood why, of all the attitudes which are not

enuine, the latter is the most widespread; because every man was first a
1ild. After having lived under the eyes of the gods, having been given the
romise of divinity, one does not readily accept becoming simply a man with
l his anxiety and doubt. What is to be done? What is to be believed? Often
1e young man, who has not, like the sub-man, first rejected existence, so
1at these questions are not even raised, is nevertheless frightened at having
) answer them. After a more or less long crisis, either he turns back toward
1e world of his parents and teachers or he adheres to the values which are
ew but seem to him just as sure. Instead of assuming an affectivity which
ould throw him dangerously beyond himself, he represses it. Liquidation,
1 its classic form of transference and sublimation,[8] is the passage from the
ffective to the serious in the propitious shadow of dishonesty. The thing that
1atters to the serious man is not so much the nature of the object which he
refers to himself, but rather the fact of being able to lose himself in it. So
1uch so, that the movement toward the object is, in fact, through his
rbitrary act the most radical assertion of subjectivity: to believe for belief's
1ke, to will for will's sake is, detaching transcendence from its end, to realize
ne's freedom in its empty and absurd form of freedom of indifference.

The serious man's dishonesty issues from his being obliged ceaselessly
) renew the denial of this freedom. He chooses to live in an infantile world,
ut to the child the values are really given. The serious man must mask the
1ovement by which he gives them to himself, like the mythomaniac who
vhile reading a love-letter pretends to forget that she has sent it to herself.
Ve have already pointed out that certain adults can live in the universe of the
erious in all honesty, for example, those who are denied all instruments of
scape, those who are enslaved or who are mystified. The less economic and
ocial circumstances allow an individual to act upon the world, the more this
vorld appears to him as given. This is the case of women who inherit a long
radition of submission and of those who are called "the humble." There is
ften laziness and timidity in their resignation; their honesty is not quite
omplete; but to the extent that it exists, their freedom remains available, it is
ot denied. They can, in their situation of ignorant and powerless individ-
als, know the truth of existence and raise themselves to a properly moral
fe. It even happens that they turn the freedom which they have thus won
gainst the very object of their respect; thus, in A Doll's House,[9] the childlike
aivete of the heroine leads her to rebel against the lie of the serious. On the
ontrary, the man who has the necessary instruments to escape this lie and
vho does not want to use them consumes his freedom in denying them. He
1akes himself serious. He dissimulates his subjectivity under the shield of
ights which emanate from the ethical universe recognized by him; he is no
1nger a man, but a father, a boss, a member of the Christian Church or the
:ommunist Party.

If one denies the subjective tension of freedom one is evidently forbid-
ing himself universally to will freedom in an indefinite movement. By virtue

of the fact that he refuses to recognize that he is freely establishing the value of the end he sets up, the serious man makes himself the slave of that end. He forgets that every goal is at the same time a point of departure and that human freedom is the ultimate, the unique end to which man should destine himself. He accords an absolute meaning to the epithet *useful*, which, in truth, has no more meaning if taken by itself than the words *high, low, right,* and *left*. It simply designates a relationship and requires a complement: useful *for* this or that. The complement itself must be put into question, and, as we shall see later on, the whole problem of action is then raised.

But the serious man puts nothing into question. For the military man, the army is useful; for the colonial administrator, the highway; for the serious revolutionary, the revolution—army, highway, revolution, productions becoming inhuman idols to which one will not hesitate to sacrifice man himself. Therefore, the serious man is dangerous. It is natural that he makes himself a tyrant. Dishonestly ignoring the subjectivity of his choice, he pretends that the unconditioned value of the object is being asserted through him; and by the same token he also ignores the value of the subjectivity and the freedom of others, to such an extent that, sacrificing them to the thing, he persuades himself that what he sacrifices is nothing. The colonial administrator who has raised the highway to the stature of an idol will have no scruple about assuring its construction at the price of a great number of lives of the natives; for, what value has the life of a native who is incompetent, lazy, and clumsy when it comes to building highways? The serious leads to a fanaticism which is as formidable as the fanaticism of passion. It is the fanaticism of the Inquisition[10] which does not hesitate to impose a credo, that is, an internal movement, by means of external constraints. It is the fanaticism of the Vigilantes of America who defend morality by means of lynchings. It is the political fanaticism which empties politics of all human content and imposes the State, not *for* individuals, but *against* them.

In order to justify the contradictory, absurd, and outrageous aspects of this kind of behavior, the serious man readily takes refuge in disputing the serious, but it is the serious of others which he disputes, not his own. Thus, the colonial administrator is not unaware of the trick of irony. He contests the importance of the happiness, the comfort, the very life of the native, but he reveres the Highway, the Economy, the French Empire; he reveres himself as a servant of these divinities. . . .

The first of virtues, in his eyes, is prudence. He escapes the anguish of freedom only to fall into a state of preoccupation, of worry. Everything is a threat to him, since the thing which he has set up as an idol is an externality and is thus in relationship with the whole universe and consequently threatened by the whole universe; and since, despite all precautions, he will never be the master of this exterior world to which he has consented to submit, he will be constantly upset by the uncontrollable course of events. He will always be saying that he is disappointed, for his wish to have the world arden into a thing is belied by the very movement of life. The future will ontest his present successes; his children will disobey him, his will will be pposed by those of strangers; he will be a prey to ill-humor and bitterness. His very successes have a taste of ashes, for the serious is one of those ways of trying to realize the impossible synthesis of the in-itself and the for-itself.[11] The serious man wills himself to be a god; but he is not one and knows it. He wishes to rid himself of his subjectivity, but it constantly risks being unmasked; it is unmasked. Transcending all goals, reflection wonders, "What's the use?" There then blazes forth the absurdity of a life which has sought utside of itself the justifications which it alone could give itself. Detached om the freedom which might have genuinely grounded them, all the ends that have been pursued appear arbitrary and useless.

This failure of the serious sometimes brings about a radical disorder. Conscious of being unable to be anything, man then decides to be nothing. We shall call this attitude nihilistic. The nihilist is close to the spirit of seriousness, for instead of realizing his negativity as a living movement, he conceives his annihilation in a substantial way. He wants to *be* nothing, and his nothing that he dreams of is still another sort of being. . . . Nihilism is disappointed seriousness which has turned back upon itself. A choice of this kind is not encountered among those who, feeling the joy of existence, assume its gratuity. It appears either at the moment of adolescence, when the individual, seeing his child's universe flow away, feels the lack which is in his heart, or, later on, when the attempts to fulfill himself as a being have failed; in any case, among men who wish to rid themselves of the anxiety of their freedom by denying the world and themselves. By this rejection, they draw near to the sub-man. The difference is that their withdrawal is not their original movement. At first, they cast themselves into the world, sometimes even with a largeness of spirit. They exist and they know it.

It sometimes happens that, in his state of deception, a man maintains a sort of affection for the serious world; this is how Sartre describes Baudelaire[12] in his study of the poet. Baudelaire felt a burning rancor in regard to the values of his childhood, but his rancor still involved some respect. Scorn alone liberated him. It was necessary for him that the universe which he rejected continue in order for him to detest it and scoff at it. . . .

One can go much further in rejection by occupying himself not in scorning but in annihilating the rejected world and himself along with it. For example, the man who gives himself to a cause which he knows to be lost chooses to merge the world with one of its aspects which carries within it the germ of its ruin, involving himself in this condemned universe and condemning himself with it. Another man devotes his time and energy to an undertaking which was not doomed to failure at the start but which he himself is bent on ruining. Still another rejects each of his projects one after the other, frittering them away in a series of caprices and thereby systematically annulling the ends which he is aiming at. . . .

But this will to negation is forever belying itself, for it manifests itself as a presence at the very moment that it displays itself. It therefore implies a constant tension, inversely symmetrical with the existential and more painful tension, for if it is true that man is not, it is also true that he exists, and in order to realize his negativity positively he will have to contradict constantly the movement of existence. . . .

The nihilist attitude manifests a certain truth. In this attitude one experiences the ambiguity of the human condition. But the mistake is that it defines man not as the positive existence of a lack, but as a lack at the heart of existence, whereas the truth is that existence is not a lack as such. And if freedom is experienced in this case in the form of rejection, it is not genuinely fulfilled. The nihilist is right in thinking that the world *possesses* no justification and that he himself *is* nothing. But he forgets that it is up to him to justify the world and to make himself exist validly. Instead of integrating death into life, he sees in it the only truth of the life which appears to him as a disguised death. However, there is life, and the nihilist knows that he is alive. That's where his failure lies. He rejects existence without managing to eliminate it. He denies any meaning to his transcendence, and yet he transcends himself. A man who delights in freedom can find an ally in the nihilist because they contest the serious world together, but he also sees in him an enemy insofar as the nihilist is a systematic rejection of the world and man, and if this rejection ends up in a positive desire for destruction, it then establishes a tyranny which freedom must stand up against.

The fundamental fault of the nihilist is that, challenging all given values, he does not find, beyond their ruin, the importance of that universal, absolute end which freedom itself is. It is possible that, even in this failure, a man may nevertheless keep his taste for an existence which he originally felt as a joy. Hoping for no justification, he will nevertheless take delight in living. He will not turn aside from things which he does not believe in. He will seek a pretext in them for a gratuitous display of activity. Such a man is what is generally called an adventurer. He throws himself into his undertakings with zest, into exploration, conquest, war, speculation, love, politics, but he does not attach himself to the end at which he aims; only to his conquest. He likes action for its own sake. He finds joy in spreading through the world a freedom which remains indifferent to its content. Whether the taste of adventure appears to be based on nihilistic despair or whether it is born directly from the experience of the happy days of childhood, it always implies that freedom is realized as an independence in regard to the serious world and that, on the other hand, the ambiguity of existence is felt not as a lack but in its positive aspect. This attitude dialectically envelops nihilism's opposition to the serious and the opposition to nihilism by existence as such. But, of course, the concrete history of an individual does not necessarily espouse this dialectic, by virtue of the fact that his condition is wholly present to him at each moment and because his freedom before it is, at every moment, total. From

he time of his adolescence a man can define himself as an adventurer. The
nion of an original, abundant vitality and a reflective scepticism will particu-
rly lead to this choice. . . .

Adventure . . . appears to us to be satisfying only as a subjective
moment, which, in fact, is a quite abstract moment. The adventurer always
meets others along the way; the conquistador meets the Indians; the condot-
ere hacks out a path through blood and ruins; the explorer has comrades
bout him or soldiers under his orders; every Don Juan is confronted with
lviras.[13] Every undertaking unfolds in a human world and affects men.
Vhat distinguishes adventure from a simple game is that the adventurer does
ot limit himself to asserting his existence in solitary fashion. He asserts it in
elationship to other existences. He has to declare himself.

Two attitudes are possible. He can become conscious of the real require-
ents of his own freedom, which can will itself only by destining itself to an
pen future, by seeking to extend itself by means of the freedom of others.
herefore, in any case, the freedom of other men must be respected and they
ust be helped to free themselves. Such a law imposes limits upon action and
t the same time immediately gives it a content. Beyond the rejected se-
ousness is found a genuine seriousness. But the man who acts in this way,
hose end is the liberation of himself and others, who forces himself to
espect this end through the means which he uses to attain it, no longer
eserves the name of adventurer. One would not dream, for example, of
pplying it to a Lawrence,[14] who was so concerned about the lives of his
ompanions and the freedom of others, so tormented by the human problems
hich all action raises. One is then in the presence of a genuinely free man.

The man we call an adventurer, on the contrary, is one who remains
ndifferent to the content, that is, to the human meaning of his action, who
inks he can assert his own existence without taking into account that of
thers. The fate of Italy mattered very little to the Italian condottiere; the
assacres of the Indians meant nothing to Pizarro;[15] Don Juan was un-
ffected by Elvira's tears. Indifferent to the ends they set up for themselves,
ey were still more indifferent to the means of attaining them; they cared
nly for their pleasure or their glory. This implies that the adventurer shares
e nihilist's contempt for men. And it is by this very contempt that he
elieves he breaks away from the contemptible condition in which those who
o not imitate his pride are stagnating. Thus, nothing prevents him from
acrificing these insignificant beings to his own will for power. He will treat
em like instruments; he will destroy them if they get in his way. But
eanwhile he appears as an enemy in the eyes of others. His undertaking is
ot only an individual wager; it is a combat. He cannot win the game without
aking himself a tyrant or a hangman. And as he cannot impose this tyranny
ithout help, he is obliged to serve the regime which will allow him to
xercise it. He needs money, arms, soldiers, or the support of the police and
e laws. It is not a matter of chance, but a dialectical necessity which leads

the adventurer to be complacent regarding all regimes which defend the privilege of a class or a party, and more particularly authoritarian regimes and fascism. He needs fortune, leisure, and enjoyment, and he will take these goods as supreme ends in order to be prepared to remain free in regard to any end. Thus, confusing a quite external availability with real freedom, he falls, with a pretext of independence, into the servitude of the object. He will range himself on the side of the regimes which guarantee him his privileges, and he will prefer those which confirm him in his contempt regarding the common herd. He will make himself its accomplice, its servant, or even its valet, alienating a freedom which, in reality, cannot confirm itself as such if it does not wear its own face. In order to have wanted to limit it to itself, in order to have emptied it of all concrete content, he realizes it only as an abstract independence which turns into servitude. He must submit to masters unless he makes himself the supreme master. Favorable circumstances are enough to transform the adventurer into a dictator. He carries the seed of one within him, since he regards mankind as indifferent matter destined to support the game of his existence. But what he then knows is the supreme servitude of tyranny. . . .

The passionate man is, in a way, the antithesis of the adventurer. In him too there is a sketch of the synthesis of freedom and its content. But in the adventurer it is the content which does not succeed in being genuinely fulfilled, whereas in the passionate man it is subjectivity which fails to fulfill itself genuinely.

What characterizes the passionate man is that he sets up the object as an absolute, not, like the serious man, as a thing detached from himself, but as a thing disclosed by his subjectivity. There are transitions between the serious and passion. A goal which was first willed in the name of the serious can become an object of passion; inversely, a passionate attachment can wither into a serious relationship. But real passion asserts the subjectivity of its involvement. In amorous passion particularly, one does not want the beloved being to be admired objectively; one prefers to think her unknown, unrecognized; the lover thinks that his appropriation of her is greater if he is alone in revealing her worth. That is the genuine thing offered by all passion. The moment of subjectivity therein vividly asserts itself, in its positive form, in a movement toward the object. It is only when passion has been degraded to an organic need that it ceases to choose itself. But as long as it remains alive it does so because subjectivity is animating it; if not pride, at least complacency and obstinacy. At the same time that it is an assumption of this subjectivity, it is also a disclosure of being. It helps populate the world with desirable objects, with exciting meanings. However, in the passions which we shall call maniacal, to distinguish them from the generous passions, freedom does not find its genuine form. The passionate man seeks possession; he seeks to attain being. The failure and the hell which he creates for himself have been

escribed often enough. He causes certain rare treasures to appear in the
'orld, but he also depopulates it. Nothing exists outside of his stubborn
roject; therefore nothing can induce him to modify his choices. And having
ivolved his whole life with an external object which can continually escape
im, he tragically feels his dependence. Even if it does not definitely disap-
ear, the object never gives itself. The passionate man makes himself a lack of
eing not that there might *be* being, but in order to be. And he remains at a
istance; he is never fulfilled.

That is why, though the passionate man inspires a certain admiration,
e also inspires a kind of horror at the same time. One admires the pride of a
ubjectivity which chooses its end without bending itself to any foreign law,
nd the precious brilliance of the object revealed by the force of this assertion.
ut one also considers the solitude in which this subjectivity encloses itself as
ijurious. Having withdrawn into an unusual region of the world, seeking
ot to communicate with other men, this freedom is realized only as a
eparation. Any conversation, any relationship with the passionate man is
npossible. In the eyes of those who desire a communion of freedom, he
ierefore appears as a stranger, an obstacle. He opposes an opaque resistance
) the movement of freedom which wills itself infinite. The passionate man is
ot only an inert facticity. He too is on the way to tyranny. He knows that his
ill emanates only from him, but he can nevertheless attempt to impose it
pon others. He authorizes himself to do that by a partial nihilism. Only the
bject of his passion appears real and full to him. All the rest are insignificant.
Vhy not betray, kill, grow violent? It is never *nothing* that one destroys. The
'hole universe is perceived only as an ensemble of means or obstacles
irough which it is a matter of attaining the thing in which one has engaged
is being. Not intending his freedom for men, the passionate man does not
:cognize them as freedoms either. He will not hesitate to treat them as
iings. If the object of his passion concerns the world in general, this tyranny
ecomes fanaticism. . . .

There is no way for a man to escape from this world. It is in this world
iat—avoiding the pitfalls we have just pointed out—he must realize himself
iorally. Freedom must project itself toward its own reality through a content
'hose value it establishes. An end is valid only by a return to the freedom
'hich established it and which willed itself through this end. But this will
nplies that freedom is not to be engulfed in any goal; neither is it to dissipate
self vainly without aiming at a goal. It is not necessary for the subject to seek
) be, but it must desire that there *be* being. To will oneself free and to will that
nere be *being* are one and the same choice, the choice that man makes of
imself as a presence in the world. We can neither say that the free man
'ants freedom in order to desire being, nor that he wants the disclosure of
eing by freedom. These are two aspects of a single reality. And whichever be
ie one under consideration, they both imply the bond of each man with all
thers.

This bond does not immediately reveal itself to everybody. A young man wills himself free. He wills that there be being. This spontaneous liberality which casts him ardently into the world can ally itself to what is commonly called egoism. Often the young man perceives only that aspect of his relationship to others whereby others appear as enemies. In the preface to *The Inner Experience* Georges Bataille[16] emphasizes very forcefully that each individual wants to be All. He sees in every other man and particularly in those whose existence is asserted with most brilliance, a limit, a condemnation of himself. "Each consciousness," said Hegel,[17] "seeks the death of the other." And indeed at every moment others are stealing the whole world away from me. The first movement is to hate them. But this hatred is naive, and the desire immediately struggles against itself. If I were really everything there would be nothing beside me; the world would be empty. There would be nothing to possess, and I myself would be nothing. If he is reasonable, the young man immediately understands that by taking the world away from me, others also give it to me, since a thing is given to me only by the movement which snatches it from me. To will that there be being is also to will that there be men by and for whom the world is endowed with human significations. One can reveal the world only on a basis revealed by other men. No project can be defined except by its interference with other projects. To make being "be" is to communicate with others by means of being.

The truth is found in another form when we say that freedom cannot will itself without aiming at an open future. The ends of which it gives itself must be unable to be transcended by any reflection, but only the freedom of other men can extend them beyond our life. I have tried to show in *Pyrrhus and Cinéas* that every man needs the freedom of other men and, in a sense, always wants it, even though he may be a tyrant; the only thing he fails to do is to assume honestly the consequences of such a wish. Only the freedom of others keeps each one of us from hardening in the absurdity of facticity. And if we are to believe the Christian myth of creation, God himself was in agreement on this point with the existentialist doctrine since, in the words of an anti-fascist priest, "He had such respect for man that He created him free."

Thus, it can be seen to what an extent those people are mistaken—or are lying—who try to make existentialism a solipsism[18] that would exalt, like Nietzsche,[19] the bare will to power. According to this interpretation, as widespread as it is erroneous, the individual, knowing himself and choosing himself as the creator of his own values, would seek to impose them on others. The result would be a conflict of opposed wills enclosed in their solitude. But we have seen that, on the contrary, to the extent that passion, pride, and the spirit of adventure lead to this tyranny and its conflicts, existentialist ethics condemns them; and it does so not in the name of an abstract law, but because, if it is true that every project emanates from subjectivity, it is also true that this subjective movement establishes by itself a surpassing of subjectivity. Man can find a justification of his own existence only in the existence of other men. Now, he needs such a justification; there is o escaping it. Moral anxiety does not come to man from without; he finds within himself the anxious question, "What's the use?" Or, to put it better, he himself is this urgent interrogation. He flees it only by fleeing himself, and as soon as he exists he answers. It may perhaps be said that it is for *himself* that e is moral, and that such an attitude is egoistic. But there is no ethics against which this charge, which immediately destroys itself, can not be leveled; for ow can I worry about what does not concern me? I concern others and they concern me. There we have an irreducible truth. The me-others relationship is s indissoluble as the subject-object relationship.

At the same time the other charge which is often directed at existen-alism also collapses: of being a formal doctrine, incapable of proposing any ontent to the freedom which it wants engaged. To will oneself free is also to will others free.

NOTES

1. René Descartes (1596–1650) was a French philosopher. See the introduction to Chapter 7. [D.C.A.]
2. In existentialist terminology, *being* is a property of objects; *existence* is a property of human persons, who differ from objects because they have consciousness and freedom. To believe in the being of parents and teachers is mistakenly to view these persons as objects defined by their roles "for others," and not to view them as free persons. [D.C.A.]
3. Beauvoir adopts Sartre's doctrine that all human persons want to become objects (and thereby gain the comfort of not having freedom) while still retaining their consciousness of objects. This is an impossible goal; to achieve it would be to become a god. [D.C.A.]
4. To discover one's subjectivity is to realize that one is a subject and not an object, that consciousness and freedom make human persons radically different from objects. As subjects, persons impart values to objects: Objects are not valuable in themselves but only insofar as persons choose to value them. [D.C.A.]
5. As already noted, *existence* is a property of human persons, while *being* is a property of objects. Hence to exist is to "*make oneself* a lack of being" in the sense of living not as an object but as a conscious and free person. To exist is to "*cast* oneself into the world" as a person among objects. [D.C.A.]
6. *facticity*: the "facts" of a person's situation; the set of circumstances within which freedom is exercised. Facticity includes things such as time and place of birth, physical constitution, past actions, environment, and attitudes of others toward oneself. [D.C.A.]
7. Nothingness (no-thing-ness) is at the heart of the human person because con-sciousness is not a "thing" (object). [D.C.A.]
8. *transference*: the process of redirecting (transferring) the feelings we have about one person to another person
   sublimation: the process of diverting an instinct from an original and socially objectionable form of expression to one that is socially acceptable [D.C.A.]

9. *A Doll's House*: a play by the Norwegian writer Henrik Ibsen (1828–1906) [D.C.A.]
10. *Inquisition*: a former tribunal of the Roman Catholic Church for discovering and punishing heretics [D.C.A.]
11. The "in-itself" is an object; the "for-itself" is consciousness. The desire to synthesize these (the impossible goal we all seek) is the desire to become a god. [D.C.A.]
12. Charles-Pierre Baudelaire (1821–1867) was a French poet. [D.C.A.]
13. *Don Juan*: a legendary seducer of women
    Elvira: the woman Don Juan abducted, married, and then abandoned [D.C.A.]
14. T. E. (Thomas Edward) Lawrence (1888–1935) was a British soldier, archeologist, and writer—better known as "Lawrence of Arabia." [D.C.A.]
15. Francisco Pizarro (about 1475–1541) was the Spanish conqueror of Peru. [D.C.A.]
16. Georges Bataille (1897–1962) was a French author. [D.C.A.]
17. Georg Wilhelm Friedrich Hegel (1770–1831) was a German philosopher. [D.C.A.]
18. *solipsism*: the theory that the self and its states are all that can be known. [D.C.A.]
19. Friedrich Nietzsche (1844–1900) was a German philosopher. See the introduction to Chapter 10. [D.C.A.]

QUESTIONS FOR REFLECTION AND DISCUSSION

1. Is the crisis of adolescence caused mainly by the discovery that objects have value only insofar as we, as free subjects, choose to value them?
2. Do we deny our freedom when we accept any absolute moral values other than freedom itself?
3. Is freedom the ultimate human value?
4. Is it morally wrong to deny one's radical freedom?
5. Can I will my own freedom without willing the freedom of others?

SUGGESTIONS FOR FURTHER READING

I. Primary Sources

The Ethics of Ambiguity, trans. Bernard Frechtman. New York: Philosophical Library, 1948, 162 pp.

"Myth and Reality," in *The Second Sex*, ed. and trans. H. M. Parshley. 1953; reprint ed., New York: Vintage, Book 1, chap. 11, pp. 235–263.

> Beauvoir contrasts the myth of the "eternal feminine" with how women actually are and explains how the myth works to the detriment of women.

The Blood of Others, trans. Roger Senhouse and Yvonne Moyse. 1948; reprint ed., New York: Pantheon, Modern Writers Ser., 1984, 292 pp.

> A novel about the political involvement of a man and a woman during the Nazi occupation of France, written as a conversation at the bedside of the woman as she is dying of wounds suffered in a sabotage mission for a resistance group.

Beauvoir stresses the inescapability of choice: The characters must decide whether they will or will not shed the blood of others.

e Mandarins, trans. Leonard M. Friedman. 1956; reprint ed., South Bend, Ind.: Regnery Gateway, 1979, 610 pp.

. Beauvoir's prize-winning novel about the attempts of some leftist French intellectuals, after World War II, to become political activists and to change society. The novel is rich in existentialist themes, especially the importance of moral choice, the conflict between moral ideals and political reality, and the complexity of human relationships.

. Secondary Sources

ttrell, Robert D. *Simone de Beauvoir*. New York: Ungar, Modern Literature Monographs, 1975, 168 pp.

Chap. 3, "Ethics and the Moral Phase," pp. 45–85, gives exposition and criticism of *Pyrrhus et Cinéas* (never translated into English), *The Blood of Others*, *Les Bouches inutiles* (Beauvoir's 1945 play, never translated into English), *All Men Are Mortal*, *The Ethics of Ambiguity*, and *L'Existentialisme et la sagesse des nations* (never translated into English).

anston, Maurice. "Simone de Beauvoir," in *The Novelist as Philosopher: Studies in French Fiction, 1935–1960*, ed. J. Cruickshank. 1962; reprint ed., Westport, Conn.: Greenwood, 1978, pp. 166–182.

Cranston explains why the novel was an essential means of philosophical expression for Beauvoir and discusses the philosophical themes in several of her novels.

eefe, Terry. *Simone de Beauvoir: A Study of Her Writings*. Totowa, N.J.: Barnes & Noble, 1983, 247 pp.

Chap. 4, "Moral Essays," pp. 74–93, summarizes and evaluates *Pyrrhus et Cinéas*, *The Ethics of Ambiguity*, and *L'Existentialisme et la sagesse des nations*. Keefe's quotations from Beauvoir are in French; an appendix translates the longer quotations, but the shorter ones are untranslated.

mons, Margaret A. "Beauvoir and Sartre: The Philosophical Relationship," in *Simone de Beauvoir: Witness to a Century*, ed. Hélène Vivienne Wenzel. New Haven, Conn.: Yale University Press, Yale French Studies, 1986, pp. 165–179.

This article examines the differences between the philosophies of Beauvoir and Sartre and points out ways in which Beauvoir influenced Sartre.

itmarsh, Anne. *Simone de Beauvoir and the Limits of Commitment*. Cambridge, England: Cambridge University Press, 1981, 212 pp.

Chap. 2, "Freedom and Responsibility," pp. 30–52, examines Beauvoir's existentialist views on the meaning of human freedom and the implications of freedom for our relationships with others.

14

B. F. Skinner

B. F. Skinner was born in Susquehanna, Pennsylvania, in 1904. He attended Hamilton College in Clinton, New York, graduating in 1926 with a degree in English. He briefly pursued a career as a writer but then became interested in psychology, especially the psychology of human behavior. Skinner was attracted by the views of the American psychologist John B. Watson (1878–1958), the founder of behaviorism. Watson rejected the views traditional of the psychology as the study of mental states, redefining it as "a science of behavior."

Skinner began graduate studies in psychology at Harvard University in 1928 and received his doctorate three years later. He did postgraduate work at Harvard until 1936, when he accepted a teaching position at the University of Minnesota. In 1938 he published *The Behavior of Organisms*, a study based on his doctoral dissertation. He remained at the University of Minnesota for nine years and then joined the faculty at Indiana University. In 1948 he returned to Harvard. That same year, fulfilling to some extent his original ambition to become a writer, he published *Walden Two*, a novel describing a community run on behaviorist principles. *Science and Human Behavior*, an explanation of how human behavior can be analyzed and controlled, appeared in 1953. Five years later he became Edgar Pierce Professor of Psychology at Harvard and received the Distinguished Scientific Award from the American Psychological Association.

In 1971 Skinner published his controversial book *Beyond Freedom and Dignity*, which argues that since our behavior is due entirely to heredity and environment, we have neither freedom nor dignity. Skinner remained at Harvard until his retirement in 1974 as Professor Emeritus of Psychology and Social Relations. That same year he published *About Behaviorism,* a general account of his view that human behavior is caused by heredity and environment, not by mental entities such as thoughts, desires, motives, and feelings. Skinner published a number of works after his retirement, including a three-volume autobiography in 1976, 1979, and 1983 and a book entitled *Enjoy Old Age*, coauthored with psychologist Margaret E. Vaughan. He died in 1990 in Cambridge, Massachusetts, at the age of eighty-six.

Our selection is from *About Behaviorism*. Since the book is more philo-ophical than psychological (Skinner states in his introduction that behav-rism "is not the science of human behavior, [but] the philosophy of that cience"), it may be helpful, as background, to explain briefly the basic oncepts of Skinner's psychological theory. Skinner distinguishes two kinds f behavior, respondent and operant. He defines as *respondent behavior* action erformed in response to a stimulus, whereas *operant behavior* "operates on" ie environment, i.e., it is followed by environmental consequences that, in irn, affect future behavior.

In Skinner's theory of operant behavior, a consequence that makes a ehavior more likely to be repeated is called a *reinforcer*. Reinforcers can be ositive or negative: A positive reinforcer will strengthen a behavior by dding something positive (e.g., a person is more likely to repeat a behavior if is followed by praise); a negative reinforcer will strengthen a behavior by emoving something negative (e.g., a person is more likely to repeat an action it relieves discomfort). Negative reinforcement differs from punishment ecause the latter tends to *prevent* the recurrence of the preceding behavior, ot strengthen it.

Both respondent and operant behavior can be modified. In *respondent* (or *lassical*) *conditioning*, one modifies a person's (or an animal's) behavior by ontrolling the stimuli that precede the behavior. This was the method used y the Russian physiologist Ivan Pavlov (1849–1936) and by John B. Watson. i *operant conditioning*, one modifies behavior by controlling the consequences einforcers or punishment) that follow it. This is the type of behavior modifi-ation that was the focus of Skinner's research.

Skinner was convinced that the best hope for improving society lies in ie systematic use of operant conditioning. He recommended that operant onditioning be based on positive reinforcement rather than on negative einforcement or punishment, since positive reinforcement produces more isting and more constructive results.

In our selection from *About Behaviorism*, Skinner rejects the "mentalistic" xplanation of human behavior. Mentalists claim that thoughts and feelings re not physical, and also that thoughts and feelings cause our physical odily) behavior. But mentalists have not been able to explain how entities iat are *not* physical can affect physical behavior. Skinner maintains that uman beings are wholly physical organisms: What we call thoughts and elings are bodily activities, not mental entities. Skinner proceeds to show ow dozens of mentalistic terms (only a sample is included in our selection) an be "translated" into descriptions of physical behavior. He then presents is view that human behavior is completely determined by heredity and nvironment. Free will is a mentalistic illusion; given our particular genetic nd environmental histories, we must act the way we do. At the end of the election, Skinner responds to the objection that behaviorism "dehumanizes" uman beings.

ABOUT BEHAVIORISM

CHAPTER 1. THE CAUSES OF BEHAVIOR

Why do people behave as they do? It was probably first a practical question: How could a person anticipate and hence prepare for what another person would do? Later it would become practical in another sense: How could another person be induced to behave in a given way? Eventually it became a matter of understanding and explaining behavior. It could always be reduced to a question about causes.

We tend to say, often rashly, that if one thing follows another, it was probably caused by it—following the ancient principle of *post hoc, ergo propter hoc* (after this, therefore because of this). Of many examples to be found in the explanation of human behavior, one is especially important here. The person with whom we are most familiar is ourself; many of the things we observe just before we behave occur within our body, and it is easy to take them as the causes of our behavior. If we are asked why we have spoken sharply to a friend, we may reply, "Because I felt angry." It is true that we felt angry before, or as, we spoke, and so we take our anger to be the cause of our remark. Asked why we are not eating our dinner, we may say, "Because I do not feel hungry." We often feel hungry when we eat and hence conclude that we eat because we feel hungry. Asked why we are going swimming, we may reply, "Because I feel like swimming." We seem to be saying, "When I have felt like this before, I have behaved in such and such a way." Feelings occur at just the right time to serve as causes of behavior, and they have been cited as such for centuries. We assume that other people feel as we feel when they behave as we behave.

But where are these feelings and states of mind? Of what stuff are they made? The traditional answer is that they are located in a world of non-physical dimensions called the mind and that they are mental. But another question then arises: How can a mental event cause or be caused by a physical one? If we want to predict what a person will do, how can we discover the mental causes of his behavior, and how can we produce the feelings and states of mind which will induce him to behave in a given way? Suppose, for

xample, that we want to get a child to eat a nutritious but not very palatable
ood. We simply make sure that no other food is available, and eventually he
ats. It appears that in depriving him of food (a physical event) we have made
im feel hungry (a mental event), and that because he has felt hungry, he has
aten the nutritious food (a physical event). But how did the physical act of
eprivation lead to the feeling of hunger, and how did the feeling move the
uscles involved in ingestion? There are many other puzzling questions of
is sort. What is to be done about them?

The commonest practice is, I think, simply to ignore them. It is possible
 believe that behavior expresses feelings, to anticipate what a person will do
y guessing or asking him how he feels, and to change the environment in
e hope of changing feelings while paying little if any attention to theoretical
roblems. Those who are not quite comfortable about such a strategy some-
mes take refuge in physiology. Mind, it is said, will eventually be found to
ave a physical basis. As one neurologist recently put it, "Everyone now
ccepts the fact that the brain provides the physical basis of human thought."
reud[1] believed that his very complicated mental apparatus would eventually
e found to be physiological, and early introspective psychologists called
eir discipline Physiological Psychology. The theory of knowledge called
hysicalism holds that when we introspect or have feelings we are looking at
ates or activities of our brains. But the major difficulties are practical: we
annot anticipate what a person will do by looking directly at his feelings *or*
is nervous system, nor can we change his behavior by changing his mind *or*
is brain. But in any case we seem to be no worse off for ignoring philosoph-
al problems.

tructuralism

 more explicit strategy is to abandon the search for causes and simply
escribe what people do. Anthropologists can report customs and manners,
olitical scientists can take the line of "behavioralism" and record political
ction, economists can amass statistics about what people buy and sell, rent
nd hire, save and spend, and make and consume, and psychologists can
ample attitudes and opinions. All this may be done through direct observa-
on, possibly with the help of recording systems, and with interviews,
uestionnaires, tests, and polls. The study of literature, art, and music is
ften confined to the forms of these products of human behavior, and lin-
uists may confine themselves to phonetics, semantics, and syntax. A kind of
rediction is possible on the principle that what people have often done they
re likely to do again; they follow customs because it is customary to follow
em, they exhibit voting or buying habits, and so on. The discovery of
rganizing principles in the structure of behavior—such as "universals" in
ultures or languages, archetypal patterns in literature, or psychological
ypes—may make it possible to predict instances of behavior that have not
reviously occurred.

The structure or organization of behavior can also be studied as a function of time or age, as in the development of a child's verbal behavior or his problem-solving strategies or in the sequence of stages through which a person passes on his way from infancy to maturity, or in the stages through which a culture evolves. History emphasizes changes occurring in time, and if patterns of development or growth can be discovered, they may also prove helpful in predicting future events.

Control is another matter. Avoiding mentalism . . . by refusing to look at causes exacts its price. Structuralism and developmentalism do not tell us why customs are followed, why people vote as they do or display attitudes or traits of character, or why different languages have common features. Time or age cannot be manipulated; we can only wait for a person or a culture to pass through a developmental period.

In practice the systematic neglect of useful information has usually meant that the data supplied by the structuralist are acted upon by others—for example, by decision-makers who in some way manage to take the causes of behavior into account. In theory it has meant the survival of mentalistic concepts. When explanations are demanded, primitive cultural practices are attributed to "the mind of the savage," the acquisition of language to "innate rules of grammar," the development of problem-solving strategies to the "growth of mind," and so on. In short, structuralism tells us how people behave but throws very little light on why they behave as they do. It has no answer to the question with which we began.

Methodological Behaviorism

The mentalistic problem can be avoided by going directly to the prior physical causes while bypassing intermediate feelings or states of mind. . . . If all linkages are lawful, nothing is lost by neglecting a supposed nonphysical link. Thus, if we know that a child has not eaten for a long time, and if we know that he therefore feels hungry and that because he feels hungry he then eats, then we know that if he has not eaten for a long time, he will eat. And if by making other food inaccessible, we make him feel hungry, and if because he feels hungry he then eats a special food, then it must follow that by making other food inaccessible, we induce him to eat the special food. . . .

There is, of course, nothing new in trying to predict or control behavior by observing or manipulating prior public events. Structuralists and developmentalists have not entirely ignored the histories of their subjects, and historians and biographers have explored the influences of climate, culture, persons, and incidents. People have used practical techniques of predicting and controlling behavior with little thought to mental states. Nevertheless, for many centuries there was very little systematic inquiry into the role of the physical environment, although hundreds of highly technical volumes were written about human understanding and the life of the mind. A program of methodological behaviorism became plausible only when progress began to e made in the scientific observation of behavior, because only then was it ossible to override the powerful effect of mentalism in diverting inquiry way from the role of the environment.

Mentalistic explanations allay curiosity and bring inquiry to a stop. It is) easy to observe feelings and states of mind at a time and in a place which ake them seem like causes that we are not inclined to inquire further. Once le environment begins to be studied, however, its significance cannot be enied. . . .

With respect to its own goals, methodological behaviorism was suc- essful. It disposed of many of the problems raised by mentalism and freed self to work on its own projects without philosophical digressions. By irecting attention to genetic and environmental antecedents, it offset an nwarranted concentration on an inner life. It freed us to study the behavior f lower species, where introspection (then regarded as exclusively human) 'as not feasible, and to explore similarities and differences between man and ther species. Some concepts previously associated with private events were ormulated in other ways.

But problems remained. Most methodological behaviorists granted the xistence of mental events while ruling them out of consideration. Did they eally mean to say that they did not matter, that the middle stage in that aree-stage sequence of physical-mental-physical contributed nothing—in ther words, that feelings and states of mind were merely epiphenomena?[2] It 'as not the first time that anyone had said so. The view that a purely physical 'orld could be self-sufficient had been suggested centuries before, in the octrine of psychophysical parallelism, which held that there were two 'orlds—one of mind and one of matter—and that neither had any effect on le other. Freud's demonstration of the unconscious, in which an awareness f feelings or states of mind seemed unnecessary, pointed in the same irection.

But what about other evidence? Is the traditional *post hoc, ergo propter hoc* rgument entirely wrong? Are the feelings we experience just before we ehave wholly unrelated to our behavior? What about the power of mind over natter in psychosomatic medicine? What about psychophysics and the math- matical relation between the magnitudes of stimuli and sensations? What bout the stream of consciousness? What about the intrapsychic processes of sychiatry, in which feelings produce or suppress other feelings and memo- es evoke or mask other memories? What about the cognitive processes said) explain perception, thinking, the construction of sentences, and artistic reation? Must all this be ignored because it cannot be studied objectively?

Radical Behaviorism

he statement that behaviorists deny the existence of feelings, sensations, leas, and other features of mental life needs a good deal of clarification. 1ethodological behaviorism . . . ruled private events out of bounds because there could be no public agreement about their validity. Introspection could not be accepted as a scientific practice. . . . Radical behaviorism, however, takes a different line. It does not deny the possibility of self-observation or self-knowledge or its possible usefulness, but it questions the nature of what is felt or observed and hence known. It restores introspection but not what philosophers and introspective psychologists had believed they were "specting," and it raises the question of how much of one's body one can actually observe.

Mentalism kept attention away from the external antecedent events which might have explained behavior, by seeming to supply an alternative explanation. Methodological behaviorism did just the reverse: by dealing exclusively with external antecedent events it turned attention away from self-observation and self-knowledge. Radical behaviorism restores some kind of balance. It does not insist upon truth by agreement and can therefore consider events taking place in the private world within the skin. It does not call these events unobservable, and it does not dismiss them as subjective. It simply questions the nature of the object observed and the reliability of the observations.

The position can be stated as follows: what is felt or introspectively observed is not some nonphysical world of consciousness, mind, or mental life but the observer's own body. This does not mean . . . that introspection is a kind of physiological research, nor does it mean (and this is the heart of the argument) that what are felt or introspectively observed are the causes of behavior. An organism behaves as it does because of its current structure, but most of this is out of reach of introspection. At the moment we must content ourselves, as the methodological behaviorist insists, with a person's genetic and environmental histories. What are introspectively observed are certain collateral products of those histories. . . .

Our increasing knowledge of the control exerted by the environment makes it possible to examine the effect of the world within the skin and the nature of self-knowledge. It also makes it possible to interpret a wide range of mentalistic expressions. For example, we can look at those features of behavior which have led people to speak of an act of will, of a sense of purpose, of experience as distinct from reality, of innate or acquired ideas, of memories, meanings, and the personal knowledge of the scientist, and of hundreds of other mentalistic things or events. Some can be "translated into behavior," others discarded as unnecessary or meaningless.

In this way we repair the major damage wrought by mentalism. When what a person does is attributed to what is going on inside him, investigation is brought to an end. Why explain the explanation? For twenty-five hundred years people have been preoccupied with feelings and mental life, but only recently has any interest been shown in a more precise analysis of the role of the environment. Ignorance of that role led in the first place to mental fictions, and it has been perpetuated by the explanatory practices to which they gave rise. . . .

Few Words of Caution

. . A word about my own verbal behavior. The English language is heavy-den with mentalism. Feelings and states of mind have enjoyed a command-g lead in the explanation of human behavior; and literature, preoccupied as is with how and what people feel, offers continuing support. As a result, it impossible to engage in casual discourse without raising the ghosts of entalistic theories. The role of the environment was discovered very late, nd no popular vocabulary has yet emerged.

For purposes of casual discourse I see no reason to avoid such an xpression as "I have chosen to discuss . . ." (though I question the possibility free choice), or "I have in mind . . ." (though I question the existence of a ind), or "I am aware of the fact . . ." (though I put a very special interpreta-on on awareness). The neophyte behaviorist is sometimes embarrassed hen he finds himself using mentalistic terms, but the punishment of which s embarrassment is one effect is justified only when the terms are used in a chnical discussion. When it is important to be clear about an issue, nothing ut a technical vocabulary will suffice. It will often seem forced or round-bout. Old ways of speaking are abandoned with regret, and new ones are wkward and uncomfortable, but the change must be made.

This is not the first time a science has suffered from such a transition. here were periods when it was difficult for the astronomer not to sound like a astrologer (or to be an astrologer at heart) and when the chemist had by no eans freed himself from alchemy. We are in a similar stage in a science of ehavior, and the sooner the transition is completed the better. The practical nsequences are easily demonstrated: education, politics, psychotherapy, nology, and many other fields of human affairs are suffering from the lectic use of a lay vocabulary. The theoretical consequences are harder to emonstrate but, as I hope to show in what follows, equally important. . . .

HAPTER 3. INNATE BEHAVIOR

he human species, like all other species, is the product of natural selection.[3] ach of its members is an extremely complex organism, a living system, the bject of anatomy and physiology. Fields such as respiration, digestion, rculation, and immunization have been set apart for special study, and nong them is the field we call behavior.

It usually involves the environment. The newborn infant is so con-ructed that it takes in air and food and puts out wastes. Breathing, suckling, rination, and defecation are things the newborn infant *does*, but so, of urse, are all its other physiological activities. . . .

Darwin's theory of natural selection came very late in the history of ought. Was it delayed because it opposed revealed truth, because it was an entirely new subject in the history of science, because it was characteristic only of living things, or because it dealt with purpose and final causes without postulating an act of creation? I think not. Darwin simply discovered the role of selection, a kind of causality very different from the push-pull mechanisms of science up to that time. The origin of a fantastic variety of living things could be explained by the contribution which novel features, possibly of random provenance, made to survival. There was little or nothing in physical or biological science that foreshadowed selection as a causal principle.

Although we still do not know much about the anatomy and physiology underlying behavior, we can speculate about the process of selection which made them part of a genetic endowment. Survival may be said to be *contingent upon* certain kinds of behavior. For example, if members of a species did not mate, care for their young, or defend themselves against predators, the species would not survive. It is not easy to study these "contingencies of survival" experimentally because selection is a slow process, but some effects may be shown by studying species which quickly mature to breeding age and by carefully arranging conditions of selection. . . .

Preparation for New Environments

[An important] process through which a person comes to deal effectively with a new environment is operant conditioning. Many things in the environment, such as food and water, sexual contact, and escape from harm, are crucial for the survival of the individual and the species, and any behavior which produces them therefore has survival value. Through the process of operant conditioning, behavior having this kind of consequence becomes more likely to occur. The behavior is said to be *strengthened* by its consequences, and for that reason the consequences themselves are called "reinforcers." Thus, when a hungry organism exhibits behavior that *produces* food, the behavior is reinforced by that consequence and is therefore more likely to recur. Behavior that *reduces* a potentially damaging condition, such as an extreme of temperature, is reinforced by that consequence and therefore tends to recur on similar occasions. . . .

"The Evolution of Mind"

The concept of mind had been thoroughly elaborated before the advent of evolutionary theory, and some accommodation was needed. When and how did mind evolve? What kind of mutation could have given rise to the first mental state or process which, in contributing to the survival of the person in whom it occurred, became part of the human genetic endowment? The question is not unlike that raised by the conversion of reality into experience or of thought into action. What sort of physical gene could carry the potentia

mind, and how could mind satisfy physical contingencies of survival? If
ind is nothing more than a manifestation of physiology, such questions can
e answered, or at least postponed without anxiety until physiology can
iswer them, but not all who subscribe to mentalism accept that position.
Iind has been said by some—Teilhard de Chardin,[4] for example—to be the
id and purpose of evolution, if not something beyond it. The distinguished
:ientist Vannevar Bush[5] has put it this way:

> We seem, thus, to have arrived at a concept of how the physical universe
> about us—all the life that inhabits the speck we occupy in this universe—has
> evolved over the eons of time by simple material processes, the sort of pro-
> cesses we examine experimentally, which we describe by equations, and call
> the "laws of nature." Except for one thing! Man is conscious of his existence.
> Man also possesses, so most of us believe, what he calls his free will. Did
> consciousness and free will too arise merely out of "natural" processes? The
> question is central to the contention between those who see nothing beyond
> a new materialism and those who see—Something.

The behaviorist has a simpler answer. What has evolved is an organism,
art of the behavior of which has been tentatively explained by the invention
: the concept of mind. No special evolutionary process is needed when the
cts are considered in their own right.

HAPTER 4. OPERANT BEHAVIOR

ne process of operant conditioning described in the preceding chapter is
mple enough. When a bit of behavior has the kind of consequence called
inforcing, it is more likely to occur again. A positive reinforcer strengthens
iy behavior that produces it: a glass of water is positively reinforcing when
e are thirsty, and if we then draw and drink a glass of water, we are more
kely to do so again on similar occasions. A negative reinforcer strengthens
iy behavior that reduces or terminates it: when we take off a shoe that is
nching, the reduction in pressure is negatively reinforcing, and we are more
kely to do so again when a shoe pinches.

The process supplements natural selection. Important consequences of
:havior which could not play a role in evolution because they were not
ifficiently stable features of the environment are made effective through
erant conditioning during the lifetime of the individual, whose power in
:aling with his world is thus vastly increased.

he Feelings of Reinforcers

he fact that operant conditioning, like all physiological processes, is a prod-
:t of natural selection throws light on the question of what kinds of
nsequences are reinforcing and why. It is commonly said that a thing is

reinforcing because it feels, looks, sounds, smells, or tastes good, but from the point of view of evolutionary theory a susceptibility to reinforcement is due to its survival value and not to any associated feelings.

The point may be made for the reinforcers which play a part in the conditioning of reflexes. Salivation is elicited by certain chemical stimuli on the tongue (as other secretions are elicited by other stimuli in later stages of digestion) because the effect has contributed to the survival of the species. A person may report that a substance tastes good, but it does not elicit salivation because it tastes good. Similarly, we pull our hand away from a hot object, but not because the object *feels* painful. The behavior occurs because appropriate mechanisms have been selected in the course of evolution. The feelings are merely collateral products of the conditions responsible for the behavior.

The same may be said of operant reinforcers. Salt and sugar are critical requirements, and individuals who were especially likely to be reinforced by them have more effectively learned and remembered where and how to get them and have therefore been more likely to survive and transmit this susceptibility to the species. It has often been pointed out that competition for a mate tends to select the more skillful and powerful members of a species, but it also selects those more susceptible to sexual reinforcement. As a result, the human species, like other species, is powerfully reinforced by sugar, salt, and sexual contact. This is very different from saying that these things reinforce *because* they taste or feel good.

Feelings have dominated the discussion of rewards and punishments for centuries. One reason is that the conditions we report when we say that a taste, odor, sound, picture, or piece of music is delicious, pleasant, or beautiful are part of the immediate situation, whereas the effect they may have in changing our behavior is much less salient—and much less likely to be "seen," because the verbal environment cannot establish good contingencies.[6] According to the philosophy of hedonism, people act to achieve pleasure and escape from or avoid pain, and the effects referred to in Edward L. Thorndike's famous Law of Effect[7] were feelings: "satisfying" or "annoying." The verb "to like" is a synonym of "to be pleased with"; we say "If you like" and "If you please" more or less interchangeably.

Some of these terms refer to other effects of reinforcers—satisfying, for example, is related to satiation—but most refer to the bodily states generated by reinforcers. It is sometimes possible to discover what reinforces a person simply by asking him what he likes or how he feels about things. What we learn is similar to what we learn by testing the effect of a reinforcer: he is talking about what has reinforced him in the past or what he sees himself "going for." But this does not mean that his feelings are causally effective; his answer reports a collateral effect.

The expressions "I like Brahms," "I love Brahms," "I enjoy Brahms," and "Brahms pleases me" may easily be taken to refer to feelings, but they can be regarded as statements that the music of Brahms is reinforcing. A person of whom the expressions are true will listen to the radio when it plays

ahms rather than turn it off, buy and play records of Brahms, and go to
ncerts where Brahms is played. The expressions have antonyms ("I dislike
ahms," "I hate Brahms," "I detest Brahms," and "Brahms bores me"), and
person for whom Brahms is thus aversive[8] will act to avoid or escape from
aring him. These expressions do not refer to instances of reinforcement but
ther to a general susceptibility or the lack of it.

The allusion to what is felt needs to be carefully examined. Feelings are
pecially plausible when the experience is directed toward a living person.
ne statement "I love my wife" seems to be a report of feelings, but it also
volves a probability of action. We are disposed to do to a person we love the
ings he likes or loves to have done. We are not disposed to do to a person
e dislike (or especially to a person we hate) the things he likes or loves to
ave done; on the contrary we are disposed to do the things he dislikes or
ates to have done. With respect to a person with whom we interact, then, to
ove" is to behave in ways having certain kinds of effects, possibly with
companying conditions which may be felt.

ants, Needs, Desires, and Wishes

ome mentalistic terms refer to conditions which affect both the susceptibility
reinforcement and the strength of already reinforced behavior. We use
want" to describe a shortage: a hungry man wants food in the simple sense
at food is wanting. "Needs" originally meant violent force, restraint, or
mpulsion, and we still make a distinction between wanting to act (because
positively reinforcing consequences) and needing to act (because not acting
ill have aversive consequences), but for most purposes the terms are inter-
angeable. We say that a car needs gasoline and, much less idiomatically,
at gasoline is wanting, but to say that a person "wants to get out" suggests
ersive control.[9] The significant fact is that a person who needs or wants
od is particularly likely to be reinforced by food and that he is particularly
ely to engage in any behavior which has previously been reinforced with
od. A person under aversive control is particularly likely to be reinforced if
escapes and to engage in any behavior which has led to escape.

If we know the level of deprivation or aversive stimulation, we can more
curately predict how reinforcing a given event will be and how likely it is
at a person will engage in relevant behavior. The knowledge has long been
sed for purposes of control. People have been made hungry so that they will
work for food" and so that they can be reinforced with food, as they have
een made miserable so that they will act in ways which reduce their misery.

An event is not reinforcing *because* it reduces a need. Food is reinforcing
ven when it does not satiate, and deprivation can be changed in ways which
e not reinforcing. The relation between a state of deprivation and the
rength of appropriate behavior is presumably due to survival value. If

behavior leading to ingestion were strong at all times, a person would grossly overeat and use his energies inefficiently.

It is a mistake to say that food is reinforcing *because* we feel hungry or *because* we feel the need for food, or that we are more likely to engage in food-reinforced behavior because we feel hungry. It is the *condition* felt as hunger which would have been selected in the evolution of the species as most immediately involved in operant reinforcement.

The states associated with wanting and needing are more likely to be felt if no relevant behavior is at the moment possible. The lover writes "I want you" or "I need you" when nothing else can be done, and if he is doing anything else, aside from writing, it must be a matter of existing in the state which he describes with these expressions. If behavior then becomes possible, it is easy to say that it was caused by the want or need, rather than by the deprivation or aversive stimulation responsible for both the behavior and the state felt.

Desiring, longing, hoping, and yearning are more closely related to a current absence of appropriate behavior because they terminate when action begins. "I miss you" could almost be thought of as a metaphor based on target practice, equivalent to "My behavior with respect to you as a person cannot reach its mark" or "I look for you and fail to find you." The lover in the arms of his beloved is not instantly free of wanting and needing her, but he is no longer missing her or longing or yearning for her. Wishing is perhaps most exclusively a reference to a heightened state of deprivation or aversive stimulation when no behavior is possible. A person may wish that he could act ("I wish I could go") or he may wish for the consequences ("I wish I were there").

The effects of operant reinforcement are often represented as inner states or possessions. When we reinforce a person we are said to give him a motive or incentive, but we infer the motive or the incentive from the behavior. We call a person highly motivated when all we know is that he behaves energetically. . . .

The Mind in Operant Behavior

In most of this chapter I have been concerned with feelings or states of mind which may be interpreted as collateral products of the contingencies which generate behavior. It remains for us to consider other mentalistic processes which are said to be needed if operant conditioning is to take place. The mind is not merely a spectator; it is said to play an active role in the determination of behavior.

Many English idioms containing the word "mind" suggest a probability of action, as in "I have a mind to go." Mind is often represented as an agent scarcely to be distinguished from the person who has the mind. "It crossed my *mind* that I should go" is scarcely more than "It occurred to *me* that

ould go." When responses of glands or smooth muscle (under control of
e autonomic nervous system) are brought under operant control by making
inforcement contingent upon them, the result is said to demonstrate the
ntrol of "mind over matter"; but what it demonstrates is that a person may
spond with his glands or his smooth muscles under operant contingencies.

mechanical arm designed to be operated by muscles normally operating
me other part of the body is said to be "thought-operated" or "operated by
e mind," although it is operated by the person who originally moved some
her part of his body. When people shoot other people, it is said that "minds
ll, not guns," and that "a man's mind was the instrument directly respon-
ble for the assassination of John F. Kennedy and Martin Luther King," but
eople are shot by people, not by minds.

The view that mental activity is essential to operant behavior is an
xample of the view that feelings or introspectively observed states are
usally effective. When a person replies to the question "Will you go tomor-
w?" by saying, "I don't know, I never know how I will feel," the assump-
on is that what is in doubt is the feeling rather than the behavior—that the
erson will go if he feels like going rather than that he will feel like going if he
oes. Neither statement is, of course, an explanation.

There are other words referring to mental activites said to be more
ecifically required by behavior. People must "judge" what will or will not
ccur if they do or do not act in certain ways. The dog in the Pavlovian
xperiment[10] salivates in anticipation of food or because it "expects" food. In
perant experiments a rat presses a lever because it "anticipates" that food
ill be delivered or expects food to be delivered when it does so. "In social
arning theory the potential of the occurrence of a behavior is considered to
e a function of the expectancy that the behavior will lead to a particular
inforcement or reinforcements and the value of these reinforcements in a
ven situation." We should have to translate these statements in some such
ay as this: "The probability of behavior depends upon the kind or frequency
f reinforcement in similar situations in the past." A person may well feel
onditions associated with "judging," "anticipating," and "expecting," but
e does not need to do so. . . .

It is sometimes said that operant conditioning is simply one aspect of the
ursuit of happiness, and the expression will help to summarize several
oints in this chapter. Happiness is a feeling, a by-product of operant rein-
rcement. The things which make us happy are the things which reinforce
s, but it is the things, not the feelings, which must be identified and used in
rediction, control, and interpretation. Pursuit suggests purpose: we act to
chieve happiness. But pursuit, like search, is simply behavior which has
een reinforced by achieving something. Behavior becomes pursuit only after
inforcement. It has been said that the pursuit of happiness cannot be an
xplanation of behavior because "nothing proves that men in modern so-
eties are happier than men in archaic societies," but operant reinforcement

is effective quite apart from any ultimate gain, as the negative utility of gambling abundantly demonstrates. . . .

CHAPTER 12. THE QUESTION OF CONTROL

A scientific analysis of behavior must, I believe, assume that a person's behavior is controlled by his genetic and environmental histories rather than by the person himself as an initiating, creative agent; but no part of the behavioristic position has raised more violent objections. We cannot prove, of course, that human behavior as a whole is fully determined, but the proposition becomes more plausible as facts accumulate, and I believe that a point has been reached at which its implications must be seriously considered.

We often overlook the fact that human behavior is also a form of control. That an organism should act to control the world around it is as characteristic of life as breathing or reproduction. A person acts upon the environment, and what he achieves is essential to his survival and the survival of the species. Science and technology are merely manifestations of this essential feature of human behavior. Understanding, prediction, and explanation, as well as technological applications, exemplify the control of nature. They do not express an "attitude of domination" or a "philosophy of control." They are the inevitable results of certain behavioral processes.

We have no doubt made mistakes. We have discovered, perhaps too rapidly, more and more effective ways of controlling our world, and we have not always used them wisely, but we can no more stop controlling nature than we can stop breathing or digesting food. Control is not a passing phase. No mystic or ascetic has ever ceased to control the world around him; he controls it in order to control himself. We cannot choose a way of life in which there is no control. We can only change the controlling conditions.

Countercontrol

Organized agencies or institutions, such as governments, religions, and economic systems, and to a lesser extent educators and psychotherapists, exert a powerful and often troublesome control. It is exerted in ways which most effectively reinforce those who exert it, and unfortunately this usually means in ways which either are immediately aversive to those controlled or exploit them in the long run.

Those who are so controlled then take action. They escape from the controller—moving out of range if he is an individual, or defecting from a government, becoming an apostate from a religion, resigning, or playing truant—or they may attack in order to weaken or destroy the controlling power, as in a revolution, a reformation, a strike, or a student protest. In other words, they oppose control with countercontrol. . . .

CHAPTER 13. WHAT IS INSIDE THE SKIN?

behavioristic analysis rests on the following assumptions: A person is first of all an organism, a member of a species and a subspecies, possessing a genetic endowment of anatomical and physiological characteristics, which are the product of the contingencies of survival to which the species has been exposed in the process of evolution. The organism becomes a person as it acquires a repertoire of behavior under the contingencies of reinforcement to which it is exposed during its lifetime. The behavior it exhibits at any moment is under the control of a current setting. It is able to acquire such a repertoire under such control because of processes of conditioning which are also part of its genetic endowment.

In the traditional mentalistic view, on the other hand, a person is a member of the human species who behaves as he does because of many internal characteristics or possessions, among them sensations, habits, intelligence, opinions, dreams, personalities, moods, decisions, fantasies, skills, percepts, thoughts, virtues, intentions, abilities, instincts, daydreams, incentives, acts of will, joy, compassion, perceptual defenses,[11] beliefs, complexes,[12] expectancies, urges, choice, drives, ideas, responsibilities, elation, memories, needs, wisdom, wants, a death instinct, a sense of duty, sublimation,[13] impulses, capacities, purposes, wishes, an id,[14] repressed fears, a sense of shame, extraversion,[15] images, knowledge, interests, information, a superego,[16] propositions, experiences, attitudes, conflicts, meanings, reaction formations,[17] a will to live, consciousness, anxiety, depression, fear, reason, libido,[18] psychic energy, reminiscences, inhibitions, and mental illnesses.

How are we to decide between these two views?

Grounds for Comparison

Simplicity. We cannot say that one is simpler than the other, since references to mental states and activities make distinctions which must be recast in terms of contingencies of survival or reinforcement. It is possible, indeed, that a behavioral analysis will be more complex. Although some schedules of reinforcement,[19] for example, produce familiar effects which have been introspectively observed and named, many yield entirely unexpected results.

Ease in Control Accessibility is a different matter. No one has ever directly modified any of the *mental* activities or traits listed above. There is no way in which one can make contact with them. The bodily conditions felt as such can be changed surgically, electrically, or with drugs, but for most practical purposes they are changed only through the environment. When a devotee of mentalism confesses that "we have not learned much about these problems in somewhat over two thousand years of reflective thought," we may ask why

reflective thought has not sooner come under suspicion. Behavior modification, although still in its infancy, has been successful, whereas mentalistic
approaches continue to fail, and once the role of the environment has been
made clear, its accessibility is often surprising.

Use in Prediction A decision is perhaps more difficult if we simply want to
predict behavior. What a person feels is a product of the contingencies of
which his future behavior will also be a function, and there is therefore a
useful connection between feelings and behavior. It would be foolish to rule
out the knowledge a person has of his current condition or the uses to which
it may be put. He may say that he does what he "feels like doing" without
asking why he feels that way, and we may ask him to tell us what he feels like
doing and use his answer without further inquiry, as we prepare for his
behavior. In casual discourse the limits of accuracy [of a person's self-reports]
are not necessarily serious, but we can nevertheless predict behavior more
accurately if we have direct knowledge about the history to which feelings are
to be traced.

    Attitudes, opinions, or intelligence, as states inferred from behavior, are
also useless in control, but they permit us to predict one kind of behavior
from another kind known to be associated with it, presumably because of a
common cause.

Use in Interpretation When human behavior is observed under conditions
which cannot be exactly described and where histories are out of reach, very
little prediction or control is possible, but a behavioristic account is still more
useful than a mentalistic one in interpreting what a person is doing or why he
behaves as he does under such circumstances. A listener usually has no
trouble in identifying the ideas a speaker is expressing, although he has no
independent evidence, but if we are going to guess, it is more helpful to guess
about genetic endowment and environmental history than about the feelings
which have resulted from them.

How Far Back? When a person says that he acted "because he felt like
acting," we can put little faith in the "because" until we have explained why
he had the feeling, but it has been objected that we must stop somewhere in
following a causal chain into the past and may as well stop at the psychic
level. Clearly that is what is done most of the time in mentalistic discussions,
and that is why they block further inquiry. It is true that we could trace
human behavior not only to the physical conditions which shape and maintain it but also to the causes of those conditions and the causes of those
causes, almost *ad infinitum*,[20] but there is no point in going back beyond the
point at which effective action can be taken. That point is not to be found in
the psyche, and the explanatory force of mental life has steadily declined as
the promise of the environment has come to be more clearly understood. . .

a **Choice Necessary?** There are those who would have it both ways and
ho continue to call psychology the science of behavior *and* mental life. To do
) is to return to that three-stage sequence in which the physical environment
:ts upon the organism to generate mental or psychic activities, some of
'hich ultimately find expression in physical action. The puzzling question of
ow a physical event causes a mental event, which in turn causes a physical
'ent, remains to be answered or dismissed as unanswerable (a specialist in
le physiology of vision has said that "the transition from the excitations in
le cortex to the subjective experience defies explanation").

The problem could be avoided if we could stay within the mental or
sychic stage. In the "intrapsychic life of the mind" mental causes have
iental effects, and among them are states of awareness or consciousness,
id if this inner world could be observed in a purely solipsistic[21] way, if the
udent of mental life had no reason to appeal to physical action, even in
ommunicating with others, and if mental life played no disruptive role to be
ken into account by the behaviorist, everyone would be satisfied. But
sychology as the study of subjective phenomena, distinct from the study of
bjective behavior, would then not be a science and would have no reason to
e. . . .

CHAPTER 14. SUMMING UP

. . Methodological behaviorism . . . could be said to ignore consciousness,
·elings, and states of mind, but radical behaviorism does not thus "behead
le organism"; it does not "sweep the problem of subjectivity under the rug";
 does not "maintain a strictly behavioristic methodology by treating reports
f introspection merely as verbal behavior"; and it was not designed to
permit consciousness to atrophy." What it has to say about consciousness is
lis: (a) Stimulation arising inside the body plays an important part in behav-
·r. (b) The nervous systems through which it is effective evolved because of
leir role in the internal and external economy of the organism. (c) In the
·nse in which we say that a person is conscious of his surroundings, he is
mscious of states or events in his body; he is under their control as stimuli.
 boxer who has been "knocked unconscious" is not responding to current
imuli either within or outside his skin, and a person may continue to talk,
unconscious of the effect he is having on his listeners" if that effect is not
:erting control over his behavior. Far from ignoring consciousness in this
·nse, a science of behavior has developed new ways of studying it. (d) A
erson becomes conscious in a different sense when a verbal community
·ranges contingencies under which he not only sees an object but sees that
e is seeing it. In this special sense, consciousness or awareness is a social
roduct. (e) Introspective knowledge of one's body—self-knowledge—is de-
·ctive for two reasons: the verbal community cannot bring self-descriptive

behavior under the precise control of private stimuli, and there has been no opportunity for the evolution of a nervous system which would bring some very important parts of the body under that control. (f) Within these limits self-knowledge is useful. The verbal community asks questions about private events because they are the collateral products of environmental causes, about which it can therefore make useful inferences, and self-knowledge becomes useful to the individual for similar reasons. (g) No special kind of mind stuff is assumed. A physical world generates both physical action and the physical conditions within the body to which a person responds when a verbal community arranges the necessary contingencies.

Other species are also conscious in the sense of being under stimulus control. They feel pain in the sense of responding to painful stimuli, as they see a light or hear a sound in the sense of responding appropriately, but no verbal contingencies make them conscious of pain in the sense of feeling that they are feeling, or of light or sound in the sense of seeing that they are seeing or hearing that they are hearing.

A completely independent science of subjective experience would have no more bearing on a science of behavior than a science of what people feel about fire would have on the science of combustion. Nor could experience be divorced from the physical world in the way needed to make such a science possible. Different verbal communities generate different kinds and amounts of consciousness or awareness. Eastern philosophies, psychoanalysis, experimental psychology, phenomenology, and the world of practical affairs lead to the observation of very different feelings and states of mind. An independent science of the subjective would be an independent science of verbal communities.

Must we conclude that all those who have speculated about consciousness as a form of self-knowledge—from the Greeks to the British empiricists to the phenomenologists[22] —have wasted their time? Perhaps we must. They deserve credit for directing attention to the relation between a person and his environment (the scientific study of stimulus control in the name of sensation and perception emerged from philosophical interests of that sort), but they have directed inquiry away from antecedent events in his environmental history. . . .

It is not always clear what is meant when it is said that a behavioral analysis dehumanizes man or destroys man qua[23] man. Sometimes the implication seems to be that its picture of man is incomplete: "Behaviorism tried to build a psychology without including man in his full complexity," or, "Behaviorism has omitted human phenomena which do not fit a physicalistic model." (Humanistic psychology,[24] on the other hand, is said to be a science "appropriate to man as a subject matter," "committed to dealing with humanness in its own right," and "comprehensively human.") But phrases like "man qua man" or "man in his humanity" tell us very little about what has been left out.

Sometimes the implication is that behaviorism neglects something a person does because he is a member of the human species or keeps him from doing something he would otherwise do as such a member. The position of the French philosopher Georges Sorel[25] has been paraphrased in this way:

> Man, at his best, that is, at his most human, seeks to fulfill himself, individually and with those close to him, in spontaneous, unended, creative activity, in work that consists of the imposition of his personality on a recalcitrant environment. . . . He acts and is not acted upon, he chooses and is not chosen for. . . . He resists every force that seeks to reduce his energy, to rob him of his independence and his dignity, to kill the will, to crush everything in him that struggles for unique self-expression and reduce him to uniformity, impersonality, monotony, and, ultimately, extinction.

This characterization of the species is likely to be subscribed to by all those members of the species who can understand it, but it does not identify anything essentially human, as can be shown by applying it to another species. We can readily agree that a lion jumping through a hoop in a circus is not behaving *qua* lion, and we might elaborate in this way:

> The lion at his best, that is, at his most leonine, seeks to fulfill himself, individually and with those close to him, in spontaneous, unended, creative activity, in work that consists of the imposition of his leoninity on a recalcitrant environment. . . . He acts and is not acted upon. He chooses and is not chosen for. . . . He resists every force that seeks to reduce his energy, to rob him of his independence and his dignity, to kill the will, to crush everything in him that struggles for unique self-expression and reduces him to uniformity, unleoninity, monotony, and, ultimately, extinction.

I suspect that most lions would subscribe to this reassuring picture if they could.

It is often said that a behavioristic account somehow neglects something of what a person can be or do because it treats him as a machine. "Man comes to think of himself," as Martin Buber[26] put it, "as if he were determined by the same mechanical laws that govern his refrigerator." But to assert that human behavior is lawful is not to say that the laws which govern it are as simple or as "mechanical" as those that apply to the operation of a refrigerator. Nor is the choice between (a) an entirely technological society in which persons are run by machines and (b) "an era of humanity with man at peace with himself by comporting with his natural environment." And we can scarcely deny that man *is* an animal, though a remarkable one. The complaint that Pavlov converted Hamlet's "How like a god!" into "How like a dog!" was answered by Hamlet himself: "In action how like an angel! In apprehension how like a god! The beauty of the world! The paragon of animals!" Man *is* the paragon of animals.

What is usually meant in saying that behaviorism dehumanizes man is that it neglects important capacities which are not to be found in machines or animals, such as the capacity to choose, have purposes, and behave creatively. But the behavior from which we infer choice, intention, and originality is within reach of a behavioral analysis, and it is not clear that it is wholly out of reach of other species. Man is perhaps unique in being a moral animal, but not in the sense that he possesses morality; he has constructed a social environment in which he behaves with respect to himself and others in moral ways.

Many of these issues were no doubt neglected in early versions of behaviorism, and methodological behaviorism systematically ruled some of them out of account, but I know of no essentially human feature that has been shown to be beyond the reach of a scientific analysis, and I doubt whether those who charge dehumanization would wish to rest their case on the inadequacy of a behavioral account, since the future might turn too heavily against them.

Behavior is the achievement of a person, and we seem to deprive the human organism of something which is his natural due when we point instead to the environmental sources of his behavior. We do not dehumanize him; we dehomunculize[27] him. The essential issue is autonomy. Is man in control of his own destiny or is he not? The point is often made by arguing that a scientific analysis changes man from victor to victim. But man remains what he has always been, and his most conspicuous achievement has been the design and construction of a world which has freed him from constraints and vastly extended his range.

No doubt he has been careless. In the nineteenth century man's overriding inhumanity to man came from the Industrial Revolution—the payment of wages to a hungry labor force, for example, neglected serious side effects. Marx[28] is said to have described this under the influence of earlier romantic writers. Schiller,[29] for example, had written: "Enjoyment was separated from labor, the means from the end, exertion from recompense. Eternally fettered only to a single little fragment of the whole, man fashions himself only as a fragment; ever hearing only the monotonous whirl of the wheel which he turns, he never displays the full harmony of his being." In other words, labor no longer had the reinforcing consequences which generate the condition felt as joy; the contingencies sustained a very narrow repertoire; a person had no chance to acquire most of the behavior of which he was capable.

Today other side effects are attracting more attention. Man continues to build machines which dehumanize him by dispensing with behaviors that contribute to his status as a person, but he is also breeding at a dangerous rate, exhausting the world's resources, polluting the environment, and doing little to relieve the threat of a nuclear holocaust. Nevertheless, if the position I have presented here is correct, he can remedy these mistakes and at the same time build a world in which he will feel freer than ever before and achieve greater things.

He can do this only if he recognizes himself for what he is. He has failed

solve his problems because he has looked in the wrong place for solutions.
he extraordinary role of the environment opens the prospect of a much more
accessful future, in which he will be most human and humane, and in which
e will manage himself skillfully because he will know himself accurately.

A science of behavior has been said to dehumanize man because it is
·ductionistic.[30] It is said to deal with one kind of fact as if it were a different
nd—as is done, for example, by physiological psychology. But behaviorism
oes not move from one dimensional system to another. It simply provides
1 alternative account of the same facts. It does not *reduce* feelings to bodily
ates; it simply argues that bodily states are and always have been what are
lt. It does not *reduce* thought processes to behavior; it simply analyzes the
ehavior previously explained by the invention of thought processes. It does
ot *reduce* morality to certain features of the social environment; it simply
isists that those features have always been responsible for moral behavior.

Even so, something in traditional formulations may seem to be missing.
he problem is not peculiar to the behavioral sciences. Hold a slip of paper
ist above a candle flame and it will "catch fire." We speak of fire as some-
iing things catch and then possess. When we stop the burning, we are said
• "put the fire out"; we "quench" it in the sense of causing it to vanish. The
ietaphor is probably harmless enough in casual discourse, but it is not
articularly useful to the physicist, and a person who is accustomed to
uenching fires by throwing water on them will be unhappy when he is told
iat water simply *cools* or *smothers* a fire. Cooling and smothering do not seem
ke quenching. But it would be wrong to say that the process of quenching
ad been "reduced" to cooling and smothering. The term has simply been
anslated into terms having a broader reference, and, as in similar instances
i a behavioral analysis, what seems to be missing is nothing to be taken
priously, nor does it justify the charge of reductionism. . . .

A common reaction to behaviorism runs as follows: "What you have
iid may all be true, but I am not interested in my behavior. I am interested in
iy feelings—and in the feelings of others. I read books because they intrigue
r excite me; I listen to music because it exhilarates me; I look at pictures
ecause I find them beautiful; I associate with people I love or with whom I
njoy talking about everyday things with everyday words." The same could
e said, of course, about any science: "I do not care about immunology, I
mply want to avoid disease"; "I do not care about genetics, I simply want
ealthy children"; "I do not care where energy comes from, I simply want
omfort and convenience." A knowledge of medicine, genetics, and tech-
ology does not interfere with feeling well, having healthy children, or being
omfortable, and no one is likely to suppose that it does, but similar state-
ients about behavior are debated. Yet there is nothing in a science of
ehavior or its philosophy which need alter feelings or introspective observa-
ons. The bodily states which are felt or observed are acknowledged, but
iere is an emphasis on the environmental conditions with which they are

associated and an insistence that it is the conditions rather than the feelings which enable us to explain behavior.

Those who understand the theory or history of music do not find music therefore any less enjoyable, nor are those who understand the techniques of the artist or the history of art less likely to enjoy paintings. It is true that a touch of mystery may be reinforcing, and we may be particularly moved by the apparently inexplicable, but if there were no offsetting gains, educators would have a good deal to explain.

A distinguished critic of science has expressed an opposing view in the following way: ". . . according to [ethology] Keats[31] is all wrong: the bird is not pouring forth its soul in ecstasy, for now we *know that all it is doing* is serving notice on its fellows that it claims a certain territory for worm grubbing." And he insists that we shall never know why birds sing, "but as poets we know—none better—how their singing affects us and as to this datum science has not a word to say; it can only listen too."

It seems to be implied that to understand why birds sing would interfere with the effect of their singing upon us, and upon the poet, and upon us when we read what he has to say. The ethologist would be wrong to take these effects into account in trying to discover why birds sing, but he can nevertheless enjoy bird song and also what a poet says about it. The bird sings not because of how it feels but because of certain contingencies of survival. How the poet feels upon hearing it is doubly irrelevant to why it sings, but there is no reason why the poet cannot tell us how he feels or, if he is a good poet, induce in us a condition felt in the same way.

If we stop to listen to a bird, it is because we are reinforced for doing so, and science can listen for other reasons. It can survey the extent to which sound patterns are or become reinforcing, and in doing so it may contribute to an explanation of why people compose and listen to music. The conditions generated within the body of the listener remain forever private, but the behavioral scientist may still investigate the reinforcing effects they are associated with and possibly discover how more reinforcing effects may be achieved.

Not only has the most ardent behaviorist feelings like everyone else; on balance he has quite possibly more enjoyable ones, because there are states of the body—associated, for example, with failure, frustration, or loss—which are far from enjoyable or reinforcing, and they are less likely to be experienced by those who practice scientific self-knowledge and self-management.

NOTES

1. Sigmund Freud (1856–1939) was the Austrian neurologist who founded psychoanalysis. See the introduction to Chapter 11. [D.C.A.]

. *epiphenomena*: phenomena that accompany and are caused by other phenomena; here, the feelings and states of mind that accompany and are caused by physical processes in the brain [D.C.A.].

. *natural selection*: the theory of the English naturalist Charles Darwin (1809–1882) that if an organism develops traits that enable it to adapt to its environment, it will survive and transmit these traits to its offspring, and if the organism *fails* to develop adaptive traits, it will perish. Darwin used the theory of natural selection to explain the origin of the various species. [D.C.A.]

. Pierre Teilhard de Chardin (1881–1955) was a French philosopher and paleontologist. [D.C.A.]

. Vannevar Bush (1890–1974) was an American electrical engineer. The quotation is from his article "Science Pauses" (*Fortune*, May 1965, p. 118). [D.C.A.]

. Skinner is referring to contingencies of reinforcement, i.e., reinforcing consequences that are *contingent* ("dependent") upon certain kinds of behavior. [D.C.A.]

. Edward L. Thorndike (1874–1949) was an American educator and psychologist. His "Law of Effect" states that a stimulus will come to elicit a response in an organism if the response is regularly followed by satisfaction and that a stimulus will *stop* eliciting a response if the response is followed by annoyance. [D.C.A.]

. *aversive*: negative [D.C.A.]

. *aversive control*: controlling behavior by threatening negative consequences if the person does not behave as requested [D.C.A.]

. Pavlov was able to condition dogs to salivate upon the presentation of stimuli, such as the sound of a bell, that had no natural connection with food. [D.C.A.]

. *perceptual defense*: an attempt to defend oneself against emotionally negative perceptual stimuli by distorting one's perceptions [D.C.A.]

. *complex*: a group of repressed wishes and memories that influences one's personality [D.C.A.]

. *sublimation*: the process of diverting an instinct from an original and socially objectionable form of expression to one that is socially acceptable [D.C.A.]

. In psychoanalytic theory, the id is the part of the psyche that contains the instincts. [D.C.A.]

. *extraversion*: the orientation of the personality to the external world [D.C.A.]

. In psychoanalytic theory, the superego is the part of the psyche that includes conscience and an idealized image of oneself. [D.C.A.]

. In psychoanalytic theory, a reaction formation is a mental force that reacts against a desire to satisfy an instinct by creating or strengthening an opposing desire. [D.C.A.]

. In psychoanalytic theory, libido is sexual energy. [D.C.A.]

. *schedule of reinforcement*: the pattern of reinforcement that goes with a given type of behavior. There are two basic patterns: continuous and intermittent. In a *continuous schedule*, every instance of the behavior is reinforced; in an *intermittent schedule*, only some instances are reinforced. [D.C.A.]

. *ad infinitum*: without end. The Latin phrase means, literally, "to the infinite." [D.C.A.]

. *solipsism*: the theory that the self and its states are all that can be known. A solipsist may hold, in addition, that the self is all that exists. [D.C.A.]

. *empiricism*: the theory that experience is the source of all knowledge. The three principal British empiricists were John Locke (1632–1704), George Berkeley

(1685–1753), and David Hume (1711–1776). For more information on Hume, see the introduction to Chapter 8.

phenomenology: the study of *phenomena* (things as they appear to our consciousness). The pioneer of modern phenomenology was the German philosopher Edmund Husserl (1859–1938). [D.C.A.]

23. *qua*: as [D.C.A.]
24. *humanistic psychology*: psychological theories built on the premise that human beings are intrinsically good and have an inner potential for healthy growth. The theories emphasize human values. The chief proponents of humanistic psychology were the American psychologists Carl Rogers (1902–1987) and Abraham Maslow (1908–1970). [D.C.A.]
25. Georges Sorel (1847–1922) was a French social philosopher. [D.C.A.]
26. Martin Buber (1878–1965) was an Israeli (Austrian-born) philosopher. [D.C.A.]
27. *dehomunculize*: to deny the theory that there is a little human being (*homunculus* in Latin) inside a person that causes a person's behavior [D.C.A.]
28. Karl Marx (1818–1883) was a German social philosopher. See the introduction to Chapter 9. [D.C.A.]
29. Friedrich von Schiller (1759–1805) was a German poet, dramatist, and historian. [D.C.A.]
30. A reductionistic theory holds that something of a higher complexity (e.g., an organism) can be fully explained in terms of things of a lower complexity (e.g., chemicals); the higher level can be "reduced" to the lower. [D.C.A.]
31. John Keats (1795–1821) was an English poet. [D.C.A.]

QUESTIONS FOR REFLECTION AND DISCUSSION

1. Can all human behavior be explained without reference to thoughts or feelings?
2. Could mind (a nonphysical entity) have resulted from the evolutionary process?
3. Can the notions of positive and negative reinforcement be explained without reference to feelings of pleasure and pain?
4. Are all our actions completely determined by heredity and environment?
5. Does behaviorism dehumanize human beings?

SUGGESTIONS FOR FURTHER READING

I. Primary Sources

About Behaviorism. 1974; reprint ed., New York: Vintage, 1976, 291 pp.

Beyond Freedom and Dignity. 1971; reprint ed., New York: Bantam and Random House, 1972, 215 pp.

A call for the use of behavioral technology to remedy society's problems. Skinner argues that traditional approaches to social problems fail because they are based on the mistaken assumption that human beings are free. Since behavior is completely determined by heredity and environment, human beings have neither freedom nor dignity.

ience and Human Behavior. New York: Macmillan, 1953, 461 pp.

Skinner gives a detailed explanation of his view that human behavior can be studied and controlled by scientific, behaviorist methods.

alden Two. 1948; reprint ed., New York: Macmillan, 1976, 301 pp.

Skinner's novel about a utopian community run on the principles of operant conditioning. The title alludes to Henry David Thoreau's book *Walden* (1854), in which Thoreau describes his solitary life on the shore of Walden Pond near Concord, Massachusetts.

I. Secondary Sources

arpenter, Finley. *The Skinner Primer: Behind Freedom and Dignity*. New York: Free Press, 1974, 224 pp.

An examination of Skinner's thesis that human beings are not free. Carpenter argues that we are free and that Skinner errs by having a notion of freedom that is too restricted. Chap. 1, pp. 3–35, gives an overview of Skinner's psychology.

vans, Richard I. *B. F. Skinner: The Man and His Ideas*. New York: Dutton, Dialogues with Notable Contributors to Personality Theory Ser., 1968, 140 pp.

Edited transcripts of interviews that Evans conducted with Skinner. Topics include Skinner's assessment of Freud, operant conditioning, and the application of behaviorist principles to our educational system.

ye, Robert D. *What Is B. F. Skinner Really Saying?* Englewood Cliffs, N.J.: Prentice-Hall, 1979, 198 pp.

An accessible and sympathetic introduction that also responds to some common objections to Skinner's views. See chap. 3, "What Are the Basic Concepts of Skinnerian Psychology?" pp. 22–75.

uligandla, Ramakrishna. *Fact and Fiction in B. F. Skinner's Science and Utopia: An Essay on Philosophy of Psychology*. St. Louis: Warren H. Green, 1974, 101 pp.

Puligandla argues that Skinner's behaviorism is not genuine science and that it cannot deal adequately with the question of values. He criticizes Skinner's ideal of basing a society on behaviorist principles.

eigel, John A. *B. F. Skinner*. Boston: Twayne, Twayne's World Leaders Ser. 1977, 125 pp.

Gives a biographical sketch of Skinner and a clear and sympathetic explanation of his basic ideas. Contains a brief exposition of *About Behaviorism* (pp. 97–102).

15

Edward O. Wilson

Edward O. Wilson was born in 1929 in Birmingham, Alabama. As a young boy he was fascinated with nature, and he decided, at age nine, to become an *entomologist* (a scientist who studies insects). Following through on his boyhood resolution, he completed a bachelor's degree in biology at the University of Alabama in 1949. He began doctoral studies in entomology at the University of Tennessee in 1950, but later that year he transferred to Harvard University, which had better resources for studying the insect that interested him most, the ant. He received his doctorate from Harvard in 1955 and began teaching there the following year. In 1976 he was appointed Frank B. Baird Jr. Professor of Science. He has been Curator of Entomology at Harvard's Museum of Comparative Zoology since 1973.

As a graduate student at Harvard, Wilson discovered that the social behavior of ants is governed by message-bearing chemical substances they secrete. His further study of the social behavior of ants and other insects led to the publication of *The Insect Societies* in 1971. Subsequent research indicated the social behavior of *all* animals is biologically based, and Wilson presented his findings in *Sociobiology: The New Synthesis* (1975). The final chapter of this book, which outlines how sociobiological theory applies to the human animal, aroused considerable interest. In 1978 he published a more detailed examination of human sociobiology entitled *On Human Nature*, which won the 1979 Pulitzer Prize for general nonfiction.

Intrigued by the question of how the human mind evolved, Wilson collaborated with physicist Charles J. Lumsden to explore this topic. In 1981 they published *Genes, Mind, and Culture: The Coevolutionary Process*, in which they argue that the mind arose through the interaction of genetic change and cultural history. Three years later, Wilson published *Biophilia*, a discussion of the innate interest human beings have in life and lifelike processes; it was also an appeal to prevent the extinction of species and to preserve natural habitats. In 1990 he and German entomologist Bert Hölldobler published *The Ants*, a comprehensive study of the creature that continues to interest Wilson more

an any other insect. In 1990 Wilson was also named co-winner of the
rafoord Prize, an award given by the Royal Swedish Academy of Sciences to
cholars working in fields not covered by the Nobel prizes.

Our selection is from *On Human Nature*. Since Wilson's arguments in
his book are based on evolutionary biology, a few words of background may
rove helpful. Modern evolutionary theory begins with the work of the
nglish naturalist Charles Darwin (1809–1882), who explained in *The Origin of
pecies* (1859) that various species have certain traits because of natural selec-
on: If an organism develops traits that enable it to adapt to its environment,
 survives; if it *fails* to develop these adaptive traits, it perishes. Darwin was
nable to explain the mechanism through which new traits were acquired and
ansmitted from parents to offspring, but the answer was later provided by
e science of genetics: Changes in an organism's genes cause changes in its
aits, and the new genes (and hence the new traits) are passed on to
ffspring. Organisms with adaptive genetic mutations are more likely to
rvive and reproduce; those with maladaptive mutations are less likely to
 so.

Until recently, evolutionary biology was used mainly to account for the
olution and transmission of physical traits, e.g., eye color. Wilson's innova-
on was to extend the principles of evolutionary biology to behavioral traits,
g., the tendency to avoid incest. The new discipline of sociobiology, as
Vilson states in our selection, is precisely "the systematic study of the
iological basis of all social behavior, in all kinds of organisms, including
an."

Our reading from *On Human Nature* begins with Wilson's description of
vo "spiritual dilemmas" that result from the fact of evolution. First, human
eings, like all other organisms, have no purpose in life other than to survive
nd reproduce; we have no higher calling, "no particular place to go." The
igher goals posited by religion and ideology are no longer tenable, and their
ower to marshal the energy of societies is fading. It is not clear what can
place these goals as mobilizers of societal action. The goals of life must lie
side us, within our biological nature, and this leads to the second dilemma:
'e must choose which of our varied inherited ethical tendencies we should
llow. Although each of our tendencies was adaptive in some way in our
olutionary past (and probably still is adaptive in some ways), these tenden-
es can come into conflict.

After making these introductory comments, Wilson explains the general
rinciples of sociobiology, which state that not only our behavior but our
oral values (including altruism) are genetically based. Wilson admits that
lture has some influence on behavior and values but holds that the ultimate
xplanation is always genetic. As he succinctly puts it: "Biology is the key to
uman nature."

In the final section of our reading, Wilson responds to the two spiritual
ilemmas he raised at the outset. He argues that scientific research will

uncover goals that can mobilize societal action, and he proposes that ethical conflicts be resolved on the basis of a new "biology of ethics" in which the ultimate value is the survival of the human gene pool. Our selection ends with Wilson pointing to a new dilemma that will soon confront us: Once scientists are able to alter the human gene complex, we will have to decide whether and how we wish to alter human nature itself.

ON HUMAN NATURE

CHAPTER 1. DILEMMA

ese are the central questions that the great philosopher David Hume[1] said e of unspeakable importance: How does the mind work, and beyond that hy does it work in such a way and not another, and from these two nsiderations together, what is man's ultimate nature?

We keep returning to the subject with a sense of hesitancy and even ead. For if the brain is a machine of ten billion nerve cells and the mind can mehow be explained as the summed activity of a finite number of chemical d electrical reactions, boundaries limit the human prospect—we are biolog- l and our souls cannot fly free. If humankind evolved by Darwinian tural selection,[2] genetic chance and environmental necessity, not God, ade the species. Deity can still be sought in the origin of the ultimate units matter, in quarks and electron shells (Hans Küng[3] was right to ask atheists hy there is something instead of nothing) but not in the origin of species. owever much we embellish that stark conclusion with metaphor and image- , it remains the philosophical legacy of the last century of scientific re arch.

No way appears around this admittedly unappealing proposition. It is e essential first hypothesis for any serious consideration of the human ndition. Without it the humanities and social sciences are the limited scriptors of surface phenomena, like astronomy without physics, biology ithout chemistry, and mathematics without algebra. With it, human nature n be laid open as an object of fully empirical research, biology can be put to e service of liberal education, and our self-conception can be enormously d truthfully enriched.

But to the extent that the new naturalism[4] is true, its pursuit seems rtain to generate two great spiritual dilemmas. The first is that no species, rs included, possesses a purpose beyond the imperatives created by its genetic history. Species may have vast potential for material and mental progress but they lack any immanent purpose or guidance from agents beyond their immediate environment or even an evolutionary goal toward which their molecular architecture automatically steers them. I believe that the human mind is constructed in a way that locks it inside this fundamental constraint and forces it to make choices with a purely biological instrument. If the brain evolved by natural selection, even the capacities to select particular esthetic judgments and religious beliefs must have arisen by the same mechanistic process. They are either direct adaptations to past environments in which the ancestral human populations evolved or at most constructions thrown up secondarily by deeper, less visible activities that were once adaptive in this stricter, biological sense.

The essence of the argument, then, is that the brain exists because it promotes the survival and multiplication of the genes that direct its assembly. The human mind is a device for survival and reproduction, and reason is just one of its various techniques. Steven Weinberg* has pointed out that physical reality remains so mysterious even to physicists because of the extreme improbability that it was constructed to be understood by the human mind. We can reverse that insight to note with still greater force that the intellect was not constructed to understand atoms or even to understand itself but to promote the survival of human genes. The reflective person knows that his life is in some incomprehensible manner guided through a biological ontogeny, a more or less fixed order of life stages. He senses that with all the drive, wit, love, pride, anger, hope, and anxiety that characterize the species he will in the end be sure only of helping to perpetuate the same cycle. . .

The first dilemma, in a word, is that we have no particular place to go. The species lacks any goal external to its own biological nature. It could be that in the next hundred years humankind will thread the needles of technology and politics, solve the energy and materials crises, avert nuclear war, and control reproduction. The world can at least hope for a stable ecosystem and a well-nourished population. But what then? Educated people everywhere like to believe that beyond material needs lie fulfillment and the realization of individual potential. But what is fulfillment, and to what ends may potential be realized? Traditional religious beliefs have been eroded, not so much by humiliating disproofs of their mythologies as by the growing awareness that beliefs are really enabling mechanisms for survival. Religions, like other human institutions, evolve so as to enhance the persistence and influence of their practitioners. Marxism[5] and other secular religions offer little more than promises of material welfare and a legislated escape from the consequences of human nature. They, too, are energized by the goal of collective self-aggrandizement. The French political observer Alain Peyrefitte

* Steven Weinberg, "The Forces of Nature," *Bulletin of the American Academy of Arts and Sciences* 29 (4): 13–29 (1976) [E.O.W.]

nce said admiringly of Mao Tse-tung[6] that "the Chinese knew the nar-
ssistic joy of loving themselves in him. It is only natural that he should have
ved himself through them."* Thus does ideology bow to its hidden masters
e genes, and the highest impulses seem upon closer examination to be
etamorphosed into biological activity. . . .

Thus the danger implicit in the first dilemma is the rapid dissolution of
anscendental goals toward which societies can organize their energies.
nose goals, the true moral equivalents of war, have faded; they went one by
ne, like mirages, as we drew closer. In order to search for a new morality
ised upon a more truthful definition of man, it is necessary to look inward,
 dissect the machinery of the mind and to retrace its evolutionary history.
ut that effort, I predict, will uncover the second dilemma, which is the
noice that must be made among the ethical premises inherent in man's
ological nature.

At this point let me state in briefest terms the basis of the second
lemma, while I defer its supporting argument to the next chapter: innate
nsors and motivators exist in the brain that deeply and unconsciously affect
ir ethical premises; from these roots, morality evolved as instinct. If that
erception is correct, science may soon be in a position to investigate the very
rigin and meaning of human values, from which all ethical pronouncements
nd much of political practice flow.

Philosophers themselves, most of whom lack an evolutionary perspec-
ve, have not devoted much time to the problem. They examine the precepts
f ethical systems with reference to their consequences and not their origins.
hus John Rawls opens his influential *A Theory of Justice* (1971) with a proposi-
on he regards as beyond dispute: "In a just society the liberties of equal
tizenship are taken as settled; the rights secured by justice are not subject to
olitical bargaining or to the calculus of social interests." Robert Nozick
egins *Anarchy, State, and Utopia* (1974) with an equally firm proposition:
ndividuals have rights, and there are things no person or group may do to
iem (without violating their rights). So strong and far-reaching are these
ghts they raise the question of what, if anything, the state and its officials
iay do." These two premises are somewhat different in content, and they
ad to radically different prescriptions. Rawls would allow rigid social control
 secure as close an approach as possible to the equal distribution of society's
ewards. Nozick sees the ideal society as one governed by a minimal state,
npowered only to protect its citizens from force and fraud, and with un-
qual distribution of rewards wholly permissible. Rawls rejects the meri-
cracy; Nozick accepts it as desirable except in those cases where local
ommunities voluntarily decide to experiment with egalitarianism. Like

Alain Peyrefitte, *The Chinese: Portrait of a People*, translated from the French by Graham Webb
obbs-Merrill, New York, 1977) [E.O.W.]

everyone else, philosophers measure their personal emotional responses to
various alternatives as though consulting a hidden oracle.

That oracle resides in the deep emotional centers of the brain, most
probably within the limbic system, a complex array of neurons and hormone-
secreting cells located just beneath the "thinking" portion of the cerebral
cortex. Human emotional responses and the more general ethical practices
based on them have been programmed to a substantial degree by natural
selection over thousands of generations. The challenge to science is to measure the tightness of the constraints caused by the programming, to find their
source in the brain, and to decode their significance through the reconstruction of the evolutionary history of the mind. This enterprise will be the logical
complement of the continued study of cultural evolution.

Success will generate the second dilemma, which can be stated as
follows: Which of the censors and motivators should be obeyed and which
ones might better be curtailed or sublimated? These guides are the very core
of our humanity. They and not the belief in spiritual apartness distinguish us
from electronic computers. At some time in the future we will have to decide
how human we wish to remain—in this ultimate, biological sense—because
we must consciously choose among the alternative emotional guides we have
inherited. To chart our destiny means that we must shift from automatic
control based on our biological properties to precise steering based on biological knowledge.

Because the guides of human nature must be examined with a compli
cated arrangement of mirrors, they are a deceptive subject, always the philos
opher's deadfall. The only way forward is to study human nature as part of
the natural sciences, in an attempt to integrate the natural sciences with the
social sciences and humanities. I can conceive of no ideological or formalistic
shortcut. Neurobiology cannot be learned at the feet of a guru. The conse
quences of genetic history cannot be chosen by legislatures. Above all, for our
own physical well-being if nothing else, ethical philosophy must not be left in
the hands of the merely wise. Although human progress can be achieved by
intuition and force of will, only hard-won empirical knowledge of our biolog
ical nature will allow us to make optimum choices among the competing
criteria of progress.. . .

It is all too easy to be seduced by the . . . view that science is competent
to generate only a few classes of information, that its cold, clear Apollonian
method will never be relevant to the full Dionysian life of the mind,[7] that
single-minded devotion to science is dehumanizing. Expressing the mood of
the counterculture, Theodore Roszak suggested a map of the mind "as a
spectrum of possibilities, all of which properly blend into one another . . . At
one end, we have the hard, bright lights of science; here we find information
In the center we have the sensuous hues of art; here we find the aesthetic
shape of the world. At the far end, we have the dark, shadowy tones of

ligious experience, shading off into wave lengths beyond all perception;
ere we find meaning."*

No, here we find obscurantism! And a curious underestimate of what
e mind can accomplish. The sensuous hues and dark tones have been
roduced by the genetic evolution of our nervous and sensory tissues; to treat
em as other than objects of biological inquiry is simply to aim too low.

The heart of the scientific method is the reduction of perceived phe-
omena to fundamental, testable principles. The elegance, we can fairly say
e beauty, of any particular scientific generalization is measured by its
mplicity relative to the number of phenomena it can explain. Ernst Mach,[8] a
hysicist and forerunner of the logical positivists, captured the idea with a
efinition: "Science may be regarded as a minimal problem consisting of the
ompletest presentation of facts with the least possible expenditure of
ought."†

Although Mach's perception has an undeniable charm, raw reduction is
nly half of the scientific process. The remainder consists of the reconstruc-
on of complexity by an expanding synthesis under the control of laws newly
emonstrated by analysis. This reconstruction reveals the existence of novel,
nergent phenomena. When the observer shifts his attention from one level
f organization to the next, as from physics to chemistry or from chemistry to
iology, he expects to find obedience to all the laws of the levels below. But to
constitute the upper levels of organization requires specifying the arrange-
ent of the lower units and this in turn generates richness and the basis of
ew and unexpected principles. . . .

Reduction is the traditional instrument of scientific analysis, but it is
ared and resented. If human behavior can be reduced and determined to
ny considerable degree by the laws of biology, then mankind might appear
 be less than unique and to that extent dehumanized. Few social scientists
nd scholars in the humanities are prepared to enter such a conspiracy, let
one surrender any of their territory. But this perception, which equates the
ethod of reduction with the philosophy of diminution, is entirely in error.
he laws of a subject are necessary to the discipline above it, they challenge
nd force a mentally more efficient restructuring, but they are not sufficient
r the purposes of the discipline. Biology is the key to human nature, and
cial scientists cannot afford to ignore its rapidly tightening principles. But
e social sciences are potentially far richer in content. Eventually they will
sorb the relevant ideas of biology and go on to beggar them. The proper
udy of man is, for reasons that now transcend anthropocentrism, man.

Theodore Roszak, "The Monster and the Titan: Science, Knowledge, and Gnosis," *Daedalus* 103
): 17–32 (1974) [E.O.W.]

Ernst Mach, *The Science of Mechanics*, ninth edition (Open Court, La Salle, Illinois, 1942) [E.O.W.]

CHAPTER 2. HEREDITY

We live on a planet of staggering organic diversity. Since Carolus Linnaeus began the process of formal classification in 1758, zoologists have catalogued about one million species of animals and given each a scientific name, a few paragraphs in a technical journal, and a small space on the shelves of one museum or another around the world. Yet despite this prodigious effort, the process of discovery has hardly begun. In 1976 a specimen of an unknown form of giant shark, fourteen feet long and weighing sixteen hundred pounds, was captured when it tried to swallow the stabilizing anchor of a United States Naval vessel near Hawaii. About the same time entomologists found an entirely new category of parasitic flies that resemble large reddish spiders and live exclusively in the nests of the native bats of New Zealand. Each year museum curators sort out thousands of new kinds of insects, copepods, wireworms, echinoderms, priapulids, pauropods, hypermastigotes, and other creatures collected on expeditions around the world. Projections based on intensive surveys of selected habitats indicate that the total number of animal species is between three and ten million. Biology, as the naturalist Howard Evans expressed it in the title of a recent book, is the study of life "on a little known planet."*

Thousands of these species are highly social. The most advanced among them constitute what I have called the three pinnacles of social evolution in animals: the corals, bryozoans, and other colony-forming invertebrates; the social insects, including ants, wasps, bees, and termites; and the social fish, birds, and mammals. The communal being of the three pinnacles are among the principal objects of the new discipline of sociobiology, defined as the systematic study of the biological basis of all forms of social behavior, in all kinds of organisms, including man. . . .

Sociobiology is a subject based largely on comparisons of social species. Each living form can be viewed as an evolutionary experiment, a product of millions of years of interaction between genes and environment. By examining many such experiments closely, we have begun to construct and test the first general principles of genetic social evolution. It is now within our reach to apply this broad knowledge to the study of human beings.

Sociobiologists consider man as though seen through the front end of a telescope, at a greater than usual distance and temporarily diminished in size, in order to view him simultaneously with an array of other social experiments. They attempt to place humankind in its proper place in a catalog of the social species on Earth. They agree with Rousseau[10] that "One needs to look

* Howard E. Evans, *Life on a Little-Known Planet* (Dutton, New York, 1968) [E.O.W.]

ar at hand in order to study men, but to study man one must look from ar."*

This macroscopic view has certain advantages over the traditional anthropocentrism of the social sciences. In fact, no intellectual vice is more crippling than defiantly self-indulgent anthropocentrism. I am reminded of the clever way Robert Nozick makes this point when he constructs an argument in favor of vegetarianism. Human beings, he notes, justify the eating of meat on the grounds that the animals we kill are too far below us in sensitivity and intelligence to bear comparison. It follows that if representatives of a truly superior extraterrestrial species were to visit Earth and apply the same criterion, they could proceed to eat us in good conscience. By the same token, scientists among these aliens might find human beings uninteresting, our intelligence weak, our passions unsurprising, our social organization of a kind already frequently encountered on other planets. To our chagrin they might then focus on the ants, because these little creatures, with their haplodiploid form of sex determination[11] and bizarre female caste system, are the truly novel productions of the Earth with reference to the Galaxy. We can imagine the log declaring, "A scientific breakthrough has occurred; we have finally discovered haplodiploid social organisms in the one- to ten-millimeter range." Then the visitors might inflict the ultimate indignity: in order to be sure they had not underestimated us, they would simulate human beings in the laboratory. Like chemists testing the structural characterization of a problematic organic compound by assembling it from simpler components, the alien biologists would need to synthesize a hominoid or two.

This scenario from science fiction has implications for the definition of man. The impressive recent advances by computer scientists in the design of artificial intelligence suggests the following test of humanity: that which behaves like man *is* man. Human behavior is something that can be defined with fair precision, because the evolutionary pathways open to it have not all been equally negotiable. Evolution has not made culture all-powerful. It is a misconception among many of the more traditional Marxists, some learning theorists, and a still surprising proportion of anthropologists and sociologists that social behavior can be shaped into virtually any form. Ultra-environmentalists start with the premise that man is the creation of his own culture: "culture makes man," the formula might go, "makes culture makes man." Theirs is only a half truth. Each person is molded by an interaction of his environment, especially his cultural environment, with the genes that affect social behavior. Although the hundreds of the world's cultures seem enormously variable to those of us who stand in their midst, all versions of human social behavior together form only a tiny fraction of the realized organizations

___
J. J. Rousseau, *Essai sur l'origine des langues*, Oeuvres Posthumes, Vol. 2 (London, 1783); quoted by Claude Lévi-Strauss in *La Pensée Sauvage* (Plon, Paris, 1964) [E.O.W.]

of social species on this planet and a still smaller fraction of those that can be readily imagined with the aid of sociobiological theory.

The question of interest is no longer whether human social behavior is genetically determined; it is to what extent. The accumulated evidence for a large hereditary component is more detailed and compelling than most persons, including even geneticists, realize. I will go further: it already is decisive.

That being said, let me provide an exact definition of a genetically determined trait. It is a trait that differs from other traits at least in part as a result of the presence of one or more distinctive genes. The important point is that the objective estimate of genetic influence requires comparison of two or more states of the same feature. To say that blue eyes are inherited is not meaningful without further qualification, because blue eyes are the product of an interaction between genes and the largely physiological environment that brought final coloration to the irises. But to say that the *difference* between blue and brown eyes is based wholly or partly on differences in genes is a meaningful statement because it can be tested and translated into the laws of genetics. . . .

Human social behavior can be evaluated . . . first by comparison with the behavior of other species and then, with far greater difficulty and ambiguity, by studies of variation among and within human populations. The picture of genetic determinism emerges most sharply when we compare selected major categories of animals with the human species. Certain general human traits are shared with a majority of the great apes and monkeys of Africa and Asia, which on grounds of anatomy and biochemistry are our closest living evolutionary relatives:

- Our intimate social groupings contain on the order of ten to one hundred adults, never just two, as in most birds and marmosets, or up to thousands, as in many kinds of fishes and insects.
- Males are larger than females. This is a characteristic of considerable significance within the Old World monkeys and apes and many other kinds of mammals. The average number of females consorting with successful males closely corresponds to the size gap between males and females when many species are considered together. The rule makes sense: the greater the competition among males for females, the greater the advantage of large size and the less influential are any disadvantages accruing to bigness. Men are not very much larger than women; we are similar to chimpanzees in this regard. When the sexual size difference in human beings is plotted on the curve based on other kinds of mammals, the predicted average number of females per successful male turns out to be greater than one but less than three. The prediction is close to reality; we know we are a mildly polygynous species.

The young are molded by a long period of social training, first by closest associations with the mother, then to an increasing degree with other children of the same age and sex.
Social play is a strongly developed activity featuring role practice, mock aggression, sex practice, and exploration.

These and other properties together identify the taxonomic group consisting of Old World monkeys, the great apes, and human beings. It is inconceivable that human beings could be socialized into the radically different repertories of other groups such as fishes, birds, antelopes, or rodents. Human beings might self-consciously *imitate* such arrangements, but it would be a fiction played out on a stage, would run counter to deep emotional responses and have no chance of persisting through as much as a single generation. To adopt with serious intent, even in broad outline, the social system of a nonprimate species would be insanity in the literal sense. Personalities would quickly dissolve, relationships disintegrate, and reproduction cease. . . .

Chimpanzees are close enough to ourselves in the details of their social life and mental properties to rank as nearly human in certain domains where it was once considered inappropriate to make comparisons at all. These facts are in accord with the hypothesis that human social behavior rests on a genetic foundation—that human behavior is, to be more precise, organized by some genes that are shared with closely related species and others that are unique to the human species. The same facts are unfavorable for the competing hypothesis which has dominated the social sciences for generations, that mankind has escaped its own genes to the extent of being entirely culture-bound.

Let us pursue this matter systematically. The heart of the genetic hypothesis is the proposition, derived in a straight line from neo-Darwinian evolutionary theory, that the traits of human nature were adaptive during the time that the human species evolved and that genes consequently spread through the population that predisposed their carriers to develop those traits. Adaptiveness means simply that if an individual displayed the traits he stood a greater chance of having his genes represented in the next generation than if he did not display the traits. The differential advantage among individuals in this strictest sense is called genetic fitness. There are three basic components of genetic fitness: increased personal survival, increased personal reproduction, and the enhanced survival and reproduction of close relatives who share the same genes by common descent. An improvement in any one of the factors or in any combination of them results in greater genetic fitness. The process, which Darwin called natural selection, describes a tight circle of causation. If the possession of certain genes predisposes individuals toward a particular trait, say a certain kind of social response, and the trait in turn conveys superior fitness, the genes will gain an increased representation in the next generation. If natural selection is continued over many generations, the favored genes will spread throughout the population, and the trait will become characteristic of the species. In this way human nature is postulated by many sociobiologists, anthropologists, and others to have been shaped by natural selection. . . .

To illustrate the [sociobiological] method [of explaining human behavior], let me present [an example]:

Incest taboos are among the universals of human social behavior. The avoidance of sexual intercourse between brothers and sisters and between parents and their offspring is everywhere achieved by cultural sanctions. But at least in the case of the brother-sister taboo, there exists a far deeper, less rational form of enforcement: a sexual aversion automatically develops between persons who have lived together when one or all grew to the age of six. Studies in Israeli kibbutzim,[12] the most thorough of which was conducted by Joseph Shepher of the University of Haifa, have shown that the aversion among people of the same age is not dependent on an actual blood relationship. Among 2,769 marriages recorded, none was between members of the same kibbutz peer group who had been together since birth. There was not even a single recorded instance of heterosexual activity, despite the fact that the kibbutzim adults were not opposed to it.* Where incest of any form does occur at low frequencies in less closed societies, it is ordinarily a source of shame and recrimination. In general, mother-son-intercourse is the most offensive, brother-sister intercourse somewhat less and father-daughter intercourse the least offensive. But all forms are usually proscribed. In the United States at the present time, one of the forms of pornography considered most shocking is the depiction of intercourse between fathers and their immature daughters.

What advantage do the incest taboos confer? A favored explanation among anthropologists is that the taboos preserve the integrity of the family by avoiding the confusion in roles that would result from incestuous sex. Another, originated by Edward Tylor and built into a whole anthropological theory by Claude Lévi-Strauss in his seminal *Les Structures Élémentaires de la Parenté*, is that it facilitates the exchange of women during bargaining between social groups. Sisters and daughters, in this view, are not used for mating but to gain power.

In contrast, the prevailing sociobiological explanation regards family integration and bridal bargaining as by-products or at most as secondary contributing factors. It identifies a deeper, more urgent cause, the heavy physiological penalty imposed by inbreeding. Several studies by human

---

* Joseph Shepher, "Mate Selection among Second-Generation Kibbutz Adolescents and Adults: Incest Avoidance and Negative Imprinting," *Archives of Sexual Behavior* 1 (4): 293–307 (1971). [E.O.W.]

eneticists have demonstrated that even a moderate amount of inbreeding
sults in children who are diminished in overall body size, muscular coordi-
ation, and academic performance. More than one hundred recessive genes
ave been discovered that cause hereditary disease in the undiluted, homo-
gous[13] state, a condition vastly enhanced by inbreeding. One analysis of
merican and French populations produced the estimate that each person
rries an average of four lethal gene equivalents: either four genes that cause
eath outright when in the homozygous state, eight genes that cause death in
fty percent of homozygotes, or other, arithmetically equivalent combina-
ons of lethal and debilitating effects. These high numbers, which are typical
f animal species, mean that inbreeding carries a deadly risk. Among 161
ildren born to Czechoslovakian women who had sexual relations with their
thers, brothers, or sons, fifteen were stillborn or died within the first year of
fe, and more than 40 percent suffered from various physical and mental
efects, including severe mental retardation, dwarfism, heart and brain de-
rmities, deaf-mutism, enlargement of the colon, and urinary-tract abnor-
alities. In contrast, a group of ninety-five children born to the same women
rough nonincestuous relations were on the average as normal as the popu-
tion at large. Five died during the first year of life, none had serious mental
eficiencies, and only five others had apparent physical abnormalities.

The manifestations of inbreeding pathology constitute natural selection
 an intense and unambiguous form. The elementary theory of population
enetics predicts that any behavioral tendency to avoid incest, however slight
 devious, would long ago have spread through human populations. So
owerful is the advantage of outbreeding that it can be expected to have
rried cultural evolution along with it. Family integrity and leverage during
olitical bargaining may indeed be felicitous results of outbreeding, but they
e more likely to be devices of convenience, secondary cultural adaptations
at made use of the inevitability of outbreeding for direct biological reasons.

Of the thousands of societies that have existed through human history,
nly several of the most recent have possessed any knowledge of genetics.
ery few opportunities presented themselves to make rational calculations of
e destructive effects of inbreeding. Tribal councils do not compute gene
equencies and mutational loads. The automatic exclusion of sexual bonding
etween individuals who have previously formed certain other kinds of
lationships—the "gut feeling" that promotes the ritual sanctions against
cest—is largely unconscious and irrational. Bond exclusion of the kind
isplayed by the Israeli children is an example of what biologists call a
roximate (near) cause; in this instance, the direct psychological exclusion is
e proximate cause of the incest taboo. The ultimate cause suggested by the
iological hypothesis is the loss of genetic fitness that results from incest. It is
 fact that incestuously produced children leave fewer descendants. The
iological hypothesis states that individuals with a genetic predisposition for
ond exclusion and incest avoidance contribute more genes to the next

generation. Natural selection has probably ground away along these lines for thousands of generations, and for that reason human beings intuitively avoid incest through the simple, automatic rule of bond exclusion. To put the idea in its starkest form, one that acknowledges but temporarily bypasses the intervening developmental process, human beings are guided by an instinct based on genes. Such a process is indicated in the case of brother-sister intercourse, and it is a strong possibility in the other categories of incest taboo. . . .

CHAPTER 7. ALTRUISM

"The blood of martyrs is the seed of the church." With that chilling dictum the third-century theologian Tertullian[14] confessed the fundamental flaw of human altruism, an intimation that the purpose of sacrifice is to raise one human group over another. Generosity without hope of reciprocation is the rarest and most cherished of human behaviors, subtle and difficult to define, distributed in a highly selective pattern, surrounded by ritual and circumstance, and honored by medallions and emotional orations. We sanctify true altruism in order to reward it and thus to make it less than true, and by that means to promote its recurrence in others. Human altruism, in short, is riddled to its foundations with the expected mammalian ambivalence.

As mammals would be and ants would not, we are fascinated by the extreme forms of self-sacrifice. In the First and Second World Wars, Korea, and Vietnam, a large percentage of Congressional Medals of Honor were awarded to men who threw themselves on top of grenades to shield comrades, aided the rescue of others from battle sites at the cost of certain death to themselves, or made other extraordinary decisions that led to the same fatal end. Such altruistic suicide is the ultimate act of courage and emphatically deserves the country's highest honor. But it is still a great puzzle. What could possibly go on in the minds of these men in the moment of desperation? "Personal vanity and pride are always important factors in situations of this kind," James Jones wrote in WWII,

> and the sheer excitement of battle can often lead a man to death willingly, where without it he might have balked. But in the absolute, ultimate end, when your final extinction is right there only a few yards farther on staring back at you, there may be a sort of penultimate national, and social, and even racial, masochism—a sort of hotly joyous, almost-sexual enjoyment and acceptance—which keeps you going the last few steps. The ultimate luxury of just *not giving a damn* any more.*

The annihilating mixture of reason and passion, which has been described often in first-hand accounts of the battlefield, is only the extreme

* James Jones, WWII (Ballantine Books, New York, 1976) [E.O.W.]

henomenon that lies beyond the innumerable smaller impulses of courage
id generosity that bind societies together. One is tempted to leave the
atter there, to accept the purest elements of altruism as simply the better
de of human nature. Perhaps, to put the best possible construction on the
atter, conscious altruism is a transcendental quality that distinguishes
iman beings from animals. But scientists are not accustomed to declaring
iy phenomenon off limits, and it is precisely through the deeper analysis of
truism that sociobiology seems best prepared at this time to make a novel
mtribution.

I doubt if any higher animal, such as an eagle or a lion, has ever
eserved a Congressional Medal of Honor by the ennobling criteria used in
ir society. Yet minor altruism does occur frequently, in forms instantly
nderstandable in human terms, and is bestowed not just on offspring but on
:her members of the species as well. Certain small birds, robins, thrushes
id titmice, for example, warn others of the approach of a hawk. They crouch
w and emit a distinctive thin, reedy whistle. Although the warning call has
:oustic properties that make its source difficult to locate in space, to whistle
all seems at the very least unselfish; the caller would be wiser not to betray
s presence but rather to remain silent.

Other than man, chimpanzees may be the most altruistic of all mam-
als. In addition to sharing meat after their cooperative hunts, they also
ractice adoption. Jane Goodall[15] has observed three cases at the Gombe
tream National Park in Tanzania, all involving orphaned infants taken over
y adult brothers and sisters. It is of considerable interest, for more theoretical
:asons to be discussed shortly, that the altruistic behavior was displayed by
ie closest possible relatives rather than by experienced females with children
f their own, females who might have supplied the orphans with milk and
iore adequate social protection.

In spite of a fair abundance of such examples among vertebrates, it is only
i the lower animals, and in the social insects particularly, that we encounter
truistic suicide comparable to man's. Many members of ant, bee, and wasp
)lonies are ready to defend their nests with insane charges against intruders.
his is the reason that people move with circumspection around honeybee
ives and yellow-jacket burrows, but can afford to relax near the nests of
)litary species such as sweat bees and mud daubers.

The social stingless bees of the tropics swarm over the heads of human
eings who venture too close and lock their jaws so tightly onto tufts of hair
iat their bodies are pulled loose from their heads when they are combed out.
ome species pour a burning glandular secretion onto the skin during these
icrificial attacks. In Brazil, they are called *cagafogos* ("fire defecators"). The
reat entomologist William Morton Wheeler[16] described an encounter with
ie "terrible bees," during which they removed patches of skin from his face,
s the worst experience of his life.

Honeybee workers have stings lined with reversed barbs like those on fishhooks. When a bee attacks an intruder at the hive, the sting catches in the skin; as the bee moves away, the sting remains embedded, pulling out the entire venom gland and much of the viscera with it. The bee soon dies, but its attack has been more effective than if it withdrew the sting intact. The reason is that the venom gland continues to leak poison into the wound, while a bananalike odor emanating from the base of the sting incites other members of the hive to launch kamikaze attacks of their own at the same spot. From the point of view of the colony as a whole, the suicide of an individual accomplishes more than it loses. The total worker force consists of twenty thousand to eighty thousand members, all sisters born from eggs laid by the mother queen. Each bee has a natural life span of only about fifty days, after which it dies of old age. So to give a life is only a little thing, with no genes being spilled.

My favorite example among the social insects is provided by an African termite with the orotund technical name *Globitermes sulfureus*. Members of this species' soldier caste are quite literally walking bombs. Huge paired glands extend from their heads back through most of their bodies. When they attack ants and other enemies, they eject a yellow glandular secretion through their mouths; it congeals in the air and often fatally entangles both the soldiers and their antagonists. The spray appears to be powered by contractions of the muscles in the abdominal wall. Sometimes the contractions become so violent that the abdomen and gland explode, spraying the defensive fluid in all directions.

Sharing the capacity for extreme sacrifice does not mean that the human mind and the "mind" of an insect (if such exists) work alike. But it does mean that the impulse need not be ruled divine or otherwise transcendental, and we are justified in seeking a more conventional biological explanation. A basic problem immediately arises in connection with such an explanation: fallen heroes do not have children. If self-sacrifice results in fewer descendants, the genes that allow heroes to be created can be expected to disappear gradually from the population. A narrow interpretation of Darwinian natural selection would predict this outcome: because people governed by selfish genes must prevail over those with altruistic genes, there should also be a tendency over many generations for selfish genes to increase in prevalence and for a population to become ever less capable of responding altruistically.

How then does altruism persist? In the case of social insects, there is no doubt at all. Natural selection has been broadened to include kin selection. The self-sacrificing termite soldier protects the rest of its colony, including the queen and king, its parents. As a result, the soldier's more fertile brothers and sisters flourish, and through them the altruistic genes are multiplied by a greater production of nephews and nieces.

It is natural, then, to ask whether through kin selection the capacity for altruism has also evolved in human beings. In other words, do the emotions we feel, which in exceptional individuals may climax in total self-sacrifice,

em ultimately from hereditary units that were implanted by the favoring of
latives during a period of hundreds or thousands of generations? This
xplanation gains some strength from the circumstance that during most of
ankind's history the predominant social unit was the immediate family and
tight network of other close relatives. Such exceptional cohesion, combined
ith detailed kin classifications made possible by high intelligence, might
xplain why kin selection has been more forceful in human beings than in
onkeys and other mammals.

To anticipate a common objection raised by many social scientists and
thers, let me grant at once that the form and intensity of altruistic acts are to
large extent culturally determined. Human social evolution is obviously
ore cultural than genetic. The point is that the underlying emotion, power-
lly manifested in virtually all human societies, is what is considered to
volve through genes. The sociobiological hypothesis does not therefore
ccount for differences among societies, but it can explain why human beings
iffer from other mammals and why, in one narrow aspect, they more closely
esemble social insects.

The evolutionary theory of human altruism is greatly complicated by the
ltimately self-serving quality of most forms of that altruism. No sustained
rm of human altruism is explicitly and totally self-annihilating. Lives of the
ost towering heroism are paid out in the expectation of great reward, not
e least of which is a belief in personal immortality. When poets speak of
appy acquiescence in death they do not mean death at all but apotheosis, or
irvana. . . . Near the end of *Pilgrim's Progress*[17] we learn of the approaching
eath of Valiant-for-Truth:

> Then said he, "I am going to my fathers, and though with great difficulty I
> am got hither, yet now I do not repent me of all the trouble I have been at to
> arrive where I am. My sword, I gave to him that shall succeed me in my pil-
> grimage, and my courage and skill, to him that can get it. My marks and my
> scars I carry with me, to be a witness for me that I have fought his battles
> who now will be my rewarder."

aliant-for-Truth then utters his last words, *Grave where is thy victory?*, and
eparts as his friends hear trumpets sounded for him on the other side.

Compassion is selective and often ultimately self-serving. Hinduism
ermits lavish preoccupation with the self and close relatives but does not
ncourage compassion for unrelated individuals or, least of all, outcastes. A
ntral goal of Nibbanic Buddhism is preserving the individual through al-
uism. The devotee earns points toward a better personal life by performing
enerous acts and offsets bad acts with meritorious ones. While embracing
e concept of universal compassion, both Buddhist and Christian countries
ave found it expedient to wage aggressive wars, many of which they justify
the name of religion.

Compassion is flexible and eminently adaptable to political reality; that
to say it conforms to the best interests of self, family, and allies of the

moment. The Palestinian refugees have received the sympathy of the world and have been the beneficiaries of rage among the Arab nations. But little is said about the Arabs killed by King Hussein or those who live in Arab countries with fewer civil rights and under far worse material conditions than the displaced people of the West Bank. When Bangladesh began its move toward independence in 1971, the President of Pakistan unleashed the Punjab army in a campaign of terror that ultimately cost the lives of a million Bengalis and drove 9.8 million others into exile. In this war more Moslem people were killed or driven from their homes than make up the entire population of Syria and Jordan. Yet not a single Arab state, conservative or radical, supported the Bangladesh struggle for independence. Most denounced the Bengalis while proclaiming Islamic solidarity with West Pakistan.

To understand this strange selectivity and resolve the puzzle of human altruism we must distinguish two basic forms of cooperative behavior. The altruistic impulse can be irrational and unilaterally directed at others; the bestower expresses no desire for equal return and performs no unconscious actions leading to the same end. I have called this form of behavior "hard-core" altruism, a set of responses relatively unaffected by social reward or punishment beyond childhood. Where such behavior exists, it is likely to have evolved through kin selection or natural selection operating on entire, competing family or tribal units. We would expect hard-core altruism to serve the altruist's closest relatives and to decline steeply in frequency and intensity as relationship becomes more distant. "Soft-core" altruism, in contrast, is ultimately selfish. The "altruist" expects reciprocation from society for himself or his closest relatives. His good behavior is calculating, often in a wholly conscious way, and his maneuvers are orchestrated by the excruciatingly intricate sanctions and demands of society. The capacity for soft-core altruism can be expected to have evolved primarily by selection of individuals and to be deeply influenced by the vagaries of cultural evolution. Its psychological vehicles are lying, pretense, and deceit, including self-deceit, because the actor is most convincing who believes that his performance is real.

A key question of social theory, then, must be the relative amounts of hard-core as opposed to soft-core altruism. In honeybees and termites, the issue has already been settled: kin selection is paramount, and altruism is virtually all hard-core. There are no hypocrites among the social insects. This tendency also prevails among the higher animals. It is true that a small amount of reciprocation is practiced by monkeys and apes. When male anubis baboons struggle for dominance, they sometimes solicit one another's aid. A male stands next to an enemy and a friend and swivels his gaze back and forth between the two while continuously threatening the enemy. Baboons allied in this manner are able to exclude solitary males during competition for estrous females. Despite the obvious advantages of such arrangements, however, coalitions are the rare exception in baboons and other intelligent animals.

But in human beings soft-core altruism has been carried to elaborate

xtremes. Reciprocation among distantly related or unrelated individuals is
ae key to human society. The perfection of the social contract has broken the
ncient vertebrate constraints imposed by rigid kin selection. Through the
onvention of reciprocation, combined with a flexible, endlessly productive
nguage and a genius for verbal classification, human beings fashion long-
emembered agreements upon which cultures and civilizations can be built.

Yet the question remains: Is there a foundation of hard-core altruism
eneath all of this contractual superstructure? The conception is reminiscent
f David Hume's striking conjecture that reason is the slave of the passions.
o we ask, to what biological end are the contracts made, and just how
:ubborn is nepotism?

The distinction is important because pure, hard-core altruism based on
in selection is the enemy of civilization. If human beings are to a large extent
uided by programmed learning rules and canalized emotional development
o favor their own relatives and tribe, only a limited amount of global har-
nony is possible. International cooperation will approach an upper limit,
·om which it will be knocked down by the perturbations of war and eco-
omic struggle, canceling each upward surge based on pure reason. The
nperatives of blood and territory will be the passions to which reason is
lave. One can imagine genius continuing to serve biological ends even after
· has disclosed and fully explained the evolutionary roots of unreason.

My own estimate of the relative proportions of hard-core and soft-core
ltruism in human behavior is optimistic. Human beings appear to be suffi-
iently selfish and calculating to be capable of indefinitely greater harmony
nd social homeostasis. This statement is not self-contradictory. True self-
shness, if obedient to the other constraints of mammalian biology, is the key
o a more nearly perfect social contract . . .

Malcolm Muggeridge[18] once asked me, What about Mother Theresa?
low can biology account for the living saints among us? Mother Theresa, a
aember of the Missionaries of Charity, cares for the desperately poor of
alcutta; she gathers the dying from the sidewalks, rescues abandoned babies
:rom garbage dumps, attends the wounds and diseases of people no one else
vill touch. Despite international recognition and rich awards, Mother
'heresa lives a life of total poverty and grinding hard work. In *Something
;eautiful for God*, Muggeridge wrote of his feelings after observing her closely
n Calcutta: "Each day Mother Theresa meets Jesus; first at the Mass, whence
he derives sustenance and strength; then in each needing, suffering soul she
ees and tends. They are one and the same Jesus; at the altar and in the
treets. Neither exists without the other."*

Can culture alter human behavior to approach altruistic perfection?
Aight it be possible to touch some magical talisman or design a Skinnerian
echnology[19] that creates a race of saints? The answer is no. In sobering

Malcolm Muggeridge, *Something Beautiful for God* (Harper & Row, New York, 1971) [E.O.W.]

reflection, let us recall the words of Mark's Jesus: "Go forth to every part of the world, and proclaim the Good News to the whole creation. Those who believe it and receive baptism will find salvation; those who do not believe will be condemned."* There lies the fountainhead of religious altruism. Virtually identical formulations, equally pure in tone and perfect with respect to ingroup altruism, have been urged by the seers of every major religion, not omitting Marxism-Leninism.[20] All have contended for supremacy over others. Mother Theresa is an extraordinary person but it should not be forgotten that she is secure in the service of Christ and the knowledge of her Church's immortality. Lenin, who preached a no less utopian, if rival, covenant, called Christianity unutterably vile and a contagion of the most abominable kind; that compliment has been returned many times by Christian theologians.

"If only it were all so simple!," Aleksandr Solzhenitsyn wrote in *The Gulag Archipelago*. "If only there were evil people somewhere insidiously committing evil deeds, and it were necessary only to separate them from the rest of us and destroy them. But the line dividing good and evil cuts through the heart of every human being. And who is willing to destroy a piece of his own heart?"†

Sainthood is not so much the hypertrophy[21] of human altruism as its ossification. It is cheerfully subordinate to the biological imperatives above which it is supposed to rise. The true humanization of altruism, in the sense of adding wisdom and insight to the social contract, can come only through a deeper scientific examination of morality. Lawrence Kohlberg, an educational psychologist, has traced what he believes to be six sequential stages of ethical reasoning through which each person progresses as part of his normal mental development. The child moves from an unquestioning dependence on external rules and controls to an increasingly sophisticated set of internalized standards, as follows: (1) simple obedience to rules and authority to avoid punishment, (2) conformity to group behavior to obtain rewards and exchange favors, (3) good-boy orientation, conformity to avoid dislike and rejection by others, (4) duty orientation, conformity to avoid censure by authority, disruption of order, and resulting guilt, (5) legalistic orientation, recognition of the value of contracts, some arbitrariness in rule formation to maintain the common good, (6) conscience or principle orientation, primary allegiance to principles of choice, which can overrule law in cases the law is judged to do more harm than good.‡

The stages were based on children's verbal responses, as elicited by questions about moral problems. Depending on intelligence and training,

---

* Jesus to the Apostles, Mark 16:15–16 [E.O.W.]
† Aleksandr I. Solzhenitsyn, *The Gulag Archipelago 1918–1956*, Vols. 1 and 2, translated by Thomas P. Whitney (Harper & Row, New York, 1973) [E.O.W.]
‡ Lawrence Kohlberg, "Stage and Sequence: The Cognitive Developmental Approach to Socialization," in D. A. Goslin, ed., *Handbook of Socialization Theory and Research* (Rand-McNally Co., Chicago, 1969), pp. 347–380 [E.O.W.]

.dividuals can stop at any rung on the ladder. Most attain stages four or five.
y stage four they are at approximately the level of morality reached by
aboon and chimpanzee troops. At stage five, when the ethical reference
:comes partly contractual and legalistic, they incorporate the morality on
hich I believe most of human social evolution has been based. To the extent
.at this interpretation is correct, the ontogeny of moral development is likely
• have been genetically assimilated and is now part of the automatically
uided process of mental development. Individuals are steered by learning
.les and relatively inflexible emotional responses to progress through stage
ve. Some are diverted by extraordinary events at critical junctures. So-
opaths do exist. But the great majority of people reach stages four or five
nd are thus prepared to exist harmoniously—in Pleistocene hunter-gatherer
amps.

Since we no longer live as small bands of hunter-gatherers, stage six is
ie most nearly nonbiological and hence susceptible to the greatest amount of
ypertrophy. The individual selects principles against which the group and
ie law are judged. Precepts chosen by intuition based on emotion are
rimarily biological in origin and are likely to do no more than reinforce the
rimitive social arrangements. Such a morality is unconsciously shaped to
ive new rationalizations for the consecration of the group, the proselytizing
ole of altruism, and the defense of territory.

But to the extent that principles are chosen by knowledge and reason
:mote from biology, they can at least in theory be non-Darwinian. This leads
s ineluctably back to the second great spiritual dilemma. The philosophical
uestion of interest that it generates is the following: Can the cultural evolu-
on of higher ethical values gain a direction and momentum of its own and
ompletely replace genetic evolution? I think not. The genes hold culture on a
ash. The leash is very long, but inevitably values will be constrained in
ccordance with their effects on the human gene pool. The brain is a product
f evolution. Human behavior—like the deepest capacities for emotional
:sponse which drive and guide it—is the circuitous technique by which
uman genetic material has been and will be kept intact. Morality has no
ther demonstrable ultimate function. . . .

CHAPTER 9. HOPE

he first dilemma has been created by the seemingly fatal deterioration of the
iyths of traditional religion and its secular equivalents, principal among
which are ideologies based on a Marxian interpretation of history. The price
f these failures has been a loss of moral consensus, a greater sense of
.elplessness about the human condition and a shrinking of concern back
oward the self and the immediate future. The intellectual solution of the first
ilemma can be achieved by a deeper and more courageous examination of

human nature that combines the findings of biology with those of the social sciences. The mind will be more precisely explained as an epiphenomenon[22] of the neuronal machinery of the brain. That machinery is in turn the product of genetic evolution by natural selection acting on human populations for hundreds of thousands of years in their ancient environments. By a judicious extension of the methods and ideas of neurobiology, ethology, and sociobiology a proper foundation can be laid for the social sciences, and the discontinuity still separating the natural sciences on the one side and the social sciences and humanities on the other might be erased.

If this solution to the first dilemma proves even partially correct, it will lead directly to the second dilemma: the conscious choices that must be made among our innate mental propensities. The elements of human nature are the learning rules, emotional reinforcers, and hormonal feedback loops that guide the development of social behavior into certain channels as opposed to others. Human nature is not just the array of outcomes attained in existing societies. It is also the potential array that might be achieved through conscious design by future societies. By looking over the realized social systems of hundreds of animal species and deriving the principles by which these systems have evolved, we can be certain that all human choices represent only a tiny subset of those theoretically possible. Human nature is, moreover, a hodgepodge of special genetic adaptations to an environment largely vanished, the world of the Ice-Age hunter-gatherer. Modern life, as rich and rapidly changing as it appears to those caught in it, is nevertheless only a mosaic of cultural hypertrophies of the archaic behavioral adaptations. And at the center of the second dilemma is found a circularity: we are forced to choose among the elements of human nature by reference to value systems which these same elements created in an evolutionary age now long vanished.

Fortunately, this circularity of the human predicament is not so tight that it cannot be broken through an exercise of will. The principal task of human biology is to identify and to measure the constraints that influence the decisions of ethical philosophers and everyone else, and to infer their significance through neurophysiological and phylogenetic reconstructions of the mind. This enterprise is a necessary complement to the continued study of cultural evolution. It will alter the foundation of the social sciences but in no way diminish their richness and importance. In the process it will fashion a biology of ethics, which will make possible the selection of a more deeply understood and enduring code of moral values.

In the beginning the new ethicists will want to ponder the cardinal value of the survival of human genes in the form of a common pool over generations. Few persons realize the true consequences of the dissolving action of sexual reproduction and the corresponding unimportance of "lines" of descent. The DNA[23] of an individual is made up of about equal contributions of all the ancestors in any given generation, and it will be divided about equally

mong all descendants at any future moment. All of us have more than two
undred ancestors who were living in 1700—each of whom contributed far
ss than one chromosome to the living descendant—and, depending on the
mount of outbreeding that took place, up to millions in 1066. Henry
dams[24] put it nicely for those of Norman-English descent when he noted
at if "we could go back and live again in all our two hundred and fifty
illion arithmetical ancestors of the eleventh century, we should find our-
lves doing many surprising things, but among the rest we should certainly
e ploughing most of the fields of the Contentin and Calvados; going to mass
 every parish church in Normandy; rendering military service to every lord,
iritual or temporal, in all this region; and helping to build the Abbey
hurch at Mont-Saint-Michel."* Go back another few thousands of years—
nly a tick in the evolutionary clock—and the gene pool from which one
odern Briton has emerged spreads over Europe, to North Africa, the Middle
ast, and beyond. The individual is an evanescent combination of genes
rawn from this pool, one whose hereditary material will soon be dissolved
ack into it. Because natural selection has acted on the behavior of individuals
ho benefit themselves and their immediate relatives, human nature bends
s to the imperatives of selfishness and tribalism. But a more detached view
f the long-range course of evolution should allow us to see beyond the blind
ecision-making process of natural selection and to envision the history and
iture of our own genes against the background of the entire human species.
 word already in use intuitively defines this view: nobility. Had dinosaurs
rasped the concept they might have survived. They might have been us.
    I believe that a correct application of evolutionary theory also favors
iversity in the gene pool as a cardinal value. If variation in mental and
hletic ability is influenced to a moderate degree by heredity, as the evidence
iggests, we should expect individuals of truly extraordinary capacity to
merge unexpectedly in otherwise undistinguished families, and then fail to
ansmit these qualities to their children. The biologist George C. Williams
as written of such productions in plants and animals as Sisyphean[25] geno-
rpes; his reasoning is based on the following argument from elementary
enetics. Almost all capacities are prescribed by combinations of genès at
any sites on the chromosomes. Truly exceptional individuals, weak or
rong, are, by definition, to be found at the extremes of statistical curves, and
ie hereditary substrate of their traits come together in rare combinations that
rise from random processes in the formation of new sex cells and the fusion
f sex cells to create new organisms. Since each individual produced by the
exual process contains a unique set of genes, very exceptional combinations
f genes are unlikely to appear twice even within the same family. So if
enius is to any extent hereditary, it winks on and off through the gene pool
 a way that would be difficult to measure or predict. Like Sisyphus rolling

Henry Adams, *Mont-Saint-Michel and Chartres* (Houghton-Mifflin, Boston, 1936) [E.O.W.]

his boulder up and over to the top of the hill only to have it tumble down again, the human gene pool creates hereditary genius in many ways in many places only to have it come apart the next generation.* The genes of the Sisyphean combinations are probably spread throughout populations. For this reason alone, we are justified in considering the preservation of the entire gene pool as a contingent primary value until such time as an almost unimaginably greater knowledge of human heredity provides us with the option of a democratically contrived eugenics.

Universal human rights might properly be regarded as a third primary value. The idea is not general; it is largely the invention of recent European American civilization. I suggest that we will want to give it primary status not because it is a divine ordinance (kings used to rule by divine right) or through obedience to an abstract principle of unknown extraneous origin, but because we are mammals. Our societies are based on the mammalian plan: the individual strives for personal reproductive success foremost and that of his immediate kin secondarily; further grudging cooperation represents a compromise struck in order to enjoy the benefits of group membership. A rational ant—let us imagine for a moment that ants and other social insects had succeeded in evolving high intelligence—would find such an arrangement biologically unsound and the very concept of individual freedom intrinsically evil. We will accede to universal rights because power is too fluid in advanced technological societies to circumvent this mammalian imperative; the long term consequences of inequity will always be visibly dangerous to its temporary beneficiaries. I suggest that this is the true reason for the universal rights movement and that an understanding of its raw biological causation will be more compelling in the end than any rationalization contrived by culture to reinforce and euphemize it.

The search for values will then go beyond the utilitarian calculus of genetic fitness. Although natural selection has been the prime mover, it works through a cascade of decisions based on secondary values that have historically served as the enabling mechanisms for survival and reproductive success. These values are defined to a large extent by our most intense emotions: enthusiasm and a sharpening of the senses from exploration; exaltation from discovery; triumph in battle and competitive sports; the restful satisfaction from an altruistic act well and truly placed; the stirring of ethnic and national pride; the strength from family ties; and the secure biophilic[26] pleasure from the nearness of animals and growing plants.

There is a neurophysiology of such responses to be deciphered, and their evolutionary history awaits reconstruction. A kind of principle of the conservation of energy operates among them, such that the emphasis of any one over others still retains the potential summed power of all. . . . Although

* George C. Williams, *Sex and Evolution* (Princeton University Press, Princeton, N.J., 1975) [E.O.W.]

e means to measure these energies are lacking, I suspect psychologists ould agree that they can be rechanneled substantially without losing rength, that the mind fights to retain a certain level of order and emotional ward. Recent evidence suggests that dreams are produced when giant ers in the brainstem fire upward through the brain during sleep, stirring e cerebral cortex to activity. In the absence of ordinary sensory information m the outside, the cortex responds by calling up images from the memory nks and fabricating plausible stories. In an analogous manner the mind will ways create morality, religion, and mythology and empower them with notional force. When blind ideologies and religious beliefs are stripped vay, others are quickly manufactured as replacements. If the cerebral cortex rigidly trained in the techniques of critical analysis and packed with tested formation, it will reorder all that into some form of morality, religion, and ythology. If the mind is instructed that its pararational activity cannot be mbined with the rational, it will divide itself into two compartments so that th activities can continue to flourish side by side.

This mythopoeic[27] drive can be harnessed to learning and the rational arch for human progress if we finally concede that scientific materialism[28] is elf a mythology defined in the noble sense. So let me give again the reasons hy I consider the scientific ethos superior to religion: its repeated triumphs explaining and controlling the physical world; its self-correcting nature en to all competent to devise and conduct the tests; its readiness to examine subjects sacred and profane; and now the possibility of explaining tradi- nal religion by the mechanistic models of evolutionary biology. The last hievement will be crucial. If religion, including the dogmatic secular ide- ogies, can be systematically analyzed and explained as a product of the ain's evolution, its power as an external source of morality will be gone rever and the solution of the second dilemma will have become a practical cessity.

The core of scientific materialism is the evolutionary epic. Let me repeat minimum claims: that the laws of the physical sciences are consistent with ose of the biological and social sciences and can be linked in chains of causal planation; that life and mind have a physical basis; that the world as we low it has evolved from earlier worlds obedient to the same laws; and that e visible universe today is everywhere subject to these materialist explana- ns. The epic can be indefinitely strengthened up and down the line, but its ost sweeping assertions cannot be proved with finality.

What I am suggesting, in the end, is that the evolutionary epic is obably the best myth we will ever have. It can be adjusted until it comes as se to truth as the human mind is constructed to judge the truth. And if that the case, the mythopoeic requirements of the mind must somehow be met scientific materialism so as to reinvest our superb energies. There are ways managing such a shift honestly and without dogma. One is to cultivate ore intensely the relationship between the sciences and humanities. The great British biologist J. B. S. Haldane[29] said of science and literature, "I am absolutely convinced that science is vastly more stimulating to the imagination than are the classics, but the products of the stimulus do not normally see the light because scientific men as a class are devoid of any perception of literary form." Indeed, the origin of the universe in the big bang of fifteen billion years ago, as deduced by astronomers and physicists, is far more awesome than the first chapter of Genesis or the Ninevite epic of Gilgamesh. When the scientists project physical processes backward to that moment with the aid of mathematical models they are talking about everything—literally everything—and when they move forward in time to pulsars, supernovas, and the collision of black holes they probe distances and mysteries beyond the imaginings of earlier generations. Recall how God lashed Job with concepts meant to overwhelm the human mind:

> Who is this whose ignorant words
> cloud my design in darkness?
> Brace yourself and stand up like a man;
> I will ask questions, and you shall answer . . .
> Have you descended to the springs of the sea
> or walked in the unfathomable deep?
> Have the gates of death been revealed to you?
> Have you ever seen the door-keepers of the place of darkness?
> Have you comprehended the vast expanse of the world?
> Come, tell me all this, if you know.*

And yes, we *do* know and we have told. Jehovah's challenges have been met and scientists have pressed on to uncover and to solve even greater puzzles. The physical basis of life is known; we understand approximately how and when it started on earth. New species have been created in the laboratory and evolution has been traced at the molecular level. Genes can be spliced from one kind of organism into another. Molecular biologists have most of the knowledge needed to create elementary forms of life. Our machines, settled on Mars, have transmitted panoramic views and the results of chemical soil analysis. Could the Old Testament writers have conceived of such activity? And still the process of great scientific discovery gathers momentum. . . .

As our knowledge of human nature grows, and we start to elect a system of values on a more objective basis, and our minds at last align with our hearts, the set of trajectories will narrow still more. We already know, to take two extreme and opposite examples, that the worlds of William Graham Sumner,[30] the absolute Social Darwinist, and Mikhail Bakunin,[31] the anarchist, are biologically impossible. As the social sciences mature into predictive disciplines, the permissible trajectories will not only diminish in number but our descendants will be able to sight farther along them.

* This translation of Job 38:2–3, 16–18, is from *The New English Bible*. [E.O.W.]

Then mankind will face the third and perhaps final spiritual dilemma. uman genetics is now growing quickly along with all other branches of ience. In time, much knowledge concerning the genetic foundation of social :havior will accumulate, and techniques may become available for altering :ne complexes by molecular engineering and rapid selection through clon- g. At the very least, slow evolutionary change will be feasible through •nventional eugenics. The human species can change its own nature. What ill it choose? Will it remain the same, teetering on a jerrybuilt foundation of irtly obsolete Ice-Age adaptations? Or will it press on toward still higher •telligence and creativity, accompanied by a greater—or lesser—capacity for notional response? New patterns of sociality could be installed in bits and .eces. It might be possible to imitate genetically the more nearly perfect .iclear family of the white handed gibbon or the harmonious sisterhoods of te honeybees. But we are talking here about the very essence of humanity. :rhaps there is something already present in our nature that will prevent us om ever making such changes. In any case, and fortunately, this third lemma belongs to later generations.

OTES

. David Hume (1711–1776) was a Scottish philosopher. See the introduction to Chapter 8. [D.C.A.]
. *Darwinian natural selection*: the theory proposed by Charles Darwin to explain the origin of the various species. See the introduction to this chapter. [D.C.A.]
. Hans Küng is a Swiss Roman Catholic theologian and author. [D.C.A.]
. *naturalism*: the doctrine that all entities and events can be explained through scientific laws [D.C.A.]
. Karl Marx (1818–1883) was a German social philosopher. See the introduction to Chapter 9. [D.C.A.]
. Mao Tse-tung (1893–1976) was the Communist leader of the People's Republic of China from 1949 to 1976. [D.C.A.]
. *Apollonian* means "measured, restrained"; *Dionysian* means "emotional, frenzied." The adjectives derive from Apollo, the Greek god of light, and Dionysus, the Greek god of wine. [D.C.A.]
. Ernst Mach (1838–1916) was an Austrian physicist and philosopher. [D.C.A.]
. Carolus Linnaeus (1707–1778) was the Swedish botanist who began the system of classifying plants and animals by genus and species. [D.C.A.]
. Jean-Jacques Rousseau (1712–1778) was a French (Swiss-born) philosopher and writer. [D.C.A.]
. *haplodiploid form of sex determination*: a system of sex determination in which unfertilized eggs produce males and fertilized eggs produce females. This means that the males are *haploid* (have just one set of chromosomes) and the females *diploid* (have two sets). [D.C.A., after E.O.W.]
. *kibbutzim*: communal farms or settlements in Israel. [D.C.A.]

13. An organism is homozygous for a particular chromosome site when the two genes at that site are identical. [D.C.A., after E.O.W.]
14. Tertullian (about 160–230) was a Christian apologist born in Carthage. [D.C.A.]
15. Jane Goodall is a British ethologist. [D.C.A.]
16. William Morton Wheeler (1865–1937) was an American entomologist. [D.C.A.]
17. *The Pilgrim's Progress from This World to That Which Is to Come*: a classic Christian allegory by the English preacher and author John Bunyan (1628–1688) [D.C.A.]
18. Malcolm Muggeridge (1903–1990) was a British journalist. [D.C.A.]
19. B. F. Skinner (1904–1990) was an American psychologist. See the introduction to Chapter 14. [D.C.A.]
20. Lenin (1870–1924) was a Russian Communist leader. His given name was Vladimir Ilyich Ulyanov; he went by the pseudonyms Vladimir Ilyich Lenin and N. Lenin [D.C.A.]
21. *hypertrophy*: the excessive development of an organic structure. Wilson extends this term to apply to the excessive development of a social behavior. [D.C.A.]
22. *epiphenomenon*: a phenomenon that accompanies and is caused by another phenomenon [D.C.A.]
23. *DNA* (deoxyribonucleic *a*cid): the molecules that are the basis of heredity. Genes are parts of DNA molecules. [D.C.A.]
24. Henry Adams (1838–1918) was an American historian. [D.C.A.]
25. In Greek mythology, Sisyphus was a king punished in the underworld by having eternally to roll a heavy rock up a hill only to have it roll down again as it nears the top. [D.C.A.]
26. "Biophilia" is a word coined by Wilson by combining the Greek words for life (*bios*) and love (*philia*). He defines it as "the innate tendency to focus on life and lifelike processes." [D.C.A.]
27. *mythopoeic drive*: the drive to create myths [D.C.A.]
28. *scientific materialism*: the theory that all reality can be explained scientifically in terms of matter [D.C.A.]
29. J. B. S. Haldane lived from 1892 to 1964. [D.C.A.]
30. William Graham Sumner (1840–1910) was an American sociologist and political economist who held the "Social Darwinist" view that in the struggle for property and social status, the "fittest" (by which he meant the most industrious) should and do survive while the "unfit" should be and are eliminated. [D.C.A.]
31. Mikhail Bakunin (1814–1876) was a Russian anarchist and revolutionary leader [D.C.A.]

QUESTIONS FOR REFLECTION AND DISCUSSION

1. Is human nature essentially a biological phenomenon?
2. Does biology show that the main purpose of human life is survival and reproduction?
3. Are the moral values we hold genetically based?
4. Is human altruism essentially the same as animal altruism?
5. Are all human choices and actions genetically determined?

UGGESTIONS FOR FURTHER READING

Primary Sources

Human Nature. Cambridge, Mass.: Harvard University Press, 1978, 260 pp.

omethean Fire: Reflections on the Origin of Mind (coauthored with Charles J. Lumsden). Cambridge, Mass: Harvard University Press, 1983, 216 pp.

A sociobiological explanation of the origin of the human mind. Wilson and Lumsden argue that the mind arose through the interaction of genetic change and cultural history. The book presents in a briefer and nontechnical way the main ideas in *Genes, Mind, and Culture: The Coevolutionary Process* (Cambridge, Mass.: Harvard University Press, 1981), which was written for specialists.

ciobiology: The Abridged Edition. Cambridge, Mass.: Harvard University Press, 1980, 366 pp.

An abridgment of *Sociobiology: The New Synthesis* (Cambridge, Mass.: Harvard University Press, 1975), which was written for specialists. Wilson explains in the preface that the abridgment contains the "essential introductory parts and most interesting case histories . . . [and] is intended to serve both as a textbook and as a semi-popular general account of sociobiology."

Biology and the Social Sciences," *Daedalus,* Fall 1977, pp. 127–140, *Proceedings of the American Academy of the Arts and Sciences,* Vol. 106, No. 4.

An explanation of biology's role as the "antidiscipline" of the social sciences. Wilson discusses the extent to which disciplines such as anthropology and psychology can be "reduced" to biology.

. Secondary Sources

arash, David. *The Whisperings Within.* New York: Harper & Row, 1979, 273 pp.

A general and readable account of sociobiology, explaining how human behavior, like that of all animals, is strongly influenced by genes, the "whisperings within."

awkins, Richard. *The Selfish Gene.* Oxford, England: Oxford University Press, 1976, 224 pp.

An argument that human beings are machines created by their genes and designed to ensure the survival and reproduction of genes. Dawkins uses this "selfish-gene" theory to analyze aggression, parental care, altruism, and other human behaviors. Accessible to the general reader.

use, Michael. *Sociobiology: Sense or Nonsense?* 1979; 2d ed., Dordrecht, Holland: Reidel, 1985, 260 pp.

This explanation of the scientific claims made by sociobiology also assesses criticisms that have been raised against this new science and discusses its scientific and philosophical implications. In his review of the first edition,

Wilson called the book "the best written to date about the whole scope o
sociobiology." For more advanced students of sociobiology.

Sahlins, Marshall. *The Use and Abuse of Biology: An Anthropological Critique of So
ciobiology*. Ann Arbor: University of Michigan Press, 1976, 120 pp.

Sahlins argues in Part 1, "Biology and Culture," pp. 3–67, that sociobiology fails
in its attempt to give a biological explanation of human social behavior.

Trigg, Roger. *The Shaping of Man: Philosophical Aspects of Sociobiology*. New York
Schocken, 1983, 186 pp.

A clearly written study of the contributions and limitations of the sociobiologica
approach to human nature. Trigg argues that because we have reason and free
will, our behavior cannot be fully explained by genetics and environment alone